Popular Culture: Production and Consumption

BLACKWELL READERS IN SOCIOLOGY

Each volume in this authoritative series aims to provide students and scholars with comprehensive collections of classic and contemporary readings for all the major sub-fields of sociology. They are designed to complement single-authored works, or to be used as stand-alone textbooks for courses. The selected readings sample the most important works that students should read and are framed by informed editorial introductions. The series aims to reflect the state of the discipline by providing collections not only on standard topics but also on cutting-edge subjects in sociology to provide future directions in teaching and research.

Popular Culture: Production and Consumption

Edited by

C. Lee Harrington and Denise D. Bielby

Copyright © Blackwell Publishers Ltd 2001; editorial introductions and arrangement copyright © C. Lee Harrington and Denise D. Bielby 2001

First published 2001

2 4 6 8 10 9 7 5 3 1

Blackwell Publishers Inc.
350 Main Street
Malden, Massachusetts 02148
USA

Blackwell Publishers Ltd
108 Cowley Road
Oxford OX4 1JF
UK

Library of Congress Cataloging-in-Publication Data

Popular culture : production and consumption / edited by C. Lee Harrington and Denise D. Bielby.
    p. cm. — (Blackwell readers in sociology)
    Includes bibliographical references and index.
    ISBN 0–631–21709–6 (acid-free paper) — ISBN 0–631–21710–X (pbk. : acid-free paper)
    1. Popular culture—United States. 2. Popular culture—Economic aspects—United States. 3. Production (Economic theory) 4. Consumption (Economics) 5. United States—Civilization—1970–6. Pluralism (Social sciences)—United States. 7. Popular culture. I. Harrington, C. Lee, 1964–II. Bielby, Denise D. III. Series.

    E169.12.P643 2000
    306—dc21

                                                                        00–024886

British Library Cataloguing in Publication Data
A CIP catalogue record for this book is available from the British Library.

Typeset Sabon in 10 on 12pt
by Kolam Information Services Private Ltd., Pondicherry, India

Printed in Great Britain by MPG Books, Bodmin, Cornwall

This book is printed on acid-free paper.

Contents

The Contributors

Robert C. Allen is the James Logan Godfrey Professor of American Studies, History, and Communication Studies at the University of North Carolina at Chapel Hill. He is the author of *Speaking of Soap Operas* (1985) and the editor of several books on television, media and culture.

Howard S. Becker is Adjunct Professor of Sociology, University of California, Santa Barbara. He is a leading scholar in the social organization of art worlds, approaches to social inquiry, and the sociology of deviance.

Walter Benjamin was an independent scholar, man of letters, critic, essayist, and freelance writer. He received support during his career from the Institute for Social Research in New York. He died in 1940.

Denise D. Bielby is Professor of Sociology at the University of California, Santa Barbara. She is co-author of *Soap Fans: Pursuing Pleasure and Making Meaning in Everyday Life* (1995). Her research focuses on culture industries and television and film audiences.

John Blacking founded the first graduate program in Ethnomusicology in Europe. He also founded the European Seminar on Ethnomusicology and was President of the Society for Ethnomusicology in the US. He was a faculty member at Queen's University in Belfast and the recipient of numerous awards and honors for his work. He died in 1990.

John G. Cawelti is Professor of English at the University of Kentucky and the author of several books about American literature and popular culture, including *The Spy Story* (1987), *The Six-Gun Mystique Sequel* (1984), and *Adventure, Mystery, and Romance* (1976).

Danae Clark is Associate Professor of Media Studies in the Department of Communication at the University of Pittsburgh. She is the author of *Negotiating Hollywood: The Cultural Politics of Actors' Labor* (1995) and has contributed to journals such as *Camera Obscura*, *Journal of Film and Video* and *American Studies*. She is currently working on the role of collectibles in US culture.

Gerry P. T. Finn is Reader in the Department of Educational Studies at the University of Strathclyde in Glasgow. He is a psychologist whose main areas of research focus on societal prejudice, social identities and intergroup conflict and its resolution. He has written about these matters in relation to education and sport, and in the specific context of the conflict in Northern Ireland. He recently co-edited *Football Culture: Local Conflicts, Global Visions* (2000).

John Fiske is Professor of Communication Arts at the University of Wisconsin–Madison. He is the author of nine books and numerous articles on cultural and media studies.

Tom Frank is the founder of *The Baffler*, a journal of cultural criticism, and the author of *The Conquest of Cool: Business Culture, Counterculture, and the Rise of Hip Consumerism* (1997). He is also a contributing reporter to publications such as *The Washington Post*, *The Nation*, and *In These Times*.

Harris Friedberg teaches English at Wesleyan University. He has published on Renaissance English poetry and rock-and-roll.

Joshua Gamson is Associate Professor of Sociology at Yale University. He is the author of *Freaks Talk Back: Tabloid Talk Shows and Sexual Nonconformity* (1998), *Claims to Fame: Celebrity in Contemporary America* (1994) and a participating author of *Ethnography Unbound: Power and Resistance in the Modern Metropolis* (1991).

Richard Giulianotti is Senior Lecturer in Sociology at the University of Aberdeen and the author of *Football: A Sociology of the Global Game* (1999). He is also co-editor of *Football Culture: Local Conflicts, Global Visions* (2000), *Football Cultures and Identities* (1999), *Entering the Field* (1997), and *Football Violence and Social Identity* (1994). He is currently working on several further books, including a collection on football in Africa and a monograph on sport.

Stuart Hall, a leading contributor to the Centre for Contemporary Cultural Studies in Birmingham, is currently Professor of Sociology at The Open University.

C. Lee Harrington is Associate Professor of Sociology and Affiliate of the Women's Studies Program at Miami University. She is co-author of *Soap Fans: Pursuing Pleasure and Making Meaning in Everyday Life* (1995). Her current research interests include culture industries and death penalty cause lawyering.

Joli Jensen is Professor of Communication at the University of Tulsa, where she teaches courses in media, culture and society. She is the author of *Redeeming Modernity: Contradictions in Media Criticism* (1990) and *The Nashville Sound: Authenticity, Commercialization, and Country Music* (1998). She is currently working on a book about intellectuals and beliefs about the arts.

Laura Kipnis teaches in the Department of Radio, Television and Film at Northwestern University. Her last book was *Bound and Gagged: Pornography and the Politics of Fantasy in America* (1996).

George Lipsitz is Professor of Ethnic Studies at the University of California, San Diego. His most recent book is *The Possessive Investment in Whiteness: How White People Profit from Identity Politics* (1998). Other publications include *Rainbow at Midnight* (1994), *Dangerous Crossroads* (1994), *The Sidewalks of St. Louis* (1991),

Time Passages (1990), and *A Life in the Struggle: Ivory Perry and the Culture of Opposition* (1988).

Minelle Mahtani is currently a visiting scholar at the University of North Carolina–Chapel Hill and Duke University. Her doctoral work was on women of "mixed race" and their negotiations of gendered and racialized identities. She worked for several years as a producer in the news and current affairs unit of the Canadian Broadcasting Corporation in Toronto.

Mel McCombie is an art historian who teaches at the University of Connecticut and Wesleyan University. She does not gamble.

Andy Medhurst teaches Media and Cultural Studies at the University of Sussex. He is the co-editor of *Lesbian and Gay Studies: A Critical Introduction* (1997), the author of many articles on popular culture, and is currently working on a book about English comedy and national identity.

Scott Salmon is Assistant Professor in the Urban and Regional Planning Program and the Department of Geography at Miami University. His academic focus is the analysis of conflict and change in the contemporary capitalist city. He also maintains an active interest in the development of social theory and the changing geographies of popular music.

David Sanjek is Archives Director at Broadcast Music Incorporated (BMI).

Kimberly S. Schimmel is an Assistant Professor in the School of Exercise, Leisure and Sport at Kent State University. She conducts research in the sociology of sport and the political economy of professional sport in the urban context.

Pamela Wilson is an Assistant Professor at Reinhardt College. She has published numerous articles in cultural and media studies, including contributions to *Quarterly Review of Film and Video, Historical Journal of Film, Radio, and Television, Camera Obscura*, and *South Atlantic Quarterly*. Her current research interests focus on the practice of genealogy as amateur historiography and in the construction of cultural identity.

Acknowledgments

The authors and publishers gratefully acknowledge the following for permission to reproduce copyright material:

Allen, Robert C., "On Reading Soaps: A Semiotic Primer," from E. Ann Kaplan (ed.), *Regarding Television* (University Publications of America, Frederick, MD, 1983);

Becker, Howard S., "Art as Collective Action," *American Sociological Review* 39 (December 1974), reprinted by permission of the American Sociological Association, Washington, D.C.);

Benjamin, Walter, "The Task of the Translator: An Introduction to the Translation of Baudelaire's *Tableaux Parisiens*," from *Illuminations* by Walter Benjamin, copyright © 1955 by Suhrkamp Verlag, Frankfurt am Main. English translation by Harry Zohn copyright © 1968 and renewed 1996 by Harcourt, Inc., reprinted by permission of Harcourt, Inc.;

Blacking, John, "Making Artistic Popular Music: The Goal of True Folk," *Popular Music* 1, 1981 (Cambridge University Press, 1981);

Cawelti, John G., "The Concept of Formula in the Study of Popular Literature," *Journal of Popular Culture* 3, 1969 (Popular Press, Bowling Green University, Ohio, 1969);

Clark, Danae, "Commodity Lesbianism," from Corey K. Creekmur and Alexander Doty (eds.), *Out in Culture: Gay, Lesbian and Queer Essays on Popular Culture* (Duke University Press, Durham, NC, 1995);

Finn, Gerry, P. T. and Richard Giulianotti, "Scottish Fans, Not English Hooligans! Scots, Scottishness, and Scottish Football," from Adam Brown (ed.), *Fanatics! Power, Identity and Fandom in Football* (Routledge, London, 1998);

Fiske, John, "Intertextuality," from John Fiske *Television Culture* (Methuen, London, 1987, reprinted by permission of Reed Books);

Frank, Tom, "Alternative to What?" from Ron Sakolsky and Fred Wei-han (eds.), *Sounding Off! Music as Subversion/Resistance/Revolution* (Autonomedia, Brooklyn, New York, 1995);

Gamson, Joshua, "The Assembly Line of Greatness: Celebrity in Twentieth-Century America," *Critical Studies in Mass Communication* 9, 1992;

Hall, Stuart, "Encoding/Decoding" from S. Hall, D. Hobson, A. Lowe, and P. Willis (eds.), *Culture, Media, Language: Working Papers in Cultural Studies* (Hutchinson Publishing, London, 1980, reprinted by permission of Random House UK);

Jensen, Joli, "Fandom as Pathology: The Consequences of Characterization," from Lisa A. Lewis (ed.), *The Adoring Audience: Fan Culture and Popular Media* (Routledge, London, 1992);

Kipnis, Laura, "(Male) Desire and (Female) Disgust: Reading *Hustler*," from Lawrence Grosserg, Cary Nelson and Paula A. Treichler (eds.), *Cultural Studies* (Routledge, New York, 1991. Copyright © 1991 from *Cultural Studies* edited by

Lawrence Grossberg, Cary Nelson, and Paula A. Treichler. Reproduced by permission of Taylor & Francis/Routledge, Inc.;

Lipsitz, George, "Diasporic Noise: History, Hip Hop, and the Post-colonial Politics of Sound," from George Lipsitz *Dangerous Crossroads: Popular Music, Postmodernism and the Poetics of Place* (Verso, London and New York, 1994);

Medhurst, Andy, "Batman, Deviance, and Camp," from Roberta E. Pearson and William Uricchio (eds.), *The Many Lives of the Batman: Critical Approaches to a Superhero and His Media* (Routledge, New York, 1991. Copyright © 1991 from *The Many Lives of Batman* edited by Roberta E. Pearson and William Uricchio. Reproduced by permission of Taylor & Francis/Routledge Inc.);

Sanjek, David, "'Don't Have to DJ No More': Sampling and the 'Autonomous' Creator," from Martha Woodmansee and Peter Janszi (eds.), *The Construction of Authorship: Textual Appropriation in Law and Literature*, pp. 343–60. Copyright 1994, Duke University Press. All rights reserved. Reprinted with permission;

Wilson, Pamela, "Mountains of Contradictions: Gender, Class, and Region in the Star Image of Dolly Parton," *South Atlantic Quarterly* 94:1 (Spring 1995), pp. 109–34. Copyright 1994, Duke University Press. All rights reserved. Reprinted with permission;

Figure 5.1.   Caesars Palace resort hotel and casino, Las Vegas, Nevada. The exterior of Caesars Palace from Las Vegas Boulevard, with Nike of Samothrace reproduction right foreground; porte cochere and statuary at rear behind fountains. Courtesy of Public Relations Department, Caesars Palace, Las Vegas;

Figure 5.2.   The Forum shops at Caesars shopping mall, Las Vegas, Nevada. Entrance court of Forum Shops; statue of Fortuna seen from rear at right, slot machines behind the statue; Warner Brothers Studio Store on left. Courtesy of Public Relations Department, Caesars Palace, Las Vegas.

The publishers apologize for any errors or omissions in the above list and would be grateful to be notified of any corrections that should be incorporated in the next edition or reprint of this book.

1 Constructing the Popular: Cultural Production and Consumption

C. Lee Harrington and Denise D. Bielby

Our interest in the study of popular culture was generated by a serendipitous encounter some twelve years ago. In the late 1980s both of us were in the Department of Sociology at the University of California–Santa Barbara, Lee as a graduate student and Denise as a faculty member. Our offices happened to be located across the hall from one another, and one Spring day Lee was explaining to her officemate the ramifications of the latest plot twist on ABC's long-running soap opera "General Hospital." She was apparently talking louder than she realized because when she stepped into the hall Denise beckoned her over and said, "I couldn't help but overhearing – you're a 'General Hospital' fan too?" As it turns out, we had both watched the show since the mid-1970s. Thus was born an ongoing collaboration in the sociological study of popular culture.

We both began teaching pop culture courses in 1993, Denise to graduate students at UC-Santa Barbara and Lee to undergraduates at Miami University of Ohio. As class materials we relied on photocopied packets of individual articles since no published collection met our shared needs. We wanted our students to read works that covered a wide range of content (such as music, television, magazines, sport, advertising and comics), reflected the myriad disciplinary perspectives that might be brought to bear on the study of popular culture (including sociology, anthropology, geography, English, communications, history, fine arts, sport studies and marketing), represented a variety of theoretical frameworks (such as media studies, cultural studies, literary theory, cultural sociology and political economy), addressed issues of diversity (race, ethnicity, nationality, gender, sexuality, age and socioeconomic class), and were accessible, enjoyable and intellectually provocative. The current collection, we hope, meets these needs for our readers as well as ourselves.

Defining the Popular

In this chapter we offer readers a general introduction to the origins of pop culture research, the background and approach of three major schools of thought, and some of the key areas of consensus and debate in the scholarly literature. As we shall see, research on popular culture is extremely diverse and challenging. We will conclude the chapter by introducing the conceptual framework for this particular collection of readings. Specifically, we suggest that the concept of a *circuit of culture* (du Gay, 1997; du Gay et al., 1997) provides a useful guide for ourselves and our students as we begin to establish links between the complex processes of cultural production and consumption.

No academic writing on popular culture can proceed, however, without first attempting to define the term, a feat easier said than done. Despite the fact that we all seem to know what we are talking about when we talk about pop culture, its exact meaning has been debated for decades. Raymond Williams argues that the word "popular" has at least four current meanings. First, it can refer simply to those objects or practices that are well-liked by a lot of people.[1] Or, it can be used to refer to objects or practices deemed inferior and unworthy. In this view, popular culture is everything left over after we have identified what constitutes elite or "high" culture – that is, the paintings and sculptures and symphonies typically associated with the wealthy and well-educated (see below). The term can also refer to "work deliberately setting out to win favour with the people." In this usage, popular culture is explicitly commercial: it is work that is produced *to be* consumed. Finally, the term can refer to the objects and practices "actually made by the people for themselves" (Williams, 1983, p. 237).

These different meanings are all useful and accurate, we believe, depending on context and the particular cultural objects or practices in question. The definition that guided us in compiling this collection is that offered by Mukerji and Schudson:

> We will sidestep a great many terminological disputes with the inclusive claim that popular culture refers to the beliefs and practices, and the objects through which they are organized, that are widely shared among a population.
>
> *(Mukerji and Schudson, 1991, p. 3)*

While the readings collected here focus primarily on the various forms of mass entertainment that usually come to mind when one hears the term, we recognize that popular culture also includes other beliefs and practices that comprise our everyday lived experience: the food we eat, the clothing we wear, the people we spend time with, the gossip we share, the roadways we travel, and so forth.

Popular Culture in the Academy

Despite its embeddedness in everyday life (or perhaps because of it), popular culture's location in the academy has long been problematic. For example, it was not until the mid-twentieth century that popular culture was first legitimized as a focus of study in the US, and widespread legitimation has been a very gradual process (see Mukerji and Schudson, 1991, p. 3). Scholars of, and courses on, popular culture remain suspect in many departments and universities worldwide, reflecting the persistent disbelief that academic theories and methodologies can shed new light on phenomena whose meanings seem transparently obvious. Every year students in Lee's undergraduate course on soap operas report being derided by roommates, friends, parents and even their formal academic advisors for not signing up for a "real" class. Most of us recognize the value of scholarly guidance in our attempts to understand Chaucer's *Canterbury Tales* or the musical compositions of Philip Glass, but can the same be true for Teletubbies, motocross, and hip hop?

The answer, increasingly, is "yes." The past 50 years have witnessed a steady growth of academic interest in popular culture as reflected in both increased scholarship and gradual transformations of formal curricula. Some disciplines have clearly been more receptive than others. Sociologists, for example, have conducted pop culture research since the early twentieth century and generally take for granted its legitimacy within the academy (which is not to say, of course, that their research findings necessarily "support" pop culture). Literary studies, in contrast, was much slower to accept pop culture as a serious focus of inquiry; critics charge that its lingering preoccupation with the idea of a canon lead to an elitist dismissal of "lesser" cultural texts.[2] In many ways, the gradual infusion of popular culture throughout the academy in the past several decades has proven truly transformative. "The process of legitimating popular culture studies in recent years has...been associated with major theoretical challenges to basic assumptions" of a number of different disciplines, including history, anthropology, sociology, and literary studies. As a result, "students of popular culture...have simultaneously worked in the tradition of their disciplines and fought with their premises" (Mukerji and Schudson, 1991, pp. 4–5).[3]

The study of popular culture today takes place within a wide variety of disciplinary and theoretical frameworks. While it is difficult to categorize all approaches, if one were to take a snapshot of the academy in the late twentieth century the photo would reveal at least three predominant schools of thought: the growing field of Cultural Studies, the Production of Culture perspective, and the Popular Culture Studies tradition. These perspectives share a belief in the legitimacy of pop culture research but have different underlying assumptions about the nature and consequences of the processes of cultural production and consumption. We briefly describe each perspective below, then turn to some of the key points of consensus and debate within pop culture scholarship as a whole.

The field of Cultural Studies grew out of efforts to understand a complex set of social and economic processes, including industrialization, modernization, urbanization, mass communication and the global economy (Nelson, Treichler, and Grossberg, 1992, p. 5). It first emerged in Great Britain in the 1950s and is most closely associated with the Centre for Contemporary Cultural Studies, which was founded in Birmingham, England in 1964. The focus of inquiry in Cultural Studies is extremely broad, as its practitioners argue that culture cannot be understood apart from other aspects of social life:

> Continually engaging with the political, economic, erotic, social, and ideological, cultural studies entails the study of all relations between all the elements in a whole way of life.
> (Nelson, Treichler, and Grossberg, 1992, p. 14; see also Barker and Beezer, 1992)

Cultural Studies is often difficult for students to understand, in part because it is relentlessly interdisciplinary and often heavily theoretical. Situated somewhere between the humanities and the social sciences, Cultural Studies has no clear methodology and no clearly defined area of content. Two main features distinguishing it from other perspectives are its emphasis on subjectivity, rather than the supposedly objective positivism associated with most social inquiry, and its explicitly political or activist orientation. As scholars point out, Cultural Studies is both intellectual theory and political practice:

> [A] continuing preoccupation within cultural studies is the notion of radical social and cultural transformation and how to study it . . . its practitioners see cultural studies not simply as a chronicle of social change but as an intervention in it, and see themselves not simply as scholars providing an account but as politically engaged participants.
> *(Nelson, Treichler, and Grossberg, 1992, p. 5)*

When Italian scholar Antonio Gramsci's work became available in English in the 1970s, Cultural Studies' focus was redefined. Gramsci's concept of hegemony, defined here as the process by which relations of power are normalized for social members, generated a research trajectory in Cultural Studies (still with us today) that centers on identifying and analyzing systems of power embedded in processes of cultural production and consumption (to date, however, the emphasis has been heavily on consumption; see Curran, Morley, and Walkerdine, 1996, p. 3).[4] The field is perhaps most noted for its now widely-accepted claim that consumers of cultural texts are not passive dupes but rather active participants in the creation of meaning:

> Cultural studies has been . . . most interested in how groups with least power practically develop their own readings of, and uses for, cultural products – in fun, in resistance, or to articulate their own identity.   *(During, 1993, p. 7)*

Popular culture, in this view, is the culture of the subordinated as they actively resist their own subordination. "Popular culture is made by various factions of subordinated or disempowered people out of the resources . . . that are provided by the social system that disempowers them" (Fiske, 1989, pp. 1–2).

Cultural Studies' focus on textual consumption and moments of resistance broadened in the late 1980s and 1990s as scholars developed a "deepening concern to understand the values and strengths of the sense-making strategies used by ordinary people" in their everyday lives (Barker and Beezer, 1992, p. 8; see also Miller and McHoul, 1998). As the field becomes increasingly internationalized, the focus of inquiry has shifted to what During (1993) calls "the voices of the other," including marginalized peoples, post-colonial identities, and members of border cultures. The new Cultural Studies project is thus:

> [A] project of thinking through the implications of extending the term "culture" to include activities and meanings of ordinary people, precisely those constituencies excluded from participation in culture when its elitist definition holds sway.
> *(Barker and Beezer, 1992, p. 5)*

In contrast to Cultural Studies, the Production of Culture school focuses less attention on the various meanings of cultural texts and the process of cultural consumption than on an examination of culture as a manufactured product. Closely identified with the social sciences and the discipline of sociology in particular, the Production of Culture perspective originated in the US in the mid-1970s.[5] An early theoretical precursor to this approach was the mid-1940s work of Theodor Adorno and Max Horkheimer on what they termed "culture industries."[6] Adorno and Horkheimer argued that cultural objects are produced in much the same way as other industries produce other objects. The assembly-line production of cars, for example, is analogous to that of music or film. The standardization of production creates standardized and interchangeable cultural objects, which leads inevitably to standardization of consumption. Consumers are neither "active" nor "creative," but instead are reduced to a homogeneous, undifferentiated mass, responding to cultural objects in a predictable, uniform manner (see Negus, 1997).

The contemporary Production of Culture approach moves beyond these somewhat pessimistic beginnings in its efforts to use "analytical systems from the sociology of occupations and of organizations to see how social resources are mobilized by artists, filmmakers, and the like to make cultural production possible" (Mukerji and Schudson, 1991, p. 28; see also Negus, 1997, p. 99). Scholars do not suggest that the production of culture can be reduced to economics alone, however. Rather, processes of production are themselves cultural phenomena and should be analyzed as such. "We need to understand the meanings that are given to both the 'product' and the practices through which the product is made" (Negus, 1997, p. 101; see also du Gay, 1997). By empirically examining group dynamics, the interactional order, social networks, and organizational decision-making, this perspective attempts to situate popular culture in concrete, identifiable social and economic processes and institutions (Mukerji and Schudson, 1991, p. 32).[7]

A third predominant perspective today is the Popular Culture Studies tradition, based in the United States and most closely associated with the work of Ray Browne and his colleagues in the Department of Popular Culture at Bowling Green State University (USA). The publication of the first issue of *Journal of Popular Culture* in 1969, the formation of the Popular Culture Association in 1970, and the creation of the Department of Popular Culture in 1972 were significant steps in the institutionalization of pop culture research in the American academy. Its practitioners define Popular Culture Studies as "the active and determined enlightened analysis of a culture's culture with its strengths and weaknesses thoroughly understood" (Browne, 1996, p. 29). In this tradition, as in others, what constitutes the "popular" is defined very broadly:

> Popular culture is the everyday culture of a group, large or small, of people...It is the way of life in which and by which most people in any society live...It is the everyday world around us...It is what we do while we are awake and how we do it...Popular culture studies are scholarly examinations of those everyday cultures.
>
> *(Browne, 1996, pp. 22, 25)*

The primary goal of Popular Culture Studies since its inception has been to legitimize the study of pop culture in all fields of the humanities and social sciences. Scholars claim widespread success: "We in Popular Culture Studies have pioneered the way and opened up the territory to a vast new field of necessary understanding" (Browne, 1995, p. 25).

As this quote suggests, Popular Culture Studies sees itself as the "umbrella" field under which various theoretical, ideological, or disciplinary approaches to the study of pop culture, including Cultural Studies and the Production of Culture perspective, are situated. In other words, to its practitioners, Popular Culture Studies is identified primarily through its subject matter. To study popular culture from any perspective is to participate in the Popular Culture Studies tradition, whether scholars recognize and acknowledge that participation or not. In a recent article Ray Browne takes the broader academic community to task for "co-opting" the tradition, and argues:

> Popular Culture Studies should be . . . the mainframe of the computer system of human understanding which receives, coordinates and redistributes all efforts and accomplishments.   *(1995, p. 26)*

In his view, Popular Culture Studies "is more important than individual fields" and needs to "incorporate all of them" (1995, p. 26). As we discuss below, however, there are significant differences in the way the Popular Culture Studies tradition understands its role and its mission, as compared to other perspectives, that might make such widespread incorporation difficult.

Issues and Debates

We turn now to a discussion of some of the key points of both convergence and debate within the broader field of popular culture scholarship. We do not mean to be exhaustive but rather offer the reader a general sense of some of the dominant themes in the literature. While there are considerably more areas of debate than consensus, most scholars – despite their differences in disciplinary location, theoretical stance, methodological approach and/or overall mission – can agree on a few key issues. First, scholars agree that popular culture both reflects *and* shapes broader social forces; it is a reciprocal process rather than a unidirectional one. Second, although scholars tend to draw upon their own disciplinary traditions to guide their work, they agree that popular culture research is, and should be, a multidisciplinary endeavor. Indeed, the range of perspectives brought to bear on the topic is astounding; as noted before, scholars throughout the Humanities, the Social Sciences, Schools of Leisure Studies, and Schools of Education are actively involved in pop culture research. Third, as a result, scholars support a diversity of methodological approaches to the study of popular culture. While disciplinary preferences or constraints shape how all scholars conduct research, there is general agreement that different modes of inquiry into popular culture generate meaningfully different questions, and thus meaningfully different results.

A final point of agreement, and perhaps the most significant, relates back to the question of how "pop culture" itself is defined. As social historians have documented, a discourse emerged in the late 1800s which distinguished elite or "highbrow" culture from mass or "lowbrow" culture.[8] Elite cultural objects and practices are those favored by the socially privileged and well-educated, who are believed to be uniquely capable of understanding and appreciating them. Lowbrow or popular culture is essentially everything that is *not* elite culture. The designation of an object or practice as highbrow or lowbrow depends upon several interrelated variables. First is its degree of accessibility: the more accessible the object or practice the more likely it is to be labeled lowbrow. A second variable is the degree of emotional "distance" adopted by consumers vis-à-vis the cultural text in question: a hyper-rational or "over-distanced" experience indicates highbrow cultural consumption whereas an overly-emotional or "under-distanced" experience signals lowbrow status (see Scheff, 1979). The final variable rests on whether the object or practice is identifiably authored: that is, traceable to a uniquely gifted creative genius. In general, authored texts are more likely to be considered highbrow than are unauthored ones. Scholars agree that distinctions between highbrow and lowbrow are made less for aesthetic reasons than political ones. According to Herbert Gans:

> It is really about the nature of the good life, and thus about the purpose of life in general...It is also about which culture and whose culture should dominate in society...As such, the mass culture critique is an attack by one element of society against another. *(Gans, 1974, pp. 3–4)*

Pierre Bourdieu concurs:

> Taste classifies, and it classifies the classifier. Social subjects, classified by their classifications, distinguish themselves by the distinctions they make, between the beautiful and the ugly, the distinguished and the vulgar...the most intolerable thing for those who regard themselves as the possessors of legitimate culture is the sacrilegious reuniting of tastes which taste dictates shall be separated. *(Bourdieu, 1984, pp. 6, 57)*

The late 1960s marked the beginning of a significant trend: the gradual disintegration of high/low distinctions. Scholars from all perspectives now agree there is considerable fluidity between elite and mass culture. In other words, culture is a dynamic process rather than a static entity, and high/low distinctions can change over time, as can the social groups that engage them (also see Peterson and Kern, 1996). For example, silent movies are treated as "art" films today but were originally created for (and consumed by) a mass audience; a similar transformation occurred with Shakespeare's plays (see Levine, 1988). As such, the categories of high and low are increasingly recognized as analytically imprecise. This is not to suggest, however, that issues of taste have been resolved. Cultural objects are rendered meaningful because of aesthetic valuation, and a key point of debate among scholars is whether it is appropriate, and if so, how to evaluate the aesthetic qualities of a product. Some believe that doing so passes judgment on the implied taste of its creators and consumers, and that the proper analytic approach is one of neutral objectivity. But is it plausible to remain neutral about issues of culture and taste? We all find issues of taste relevant to our everyday lived experiences. At the end of each semester, students enrolled in Lee's soap opera class invariably confess they had expected the course to be easy because soap operas are so "trashy." To their surprise, neither turns out to be true.

While there is considerable agreement about the questions addressed by the field of popular culture, there are at least three areas of ongoing debate: the origins of popular culture; the question of whether cultural consumers are active or passive; and as noted above, the question of whether it is appropriate for scholars to take an explicitly evaluative approach in conducting pop culture research. In the following sections we outline each of these debates – but, we make no attempt to resolve them in this introductory chapter. It is our hope that the articles in this collection encourage and enable readers to examine these debates on their own.

What are the origins of popular culture? When, where and under what conditions did it emerge? Most scholars, particularly those in the Cultural Studies and Production of Culture traditions, believe that mass production (and thus mass distribution and mass consumption) was a necessary precursor to the emergence of a truly "popular" culture, and place its origins in the various transformations wrought by the Industrial Revolution in Western Europe and North America in the late 1800s. Popular Culture Studies scholars question this positioning, suggesting that research biases might obscure researchers from recognizing its true origins. Fred Schroeder (1980), for example, claims that our tendency to equate pop culture with various forms of mass entertainment (such as television, music and film) obscures our ability to recognize other objects and practices as "popular" (see also Browne, 1973). Relatedly, he suggests that our tendency to equate it with everything Western, especially everything "American," obscures our ability to recognize its presence in other regions and cultures of the world. Finally, our tendency to equate mass production with factory or assembly-line production obscures our ability to legitimize earlier forms of production as, indeed, "mass." In his edited collection titled *5000 Years of Popular Culture*, Schroeder (1980) recounts a visit to an Egyptian museum where he discovered an ancient clay mold from which figurines were produced for funerals and other spiritual practices. He writes:

> Molds are the most obvious and least ambiguous of mass-production techniques. They are indicators of the alienation of creator from the product, and producer from consumer, and they are indicators of a metropolitan (i.e. "mother-city") value system ... I later observed similar molds from Tibet, and it became clear to me that I had found a technological connecting link to Sony radios, Coke bottles, penny-dreadfuls, the Bay Psalm Book and the Gutenberg Bible. I had discovered ancient popular culture.
>
> *(Schroeder, 1980, pp. 12, 4)*

Thus, according to Schroeder, scholars' recognition of their possible research biases might significantly expand the realm of what is typically considered "popular" culture.

A second area of debate concerns the question of whether pop culture is imposed from above by social elites for purposes of social control, or is truly created "by the people, for the people." Most scholars writing in the mid-twentieth century believed that pop culture wholly reflected the interests and motivations of the dominant classes. In the most pessimistic reading of this perspective, usually termed the mass culture critique and associated with members of the Frankfurt school (including Adorno and Horkheimer, mentioned earlier), cultural consumers are completely pacified and homogenized in the process of consumption. As unquestioning recipients, consumers contribute nothing to the meaning of popular culture – and thus nothing to society at large – but instead are repetitively victimized and immobilized by it.[9]

Scholars writing today generally reject this perspective, but they disagree on the extent to which pop culture is instead an "authentic expression of the interests of the people" (Ross, 1989, p. 4). Cultural Studies asserts that popular culture is neither totally imposed from above, nor something that emerges spontaneously from below, but rather is the outcome of an ongoing interplay between the processes of production and consumption (see Storey, 1993, p. 13). As noted earlier, however, Cultural Studies tends to focus heavily on consumers. John Fiske, for example, acknowledges that while the larger social system provides cultural resources to consumers (and benefits economically from the process of consumption), it is only consumers who can popularize objects or practices. In his view, the power, ultimately, is with the people:

> Popular texts...are completed only when taken up by people and inserted into their everyday culture. The people make popular culture at the interface between everyday life and the consumption of the products of the cultural industries...Relevance can be produced only by the people, for only they can know which texts enable them to make the meanings that will function in their everyday lives.   *(Fiske, 1989, p. 6)*

Others argue that we need to be cautious in applauding the apparent power of active audiences to generate their own cultural meanings, because this power is actually quite limited. In reference to media consumption Ien Ang writes:

> audiences may be active in myriad ways using and interpreting media, but it would be utterly out of perspective to cheerfully equate "active" with "powerful," in the sense of "taking control" at an enduring, structural, or institutional level. It is a perfectly reasonable starting point to consider people's active negotiations with media texts and technologies as empowering in the context of their everyday lives...but we must not lose sight of the marginality of this power.   *(Ang, 1990, p. 247)*

In sum, the extent to which "people make the popular" has yet to be resolved.

The final area of debate speaks back to the aesthetics of pop cultural objects and practice and centers on the question of whether academic scholars should approach issues of aesthetics in an evaluative or nonevaluative way. Sociologist Herbert Gans defines aesthetics as follows:

> I use the term "aesthetic" broadly, referring not only to standards of beauty and taste but also to a variety of other emotional and intellectual values which people express or satisfy when they choose content from a culture.   *(Gans, 1974, p. 14)*

In terms of the three approaches discussed here, only Cultural Studies seems explicitly involved in evaluative research. Its origins as an activist or politically transformative project render aesthetic evaluation a necessary element in the critical analysis of power relations in the processes of production and consumption. Popular Culture Studies, in contrast, espouses a non-evaluative approach, arguing that researchers should be neutral or objective in examining cultural texts and the people who produce and consume them. Since pop culture is defined as everyday culture, "liked or disliked, approved or disapproved...the question of aesthetics plays only a tangential and relatively unimportant role" (Browne, 1996, pp. 25, 33). What researchers might think of any given object, practice or process is irrelevant to their ability to describe and/or interpret it. Rollin (1975) goes further by arguing that cultural evaluation is simply part of human nature. Making judgments about popular culture is thus inevitable:

> And because it is inevitable it is unnecessary – unnecessary at least for the serious critic of Popular Culture, and unnecessary to the construction of a critical theory for Popular Culture . . . the only real authority concerning the "beauty" or "excellence" of a work of Popular Culture is the people . . . in Popular Culture, the rule is "one person – one vote." However regrettable this may appear . . . it is a fact . . . Popular Art [thus] represents the triumph of a democratic aesthetic.   *(Rollin, 1975, p. 4, 5; emphasis deleted)*

Rollin goes on to warn that aesthetic evaluations can in fact be damaging:

> students of Popular Culture should be aware of the ways in which standards of aesthetic value can be transformed into moral imperatives which are then employed to celebrate some human beings and oppress others.   *(Rollin, 1975, p. 10)*

Cultural Studies would probably agree with this statement but would argue that scholars should examine aesthetic standards precisely *because* they are embedded in relations of power. Negotiations between producers and consumers about "goodness" and "badness" are integral to the larger struggle over cultural meaning-making, and thus should be a key focus of empirical analysis.

The discipline of sociology, in which the Production of Culture perspective originated, is still attempting to articulate its position. In the early twentieth century, sociologists were centrally involved in aesthetic evaluation as part of their widespread critique of the "evils" of mass culture (see, for example, Blumer, 1933). Newer sociological approaches, in contrast, have avoided evaluative issues, and the Production of Culture perspective essentially ignores the issues of meaning-making and aesthetics altogether. "To the extent that aesthetics is addressed among scholars, it is as a dependent variable determined by market structure or industrial organization" (Bielby and Bielby, forthcoming, p. 4). This reluctance is based on sociologists' erroneous belief that aesthetic judgment within popular culture is not empirically accessible. In the realm of elite culture, professional gatekeepers or mediators play a central role in deciphering and articulating a cultural object's value to social members. In pop culture, in contrast, the accessibility of the cultural object pre-empts the traditional gatekeeping role.[10] Instead, consumers articulate aesthetic values and make aesthetic judgments for themselves but since they are presumed to lack the critical capacity to do so they are granted little cultural authority. Consequently, sociologists treat most forms of popular culture as if they have no accessible aesthetic value at all. Bielby and Bielby suggest, however, that sociology can examine pop culture's various aesthetic systems by beginning with the interpretations and meaning-making systems of consumers themselves. In terms of television they write:

> Our point is that what makes a popular culture art form both "culture" and "popular" is that appreciation and evaluation are mediated by a widely shared and understood aesthetic, and both the art form and the aesthetic are accessible to an engaged audience that invests in acquiring the requisite knowledge without deferring to cultural authorities.   *(Bielby and Bielby, forthcoming, p. 22)*

In short, while the Production of Culture approach sidesteps the issue, Bielby and Bielby argue that a complete sociological analysis of pop culture requires scholars to treat seriously the various ways consumers construct and maintain their own aesthetic systems.

The Circuit of Culture

This collection of readings is organized around the principle of connecting the worlds of cultural production and consumption. Common sense tells us that the popularity of any given cultural text, whether it be music or television or sport, is dependent upon an integrated relationship between producers and consumers. We learn little about singers unless we also study music-buyers; we learn little about television producers unless we also study television viewers. For ease of analysis, however, pop culture research tends to focus on only one dimension. The consumptionist trajectory of Cultural Studies and the productionist trajectory of Production of Culture scholars obscure linkages between the two processes:

> [The] analytic splitting of production from consumption overstates the interpretive control exercised by consumers and understates the power of the culture industries to limit what is made available for interpretation.   *(Traube, 1996, p. xii)*

To connect production and consumption we borrow the conceptual image of a *circuit of culture*, which suggests that cultural meaning-making functions less in terms of a "transmission flow" model from producer to consumer "and more like the model of a dialogue. It is an ongoing process" (du Gay, 1997, p. 10; see also du Gay et al. 1997). Cultural meanings are produced at a number of different sites and are circulated through a complex set of reciprocal processes and practices. While production and consumption are key sites for meaning-making, other sites serve important intermediary functions.[11] Advertising, for example, "both articulates production with consumption, and draws consumption back into the process of production." Advertising thus constitutes its own moment in the circuit of culture: the moment of circulation (Nixon, 1997, p. 10).

According to du Gay and his colleagues (1997), there are at least five major cultural processes that should be emphasized in studying the circuit of culture, including representation, identity, production, consumption, and regulation. To study an object or text culturally, "one should at least explore how it is represented, what social identities are associated with it, how it is produced and consumed, and what mechanisms regulate its distribution and use" (du Gay et al., 1997, p. 3). In analyzing the circuit one can begin with any moment or site that one chooses; while they might appear to be distinct categories, they overlap and articulate with one another in myriad ways.

This collection of readings is designed to encourage and facilitate this understanding of cultural meaning-making as dialectical. Readings were selected to cover a variety of sites in the circuit of culture and to explore key themes and debates about the relationship between them. The readings reflect the richly diverse history of pop culture scholarship in that they are situated in a broad spectrum of theoretical and disciplinary perspectives. The collection is organized into five distinct sections. Part I explores the meaning of the term "popular" through a range of cultural texts including music, comics, sport, and art. This section aims to introduce readers to the variety of objects and practices that constitute the popular and to the range of scholarly perspectives that might be used to study them. Parts II and III focus explicitly on the two key sites in the circuit of culture: production and consumption. We encourage students to read across these two sections very carefully. Part II explores how mass culture is commodified and asks who profits (and loses) from that commodification. Included here are analyses of art, advertising, alternative rock, and the post-modern city. Part III examines cultural consumption, focusing on the ongoing tension between producers and consumers over the generation of cultural meaning. This section opens with a classic piece on encoding and decoding meaning in cultural texts, a process further explored through an article on pornography and three different articles on music. Part IV returns to the key element of cultural texts as explored in the first section but focuses on several new issues. The first article introduces and explores the concept of formula or genre. The articles on literature translation and music sampling address the authorship of cultural texts; as noted earlier, determinations of authorship are central in the social "worth" awarded a cultural object (i.e. highbrow/lowbrow status). The two articles on television illustrate the complexity of textual meanings and the role of the text in the circuit of culture. Finally, Part V focuses on celebrity and fandom through readings on the emergence of the concept of celebrity in America, the meanings/readings of country music legend Dolly Parton, and through two articles on the uneasy role of fans in the generation of cultural meaning. The readings in Part V are included because they concretize or materialize the circuit of culture. They illustrate that celebrity is a manufactured product (one site in the circuit) which necessarily depends on distribution and circulation (a second site) and the patronage of fan-consumers (a third site) to maintain celebrity status. The celebrity-fan relationship, in other words, might be said to literally embody the circuit of culture.[12]

The essays collected here include some of the "classics" in pop culture scholarship, more recently published selections from scholarly books and journals, and several new pieces solicited especially for this book. Readers will note that the essays emphasize various forms of mass entertainment (rather than other types of cultural content), reflect a mostly Western perspective, and are situated in contemporary (rather than historical) cultural arenas. However, we hope that readers in all areas of popular culture find this collection useful for their scholarship, teaching and learning.

Notes

1 Some believe this particular understanding of the term is justification enough for why pop culture should be studied in the academy. In this view, popularity is a significant indicator of the cultural mindset of the times, "the popularity of a given cultural element (object, person or event) is directly proportional to the degree to which that element is reflective of audience beliefs and values. The *greater* the popularity of the cultural element – in an era and/or over time – the *more* reflective of the zeitgeist this element is likely to be" (Nachbar and Lause

1992, p. 5; emphasis in original). Studying pop culture is important, then, because it tells us something significant about ourselves and our culture more broadly.

2 Today, however, literary studies has fully embraced pop culture research, especially within the Cultural Studies tradition.

3 See Mukerji and Schudson (1991) for an excellent discussion of the disciplinary origins of popular culture research.

4 To expand, Gramsci's work explores the ways that dominant classes rule without employing direct force. "The question to which 'hegemony' is an answer is, 'Why do dominated or oppressed groups accept their position in the social hierarchy?' Gramsci held that, in fact, oppressed groups accept the definition of the world of elites as common sense; their understanding of how the world works, then, leads them to collaborate in their own oppression" (Mukerji and Schudson, 1991, p. 15).

5 Keith Negus (1997) dates the emergence of this perspective to the 1976 publication of Richard Peterson's edited collection, *The Production of Culture* (London: Sage). Particularly influential was the chapter by Peterson himself titled "The production of culture: A Prolegomenon."

6 Adorno and Horkheimer, along with other members of what has been termed the Frankfurt school, were extremely influential in the development of Cultural Studies as well.

7 As Mukerji and Schudson point out, however, there are several potential drawbacks to this approach. First, the production of culture perspective is "much better at explaining the normal mechanisms for creating 'normal' culture than it is at explaining what happens when culture changes." Furthermore, this approach has a tendency to "assume that sociological factors are more determining than, in fact, they are." Finally, and perhaps more importantly, production of culture studies "assume that they study the production of 'culture.' They do not. They study the production of cultural objects, and these objects become a part of and contribute to culture. But they are not culture as such" (Mukerji and Schudson 1991, pp. 32–3).

8 There is some debate about when this distinction first occurred. Herbert Gans (1974) claims it emerged about 200 years ago in most modern societies when daily life was first divided into "work" time and "leisure" time. Other scholars argue that the late nineteenth century and the transformations heralded by the Industrial Revolution (e.g. mass production/distribution/consumption) first allowed for the distinction to be made. Levine (1988) traces the first appearance of the term "highbrow" to the late 1880s, and the term "lowbrow" to shortly after 1900 (see also Cullen 1996).

9 Writing in the mid-1970s, Herbert Gans suggests there are four major themes in most mass culture critiques. The first concerns the "negative character of popular culture creation" (i.e. pop culture is mass produced and is purely for-profit). The second addresses the "negative effects on high culture" (i.e. pop culture "steals" from high culture and thus debases it). The third theme focuses on the "negative effects on the popular culture audience" (as noted, mass culture critics believe popular culture is narcotizing and harmful to its consumers). A final theme is the potentially "negative effects on the society" (i.e. pop culture consumption reduces the level of civilization, and since it encourages consumer passivity, also encourages totalitarianism) (Gans 1974, p. 19).

10 While there are obviously professional critics of popular cultural forms, particularly forms of mass entertainment, they are not presumed to be "necessary" in terms of consumers' ability to understand and appreciate an object or practice. In elite culture, in contrast, the critics' role is believed essential to the meaning-making process.

11 DuGay and his colleagues address how the cultural economy links production and consumption, specifically through the processes of representation, identity, and regulation. By broadening conceptualization of how production and consumption occur, du Gay attends

to cultures of meaning and the identities which create them. Griswold's (1994) "cultural diamond" also considers the relationship between cultural objects and the social world. She identifies four elements: creators, cultural objects, recipients, and the social world. However, Griswold's schema is an accounting device that does not specify the content of the relationships among any of the elements. She makes clear that her schema is neither a theory nor a model of culture because it does not indicate cause and effect.

12 Marshall (1997) suggests that celebrities are manufactured commodities; using a Marxian metaphor, he suggests they have no use value in contemporary culture but instead are pure exchange value. In contrast to this conceptualization, we argue that celebrities embody the circuit of culture as a whole.

References

Ang, Ien: "Culture and communication: Toward an ethnographic critique of media consumption in the transnational media realm," *European Journal of Communication*, 5 (1990), 239–60.

Barker, Martin and Beezer, Anne: "Introduction: What's in a text?" *Reading into Cultural Studies*, ed., M. Barker and A. Beezer (London: Routledge, 1992), pp. 1–20.

Bielby, Denise D. and Bielby, William T.: "Audience aesthetics and popular culture," *The Cultural Turn*, ed. R. Friedland and J. Mohr (London: Cambridge University Press, forthcoming).

Bourdieu, Pierre: *Distinction: A Social Critique of the Judgement of Taste* (Cambridge, MA: Harvard University Press, 1984).

Blumer, Herbert: *Movies and Conduct* (New York: Macmillan, 1933).

Browne, Ray: "Coping with success: Homo Empatheia and popular culture studies in the 21st century," *Preview 2001+: Popular Culture Studies in the Future*, ed. R. B. Browne and M. Fishwick (Bowling Green, OH: Bowling Green State University Popular Press, 1995), pp. 17–28.

Browne, Ray: "Internationalizing popular culture studies," *Journal of Popular Culture*, 30 (1996), pp. 21–37.

Browne, Ray B.: "Popular culture: Notes toward a definition," *Popular Culture and the Expanding Consciousness*, ed. R. B. Browne (New York: John Wiley and Sons, 1973), pp. 14–22.

Cullen, Jim: *The Art of Democracy: A Concise History of Popular Culture in the United States* (New York: Monthly Review Press, 1996).

Curran, James, Morley, David, and Walkerdine, Valerie: "Introduction," *Cultural Studies and Communications*, ed. J. Curran, D. Morley and V. Walkerdine (London: Arnold, 1996), pp. 1–5.

Du Gay, P., Hall, S., James, L., Mackay, H., and Negus, K.: *Doing Cultural Studies: The Story of the Sony Walkman* (London: Sage/The Open University, 1997).

Du Gay, Paul: "Introduction," *Production of Culture/Cultures of Production*, ed., Paul du Gay (London: Sage, 1997), pp. 1–10.

During, Simon: "Introduction," *The Cultural Studies Reader*, ed. Simon During (London: Routledge, 1993), pp. 1–25.

Fiske, John: *Reading the Popular* (Boston, MA: Unwin Hyman, 1989).

Gans, Herbert: *Popular Culture and High Culture: An Analysis and Evaluation of Taste* (New York: Basic Books, 1974).

Griswold, Wendy: *Cultures and Societies in a Changing World* (Thousand Oaks, CA: Sage, 1994).

Levine, Lawrence W.: *Highbrow/Lowbrow: The Emergence of Cultural Hierarchy in America* (Cambridge, MA: Harvard University Press, 1988).

Marshall, P. David: *Celebrity and Power: Fame in Contemporary Culture* (Minneapolis, MN: University of Minnesota Press, 1997).

Miller, Toby and McHoul, Alec: *Popular Culture and Everyday Life* (London: Sage, 1998).

Mukerji, Chandra and Schudson, Michael: "Introduction: Rethinking popular culture," *Rethinking Popular Culture: Contemporary Perspectives in Cultural Studies*, ed. C. Mukerji and M. Schudson (Berkeley, CA: University of California Press, 1991), pp. 1–61.

Nachbar, Jack and Lause, Kevin: "Getting to know us: An introduction to the study of popular culture: What is this stuff that dreams are made of?" *Popular Culture: An Introductory Text*, ed. J. Nachbar and K. Lause (Bowling Green, OH: Bowling Green State University Popular Press, 1992), pp. 1–35.

Negus, Keith: "The production of culture," *Production of Culture/Cultures of Production*, ed. Paul du Gay (London: Sage, 1997), pp. 67–104.

Nelson, Cary, Treichler, Paula A., and Grossberg, Lawrence: "Cultural studies: An introduction," *Cultural Studies*, ed. L. Grossberg, C. Nelson, and P. A. Treichler (New York: Routledge, 1992), pp. 1–22.

Nixon, Sean: "Circulating culture," in *Production of Culture/Cultures of Production*, ed. P. du Gay (London: Sage, 1997), pp. 177–220.

Peterson, Richard A. and Roger M. Kern: "Changing highbrow taste: From snob to omnivore," *American Sociological Review*, 61 (1996), 900–8.

Rollin, Roger B.: "Against evaluation: The role of the critic of popular culture," *Journal of Popular Culture*, 9 (1975), 3–13.

Ross, Andrew: *No Respect: Intellectuals & Popular Culture* (New York, NY: Routledge, 1989).

Scheff, Thomas J.: *Catharsis in Healing, Ritual and Drama* (Berkeley and Los Angeles, CA: University of California Press, 1979).

Schroeder, Fred: *5000 Years of Popular Culture* (Bowling Green, OH: Bowling Green University Popular Press, 1980).

Storey, John: *An Introductory Guide to Cultural Theory and Popular Culture* (Athens, GA: The University of Georgia Press, 1993).

Traube, Elizabeth G.: "Introduction," in *Making and Selling Culture*, ed. R. Ohmann (Hanover, MA: Wesleyan University Press, 1996), pp. xi–xxiii

Williams, Raymond: *Keywords* (London: Fontana, 1983).

Part I

What is Popular?

2 Making Artistic Popular Music: The Goal of True Folk

John Blacking

There is good evidence that for over ninety-nine per cent of human history, and for ninety-seven per cent of the time since the emergence of our own species (*homo sapiens sapiens*) approximately 70,000 years ago, all music was popular, in so far as it was shared and enjoyed by all members of a society. If there were distinctions of style within a society's music, they were accepted as signs of functional or social differentiation rather than as barriers to mutual communication. Distinctions between sacred and secular music, between music for young and old or men and women, were generally drawn within the style of each music culture, and, at least in principle, a member of one group could perform and appreciate the music of another group in the same society.

There is, of course, no direct evidence of the antiquity of popular music: we infer it from the musical practices of non-literate societies that have been studied by folklorists, anthropologists and ethnomusicologists. Moreover, it would be quite wrong to regard any contemporary society of hunter-gatherers or horticulturalists as a survival of palaeolithic or early neolithic times: more than 10,000 years of history and constant social change separate the Aurignacians and Magdalenians of prehistoric Europe from the San of the Kalahari desert or the Aranda of Central Australia, even as they were described a hundred years ago. Nevertheless the study of music-making in small-scale, non-literate societies has made possible certain generalisations about the musical process (see Blacking 1973) which can be applied to all societies, past and present.

First, all members of the species are basically as capable of dancing, singing and making music, as they are of speaking a natural language. There is even evidence that early human species were able to dance and sing several thousand years before *homo sapiens sapiens* emerged with the capacity for speech as we now know it (see Livingstone 1973, Blacking 1976).

Second, performing music, like speaking a verbal language, is part of the process of knowing and understanding it. Performance does not require a special set of capabilities, and active listening is essentially a mental rehearsal of performance, in which a person re-invents "the text". Thus distinctions between creator, performer and listener are the consequence of assigned social roles.

Third, music and music-making can in principle be assigned almost any social, political or religious meaning, and treated like any other social activities, but the symbols that are invoked also involve the body in such a way that they sometimes acquire a force of their own. Musical performance can express and evoke sensuous experiences that can be, and often are, related to feelings. Thus music, as a category

Original publication: Blacking, John, "Making Artistic Popular Music: The Goal of True Folk," *Popular Music*, 1 (Cambridge University Press, 1981).

of action,[1] need not always be a reflective epiphenomenon of the social: it can be a primary modelling system of thought, and musical imagination can trigger off action in social fields to which its sensuous code does not directly refer, because of the effects that the bodily experiences may have on consciousness, motivation, commitment and decision-making (see Blacking 1981).

Fourth, although musical codes can express and evoke feelings as well as new sound experiences, and human emotions are broadly similar throughout the world, music is not a universal language. Attempts to trace the evolution of the musical art from simple to complex, from one-tone to twelve-tone scale, and to fit all the music of the world into the scheme, have proved fruitless: for example, the San of the Kalahari and the so-called Pygmies of the Ituri forest have simple technologies but also polyphony (see *Bushman Music and Pygmy Music*), whose invention was supposed to have been the prerogative of advanced European societies. Musical codes are derived neither from some universal emotional language nor from stages in the evolution of a musical art: they are socially accepted patterns of sound that have been invented and developed by interacting individuals in the context of different social and cultural systems.

These and other generalisations about music-making can be summed up and developed as follows: music is a social fact, and discriminating listeners are as necessary as performers for its existence; all normal human beings are capable of making music; role distinctions between creator, performer and listener, variations in musical styles, and contrasts in the apparent musical ability of composers and performers, are consequences of the division of labour in society, of the functional interrelationship of groups and of the commitment of individuals to music-making as a social activity.

But music is also a special kind of symbolic activity, in which sensuous experience and transformations of consciousness are often more highly valued than immediate practical social consequences. When people become involved in the performance of music, they suspend other kinds of decision-making. Thus the nature of the activity, and the ways in which people relate to the organisation and perception of tones, the essential symbols of a musical system, are the most interesting and problematic features of music-making.

It is not, therefore, surprising that so much music writing and musicological research have been concerned with values and with effectiveness of musical symbols, and that styles of music have been labelled and assigned categories of value. Art music was supposed to be that which displayed exceptional skill in creation and was generally written down, as distinct from folk music, which was of popular origin. Classical music was a branch of art music, initially opposed to romantic, folk, modern, or popular music; but as modern music became contemporary music, so it became linked with romantic and classical music, and labelled as serious music.

Popular music was music that did not seek "to appeal to refined or classical taste" (*Oxford English Dictionary*) and was generally thought to include folk songs. But as research into and preservation of folk music grew, so the elitism of the labellers was extended: just as addicts of serious music had regarded popular music with distaste or disgust, so folk-music performers and scholars frequently viewed popular music with disdain. There was "good", "pure" popular music, which was the authentic music of the people, and could be called "folk", or perhaps "traditional", music; and there was "bastardised", "contaminated" music of the people, which was dismissed by derogatory terms such as "popular", "commercial", or even "urban" (see Blacking 1978, pp. 7–9). Such extreme attitudes are no longer common amongst writers and researchers, but they persist in the attitudes of many organisers of folklore festivals and performers of folk music. For example, I have encountered several Irish traditional musicians who weaken their case against the elitism of Irish institutions and of individuals devoted to "art" music, by taking a similarly elitist attitude towards what they regard as "unauthentic" performances of Irish music, and indeed towards the traditional music of Africa, Asia, America and Oceania in general.

Classifications of music into "folk", "art" or "popular" reflect a concern with musical products, rather than with the dynamic process of music-making. The labels have come to identify weapons in the battles of the record companies, whose ultimate aim is surely to substitute packaged recordings for the live, genuinely popular music-making of ordinary human beings, which still exists in some societies and was almost certainly the way that all music was made for ninety-seven per cent of the history of the human species. As descriptions of different kinds of music, or even of the musical cultures of different social groups, the labels are meaningless and invariably misleading. They are also value-laden terms that are often used without specification of underlying assumptions. For example, popular music and folk music have been widely regarded as degenerations of art music: just as the popular hymn-singing of Black South African Independent Churches was said to be a consequence of members' inability to sing European hymns correctly (Blacking 1981), so the *ganga* part-songs of peasants in Bosnia and Herzegovina were said to be crude attempts to reproduce harmonies that had been heard in the sophisticated music of the cities (Petrovic 1977).

Ethnomusicological research has reminded us that music-making must always be regarded as intentional action, and that the actors' reasons for what they do must be taken into account. Art does not consist of products, but of the processes by which people make sense of certain kinds of activity and experience. Music is available-foruse (see Jones 1971), and musical value resides not in any piece or style of music, but in the ways that people address themselves to listening and performance. Supposing that popular music were music that does not seek "to appeal to refined taste" (*OED*), this would not make art music refined and popular music unrefined. Refinement is a quality that people evoke through performing or listening to music; and just as many people's attitudes to art music may lack refinement, so others' attitudes and responses to popular music may be refined.

Similarly, musical skills are not required any less for "folk" and "popular" music than for "art" music, just as William Byrd's choral music is not easier than Handel's or Verdi's or Britten's. Pop musicians are no less meticulous about rehearsal than symphony orchestras; and if they may seem a little inarticulate in defining the sounds that they want, one only has to listen to the language of orchestral conductors to appreciate how much they also are disadvantaged by working in a non-verbal medium.

Although music is "the result of certain attitudes, certain specific ways of thinking about the world, and only ultimately about the 'ways' in which music can be made" (Jones 1963, p. 153), the effectiveness of music depends on people's relationships to the organisation and perception of the musical symbols, rather than the non-musical attitudes expressed towards them or in company with them. Thus although musical value is to be measured by the ways in which people make sense of music, the relevant terms in which the sense is made must be musical. If people value music because it is political, or is religious, or has a social message, they are not being affected primarily by the musical symbols. Popular *music*, as distinct from popular sentiment, is identified when people like a tune, a sonority or a whole piece of music, without emphasising its non-musical attributes, and try to relate themselves to the organisation of rhythms, tones and timbres that they perceive.

In this sense, "popular music" is a category of value that can be applied to all styles of music:[2] it is music that is liked or admired by people in general, and it includes Bach, Beethoven, the Beatles, Ravi Shankar, Sousa's marches and the "Londonderry Air". Far from being a patronising or derogatory term, it describes positively music that has succeeded in its basic aim to communicate as *music*. The music that most people value most is popular music; but what that music is, varies according to the social class and experience of composers, performers and listeners.

Since I argue that labels such as "folk", "art" and "popular" tell us nothing substantive about different styles of music; that as categories of value they can be applied to any music; and that the most pressing tasks are to understand the musical process and ensure that no human beings are deprived of their right to make music, it may well be asked how I can serve on the Editorial Board and contribute to a publication that is called *Popular Music*.

First, I am not specially interested in popular music as defined by the Editors above, but I am very much interested in popular music as a category of value. I regard music-making (or at least some "artistic" activity) as an essential qualification of becoming fully human, so that failure to practice it means leaving some innate capabilities and resources untapped. Music-making must be an essential activity for all in a healthy, developing society; practice of music, and of the arts in general, must be part of the process of educating the feelings and the intellect. The lesson of ethnomusicological research is that, far from being a pious hope for the future in industrial societies, this situation has existed in the majority of human societies for the greater part of human history. As Eric Gill said, "it isn't that artists are special kinds of people. It's that people are special kinds of artists."

Second, the emergence of popular music, in the sense defined by the Editors, as a phenomenon of industrialised and industrialising societies, is one of the most striking examples of the power of musical symbols, and of people's general musical creativity and search for quality in life. Just as it was necessary to define and analyse class in order to dissolve it, so it is perhaps necessary to define and analyse a new type of music, and give it a name that expresses a pious hope if not an accurate fact, in order to restore musical consciousness *and practice* to their central place in human life.

Karl Marx looked forward to a society in which "*the* artist" as a special category of person would be redundant, and in which all men and women could cultivate their artistic capabilities, so that the distinction between producer and consumer of art would abolish itself and Art and Life would become one. Similarly, distinctions between "art", "folk" and "popular" music should dissolve, as human beings achieve the most important goal of ownership of the senses.

The serious study of popular music will serve a useful purpose if it helps to extend the practice of music and eliminate elitism as quite contrary to the spirit of music-making.

Notes

1 Another issue raised by the study of musical systems in non-literate societies is that many peoples lack a word for "music". I use the concepts of "music" and "musical" as ideal types, or gloss terms, for a category of human action that is widely accepted but not yet fully understood.
2 "Folk music" and "art music" can also be treated as categories of value rather than as types of music, but the argument need not be taken further here.

References

Blacking, John, *How Musical is Man?* (Seattle, 1973, and London, 1976).
"Dance, conceptual thought and production in the archaeological record", in *Problems in Economic and Social Archaeology*, ed. G. de G. Sieveking, I. H. Longworth and K. E. Wilson (London, 1976), pp. 1–13.
"Some problems of theory and method in the study of musical change", *Yearbook of the International Folk Music Council*, 9 (1978), pp. 1–26.
"Political and musical freedom in the music of some Black South African Churches", in *The Structure of Folk Models*, ed. L. Holy and M. Stuchlik, Association of Social Anthropologists monograph no. 20 (London, 1981), pp. 35–62.
Bushman Music and Pygmy Music, recording issued, with notes and transcriptions, by the Musée de l'Homme and the Peabody Museum.
Jones, Leroi, *Blues People* (New York, 1963).
Jones, Peter, "Works of art and their availability-for-use", *The British Journal of Aesthetics*, 11:2 (1971), pp. 115–22.
Livingstone, Frank, "Did the Australopithecines sing?", *Current Anthropology*, 14 (1973), pp. 25–9.
Petrovic, Ankica, "*Ganga*, a form of traditional rural singing in Yugoslavia" (The Queen's University of Belfast, unpublished PhD thesis 1977).

3 Batman, Deviance, and Camp

Andy Medhurst

Only someone ignorant of the fundamentals of psychiatry and of the psychopatholgy of sex can fail to realize a subtle atmosphere of homoerotism which pervades the adventure of the mature "Batman" and his young friend "Robin." *(Fredric Wertham)*[1]

It's embarrassing to be solemn and treatise-like about Camp. One runs the risk of having, oneself, produced a very inferior piece of Camp. *(Susan Sontag)*[2]

I'm not sure how qualified I am to write this essay. Batman hasn't been particularly important in my life since I was seven years old. Back then he was crucial, paramount, unmissable as I sat twice weekly to watch the latest episode on TV. Pure pleasure, except for the annoying fact that my parents didn't seem to appreciate the thrills on offer. Worse than that, they actually laughed. How could anyone laugh when the Dynamic Duo were about to be turned into Frostie Freezies (pineapple for the Caped Crusader, lime for his chum) by the evil Mr. Freeze?

Batman and I drifted apart after those early days. Every now and then I'd see a repeated episode and I soon began to understand and share that once infuriating parental hilarity, but this aside I hardly thought about the man in the cape at all. I knew about the subculture of comic freaks, and the new and alarmingly pretentious phrase "graphic novel" made itself known to me, but I still regarded (with the confidence of distant ignorance) such texts as violent, macho, adolescent and, well, silly.

That's when the warning bells rang. The word "silly" reeks of the complacent condescension that has at various times been bestowed on all the cultural forms that matter most to me (Hollywood musicals, British melodramas, pop music, soap operas) so what right had I to apply it to someone else's part of the popular cultural playground? I had to rethink my disdain, and 1989 has been a very good year in which to do so, because in terms of popular culture 1989 has been the Year of the Bat.

This essay, then, is not written by a devotee of Batman, someone steeped in every last twist of the mythology. I come to these texts as an interested outsider, armed with a particular perspective. That perspective is homosexuality, and what I want to try and do here is to offer a gay reading of the whole Bat-business. It has no pretension to definitiveness, I don't presume to speak for all gay people everywhere. I'm male, white, British, thirty years old (at the time of writing) and all of those

Original publication: Medhurst, Andy, "Batman, Deviance, and Camp," from Roberta E. Pearson and William Uricchio (eds.), *The Many Lives of the Batman: Critical Approaches to a Superhero and His Media* (Routledge, New York, 1991).

factors need to be taken into account. Nonetheless, I'd argue that Batman is especially interesting to gay audiences for three reasons.

Firstly, he was one of the first fictional characters to be attacked on the grounds of presumed homosexuality, by Fredric Wertham in his book *Seduction of the Innocent*. Secondly, the 1960s TV series was and remains a touchstone of camp (a banal attempt to define the meaning of camp might well start with "like the sixties' *Batman* series"). Thirdly, as a recurring hero figure for the last fifty years, Batman merits analysis as a notably successful construction of masculinity.

Nightmare on Psychiatry Street: Freddy's Obsession

Seduction of the Innocent is an extraordinary book. It is a gripping, flamboyant melodrama masquerading as social psychology. Fredric Wertham is, like Senator McCarthy, like Batman, a crusader, a man with a mission, an evangelist. He wants to save the youth of America from its own worst impulses, from its id, from comic books. His attack on comic books is founded on an astonishingly crude stimulus-and-response model of reading, in which the child (the child, for Wertham, seems an unusually innocent, blank slate waiting to be written on) reads, absorbs and feels compelled to copy, if only in fantasy terms, the content of the comics. It is a model, in other words, which takes for granted extreme audience passivity.

This is not the place to go into a detailed refutation of Wertham's work, besides which such a refutation has already been done in Martin Barker's excellent *A Haunt of Fears*.[3] The central point of audience passivity needs stressing, however, because it is crucial to the celebrated passage where Wertham points his shrill, witch-hunting finger at the Dynamic Duo and cries "queer."

Such language is not present on the page, of course, but in some ways *Seduction of the Innocent* (a film title crying out for either D. W. Griffith or Cecil B. DeMille) would be easier to stomach if it were. Instead, Wertham writes with anguished concern about the potential harm that Batman might do to vulnerable children, innocents who might be turned into deviants. He employs what was then conventional psychiatric wisdom about the idea of homosexuality as a "phase":

> Many pre-adolescent boys pass through a phase of disdain for girls. Some comic books tend to fix that attitude and instill the idea that girls are only good for being banged around or used as decoys. A homoerotic attitude is also suggested by the presentation of masculine, bad, witch-like or violent women. In such comics women are depicted in a definitely anti-erotic light, while the young male heroes have pronounced erotic overtones. The muscular male supertype, whose primary sex characteristics are usually well emphasized, is in the setting of certain stories the object of homoerotic sexual curiosity and stimulation.[4]

The implications of this are breathtaking. Homosexuality, for Wertham, is synonymous with misogyny. Men love other men because they hate women. The sight of women being "banged around" is liable to appeal to repressed homoerotic desires (this, I think, would be news to the thousands of women who are systematically physically abused by heterosexual men). Women who do not conform to existing stereotypes of femininity are another incitement to homosexuality.

Having mapped out his terms of reference, Wertham goes on to peel the lid from Wayne Manor:

> Sometimes Batman ends up in bed injured and young Robin is shown sitting next to him. At home they lead an idyllic life. They are Bruce Wayne and "Dick" Grayson. Bruce Wayne is described as a "socialite" and the official relationship is that Dick is Bruce's ward. They live in sumptuous quarters, with beautiful flowers in large vases, and have a butler, Alfred Batman is sometimes shown in a dressing gown.... It is like a wish dream of two homosexuals living together. Sometimes they are shown on a couch, Bruce reclining and Dick sitting next to him, jacket off, collar open, and his hand on his friend's arm.[5]

So, Wertham's assumptions of homosexuality are fabricated out of his interpretation of certain visual signs. To avoid being thought queer by Wertham, Bruce and Dick should have done the following: never show concern if the other is hurt, live in a shack, only have ugly flowers in small vases, call the butler "Chip" or "Joe" if you have to have one at all, never share a couch, keep your collar buttoned up, keep your jacket on, and never, ever wear a dressing gown. After all, didn't Noel Coward wear a dressing gown?

Wertham is easy to mock, but the identification of homosexuals through dress codes has a long history.[6] Moreover, such codes originate as semiotic systems adopted by gay people themselves, as a way of signalling the otherwise invisible fact of sexual preference. There is a difference, though, between sporting the secret symbols of a subculture if you form part of that subculture and the elephantine spot-the-homo routine that Wertham performs.

Bat-fans have always responded angrily to Wertham's accusation. One calls it "one of the most incredible charges ... unfounded rumours ... sly sneers"[7] and the general response has been to reassert the masculinity of the two heros, mixed with a little indignation: "If they had been actual men they could have won a libel suit."[8] This seems to me not only to miss the point, but also to *reinforce* Wertham's homophobia – it is only possible to win a libel suit over an "accusation" of homosexuality in a culture where homosexuality is deemed categorically inferior to heterosexuality.

Thus the rush to "protect" Batman and Robin from Wertham is simply the other side to the coin of his bigotry. It may reject Wertham, cast him in the role of dirty-minded old man, but its view of homosexuality is identical. Mark Cotta Vaz thus describes the imputed homosexual relationship as "licentious" while claiming that in fact Bruce Wayne "regularly squired the most beautiful women in Gotham city and presumably had a healthy sex life."[9] Licentious versus healthy – Dr. Wertham himself could not have bettered this homophobic opposition.

Despite the passions aroused on both sides (or rather the two facets of the same side), there is something comic at the heart of this dispute. It is, simply, that Bruce and Dick are *not* real people but fictional constructions, and hence to squabble over their "real" sex life is to take things a little too far. What is at stake here is the question of reading, of what readers do with the raw material that they are given. Readers are at liberty to construct whatever fantasy lives they like with the characters of the fiction they read (within the limits of generic and narrative credibility, that is). This returns us to the unfortunate patients of Dr. Wertham:

> One young homosexual during psychotherapy brought us a copy of *Detective* comic, with a Batman story. He pointed out a picture of "The Home of Bruce and Dick," a house beautifully landscaped, warmly lighted and showing the devoted pair side by side, looking out a picture window. When he was eight this boy had realized from fantasies about comic book pictures that he was aroused by men. At the age of ten or eleven, "I found my liking, my sexual desires, in comic books. I think I put myself in the position of Robin. I did want to have relations with Batman . . . I remember the first time I came across the page mentioning the 'secret batcave.' The thought of Batman and Robin living together and possibly having sex relations came to my mind . . ."[10]

Wertham quotes this to shock us, to impel us to tear the pages of *Detective* away before little Tommy grows up and moves to Greenwich Village, but reading it as a gay man today I find it rather moving and also highly recognizable.

What this anonymous gay man did was to practice that form of bricolage which Richard Dyer has identified as a characteristic reading strategy of gay audiences.[11] Denied even the remotest possibility of supportive images of homosexuality within the dominant heterosexual culture, gay people have had to fashion what we could out of the imageries of dominance, to snatch illicit meanings from the fabric of normality, to undertake a corrupt decoding for the purposes of satisfying marginalized desires.[12] This may not be as necessary as it once was, given the greater visibility of gay representations, but it is still an important practice. Wertham's patient evokes in me an admiration, that in a period of American history even more homophobic than most, there he was, raiding the citadels of masculinity, weaving fantasies of oppositional desire. What effect the dread Wertham had on him is hard to predict, but I profoundly hope that he wasn't "cured."

It wasn't only Batman who was subjected to Dr. Doom's bizarre ideas about human sexuality. Hence:

> The homosexual connotation of the Wonder Woman type of story is psychologically unmistakable. . . . For boys, Wonder Woman is a frightening image. For girls she is a morbid ideal. Where Batman is anti-feminine, the attractive Wonder Woman and her counterparts are definitely anti-masculine. Wonder Woman has her own female following . . . Her followers are the "Holiday girls", i.e. the holiday girls, the gay party girls, the gay girls.[13]

Just how much elision can be covered with one "i.e."? Wertham's view of homosexuality is not, at least, inconsistent. Strong, admirable women will turn little girls into dykes – such a heroine can only be seen as a "morbid ideal."

Crazed as Wertham's ideas were, their effectiveness is not in doubt. The mid-fifties saw a moral panic about the assumed dangers of comic books. In the United States companies were driven out of business, careers wrecked, and the Comics Code introduced. This had distinct shades of the Hays Code that had been brought in to clamp down on Hollywood in the 1930s, and under its jurisdiction comics opted for the bland, the safe and the reactionary. In Britain there was government legislation to prohibit the importing of American comics, as the comics panic slotted neatly into a whole series of anxieties about the effects on British youth of American popular culture.[14]

And in all of this, what happened to Batman? He turned into Fred MacMurray from *My Three Sons*. He lost any remaining edge of the shadowy vigilante of his earliest years, and became an upholder of the most stifling small town American values. Batwoman and Batgirl appeared (June Allyson and Bat-Gidget) to take away any lingering doubts about the Dynamic Duo's sex lives. A 1963 story called "The Great Clayface–Joker Feud" has some especially choice examples of the new, squeaky-clean sexuality of the assembled Bats.

Bat-Girl says to Robin, "I can hardly wait to get into my Bat-Girl costume again! Won't it be terrific if we could go on a crime case together like the last time? (sigh)." Robin replies, "It sure would, Betty (sigh)." The elder Bats look on approvingly. Bat-Girl is Batwoman's niece – to make her a daughter would have implied that Batwoman had had (gulp) sexual intercourse, and that would never do. This is the era of Troy Donohue and Pat Boone, and *Batman* as ever serves as a cultural thermometer, taking the temperature of the times.

The Clayface/Joker business is wrapped up (the villains of this period are wacky conjurors, nothing more, with no menace or violence about them) and the episode concludes with another tableau of terrifying heterosexual contentment. "Oh Robin," simpers Batgirl, "I'm afraid you'll just have to hold me! I'm still so shaky after fighting Clayface . . . and you're so strong!" Robin: "Gosh Batgirl, it was swell of you to calm me down when I was worried about Batman tackling Clayface alone." (One feels a distinct Wertham influence here: if Robin shows concern about Batman, wheel on a supportive female, the very opposite of a "morbid ideal," to minister in a suitably self-effacing way.) Batwoman here seizes her chance and tackles Batman: "You look worried about Clayface, Batman . . . so why don't you follow Robin's example and let me soothe you?" Batman can only reply "Gulp."

Gulp indeed. While it's easy simply to laugh at strips like these, knowing as we do the way in which such straight-faced material would be mercilessly shredded by the sixties' TV series, they do reveal the retreat into coziness forced on comics by the Wertham onslaught and its repercussions. There no doubt were still subversive readers of *Batman*, erasing Batgirl on her every preposterous appearance and reworking the Duo's capers to leave some room for homoerotic speculation, but such a reading would have had to work so much harder than before. The *Batman* of this era was such a closed text, so immune to polysemic interpretation, that its interest today is only as a symptom – or, more productively, as camp. "The Great Clayface–Joker Feud" may have been published in 1963, but in every other respect it is a fifties' text. If the 1960s began for the world in general with the Beatles, the 1960s for *Batman* began with the TV series in 1966. If the Caped Crusader had been all but Werthamed out of existence, he was about to be camped back into life.

The Camped Crusader and the Boys Wondered

Trying to define Camp is like attempting to sit in the corner of a circular room. It can't be done, which only adds to the quixotic appeal of the attempt. Try these:

To be camp is to present oneself as being committed to the marginal with a commitment greater than the marginal merits.[15]

Camp sees everything in quotation marks. It's not a lamp but a "lamp"; not a woman but a "woman"....It is the farthest extension, in sensibility, of the metaphor of life as theatre.[16]

Camp is...a way of poking fun at the whole cosmology of restrictive sex roles and sexual identifications which our society uses to oppress its women and repress its men.[17]

Camp was and is a way for gay men to re-imagine the world around them... by exaggerating, stylizing and remaking what is usually thought to be average or normal.[18]

Camp was a prison for an illegal minority, now it is a holiday for consenting adults.[19]

All true, in their way, but all inadequate. The problem with camp is that it is primarily an experiential rather than an analytical discourse. Camp is a set of attitudes, a gallery of snapshots, an inventory of postures, a *modus vivendi*, a shop-full of frocks, an arch of eyebrows, a great big pink butterfly that just won't be pinned down. Camp is primarily an adjective, occasionally a verb, but never anything as prosaic, as earth-bound, as a noun.

Yet if I propose to use this adjective as a way of describing one or more of the guises of Batman, I need to arrive at some sort of working definition. So, for the purposes of this analysis, I intend the term camp to refer to a playful, knowing, self-reflexive theatricality. *Batman*, the sixties' TV series, was nothing if not knowing. It employed the codes of camp in an unusually public and heavily signalled way. This makes it different from those people or texts who are taken up by camp audiences without ever consciously putting camp into practice. The difference may be very briefly spelled out by reference to Hollywood films. If *Mildred Pierce* and *The Letter* were taken up *as* camp, teased by primarily gay male audiences into yielding meaning not intended by their makers, then *Whatever Happened To Baby Jane?* is a piece of self-conscious camp, capitalizing on certain attitudinal and stylistic tendencies known to exist in audiences. *Baby Jane* is also, significantly, a 1960s' film, and the 1960s were the decade in which camp swished out of the ghetto and up into the scarcely prepared mainstream.

A number of key events and texts reinforced this. Susan Sontag wrote her *Notes On Camp*, which remains the starting point for researchers even now. Pop Art was in vogue (and in *Vogue*) and whatever the more elevated claims of Lichtenstein, Warhol and the rest, their art-works were on one level a new inflection of camp. The growing intellectual respectability of pop music displayed very clearly that the old barriers that once rigidly separated high and low culture were no longer in force. The James Bond films, and even more so their successors like *Modesty Blaise*, popularized a dry, self-mocking wit that makes up one part of the multifaceted diamond of camp. And on television there were *The Avengers, The Man From UNCLE, Thunderbirds*, and *Batman*.

To quote the inevitable Sontag, "The whole point of Camp is to dethrone the serious.... More precisely, Camp involves a new, more complex relation to 'the serious.' One can be serious about the frivolous, frivolous about the serious."[20]

The problem with Batman in those terms is that there was never anything truly serious to begin with (unless one swallows that whole portentous Dark Knight charade, more of which in the next section). Batman in its comic book form had, unwittingly, always been camp – it was serious (the tone, the moral homilies) about the frivolous (a man in a stupid suit). He was camp in the way that classic Hollywood was camp, but what the sixties' TV series and film did was to overlay this "innocent" camp with a thick layer of ironic distance, the self-mockery version of camp. And given the long associations of camp with the homosexual male subculture, Batman was a particular gift on the grounds of his relationship with Robin. As George Melly put it, "The real Batman series were beautiful because of their unselfconscious absurdity. The remakes, too, at first worked on a double level. Over the absorbed children's heads we winked and nudged, but in the end what were we laughing at? The fact they didn't know that Batman had it off with Robin."[21]

It was as if Wertham's fears were being vindicated at last, but his 1950s' bigot's anguish had been supplanted by a self-consciously hip 1960s' playfulness. What adult audiences laughed at in the sixties' *Batman* was a camped-up version of the fifties they had just left behind.

Batman's lessons in good citizenship. ("We'd like to feel that our efforts may help every youngster to grow up into an honest, useful citizen"[22]) were another part of the character ripe for ridiculing deconstruction – "Let's go, Robin, we've set another youth on the road to a brighter tomorrow" (the episode "It's How You Play The Game"). Everything the Adam West Batman said was a parody of seriousness, and how could it be otherwise? How could anyone take genuinely seriously the words of a man dressed like that?

The Batman/Robin relationship is never referred to directly; more fun can be had by presenting it "straight," in other words, screamingly camp. Wertham's reading of the Dubious Duo had been so extensively aired as to pass into the general consciousness (in George Melly's words, "We all knew Robin and Batman were pouves"[23]), it was part of the fabric of *Batman*, and the makers of the TV series proceeded accordingly.

Consider the Duo's encounter with Marsha, Queen of Diamonds. The threat she embodies is nothing less than heterosexuality itself, the deadliest threat to the domestic bliss of the Bat-couple. She is even about to marry Batman before Alfred intervenes to save the day. He and Batman flee the church, but have to do so in the already decorated Batmobile, festooned with wedding paraphernalia including a large "Just Married" sign. "We'll have to drive it as it is," says Batman, while somewhere in the audience a Dr. Wertham takes feverish notes. Robin, Commissioner Gordon and Chief O'Hara have all been drugged with Marsha's "Cupid's Dart," but it is of course the Boy Wonder who Batman saves first. The dart, he tells Robin, "contains some secret ingredient by which your sense and your will were affected," and it isn't hard to read that ingredient as heterosexual desire, since its result, seen in the previous episode, was to turn Robin into Marsha's slobbering slave.

We can tell with relief now, though, as Robin is "back in fighting form" (with impeccable timing, Batman clasps Robin's shoulder on the word "fighting"). Marsha has one last attempt to destroy the duo, but naturally she fails. The female temptress, the seductress, the enchantress must be vanquished. None of this is in the least subtle (Marsha's cat, for example, is called Circe) but this type of mass-market camp can't afford the luxury of subtlety. The threat of heterosexuality is similarly mobilized in the 1966 feature film, where it is Bruce Wayne's infatuation with Kitka (Catwoman in disguise) that causes all manner of problems.

A more interesting employment of camp comes in the episodes where the Duo battle the Black Widow, played by Tallulah Bankhead. The major camp coup here, of course, is the casting. Bankhead was one of the supreme icons of camp, one of its goddesses, "Too intelligent not to be self-conscious, too ambitious to bother about her self-consciousness, too insecure ever to be content, but too arrogant ever to admit insecurity, Tallulah personified camp."[24]

A heady claim, but perhaps justified, because the Black Widow episodes are, against stiff competition, the campest slices of Batman of them all. The stories about Bankhead are legendary – the time when on finding no toilet paper in her cubicle she slipped a ten dollar bill under the partition and asked the woman next door for two fives, or her whispered remark to a priest conducting a particularly elaborate service and swinging a censor of smoking incense, "Darling, I love the drag, but your purse is on fire" – and casting her in Batman was the final demonstration of the series' commitment to camp.

The plot is unremarkable, the usual Bat-shenanigans, the pleasure lies in the detail. Details like the elderly Bankhead crammed into her Super-Villainess costume, or like the way in which (through a plot detail I won't go into) she impersonates Robin, so we see Burt Ward miming to Bankhead's voice, giving the unforgettable image of Robin flirting with burly traffic cops. Best of all, and Bankhead isn't even in this scene but the thrill of having her involved clearly spurred the writer to new heights of camp, Batman has to sing a song to break free of the Black Widow's spell. Does he choose to sing "God Bless America?" Nothing so rugged. He clutches a flower to his Bat chest and sings Gilbert and Sullivan's "I'm Just Little Buttercup." It is this single image, more than any other, that prevents me from taking the post-Adam West Dark Knight at all seriously.

The fundamental camp trick which the series pulls is to make the comics speak. What was acceptable on the page, in speech balloons, stands revealed as ridiculous once given audible voice. The famous visualized sound effects (URKKK! KA-SPLOOSH!) that are for many the fondest memory of the series work along similar lines! Camp often makes its point by transposing the codes of one cultural form into the inappropriate codes of another. It thrives on mischievous incongruity.

The incongruities, the absurdities, the sheer ludicrousness of Batman were brought out so well by the sixties' version that for some audience there will never be another credible approach. I have to include myself here. I've recently read widely in post-sixties Bat-lore, and I can appreciate what the writers and artists are trying to do, but my Batman will always be Adam West. It's impossible to be sombre or pompous about Batman because if you try the ghost of West will come Bat-climbing into your mind, fortune cookie wisdom on his lips and keen young Dick by his side. It's significant, I think, that the letters I received from the editors of this book began "Dear Bat-Contributor." Writers preparing chapters about James Joyce or Ingmar Bergman do not, I suspect, receive analogous greetings. To deny the large camp component of Batman is to blind oneself to one of the richest parts of his history.

Is There Bat-Life After Bat-Camp?

The international success of the Adam West incarnation left Batman high and dry. The camping around had been fun while it lasted, but it hadn't lasted very long. Most camp humour has a relatively short life-span, new targets are always needed, and the camp aspect of Batman had been squeezed dry. The mass public had moved on to other heroes, other genres, other acres of merchandising, but there was still a hard Bat-core of fans to satisfy. Where could the Bat go next? Clearly there was no possibility of returning to the caped Eisenhower, the benevolent patriarch of the 1950s. That option had been well and truly closed down by the TV show. Batman needed to be given his dignity back, and this entailed a return to his roots.

This, in any case, is the official version. For the unreconstructed devotee of the Batman (that is, people who insist on giving him the definite article before the name), the West years had been hell – a tricksy travesty, an effeminizing of the cowled avenger. There's a scene in *Midnight Cowboy* where Dustin Hoffman tells Jon Voight that the only audience liable to be receptive to his cowboy clothes are gay men looking for rough trade. Voight is appalled – "you mean to tell me John Wayne was a fag?" (quoted, roughly, from memory). This outrage, this horror at shattered illusions, comes close to encapsulating the loathing and dread the campy Batman has received from the old guard of Gotham City and the younger born-again Bat-fans.

So what has happened since the 1960s has been the painstaking re-heterosexualization of Batman, I apologize for coining such a clumsy word, but no other quite gets the sense that I mean. This strategy has worked, too, for large audiences, reaching its peak with the 1989 film. To watch this and then come home to see a video of the 1966 movie is to grasp how complete the transformation has been. What I want to do in this section is to trace some of the crucial moments in that change, written from the standpoint of someone still unashamedly committed to Bat-camp.

If one wants to take Batman as a Real Man, the biggest stumbling block has always been Robin. There have been disingenuous claims that "Batman and Robin had a blood-brother closeness. Theirs was a spiritual intimacy forged from the stress of countless battles fought side by side"[25] (one can imagine what Tallulah Bankhead might say to *that*), but we know otherwise. The Wertham lobby and the acolytes of camp alike have ensured that any Batman/Robin relationship is guaranteed to bring on the sniggers. Besides which, in the late 1960s, Robin was getting to be a big boy, too big for any shreds of credibility to attach themselves to all that father-son smokescreen. So in 1969 Dick Grayson was packed off to college and the Bat was solitary once more.

This was a shrewd move. It's impossible to conceive of the recent, obsessive, sturm-und-drang Batman with a chirpy little Robin getting in the way.[26] A text of the disturbing power of *The Killing Joke* could not have functioned with Robin to rupture the grim dualism of its Batman/Joker struggle. There was, however, a post-Dick Robin, but he was killed off by fans in that infamous telephone poll.

It's intriguing to speculate how much latent (or blatant) homophobia lay behind that vote. Did the fans decide to kill off Jason Todd so as to redeem Batman for unproblematic heterosexuality? Impossible to say. There are other factors to take into account, such as Jason's apparent failure to live up to the expectations of what a

Robin should be like. The sequence of issues in which Jason/Robin died, *A Death in the Family*, is worth looking at in some detail, however, in order to see whether the camp connotations of Bruce and Dick had been fully purged.

The depressing answer is that they had. This is very much the Batman of the 1980s, his endless feud with the Joker this time uneasily stretched over a framework involving the Middle East and Ethiopia. Little to be camp about there, though the presence of the Joker guarantees a quota of sick jokes. The sickest of all is the introduction of the Ayatollah Khomeini, a real and important political figure, into this fantasy world of THUNK! and THER-ACKK! and grown men dressed as bats. (As someone who lived in the part of England from which Reagan's planes took off on their murderous mission to bomb Libya, I fail to see the humor in this cartoon version of American foreign policy: it's too near the real thing.)

Jason dies at the Joker's hands because he becomes involved in a search for his own origins, a clear parallel to Batman's endless returns to *his* Oedipal scenario. Families, in the Bat-mythology, are dark and troubled things, one more reason why the introduction of the fifties versions of Batwoman and Bat-Girl seemed so inappropriate. This applies only to real, biological families, though; the true familial bond is between Batman and Robin, hence the title of these issues. Whether one chooses to read Robin as Batman's ward (official. version), son (approved fantasy) or lover (forbidden fantasy), the sense of loss at his death is bound to be devastating. Batman finds Robin's body and, in the time-honored tradition of Hollywood cinema, is at least able to give him a loving embrace. Good guys hug their dead buddies, only queers smooch when still alive.

If the word "camp" is applied at all to the eighties' Batman, it is a label for the Joker. This sly displacement is the cleverest method yet devised of preserving Bat-heterosexuality. The play that the texts regularly make with the concept of Batman and the Joker as mirror images now takes a new twist. The Joker is Batman's "bad twin," and part of that badness is, increasingly, an implied homosexuality. This is certainly present in the 1989 film, a generally glum and portentous affair except for Jack Nicholson's Joker, a characterization enacted with venomous camp. The only moment when this dour film comes to life is when the Joker and his gang raid the Art Gallery, spraying the paintings and generally camping up a storm.

The film strives and strains to make us forget the Adam West Batman, to the point of giving us Vicki Vale as Bruce Wayne's lover, and certainly Michael Keaton's existential agonizing (variations on the theme of why-did-I-have-to-be-a-Bat) is a world away from West's gleeful subversion of truth, justice and the American Way. This is the same species of Batman celebrated by Frank Miller: "If your only memory of Batman is that of Adam West and Burt Ward exchanging camped-out quips while clobbering slumming guest-stars Vincent Price and Cesar Romero, I hope this book will come as a surprise . . . . For me, Batman was never funny. . . ."[27]

The most recent linkage of the Joker with homosexuality comes in *Arkham Asylum*, the darkest image of the Bat-world yet. Here the Joker has become a parody of a screaming queen, calling Batman "honey pie," given to exclamations like "oooh!" (one of the oldest homophobic cliches in the book) and pinching Batman's behind with the advice, "loosen up, tight ass." He also, having no doubt read his Wertham, follows the pinching by asking, "What's the matter? Have I touched a nerve? How is the Boy Wonder? Started shaving yet?" The Bat-response is unequivocal: "Take your filthy hands off me . . . . Filthy degenerate!"

Arkham Asylum is a highly complex reworking of certain key aspects of the mythology, of which the sexual tension between Batman and the Joker is only one small part. Nonetheless the Joker's question "Have I touched a nerve?" seems a crucial one, as revealed by the homophobic ferocity of Batman's reply. After all, the dominant cultural construction of gay men at the end of the 1980s is as plague carriers, and the word "degenerate" is not far removed from some of the labels affixed to us in the age of AIDS.

Batman: Is He or Isn't He?

The one constant factor through all of the transformations of Batman has been the devotion of his admirers. They will defend him against what they see as negative interpretations, and they carry around in their heads a kind of essence of batness, a Bat-Platonic Ideal of how Batman should really be. The Titan Books reissue of key comics from the 1970s each carry a preface by a noted fan, and most of them contain claims such as "This, I feel, is Batman as he was meant to be."[28]

Where a negative construction is specifically targeted, no prizes for guessing which one it is: "you . . . are probably also fond of the TV show he appeared in. But then maybe you prefer Elvis Presley's Vegas years or the later Jerry Lewis movies over their early stuff . . . for me, the definitive Batman was then and always will be the one portrayed in these pages."[29]

The sixties' TV show remains anathema to the serious Bat-fan precisely because it heaps ridicule on the very notion of a serious Batman. *Batman* the series revealed the man in the cape as a pompous fool, an embodiment of superseded ethics, and a closet queen. As Marsha, Queen of Diamonds, put it, "Oh Batman, darling, you're so divinely square." Perhaps the enormous success of the 1989 film will help to advance the cause of the rival Bat-archetype, the grim, vengeful Dark Knight whose heterosexuality is rarely called into question (his humorlessness, fondness for violence and obsessive monomania seem to me exemplary qualities for a heterosexual man). The answer, surely, is that they needn't be mutually exclusive.

If I might be permitted a rather camp comparison, each generation has its definitive Hamlet, so why not the same for Batman? I'm prepared to admit the validity, for some people, of the swooping eighties' vigilante, so why are they so concerned to trash my sixties' camped crusader? Why do they insist so vehemently that Adam West was a faggy aberration, a blot on the otherwise impeccably butch Bat-landscape? What *are* they trying to hide?

If I had a suspicious frame of mind, I might think that they were protesting too much, that maybe Dr. Wertham was on to something when he targeted these narratives as incitements to homosexual fantasy. And if I want Batman to be gay, then, for me, he is. After all, outside of the minds of his writers and readers, he doesn't really exist.

Notes

1 Fredric Wertham, *Seduction of the Innocent* (London: Museum Press, 1955), p. 190.

2 Susan Sontag, "Notes on Camp," in *A Susan Sontag Reader* (Harmondsworth: Penguin Books), p. 106.

3 Martin Barker, *A Haunt Of Fears* (London: Pluto Press, 1984).

4 Wertham, p. 188.

5 Wertham, p. 190.

6 See, for example, the newspaper stories on "how to spot" homosexuals printed in Britain in the fifties and sixties, and discussed in Jeffrey Weeks, *Coming Out: Homosexual Politics in Britain* (London: Quartet, 1979).

7 Phrases taken from chapters 5 and 6 of Mark Cotta Vaz, *Tales Of The Dark Knight: Batman's First Fifty Years* (London: Futura, 1989).

8 Les Daniels, *Comix: A History of Comic Books in America* (New York: Bonanza Books, 1971), p. 87.

9 Cotta Vaz, pp. 47 and 53.

10 Wertham, p. 192.

11 Richard Dyer, ed., *Gays and Film*, 2nd Edition (New York: Zoetrope, 1984), p. 1.

12 See Richard Dyer, "Judy Garland and Gay Men", in Dyer, *Heavenly Bodies* (London: BFI, 1987) and Claire Whitaker, "Hollywood Transformed: Interviews with Lesbian Viewers," in Peter Steven, ed., *Jump Cut: Hollywood, Politics and Counter-Cinema* (Toronto: Between the Lines, 1985).

13 Wertham, pp. 192–3.

14 See Barker.

15 Mark Booth, *Camp* (London: Quartet, 1983), p. 18.

16 Sontag, p. 109.

17 Jack Babuscio, "Camp and the Gay Sensibility", in Dyer, ed., *Gays and Film*, p. 46.

18 Michael Bronski, *Culture Clash: The Making of Gay Sensibility* (Boston: South End Press,), p. 42.

19 Philip Core, *Camp: The Lie That Tells The Truth* (London: Plexus), p. 7.

20 Sontag, p. 116.

21 George Melly, *Revolt Into Style: The Pop Arts in the 50s and 60s* (Oxford: Oxford University Press, 1989 (first published 1970)), p. 193.

22 "The Batman Says," *Batman* #3 (1940), quoted in Cotta Vaz, p. 15.

23 Melly, p. 192.

24 Core, p. 25.

25 Cotta Vaz, p. 53.

26 A female Robin is introduced in the *Dark Knight Returns* series, which, while raising interesting questions about the sexuality of Batman, which I don't here have the space to address, seems significant in that the Dark Knight cannot run the risk of reader speculation that a traditionally-male Robin might provoke.

27 Frank Miller, "Introduction," *Batman: Year One* (London: Titan, 1988).

28 Kim Newman, "Introduction," *Batman: The Demon Awakes* (London: Titan, 1989).

29 Jonathan Ross, "Introduction," to *Batman: Vow From the Grave* (London: Titan, 1989).

4 Take Me Out to the Ball Game: The Transformation of Production–Consumption Relations in Professional Team Sport

Kimberly S. Schimmel

> Why should we be losing money when we represent a game that people love? (William A. Hulbert, professional baseball owner, to his colleagues in 1876; quoted in Peitrusza, 1991, p. 28)

At the turn of the twentieth century, sports were occasional and unregulated events played by members of local sport clubs.[1] But as the above quote suggests, sports gradually became meaningful to more than just the people who played them. The emergence of crowds at local sport club contests provided the opportunity for risk-taking entrepreneurs to turn "games that people love" into profit-making ventures. In a relatively short time, traditional community pastimes became today's commercial urban spectacles. This rise of contemporary professional team sport necessarily involved a transformation in producer-consumer relations in US sport culture. Voluntaristic participation was replaced by binding, contractual arrangements, and small, hometown rivalries gave way to regional mega-events produced for mass consumption. The ties that once bound the sport spectator in localized ways are now attenuated by the prevailing economic arrangements of major league organization. In this transformed environment, major league teams no longer fear losing money, but local fans do fear losing their teams. In today's context, all city residents (whether sport fans or not) are called upon to provide powerful incentives to capture footloose professional sport franchises. Fans' continuing desire to "take me out to the ball game" is a necessary, but not sufficient, condition to keep a professional franchise in a host community.

The factors that fueled the evolution and rise of contemporary sport are complex; I will not attempt to present them all in this paper.[2] Instead, I will address four eras in the transformation of producer-consumer relations in professional team sport: the emergence of professional team sport in US popular culture; the organization of the major league structure; the articulation of professional sport with pro-growth politics in US cities; and the attempts by local sport consumers to influence the decisions of professional sport franchise owners. For each historical period, I provide an introduction to major transformative events by focusing on professional baseball

This chapter was specifically commissioned for this volume.

– America's Pastime – and, most importantly, professional football, the most popular sport form in US culture.[3] I illustrate many of my points with examples from Northeastern Ohio, where professional football was founded.

The Kickoff

Early attempts to launch professional team sport, though plentiful, are more notable for their failures than successes. Between 1869 and 1900, 850 men's professional sport clubs were founded (Vincent, 1981). Of these clubs, 650 folded in two years or less and only 50 lasted longer than six years. Baseball was the first sport to attempt structured leagues, forming the first league in 1870. But teams stumbled along week-to-week, uncertain of their rosters, opponents, and ultimately their futures. Many teams could not complete their schedules for financial reasons. In a practice called "revolving," players would play for whatever team offered them the most money. In the "twilight" period of league formation, as Voigt (1966) aptly named it, teams competed against one another both on the field and in the accounting ledger. During this time sport club owners emphasized making money for themselves (termed "utility maximization") and ignored the welfare of the league as a whole (or "group profit maximization"). Anyone seeking to affirm his "leading citizen" status, increase his power in the local community or increase patronage in his shop, restaurant, or saloon would give club ownership a try – provided the local team was a winner and could draw crowds (see Vincent, 1981; see also Ingham, Howell, and Schilperoort, 1987).

About 20 years after the formation of baseball leagues (circa 1890), football clubs emerged in the steel and coal producing towns of Ohio and Pennsylvania. Though they formed later, football teams and leagues experienced developmental patterns similar to baseball's. In contrast to baseball, however, football clubs were formed after football had already been embraced in the US as a cultural practice. By the 1890s college football had secured its position as king among college sports, drawing up to 40,000 spectators in East Coast campus towns (Leifer, 1995). In contrast, "independent football" (so called because it existed outside the college structure), was most popular in the medium-sized towns of the Midwest, places more likely to have a factory-sponsored team than a college team. From its founding days, professional football clashed with the amateur ethos of the more elite college game which advocated "fair play" and "sportsmanship" (McClellan, 1998). The "true" football amateur positioned sport among a variety of disinterested practices, more valued as displays of gentlemanly virtue than as opportunities to defeat opponents (see Bourdieu, 1978). But for the professionals, and the crowds who cheered them, sport was altogether something else.

Early professional football dramatized working class life. Workers identified more closely with professional players than with the mainly upper-middle and upper-class college players for whom football was believed to be a "character-building" pursuit. As symbols of working class masculinity professional players were revered for their rough-and-tumble styles, never-give-up attitudes, and willingness to tolerate (and inflict) pain in pursuit of victory. For the factory, mill, and railroad workers who supported the game, the local football team became a symbol of blue collar community pride. Unlike college football's Saturday games, professional football was played on Sundays when factories were closed. Workers embraced "their teams" by virtue of commonality and community rather than credentialism. Fans of professional football showed up to games on their day off from work. They did not have to be a college alumnus to feel a sense of attachment to local teams, "[s]corned and ridiculed by the college crowd, loved by only factory workers and a few fanatics, professional football [took] root in America's midwestern factory town" (McClellan, 1998, pp. 20–1).

Yet a blue-collar base of support was not always an advantage to the early entrepreneurs of professional football. Prior to 1915, to pay for expenses many independent teams simply "passed the hat" at the end of games. However, over the next few years football changed dramatically, marking a transition from independent, semi-professional football to professional football. While the solid popularity of the sport assured that profit-minded entrepreneurs would continue to finance teams, the utility maximizing practices of football's financial backers and the revolving practices of the players continued to escalate the cost of producing games. During these times of uncertain scheduling and revenue shortfalls, a player usually only contracted for one game at a time, thus freeing him to sell his talents weekly to the highest bidder. It was also common for players to play under assumed names so they could play for more than one team at a time. Given the low wages of football fans, pursuing profit by increasing the price of admission was not a viable option. Concerned with enhancing the profitability of their individual teams, football entrepreneurs needed to field teams that would draw large numbers of paying fans, accomplished by creating "interesting" games or by hiring talented, well known "ringers." In attempts to survive in this tenuous market, owners recruited (mostly former) college stars and promoted local rivalries (McClellan, 1998).

Ball Field Battles in the Buckeye State

As early as 1896 a state football championship was held among Ohio independent teams (Leifer, 1995; see also Becker, 1998). The fiercest rivalries in early professional football existed among teams in Northeastern Ohio including Canton, Massillon, Akron, Youngstown, and Cleveland. During these early years Cleveland fielded six different independent teams. One team, the Blepp Knights, opened the 1915 season against the Massillon Tigers with a grand parade including the Massillon High School band and football players from both teams. Two thousand spectators packed Massillon's tiny ballpark to see the hometown team win a one-sided game. The next year, a crowd of ten thousand gathered to watch Cleveland's professional football team, the Indians, play the Canton Bulldogs. While the Cleveland-Canton rivalry created interest, the crowd was drawn to this game for an additional reason: to see Jim Thorpe, hero of the 1912 Olympics and football's greatest ringer. As reported in the *Cleveland Plain Dealer*, spectators came, "to feast their eyes on the greatest athlete of all time – Jim Thorpe – and, incidentally, to see Cleveland and Canton professional football elevens wage battle" (quoted in McClellan, 1998, p. 217). Whenever Thorpe played in a game the size of the crowd doubled. The last game of the 1915 Ohio season is an excellent example of how the combination of rivalry games and star players attracted fan interest. The game was played between the Canton Bulldogs, featuring Thorpe, and the Massillon Tigers, featuring football legend Knute Rockne. Star players were hired by both teams though many played under assumed names. According to McClellan (1998), over sixty-five hundred fans paid to enter the game and another fifteen hundred climbed trees and scrambled over the fence to watch.

Despite its popularity with fans, the commercial operation of early professional football created economic instability for many teams and spelled economic disaster for most. Even winning teams found it difficult to survive in such a chaotic business environment, given that the prevailing economic arrangement was one in which supply (number of teams) exceeded demand and labor costs were driven up by players' revolving. During the early years of the twentieth century, the prospects for professional football were by no means clear.

The Huddle: Owners' Teamwork Alters the Game

A model for the reorganization of the professional team sports industry was created on February 2, 1876 when a small group of baseball owners met behind locked doors at New York's Grand Hotel. The meeting, called by William A. Hulbert, owner of the Chicago Baseball Club, was disguised to the media as a gathering of the rules committee (Vincent, 1981). But Hulbert's agenda was much different: he wanted to establish a new league for baseball. He proposed that the owners in the league, to be called the Major League, act together to ensure that each team was financially successful. With owners acting in concert, Hulbert reasoned, the Major League could emerge as *the* prestige league, thereby maximizing economic profits. The creation of one major league would stratify the game and franchise owners would be forced to apply for entry (which existing owners could deny) or try to survive alone. Games between league members and non-members were banned completely. Hulbert's meeting marked the beginning of what has been called the "cartelization era" of professional sport (see below), and baseball's National League set a precedent for the business practices that dramatically transformed and institutionalized the production and consumption of American professional team sport (Ingham, Howell, and Schilperoort, 1987; Schimmel, Ingham, and Howell, 1993).

Although we tend to think of American professional sport as the epitome of competition, it is owners' willingness to cooperate with each other that ensures league success. In the long run Hulbert's model for league structure ensured that professional sport was controlled by (mostly) men of affluence.[4] Though he could not have foreseen it, Hulbert's experimental model contained three elements that became taken-for-granted features of the American professional sports industry: *cartelization*, *monopoly*, and *monopsony*. Cartelization is the term that applies to owners of business firms (in this case sport teams) acting together to make decisions about the production and distribution of their products (in this case sports). Sport franchise owners, acting as a cartel, have a remarkably complex set of rules designed to restrict business competition for athletic labor and divide geographical markets for individual franchises. Even though each team is a separate business entity, the owners have worked out rules for conducting business in ways that represent their collective interests. For example, all leagues have rules for revenue sharing among teams, and owners vote on the placement, ownership and number of franchises in the league. In addition, television and radio broadcasts, admission to games, and the sale of team-related merchandise are all subject to league regulations. In short, monopoly practices manipulate the distribution of professional sport to consumers.

Monsopsony practices, on the other hand, manipulate the cost of acquiring sport labor. For example, league rules specify the procedures for drafting new players and binding them to contracts, thereby assuring bidding wars will not break out for athletic talent. Though sport cartelization has been challenged from time to time by rogue owners and players' unions, these business practices have established Major League Baseball, The National Football League, the National Hockey League and the National Basketball Association as some of the most powerful firms in the history of America.

It is important to note, however, that the precedent set by Hulbert and his baseball colleagues was ignored by owners in other professional sports during their formative years. Eventually, however, economic concentration and cartelization were embraced by other sport owners for exactly the same reason: the creation of artificial scarcity in the marketplace increased consumer demand. Teams literally could not survive outside of a prestige league: they merged into it or folded. For example, in the 1920s football had two leagues and 58 teams, but by the 1950s mergers, failures and exclusions reduced the number of leagues to one: the National Football League (NFL) had control of the entire US market (Schimmel, Ingham, and Howell, 1995).

Football's New League and Brown's Town

The NFL was founded in 1920 in Canton, Ohio, a city located in the middle of Ohio's football rivalries and home of football's best team at the time. Team representatives from five Midwestern states met at a Canton car dealership and formed the American Professional Football Association (renamed the National Football League a year later). Jim Thorpe, who was still competing as a football player, agreed to serve as league president. Like Hulbert's baseball model, the NFL attempted to enforce rules of exclusivity. A membership fee of $100.00 was charged to each team (though it was not collected) (Leifer, 1995). Unlike in baseball, however, game scheduling was left to individual teams; as a result, they played varying numbers of games against both members and non-members. Jim Thorpe, described as a "better athlete than organizer" (Leifer, 1995, p. 99), was replaced as president during the second year of the league. It took two more years (until 1924) for the NFL to establish a fixed schedule of games with member teams in eleven Midwestern cities. During the league's first decade three different franchises failed in Cleveland, all victims of losing seasons, dwindling finances and bad weather (Danielson, 1997). The National Football League finally took root in Northeastern Ohio in 1937 when the American Football Conference's Rams applied for and received NFL membership (Morgan, 1997). For the next forty-seven years, professional football fans in Cleveland had a team to cheer. As we will see below, however, for a short time the NFL lost its grip on the city.

Cleveland Football Goes to the "Dawgs"

In 1943, Cleveland Rams owner Dan Reeves complained that his team was losing money. Wealthy Cleveland taxicab magnate Arthur "Mickey" McBride offered to buy his hometown Rams but the NFL refused to sell to him. The next year McBride, along with five other investors, founded a rival league called the All-American Football Conference (AAFC) and designated himself as owner of a new Cleveland team. Ohio football hero Paul Brown was hired as coach and, capitalizing on his popularity, the team was named after him. Paul Brown's reputation alone was enough to run the Rams – then-reigning NFL champions – out of Cleveland. Compounding problems for the Rams, however, was the fact that they played their games at a number of different stadiums and the season ticket base consisted of only 200 fans. The Browns, by contrast, signed a long-term lease at Municipal Stadium which seated 78,000 people. Not wanting to compete with Paul Brown or his namesake franchise, Rams owner Reeves received NFL permission to relocate the Rams to Los Angeles (Morgan, 1997).

Reeves, it seems, made the right move. In their first game at Municipal Stadium on September 6, 1946 the AAFC Cleveland Browns set a new professional football attendance record when a crowd of 60,135 watched the Browns beat the Miami Seahawks. Cleveland's team went on to win four straight AAFC titles but in 1950, after a vigorous trade war, the rival conference agreed to merge with the National Football League. Three AAFC teams (San Francisco, Cleveland, and New York) joined the NFL and a special draft was held for the remaining players. The merger meant that professional football franchises existed in only fourteen cities. After more than seventy years of small town rivalries, the Browns were the only team left in Ohio.

Cleveland was once again an NFL town and fans' affinity for the team grew steadily over the decades. In the mid-1980s Browns fans seated in the end zones adopted the nickname the "Dawg Pound." Braving freezing Cleveland winters, wearing rubber dog masks and waving dog biscuits, the Dawg Pound became a staple of NFL highlight films. Fans bonded not only with the Browns but also with venerable Municipal Stadium. Built on Lake Erie's edge in the late 1920s, Municipal Stadium was a symbol of muscular, industrial downtown Cleveland. Commenting on its immensity (11 stories high and 800 feet long), Cleveland Mayor John Marshall said at the building's christening, "The ancient world never saw a structure like this" (Morgan, 1997, p. 61). However, sixty-seven years later the hulking old stadium was in dire need of repairs. In the 1930s, Municipal Stadium was partly to credit for the success of the infant Browns franchise, but in a different era it would be blamed for their departure. When do old stadiums became a liability for cities?

If You Build It

We tend to think of cities as having both tangible and intangible qualities. The tangible components are a city's structures, built from concrete, bricks and glass that make up the grids and skylines of urban form. A city's intangible aspects stem from what we imagine the city to be: a good city or a dangerous city; a vibrant community or Nowheresville. Of course these two ways of thinking about cities are not unrelated, nor are they permanent. A deeper inspection of a city's built environment reveals the impact of dynamic social, economic, and political forces. Some cities or sections of a city evidence decline and decay, while in others old structures are razed and replaced. A city's social fabric may also change as populations withdraw from some areas and are replaced by different social groups. Changing patterns of commerce and trade, production and consumption, also contour the character of urban social life. In the past twenty years nearly all US cities have been affected by changes in national and global economic systems. Responding to these changes locally entails a highly complex interaction of public and private decisions. Local-level groups made up of business leaders, developers, and politicians plan and implement urban "growth" initiatives.[5] In numerous cities, building new sports stadiums and attempting to obtain (or retain) professional sport franchises have been included in growth coalitions' strategies for stimulating the urban environment. This growth agenda not only alters the (tangible) built environment, but it also contributes to the (intangible) perception of whether or not a city is worthy of "major league" status.

One of the more troubling particularities of the US urban context is the perception that overarching social problems should be handled at the local levels and that "more development" is the solution (Molotch, 1993). Local level politicians are expected to "do something" about the impact of broad-scale social problems (unemployment resulting from structural changes in the economy, for example) that manifest themselves in local areas. Coupled with this expectation is the fact that locally elected officials are held accountable for problems that are authentically place-related, such as a declining infrastructure. The solution, for many politicians, is to "do something" by manipulating the use and regulation of urban land, one of the few autonomous realms of local-level governance. The result is the hegemony of "growth politics" and the use of public subsidies for enterprises such as convention centers, urban shopping malls, retail anchors, and cultural center development. In many cases these projects are trumpeted as successful, not because of any objective assessment about their benefits to local residents but because of the symbolic power attached to the edifices themselves. What they point to is a "something" that can be done, and their mere presence colors local perceptions and builds political careers (Molotch, 1993; Zukin, 1991; see also the article by Salmon in this volume). I suggest that sport stadiums too, have this type of symbolic power, even more if they have a team to go with it.

It is commonly believed that hosting a professional sport franchise enhances a community's prestige, "no place can really be considered to be a 'big town' if it doesn't have a professional baseball or football team" (Okner, 1974, p. 327). In turn, the cultural hegemony of professional sport and the internal economics of the league structure, combined with the hegemony of growth politics, creates a context in which cities are held hostage to the profit motives of sport franchise owners. In the 1970s and 1980s nearly all professional sport franchise owners threatened to move if their demands for new stadiums and other benefits were not met (Euchner, 1993). Under league-defined conditions of artificial scarcity (limiting the number of franchises), there are presently more cities that want teams than there are franchises available. Though most all stadiums are publicly owned, sport franchises are private business enterprises and can move to the places that promise greatest profits. Paraphrasing Ingham, Howell, and Schilperoort (1987), franchises are mobile but cities are not. Emboldened by fans' attachments to teams and mindful of the symbolic power of professional sport, urban growth coalitions compete with one another to capture footloose franchises. Cities that refuse to enter this inter-city competition risk losing their existing team(s), and the politics of stadium construction are always at the center of the game. Once again we can look for Cleveland for an example.

The Mistake on the Lake

Q: What's the difference between Cleveland and the Titanic?
A: Cleveland has a better Orchestra.[6]

Although Cleveland was once a formidable industrial giant, by the 1970s this city embodied the worst aspects of the Rustbelt. Factory closings, population loss and unsightly landscapes earned the city the nickname "The Mistake on the Lake." In 1975 Cleveland was ranked second among fifty-eight big cities with the worst social and economic problems in the country (Green, 1993). Cleveland's image as a dirty, dying city was no doubt solidified in most people's minds when in 1969 the Cuyahoga River, coated with a layer of oil and toxic waste, caught fire. Cleveland's crisis reached its height under Mayor Dennis Kucinich (1977–79), who promoted an urban populism antithetical to the corporate establishment. Kucinich opposed tax abatements and subsidies for business firms and was reluctant to increase local income taxes. The mayor's planning department invented "advocacy planning," which sought to direct urban planning on behalf of low income residents by emphasizing social equity over efficiency and stressing, for example, public housing and public transportation (see Warf and Holly, 1997). Referring to the relationship between the mayor's office and the corporate community, a senior partner at the nation's largest law firm (based in Cleveland) said:

> It was terrible...[Kucinich] made business bashing an extracurricular activity...There was a general feeling that something had to change. That things couldn't get any worse and that things couldn't go on like this.   (quoted in Green, 1993, p. A6)

The business community was so alienated by Kucinich's leadership that in 1978 local banks refused to rollover $15.5 million in short-term municipal notes, thus plunging the city into bankruptcy. Cleveland became the first US city to default on its bonds since the Great Depression, and this default precipitated the defeat of Mayor Kucinich and ushered in a new era of local politics (Swanstrom, 1985)

Pro-growth and Pro-sport: An (E)erie Solution to Cleveland's Problems

Shortly after the default of 1978, business leaders sent an emissary to the Ohio statehouse where Republican George Voinivich, a former Cuyahoga County Commissioner, was serving as Lieutenant Governor. The emissary's mission was to convince

Voinivich to return to his hometown and lead Cleveland out of its crisis. With business groups financing his campaign, Voinivich defeated Dennis Kucinich in 1980, and held the mayor's office until he was elected as Ohio's governor nine years later.

Less than 24 hours after Voinivich was elected as Cleveland's mayor he created a volunteer business task force that spent three months studying the city's finances. The business group sent 650 recommendations to the new mayor and Voinivich accepted 500 of them, ranging from privatization of certain contracts to the creation of an economic development office. Corporate leaders also created a growth coalition named "Cleveland Tomorrow," dedicated to directing downtown development (Green, 1993).

The election of George Voinivich as Cleveland's mayor was seen by many as the watershed event in the city's redevelopment. According to Richard Jacobs, one of the world's leading commercial and real estate developers:

> That's what began the renaissance of downtown Cleveland . . . There was finally an end to the bickering . . . with Voinivich's election the two sides (government and corporate leaders) began to work together, hammering out differences and setting a course for a new downtown . . . We got together just in time, our entire city was at stake.
>
> *(quoted in Green, 1993, p. A6)*

Jacobs' company has invested millions of dollars in developing Cleveland's downtown and received $225 million in tax abatements in the 1980s (Keating, Krumholz, and Metzger, 1995). Since 1986, Jacobs has also been the principal owner of Cleveland's professional baseball franchise, the Cleveland Indians.

In 1987, lead by Mayor Voinivich, Cleveland Indians (Major League Baseball) owner Richard Jacobs, and Cleveland Cavaliers (National Basketball Association) owner George Gund, the professional sport facility concept was formalized and the "Gateway Economic Development Corporation" was founded.[7] Browns owner Art Modell was an original member of Gateway, but relations between him and other coalition members soured and in 1990 he dropped out of the group. That same year "Gateway Complex" was proposed to Cuyahoga County voters, who were called upon to approve a tax increase on alcohol and cigarettes to help pay for it. Plans called for the tax-supported complex to be constructed on a downtown site that would contain a new baseball stadium for the Indians (who were then sharing Municipal Stadium with the Browns) and a new basketball arena for the Cavaliers (who were playing in a suburban stadium owned by George Gund).

To help assure voter approval, Cleveland Tomorrow financed a $1 million Pro-Gateway political campaign. Two days before the tax vote, Major League Baseball Commissioner Fay Vincent delivered a difficult-to-miss threat before the city council:

> Should this facility not be available in Cleveland, should the vote be a negative one, we may find ourselves confronting a subject that we want to avoid . . . I say to you, it would be very bad for baseball, and I am opposed to Cleveland losing its team.
>
> *(quoted in Bartimole, 1994, p. 30)*

Along with these warnings came full-page newspaper ads informing the voters that their approval would create, "28,000 good-paying jobs for the jobless, $15 million a year for schools and for our children; revenues for city and county clinics and hospitals for the sick; energy-assistance programs for the elderly" (quoted in Barti-mole, 1994, p. 30). With 383,000 votes cast Gateway was narrowly approved by voters (51.7 percent in favor; 48.3 percent against). Completed in 1994 and carrying a final price tag of $485 million (at a cost overrun of $28 million), Gateway is the largest and most expensive development project in Cleveland's history (see Rosen-traub, 1997).

Browns owner Art Modell was left out of the Gateway project, and there was no proposal to renovate 62-year old Municipal Stadium. Soon after groundbreaking on the new baseball and football stadiums he began cryptically complaining that city leaders were taking him for granted. Because of Gateway, Cleveland Tomorrow members Richard Jacobs and George Gund (both already members of *Fortune* magazine's list of wealthiest Americans; see Keating, Krumholz, and Metzger, 1995) got new, tax-payer supported sports arenas with favorable leases and revenue guarantees. Local baseball and basketball fans got to "keep" the Indians and the Cavaliers. Cuyahoga County voters, however, got more than they bargained for: contractors filed a lawsuit claiming they were owed $21.5 million for their work, and by 1996 the arenas were $20 million in debt. Gateway alone has an annual operating debt of more than $1 million and $600,000 in unpaid Cuyahoga County property taxes (Adams, 1996). Currently the arenas are teetering on the brink of bankruptcy. But even given these financial realities, Cleveland growth promoters point to the Gateway project and surrounding development as evidence of Cleveland's supposed "renaissance."

Cleveland's participation in the 1995 baseball World Series provided a national stage for growth leaders and local sports fans to display the city's new "successes." After decades of taunts from outsiders Clevelanders reveled in the opportunity to send a retort to the national television audience: during game three of the Series a handmade banner flew from the upper deck of Jacobs Field that read, "NOW do you believe in Cleveland?" (Green, 1993). Whatever national envy existed during the October World Series came to an end in November, however, when Art Modell, at last able to seemingly retaliate, announced he was moving the Browns to Baltimore.

Fumble! Cleveland Loses Possession of the Browns

> It was a very emotional game for me. There were 300-pound bearded men hugging me and crying. When I left, I saw the people in the parking lot crying. I tried not to cry, but I couldn't help it.
> *(Bob Burnett, Browns defensive end, on the last game in Municipal Stadium; quoted in Cabot, 1999, p. S-23)*

In the days leading up to the official announcement of the Browns move, politicians in Baltimore and Cleveland engaged in a bidding war for the opportunity to host the franchise. Cleveland-area residents were presented with a referendum to extend the county's sin tax on alcohol and cigarettes tax to provide $175 million to renovate Municipal Stadium. One day before the vote, Modell announced he was relocating the Browns to Baltimore. Cleveland fans, whose average game attendance exceeded seventy thousand, responded by passing the tax anyway. In the end, however,

Baltimore won the battle for the Browns by striking a clandestine deal with Modell that provided him with $75 million in moving expenses, rent-free use of a new $200 million publicly financed stadium, a $50 million signing bonus, and all revenues from ticket sales, concessions, parking, and stadium advertising. Maryland tax-payers will also have to pay Modell for "lost revenue" if the stadium does not sell out in each of the next ten years (Eitzen, 1999). It was these incentives, coupled with the poor condition and relatively less revenue potential of Cleveland's stadium, that Modell referred to when he said that keeping the Browns was "far beyond the capacity of Cleveland" (Heider, Diemer, and Theiss, 1995, p. 1Å).

What was certainly beyond the capacity of most Northeastern Ohio football fans was the ability to accept that over a century of local professional football had ended. The once proud Cleveland fans, models of loyalty to team and respect for football tradition, were now reduced to victims of a league they helped build – or were they? In the next section, I highlight Browns fans' response to Modell's move and the NFL's decision to allow it.

Out of the Bleachers and on to the Field: Fans Get in the Game

> The fans in Cleveland have always been phenomenal and they are in a part of the country where football is a cradle-to-grave love.
> *(Paul Tagliabue, NFL Commissioner; quoted in Grossi, 1999, p. 2-S)*

While research on sport fans in the US dates back at least to the 1930s (see, for example, Nash, 1938), there has been little scholarly documentation of the political or activist component of sport fandom. This is true despite the fact that fans' emotional attachments to their favorite professional sport teams have been strained time and time again by team owners' threats of (and actual) relocation. Ironically, prior to the Browns move to Baltimore, the most infamous case of professional football relocation was the 1984 shift of the NFL's Colts from Baltimore to Indianapolis. Media coverage of the move depicted dramatic outpourings of emotion from fans who felt parts of their identities had been lost (or stolen). In Baltimore, where the Colts left in the middle of the night after 31 years, fans charged that the franchise's night time departure was intended to "humiliate and degrade" them (*Indianapolis Star*, 1984).

However, while there have been many media accounts of fans' outrage over franchise relocations, there have been few scholarly attempts to analyze fans' responses to these moves. Sport historians have mostly focused on how urbanization and industrialization has fostered "spectatoritis." Sport economists have tended to focus on the economic impact (to cities) of gaining or losing a professional sport franchise. Sport sociologists have focused on the urban political economy of stadium development. In none of this research has there been a focus on fans per se. Why are fans not treated as an important part of these analyses? The answer, according to most recent sport studies scholarship, is that fans simply do not count:

> The bonds that exist between professional sports franchises and their host communities are not held together by sentiment, loyalty, or tradition. Furthermore, a community's

endearment to a professional sports team is not of primary import to franchise owners when they review their location/relocation decisions. When owners consider relocation their dialogue is with city governments or city "authorities," not with fans.

(Schimmel, 1995, p. 112)

Instead, fans are "reduced to a dependency upon monopolistic sources of supply that limits [them] to only one sanction against displeasure – the choice of not to buy" (Ingham, Howell, and Schilperoort, 1987, p. 428).

But is this still true? Are dispossessed fans merely the losers in inter-city competition for professional sport franchises? Do they have no recourse beyond the choice to stop being fans? I do believe that fans have been perceived as, and have mostly acted as, powerless victims of professional sports team owners' decisions. However, I suggest that the 1995 relocation of the Browns from Cleveland may mark a turning point in the fans-as-victims era. Through their actions, Browns fans rescued the history of professional football in Cleveland but the tool they used to do so is very much a part of the present.

Brownsfans.org: Football Fans Tackle the NFL

Internet activism is slowing making an impact – sometimes small, sometimes dramatic – on local politics....What would have taken hours of stamp-licking and hundreds of dollars in distribution costs a decade ago...takes less than 30 minutes of free keystrokes. (Riccardi, 1998)

News that Browns owner Art Modell intended to move his franchise to Baltimore sparked a massive, coordinated effort by Browns fans and the larger Cleveland community to keep the franchise in Cleveland. Though the NFL did not block the move, it did make the unprecedented decision to prohibit Modell from taking the team's name and colors with him, and to grant Cleveland an expansion team beginning with the 1999 football season. This effectively returned the Browns to Cleveland after a three year hiatus. Central to Cleveland's apparent success were the efforts of "Save Our Browns Campaign" members. Spearheaded by Cleveland's Mayor shortly after Modell's announcement, the Campaign united Browns fans, politicians and local businesses in a community-wide effort to prevent the proposed relocation.

At the heart of the Campaign were Browns fans themselves, large in number and very well organized. Particularly notable was the emergence of several Internet-based fan groups dedicated to fighting the relocation. A quick search of the Internet will locate dozens of Browns-oriented home pages and web sites, including the "Burn Art Modell Page," "The Browns Fans Headquarters," "Dawgs in Cyberspace," and "Greedwatch." While some of these sites are discussion-based, others are explicitly activist-oriented. As relocation rumors began to swirl around the time of Modell's announcement, Net-savvy Browns fans quickly established the Browns Fans Worldwide Network (BFWWN). In their own description:

Who Are We? We're the Browns Fans Worldwide Network, a group of fans who REFUSE to roll over and play dead for the NFL. We've figured out what few other have, namely that WE PAY THE BILLS! As such, we think we are owed some consideration in the big scheme of things and by God, we're going to get it!!

(www.browns-fans.com)

The group's explicit function was to coordinate fans' grassroots activism. As a key component of the larger Save Our Browns Campaign, the BFWWN helped stage a number of protests and rallies, including a demonstration at the Football Hall of Fame Induction ceremonies in Canton, Ohio, a march outside of US Congressional Hearings on sports team relocation, a protest at the annual NFL meetings, and public demonstrations in front of Cleveland's stadium. But the BFWWN used the Net as more than a place to coordinate off-line activities: The Net itself became a vehicle for protest. Websites and home pages routinely included email addresses and fax numbers for NFL owners, the NFL Commissioner, other league officials, and even US Senators and members of Congress. In their most notorious move, in mid-January 1996 Net-based fans bombarded NFL offices, team owners, Maryland web sites, media outlets, and NFL corporate sponsors with 24 million email messages and faxes. This barrage was, in the gleeful words of one BFWWN member, "The first and largest one day protest event in the history of the world" (quoted in Dyer, 1997; see also Gamboda, 1996). The electronic protest was so intense that it hampered the NFL's ability to conduct routine business. Browns fans also bombarded the comment section of the official Internet site for the state of Maryland so heavily that state officials closed it down. The protests continued for months.

Faced with unrelenting fan pressure and concerned that Cleveland would lure an existing team (thereby creating an even bigger public relations nightmare) the NFL decided to return professional football to Cleveland. In March 1996, league officials and Cleveland politicians agreed to an unprecedented deal: the city agreed to build a new $250 million stadium and the league agreed to provide a team and a $48 million loan (to be paid by the new team owner). Cleveland kept the Browns name, colors, and history (records, statistics, etc.) and the new Baltimore team was renamed the Ravens. The NFL also agreed to an outline of a lease for the new Cleveland stadium which contained provisions for the construction of a "Dawg Pound" bleacher section in honor of its most loyal fans.

Yet, despite these concessions by the NFL the price of victory was quite high for the Cleveland community. When the cost of the new football stadium is added to the investments for Gateway, financed over a period of twenty-five years, Cuyahoga County residents (whether they are sports fans or not) will pay over $1 billion for the opportunity to host professional sport (see Rosentraub, 1997). In the final analysis, the actions of Browns fans did not lead to any real structural transformation – the NFL still owns the franchise, not the fans – but they did succeed in altering the League's plans. This is the first time in the contemporary professional sport era that the sport's producers actually reversed a decision based upon the demands of its consumers. It remains to be seen if the Browns' case is unique or whether it signifies a new era in professional sport. In the meantime, Cleveland football fans awaiting the return of the Browns can monitor up-to-the-minute construction of their newest investment (the football stadium) on, ironically, a web site supported by the National Football League *(www.cleveland.com/sports/browns/)*.

Conclusion

The phenomenon of today's professional team sport derives from the extension of capitalism's production-consumption relations into the realm of sport culture.[8] Far from merely responding to sport enthusiasts' interest in local games, sport's financial backers both cultivated fan support and transformed the sporting environment in an attempt to reap financial profits. Once novelties only for the people who played them, contemporary sport events are regularized commodities produced for exchange on the market. In a little more than a century, interested supporters became loyal local fans, and eventually nation-wide sport/media event consumers. The informally organized local games of the past have been replaced by a limited stream of nationally produced urban sport spectacles that now symbolize the status of major league cities. In order to host a professional sport franchise, cities must now meet the demands of franchise owners, a condition that requires the combined resources of local politicians and city residents. At every point along the way, the transformation of production and consumption relations in professional team sport was driven by a reorganization and institutionalization of major sport leagues (Leifer, 1995).

As we look to the next century, it is safe to assume that professional sport will undergo more sweeping changes. Though I will not attempt to predict specific events, I will suggest possible catalysts. On the consumption side, I suggested in this paper that the sports fans-as-victims era might be ending. Cleveland Browns fans, for example, have been credited – both by themselves and others – with accomplishing what no other group of professional sports fans has: they got "their" team back. For the first time in the post-cartelization era the NFL was forced to respond to its consumers. Also, cities have recently turned to the courts, and local congressional representatives to their legislative bodies, in attempts to halt sport franchise relocations. Though none of these efforts has been successful, each time the major leagues have to defend their movements they risk alienating loyal fans. Finally, since the cost of hosting a professional sport franchise is escalating, more and more US citizens are drawn into debates about whether or not the symbolic benefits of major league status are worth it. With city budgets already highly strained, sport stadium proposals have become more difficult to sell to the public. On the production side, US major league sports are seeking to expand into international markets. The NFL, for example, recently launched a trial league in Europe, and in 1999 will play an exhibition game in Australia. Also, in what many have called the Americanization of sport, professional sport leagues in Europe, Australia and Canada are beginning to adopt the organizational structure of the US major leagues. In the sports market of the twenty-first century, it is likely that the familiar tune, "Take me out to the ball game," will be played in a global arena.

Notes

1 Historically team sport has been a male privilege. Though there have been recent attempts to organize women's professional sport leagues (the Women's National Basketball Association, for example), these league structures closely adhere to the one described in this paper.

2 For an overview of these factors, see Ingham and Hardy (1993) and Hardy (1997).
3 As measured by broadcast audiences and polls, football surpassed baseball in the 1970s as the nation's most popular professional sport (Danielson, 1997).
4 Descriptions of the league structure are taken from Schimmel (Forthcoming). This article also discusses the few women who have owned men's sport teams (see also Coakley, 1998).
5 This perspective on US urban development is outlined in Fainstein and Fainstein (1983); see also Fainstein (1994) and Molotch (1993).
6 From Swanstrom (1985).
7 It is not uncommon for groups of growth advocates comprised of both public officials and private entrepreneurs to plan urban development strategies. Sometimes these groups formalize, as in the case of Cleveland's Gateway group, while other times they operate out of view of public scrutiny. Examining these groups and their impact on local communities has become a dominant theme in US urban studies. Whether labelled as "growth machines" (Logan and Molotch, 1987; Molotch, 1993), "growth coalitions" (Mollenkopf, 1983; Swanstrom, 1985), "governing coalitions" (Stone, 1987), or "urban regimes" (Elkin, 1987; Fainstein and Fainstein, 1983), the basic premise about local political groups is the same: local-level development policy is produced through the proximate actions of interested actors, and the benefits and burdens of their strategies are unequally distributed throughout the city. Not until very recently, however, have there been attempts to theorize and empirically examine the connection between growth politics, local-level political actors, and US professional team sport (for an exception see Lipsitz, 1984). For example, the political economy of stadium construction has been explored by Euchner (1993), Sage (1993), Schimmel (1995) and Schimmel, Ingham, and Howell (1993). It is likely that sport stadium construction will attract more attention from urban studies scholars, however, because currently the US is undergoing a stadium boom. Thirty-nine professional sport facilities are planned to open in the next four years at an estimated cost of $8 billion, with taxpayers expected to fund half of the cost (Kalich, 1998).
8 For a discussion of the commodification of sport see Ingham and Hardy (1993).

References

Adams, D.: "Indians, Cavs to pay for Gateway's debt," *The Akron Beacon Journal*, (1996, February 2), A1, A7.

Bartimole, R.: "'If you built it, we will stay'," *The Progressive*, 44 (1994), 28–31.

Becker, C. M.: *Home and Away: The Rise and Fall of Professional Football on the Banks of the Ohio, 1919–1934* (Athens, OH: Ohio University Press, 1998).

Bourdieu, P.: "Sport and social class," *Social Science Information*, 17 (1978), 819–40.

Cabot, M. K.: "The house came crashing down," *The Cleveland Plain Dealer* (1999, August 8), 21–23S.

Coakley, J.: *Sport in Society: Issues and Controversies* (Boston, MA: Irwin McGraw-Hill, 1998).

Danielson, M. N.: *Home Team: Professional Sports and the American Metropolis* (Princeton, NJ: Princeton University Press, 1997).

Dyer, B.: "Dawgs pound the keyboard for revenge," *The Akron Beacon Journal* (1997, January 17), B1.

Eitzen, D. S.: *Fair and Foul: Beyond the Myths and Paradoxes of Sport* (New York: Rowan & Littlefield Publishers, 1999).

Elkin, D.: *City and Regime in the American Republic* (Chicago, IL: University of Chicago Press, 1987).

Euchner, C. C.: *Playing the Field: Why Sports Teams Move and Cities Fight to Keep Them* (Baltimore, MD: The Johns Hopkins University Press, 1993).

Fainstein, S. S.: *The City Builders: Property, Politics, and Planning in London and New York* (Cambridge, MA: Blackwell Publishers, 1994).

Fainstein, S. S. and Fainstein, N. I.: "Economic change, national policy, and the system of cities," *Restructuring the City: The Political Economy of Urban Development*, ed. S. S. Fainstein, N. I. Fainstein, R. C. Hill, D. R. Judd, and M. P. Smith (New York: Longman, 1983), pp. 1–26.

Gamboda, G.: "No peace for NFL, owners," *The Akron Beacon Journal*, (1996, January 12), A1, A6.

Green, R.: "Cleveland's loud and proud," *The Cincinnati Enquirer* (1993, July 26), A1, A6, A7.

Grossi, T.: "The memories never left," *The Cleveland Plain Dealer* (1999, August 8), 2-S.

Hardy, S.: "Sport in urbanizing America: A historical review," *Journal of Urban History*, 23 (1997), 675–708.

Heider, T., Diemer, T. and Theiss, E.: "Browns bolt," *The Cleveland Plain Dealer*, (1995, November 7), 1A, 6A.

Indianapolis Star. (Baltimore–UPI, April 5, 1984), p. 35.

Ingham, A. G. and Hardy, S.: "Introduction: Sport studies through the lens of Raymond Williams," *Sport in Social Development: Traditions, Transitions and Transformations*, ed. A. G. Ingham and J. W. Loy (Champaign, IL: Human Kinetics Publishers, 1993), pp. 1–19.

Ingham, A. G., Howell, J. W. and Schilperoort, T. S.: "Professional sport and community: A review and exegesis," *Exercise and Sport Science Reviews*, 15 (1987), 427–65.

Kalich, V. C.: "A public choice perspective on the subsidization of private industry: A case study of three cities and three stadiums," *Journal of Urban Affairs*, 20 (1998), 199–219.

Keating, D. W., Krumholz, N. and Metzger, J.: "Postpopulist public–private partnerships," *Cleveland: A Metropolitan Reader*, ed. W. D. Keating, N. Krumholz, and D. C. Perry (Kent, OH: Kent State University Press, 1995), pp. 332–50.

Leifer, E. M.: *Making the Majors: The Transformations of Team Sports in America* (Cambridge, MA: Harvard University Press, 1995).

Lipsitz, G. "Sports stadia and urban development: A tale of three cities," *Journal of Sport and Social Issues*, 8 (1984), 1–18.

Logan, J. R. and Molotch, H.: *Urban Fortunes: The Political Economy of Place* (Berkeley, CA: University of California Press, 1987).

McClellan, K.: *The Sunday Game: At the Dawn of Professional Football* (Akron, OH: University of Akron Press, 1998).

Mollenkopf, J.: *The Contested City* (Princeton, NJ: Princeton University Press, 1983).

Molotch, H.: "The political economy of growth machines", *Journal of Urban Affairs*, 15 (1993), 29–53.

Morgan, J.: *Glory for Sale: Fans, Dollars and the New NFL* (Baltimore, MD: Bancroft Press, 1997).

Nash, J. B.: *Spectatoritis* (New York, NY: Barnes, 1938).

Okner, B. A.: "Taxation and the sports enterprises," *Government and the Sports Business*, ed. R. Noll (Washington, D. C.: Brookings Institute, 1974), pp. 159–83.

Peitrusza, D.: *Major Leagues: The Formation, Sometimes Absorption, and Mostly Inevitable Demise of 18 Professional Baseball Organizations, 1871 to Present* (Jefferson, NJ: McFarland & Co., 1991).

Riccardi, N.: "Invasion of the gadflies in cyberspace," *Los Angeles Times* (1998, May 18), *www.latimes.com/*.

Rosentraub, M. S.: *Major League Losers: The Real Cost of Sports and Who's Paying For It* (New York, NY: Basic Books, 1997).

Sage, G.: "Stealing home: Political, economic, and media power in a publicly funded baseball stadium in Denver," *Journal of Sport and Social Issues*, 17 (1993), 110–24.

Schimmel, K. S.: "Ownership," *International Encyclopedia of Women and Sport*, ed., K. Christensen (Great Barrington, MA: Berkshire Reference Works, forthcoming).

Schimmel, K. S.: "Growth politics, urban development, and sports stadium development in the United States: A case study," *The Stadium and the City*, ed. J. Bale and O. Moen (Stafford, England: Keele University Press, 1995), pp. 111–55.

Schimmel, K. S., Ingham, A. G. and Howell, J. W.: "Professional team sport and the American city: Urban politics and franchise relocations," *Sport in Social Development: Traditions, Transitions and Transformations*, ed. A. G. Ingham and J. W. Loy (Champaign, IL: Human Kinetics Publishers, 1993), pp. 211–44.

Staudohar, P. D.: *The Sports Industry and Collective Bargaining* (New York, NY: Cornell University Press, 1986).

Stone, C.: "The study of the politics of urban development," *The Politics of Urban Development*, ed., C. N. Stone and H. T. Sanders (Lawrence, KS: University of Kansas Press, 1987), pp. 3–24.

Swanstrom, T.: *The Crisis of Growth Politics: Cleveland, Kucinich, and the Challenge of Urban Populism* (Philadelphia, PA: Temple University Press, 1985).

Vincent, T.: *Mudville's Revenge: The Rise and Fall of American Sport* (New York, NY: Seaview Press, 1981).

Voigt, D. Q.: *American Baseball: From Gentleman's Sport to Commissioner System* (Norman, OK: University of Oklahoma Press, 1966).

Warf, B. and Holly, B.: "The rise and fall of Cleveland," *The Annals of the American Academy of Political and Social Science*, 551 (1997), 208–21.

Williams, R.: *Marxism and Literature* (New York, NY: Oxford University Press, 1976).

Zukin, S.: *Landscapes of Power* (Berkeley and Los Angeles: University of California Press, 1991).

5 Art Appreciation at Caesars Palace

Mel McCombie

"Live the Legend," the ads call out, a simulation of history recreated at Caesars Palace in Las Vegas. Caesars – no apostrophe, "by imperial decree" – was the brainchild of developer Jay Sarno, a hotel operator best known for his Palo Alto Cabana Hotel. Designed by Miami architect Melvin Grossman and opened in August 1966, Caesars Palace broke with the architectural mode established by Benjamin Siegal's Flamingo, which looked to luxe modernism rather than the Old West. Unlike any previous casino-hotel in Las Vegas, Caesars was modeled on a Baroque European city, symmetrical, grand, and adorned with fountains, gardens, and statuary figure 5.1. It established the mold from which seemingly every resort in Las Vegas has been cast.

Caesars was the first Las Vegas resort to consistently embody an historical theme of time and place. As Alan Hess describes it, "it was Rome and it was not Rome. As with a dream, only a few cues were required to convey the place's identity" (1993, p. 84).[1] This dream of ancient Rome was accomplished with a Jamesonian pastiche of art and architecture, "a world in which . . . all that is left is to imitate dead styles, to speak through the masks and with the voices of the styles in the imaginary museum" (Jameson, 1983, p. 115). When Jameson wrote of "the transformation of reality into images, the fragmentation of time into a series of perpetual presents," he could have been writing a scholarly cutline for a photograph of Caesars. It creates a postmodern (a)historical space that is wildly entertaining and highly effective in marketing its gaming and shows, a postmodern demonstration of the logic of consumer capitalism (Jameson, 1983, p. 125).

Themed environments simulate history and locales with art, architecture, and theater, attempting to recreate an historical and cultural ambience and to present it as a commodity.[2] Vast "urban entertainment centers," in the parlance of the Urban Land Institute, combine retail, entertainment, and food in order to commodify leisure, broadly defined as anything people do when they are not working. These urban entertainment centers – like the South Street Seaport in New York, Universal's City Walk in Los Angeles, Faneuil Hall in Boston, or Ghiradelli Square and Pier 39 in San Francisco – commodify leisure activities, married with consumer products. They are most successful when "branded" – when fused with well-known, highly-advertised product lines like Nike sportswear, Virgin Records, Barnes and Noble books, or restaurants like the Hard Rock Cafe or Planet Hollywood (Boyer, 1992).[3] Industry newsletters offer developers brand guidelines for tenant mixes at themed urban sites. For example, in "Get A Lifestyle," the *Entertainment Real Estate Report* (1998) suggests choosing a broad theme – like Sports, or Movies and Media, or Learning and Technology, or Car Culture – and slotting in appropriate tenants. A sports-themed entertainment center, for example, might include Magic Johnson Theaters;

This chapter was specifically commissioned for this volume.

Figure 5.1   Caesars Palace resort hotel and casino, Las Vegas, Nevada. The exterior of Caesars Palace from Las Vegas Boulevard, with Nike of Samothrace reproduction right foreground; porte cochere and statuary at rear behind fountains

restaurants like ESPN Zone and The Clubhouse; museums like the Baseball Hall of Fame and the National Sports Gallery; retail stores like Just for Feet and Ron Jon Surf Shop; and family entertainment centers like Crunch Fitness and Arc Ice Sports. For Movies and Media, the report suggests Sundance and AMC Cinemas; The Bubba Gump Cafe and Screening Room restaurants; the Mary Pickford and Getty Museums; the Sundance Stores, Disney Stores, and Nickelodeon; and Jurassic Park: The Ride, and Star Trek: The Experience. Using their template, the enterprising developer can create themed entertainment centers that cater to virtually any audience.

Caesars and its Las Vegas rivals compete with state lotteries, riverboats, Indian reservations, and other recently legalized forms of gaming for the national gambling dollar. Ironically, the legalizing of gaming in so many states has not so much cannibalized Las Vegas as it has mitigated the sordid reputation of gambling in general, thus recasting Las Vegas from Sin City to River City. The over-the-top fantasy theme park that Las Vegas has become has made it the premier destination for the newly-addicted gambler, for whom the state lotto might have been the gateway. Historian Don Payne described Las Vegas's appeal with a sports metaphor, "If you see your first baseball game on a sandlot, sooner or later you'll want to see the World Series" (Bragg, 1997, p. A22).[4]

What Caesars has done is to meld gambling into a branded themed environment, a brilliant stroke that casts gambling as a kind of wholesome escapist entertainment embedded within a self-contained urban entertainment center. The simulated Greco-Roman world of Caesars also works to keep the bottom line healthy. Gambling historian John Findlay asserts that themed spaces like Caesars distance customers from the everyday world and the concerns that might put a brake on their gambling. He notes that "any device that helps to remove the bettor from his normal environment actually enhances the experience of betting. . . . The greater the player's sense of distance from the setting that makes up his daily reality, the more he is 'released' from 'conventional responsibilities and controls'" (Findlay, 1986, p. 133).[5]

Theming also enhances the entertainment value of the casino experience, particularly when extended into shopping and dining. Indeed, a poll by the Las Vegas Convention and Visitors Bureau placed gambling as only one entertainment choice for Las Vegas visitors. Forty eight percent of first-time tourists came to gamble; 67 percent came to shop (Lee, 1998, p. 2). Entertainment is the chief commodity of Las Vegas, and gambling is only one component; increasingly, entertainment in Las Vegas is being redefined as both themed and branded. There are over 40 "branded entertainment theme-store retailers," in industry parlance, and their numbers grow yearly. Stores like The Disney Store, Warner Brothers Studio Stores, Nike Town, and M&M World not only generate huge profits, but casinos have adopted them to enhance the appeal of their venues (Bobrow, 1998). Caesars excels in fusing its ancient Roman theme with known brands like Warner Brothers; indeed, Caesars is itself its own brand, with a line of fragrances and clothing touted in national magazines.

Baby boomers are the target of this trend. Glenn Schaeffer, President of Circus Circus, spoke of the imperative to theme and brand casinos in order to sell themselves to "the Woodstock generation. . . . Generation 50 has a quest for fresh pleasures . . . they are indulgers and will pay for fun. Thus if their number one goal is to have more fun, then our design standard in Vegas should be to have stuff with more fun," what he calls "gratifier central" (Bobrow, 1998, p. 10). For Schaeffer, part of the key to "gratifier central" is name brands.

The trend toward branded theming in Las Vegas extends to dining as well as shopping and gaming – casino owners vie for elite "name" restauranteurs like Wolfgang Puck (Caesars), Emeril Lagasse (MGM Grand and the Venetian), and Sergio Maccioni's Le Cirque (Bellagio). Indeed, the "name" restaurant as theme unto itself now allows the foodie to tour the culinary world without leaving Las Vegas. Other chefs lending their names to Las Vegas's upscale branded eateries include Charlie Palmer of New York, Todd English of Boston, Nobu Matsuhita of New York, Joachim Splichal of Los Angeles, Mark Miller of Santa Fe, and Jean-Louis Palladin of Washington. These star chefs farm out the scut work of their Las Vegas locations to trained sous-chefs, and rake in the profits, making occasional appearances (and perhaps to count their money).

Though these high-end restaurants abjure the blue-collar gambler, they welcome those who are happy to shell out $100 or more for dinner for two, excluding wine, tax, and tip. Todd English of Boston's Figs restaurant stated "the size of the market is amazing. There's got to be gold in them thar hills. You need just a tiny fraction of the people who live there or come to visit to make Las Vegas a dining destination" (Apple, 1998). With Gallic directness, Jean-Louis Palladin put it even more bluntly, "The money's real, but everything else is fake" (Apple, 1998, p. F6). The often bizarre disjunctions between the ambitions of the restaurant and its setting (such as the view from Chinois across the Forum Shops into FAO's World of Barbie, or the gambling carnival that surrounds Napa, Palladin's restaurant in the Rio) seem to add to the fun, if you leaven your dinner with enough irony.

Themed environments like Caesars (or Disney World or any shopping mall) contrive to control behavior by creating physical settings that prolong the beholder's immersion both physically and psychologically. The number of entries and exits are limited – and once inside, leaving is difficult. Caesars (indeed, all casinos) maximize encounters with slot machines by creating tortuous routes to elevators, bathrooms, restaurants, and pools. Finding an exit is probably the hardest task of all. It is easy to enter by car or on foot through one of Caesars five grand entrances, but once in, the visitor is confronted by faux-Latin signs at the entries that say "Non exitus." It is like driving in a city of one-way streets.

Just as shopping malls offer "rest" areas with uncomfortable chairs and views into shops, Caesars' restaurants, seating, and fountains are sited with alluring views of slots or gaming areas. A meandering, indeed vast, plan entices the visitor (or Noble Guest, in Caesar-talk) to wander, seeking new delights. The resort covers over 80 acres, and although the exterior view of Caesars evokes the grand symmetry of Versailles or Rome, the plan is a maze that would flummox Stanley and Livingston. There is no external noise or view, only simulated sky painted on the ceilings; no clocks to mark time; and since casinos are active at almost all hours, no social cues to indicate time. Caesars bears the markers of a complete city in analogous form – with theaters, housing, parks, transit systems, and banking (Hess, 1993, p. 120). One need never leave, unless you go bust.

The psychological enticement to stay is enhanced with themed entertainment. There, "Caesar" is a single person – not Caesar Augustus or Julius Caesar, but just plain "Caesar." He is accompanied by his consort, Cleopatra (who in history never went to Rome nor had anything to do with a Roman emperor). Actors impersonate the emperor and his girlfriend; urging gamblers to enjoy themselves, the pair tours the vast empire and willingly pose for pictures. Art consultant Neal Menzies (1999) described the giddy sensation the actors and environment produced: "The first time I ever went to Caesars, my staff and I went into the gaming area and were looking at a centurion and Cleopatra's handmaid; the centurion waved his arm and said, 'Caesar bids you put coin of the realm in yonder slot!' I cracked up!" The very ahistoricity of Caesars is itself entertaining, and everyone is in on the joke.

Art is both a carrier of cultural meaning and a source of entertainment at Caesars. Simulations of the sculptures of Greece, Rome, and France elevate the tone of what is at heart a gaming house. Art at Caesars flatters its spectators for their taste; it is vaguely familiar, bearing the signs of historicity without tedious wall labels, carriers of culture without the behavioral constraints and class implications found in an art museum. Caesars Palace creates a museum for the mass audience, a museum free of uniformed security guards, velvet ropes, admission fees and Plexiglass panels. Of course, though the casino appears not to be a zone of surveillance as an art museum clearly is, there is in fact no site more carefully and covertly policed than a casino.[6]

The most favored image of Caesar is the *Prima Porta Augustus* – the emperor about to harangue the legions. The early first century original (now in the Vatican Museums) depicts the emperor with his hand raised in an oratorical gesture. His cuirass depicts the return of Roman standards captured by the Parthians; the supporting Cupid reminds viewers of the Julian family's claim to have descended from Venus. This carefully crafted work of political propaganda served as a symbol of his right to rule. Today, it serves Caesars Palace as corporate spokesperson. Augustus directs traffic at the entrance to the long driveway; he greets gamblers entering the Forum Casino; he adorns the in-room guide for hotel guests; and he lifeguards at the Garden of the Gods pool complex.

Other entrances to Caesars are also marked with reproductions of statues. The elaborate entries fronting the sidewalk of Las Vegas Avenue beckon with reproductions of the equestrian Marcus Aurelius (A D 161–180); the *Apollo Belvedere* (circa second century A D); and the quadriga from atop the Mausoleum at Halicarnassus. These grand entries on the sidewalks connect to the casino and shops with people movers in a one-way flow. Once in, of course, "non exitus" applies.

A simulated *Nike of Samothrace* beckons at the entrance to the drive leading to the main porte-cochere grand entry. The original work of the second century B C in the Louvre is placed on the landing of a great staircase; its desert equivalent is ironically placed more appropriately than that of the original. At Caesars, she is sited at the head of a long reflecting pool, amid jets of water, a placement that recalls the nautical victory that the original celebrates.

A sedulous reproduction of Giovanni Bologna's 1583 *Rape of the Sabines*, a mannerist *tour de force* depicting the founding myth of Rome described by Virgil, a story of civilizing and fusing two cultures, adorns the elliptical pool at the casino end of the main drive. It was among the first sculptures to adorn the new resort in 1966, carved in Italy to exacting specifications, and the source of major bragging rights for Caesars. High-rollers who exit their limousines next to the statue seem unaware of whatever ironies its subject of abduction and cultural fusion may call forth. It is understood instead as simply classy, a fancy sculpture of naked people that marks the entry as elegant.

The massive cantilevered porte-cochere ("the world's largest cantilevered structure of its kind," according to its celebratory plaque) culminates in a series of niches featuring reproductions from 2000 years of European art. There one can view a virtual museum of simulations that includes the *Venus de Medici* (original first century A D), the *Venus de Milo* (ca. 150 B C), *Venus* by Antonio Canova (eighteenth century), and *Hebe* by Adrian de Vries (eighteenth century). Male statues include reproductions of two by Michelangelo, the 1503 *David* and the 1495 *Bacchus*. The porte-cochere entry has the most lavish sculptural simulations in the resort, perhaps because it caters to those arriving by car or limousine, not by foot – a class distinction that separates the flatfoots from the high rollers.

As Pierre Bourdieu would assert, understanding the connection between this constructed vision of culture and class is fundamental to understanding the success of Caesars. Caesars virtual museum endows its visitors with unearned cultural capital, developed upon those who cross its thresholds (see Passeron and Bourdieu, 1977). We can see how this works in the ways Caesars employs what is arguably the most famous sculpture in the world, Michelangelo's *David*.

A much-touted eighteen-foot Carrara marble indexical replica of *David* is the centerpiece of Caesars Appian Way Shops. The massive sculpture, which press material brags "weighs more than nine tons and took longer than 10 months to complete,"[7] is sited in the central court of the Appian Way Shops, home to Cartier, Ted Lapidus, and other elite venues. The original's context (the Loggia dei Lanzi in Florence) was distinctly political, a statement of Florentine liberty in the face of tyranny. At Caesars, its political connotations are transformed into the commercial vernacular of the shopping center; *David* becomes a commodity akin to those offered in the shops, while its art historical connotations simultaneously elevate the tone of the shopping area and its patrons.

The hidden persuader at the Appian Ways shops isn't subtle. One's first view of this David is from the waist down. Indeed, the sublimated homosexual longing that some scholars suggest informed Michelangelo's original work seems to be expressed more overtly at Caesars, where another replica of *David* presides over homosocial gatherings in the hot tub of the men's spa.

Other sculptures and paintings abound throughout the hotel and casino. Among the more inventive are loose reproductions of Michelangelo's tomb sculptures of the Medici Chapel of San Lorenzo in Florence, depicting Lorenzo and Guiliano de Medici. These reproduction replicate the famous poses of the originals – Lorenzo's brooding relaxed stance and Guiliano's torqued martial figure – but with twists. At Caesars, these two powerful types surmount the Quarter Mania slots. They are surrounded by lunettes based on Michelangelo's depictions of the ancestors of Christ on the Sistine Chapel ceiling in the Vatican – but at Caesars, the pensive, muscular originals are transformed into more cheerful guys and gals in ancient garb. Art consultants carefully directed the muralists painting the niches, aiming for a contemporary translation of antique art.

Michelangelo's less famed colleagues of later generations are also paid homage at Caesars. A copy of Gianlorenzo Bernini's *Triton* presides over one corridor; the *Fontainebleu Diane* guards elevators to the Palace Towers rooms. Indeed, some images, especially in the pool area, seem to refer more to Sid Caesar than to Augustus, with grinning faces surrounded by wreathes of laurel.

Sculpture serves as handmaid to commerce in the wildly successful shopping mall attached to the casino, the Forum Shops (figure 5.2). These are the most profitable square feet of retail space in the United States. One can enter only through the casino, via the Fortuna Terrace, where a monumental statue of the goddess of fortune and luck welcomes shoppers. Banks of slot machines flank the statue, whose chairs beckon the tired shopper to rest their feet and feed the slots. This over-the-top mall marries entertainment with retail for huge profits. Far outstripping its now-quaint antecedents, like Ghiradelli Square in San Francisco or Faneuil Hall in Boston, the Forum Shops provides architecturally embellished settings for a nonstop barrage of song, show, and sell.[8]

Replicas of classical statuary adorn the niches above the stores (like Versace, Estee Lauder, Saint John, Swatch, Ann Taylor), images that the visitor already recognizes – the *Venus de Medici, Hebe*, the *Prima Porta Augustus*. The mall appears to have marble-tiled "streets" that expand to piazzas with central fountains embellished with animatronic figures of Bacchus, Venus, Apollo, and Plutus, who hourly come to life and invite shoppers to revel in the glories of Rome. The laser and light shows of the

Figure 5.2   The Forum shops at Caesars shopping mall, Las Vegas, Nevada. Entrance court of Forum Shops; statue of Fortuna seen from rear at right, slot machines behind the statue; Warner Brothers Studio Store on left

mall sculptures are an attraction in themselves, drawing waiting crowds who applaud when the hourly show is completed. As the in-room guide brags, "This is not your standard mall. The statues talk. The fountains dance. The sky does tricks…Caesars, the shopping wonder of the world" (*The Emperor's Guide*, 1997, p. 75).

Retailers employ themed decor with varying degrees of postmodern irony. FAO Schwartz's toy store beckons with a giant Trojan Horse, whose secret compartments pop open regularly and feature singing animatronic toys. Within FAO, The World of Barbie features a frieze of Mattel's doll as life-size statues dressed in classical robes – what Bill and Ted might call "historical babes." The Warner Brothers Studio Store puts a lexical spin on the theme, with its faux Latin sign, "Warnerius Fraternius Studius Storius." A statue of Elmer Fudd stands at the entrance, elevated to Senatorial rank, as his purple toga declares. Above Senator Fudd, the Tasmanian Devil and Sylvester the Cat don armor and swords, cartoon statuary simulacra of the actors that stroll the casino floor. It seems natural that the Forum Shops also boast an outlet of the ultimate in high cultural simulacra, the Museum Store. There, reproductions of the Venus de Milo jostle with mouse pads bearing Raphael's contemplative angels and scarves with *ignudi* from the Sistine Chapel ceiling.

One can't help but notice the disjunction between the Imperial Roman theme of Caesars, and its arts reproduced from millennia of history and a variety of cultures. My first take on this was an ironic and superior chuckle – these yahoos just didn't know better. It turns out that I was wrong. Caesars employs designers through

Wilson and Associates in Dallas and Los Angeles who consult with art historians, such as Neal Menzies and Associates on selections. James Adams Design of Newport Beach is the theming designer for the parts of the Palace Towers area and the pools. As Menzies (1999) stresses, "the people I have worked with are intelligent; they know good art from bad art. They want art that is attractive and entertaining, not necessarily instructive or informative. If it is instructive or informative, so much the better." Menzies (1999) recalled his teenage job working at Disneyland, where the dressing-room sign reminded him to "Remember, it's for the show!" "That's what art is for at Caesars," he says. "It's always for the show."

The art choices are, therefore, informed, aware, and deliberate, akin to the cultural pastiche of Rome itself. It is, after all, a city in which the strata of history coexist in comfort. The culture of imperial Rome was one of absorption, coopting the images, arts, and religions of its tributaries. So is Caesars. Menzies (1999) agrees, stating that "the art at Caesars is like Roman art – it has been added to and subtracted from over the years."

Identity politics may also inform the art choices at Caesars. Its overall Italian-ness may reflect the casino's original whispered relationship to La Cosa Nostra. The casino developed by Jay Sarno was partially funded with Teamster pension fund money rumored to have been funneled through the mob.[9]

The purpose of art at Caesars is not didactic but entertaining. Art there exists outside the white cube of the museum, de-mystified and accessible. It democratizes privilege. The designers making art and decoration decisions are perfectly aware of this. They looked for art that looked like smart adaptations of antique art: "Caesars was about decoration, about trying to make guests feel welcome and comfortable," not intimidated as they might feel in the new Venetian (Menzies, 1999). The success of the art program at Caesars is more amazing in light of the inherent conflict between designers and corporate bean-counters. Management's sensibility has collided with the designers again and again, making the relative coherence of the themed environment all the more compelling.[10]

The art-as-entertainment formula works well. As Las Vegas has expanded, casinos are making even greater use of decontextualized history and art to create sites where culture and commerce mix to expand their markets, from middle-to-lower income families to the rich. All are invited to play in surroundings redolent of a Disneyesque version of history and art. The Excalibur mega-hotel uses an Arthurian motif to entice, complete with parking attendants in plastic armor who wave cars in with plastic swords; it offers three "authentic" jousts on horseback per day in the central court (including a dinner show joust). The Luxor mines the imagery of ancient Egypt for its allure, mixing New Age and Old Kingdom with slots and rides. New York–New York compresses the Big Apple into a clean, safe, crime-free pastiche in which the Chrysler Building, the Whitney Museum, the Empire State, and the Statue of Liberty are all within 5-minute walks of each other. Paul Goldberger (1997) describes New York–New York as "an apple in plastic shrink-wrap . . . a whole city, turned in a swoop into a theme park." It even has a roller coaster.

The new mega-casino, the Mandalay Bay Resort and Casino, not only recreates an overall themed environment (in this case, East Indian colonial tropics), but is divided into sub-colonies, each with themes of their own – from the House of Blues to the elite Four Seasons Hotel plunked like a gilded cage atop a skyscraper on the top four floors of the hotel. Observers see an increasing trend to this kind of internal specialization, like the billion-dollar mansion suites and villas at the MGM Grand (available by invitation only) that co-exist with the MGM's family-oriented 5000 standard rooms.

The latest fantasy to open as of this writing recreates the city of Venice, canals and all, an ecological disaster and a wild luxury in the parched desert. Chair of The Venetian hotel and casino, Sheldon Adelson, announced his hotel as the next step in Las Vegas's evolution, "I submit this town has not gone far enough – it has just dipped their foot [sic] into the well of change" (Bobrow, 1998). He has raised the bar, aiming to out-theme his Las Vegas rivals with a monstrous 6000-suite hotel, stating that "we are not going to build a 'faux' Venice. We're going to build what is essentially the *real* Venice" (McKee, 1997). It includes canals with gondolas piloted by men singing "O Solo Mio" who greet guests with fake Italo-American accents; a recreated Piazza San Marco and the famed campanile; and painted reproductions of Tintoretto and Tiepolo's paintings. Ironically, his Renaissance-themed hyperbole is persuasive enough that a committee of Venetians have protested the Disney-fying of their city. Venetian mayor Massimo Cacciari denounced the hotel as a project "about the 'violent' use of the image of Venice," and asked the Italian Foreign Ministry take up the issue (Binkley, 1999, p. B1). Sniffs Menzies (1999), "at least Caesars *knows* the art is fake. That appalling Venetian actually tries to look like antique art!" Adelson's Venetian's 6000 suites should have no problem being filled, however; he is the founder of the world's largest convention, Comdex. This annual computer convention fills Las Vegas with 300,000 visitors yearly.[11]

Casinos are also investing in museum-quality art, a charge led by mega-developer Steve Wynn (Binkley, 1998). Wynn's collection of French painting, valued near $300 million, is part of the decorative scheme of his $1.6 billion casino, the Bellagio. Tickets to view the collection at the Bellagio cost $12 and often require long waits to enter, just like blockbuster art shows at conventional museums. Outbidding museums, the Brazilian-themed Rio Hotel and Casino hosted an exhibition of Romanov Dynasty treasures in 1998. The art and entertainment industries are united in the museum world as well. A 1997 conference of science museum leaders emphasized the need for attracting audiences with entertainment, "not unlike Disney...the key lies in attraction and identity branding," an approach endorsed by museums all over the country (*The Entertainment Zone*, 1997, p. 5).

It seems that everyone has taken a leaf from Caesars book. The recent boom has proven that the postmodern mix of culture, (a)history, and commerce first created in Caesars Palace works. Simulations of vaguely and reassuringly familiar icons of art flatter the beholders, elevate the tone of casinos from tawdry to respectable, and bear the markers of elite culture grafted onto popular commercial enterprise.[12] Familiar icons of art, like Michelangelo's *David*, flatter, entertain and elevate the casino's tone. Recently, Caesars received the ultimate pop cultural tribute: it was drolly cited in an episode of "Xena: Warrior Princess," entitled "When In Rome...," with "Caesar's Palace" opening the episode. In that contest, I'd bet on Xena.

Acknowledgments

The staff of Caesars Palace public relations, especially Deborah Munch, assistant vice president of public relations, were most helpful. I am also grateful to Susan Prann of Wilson and Associates of Los Angeles; Neal Menzies; and William C. Murphy of Keyser Marston Associates, Inc. of San Francisco for providing valuable information.

Notes

1 Prior to 1945, casinos and hotels did adopt themed motifs that dovetailed with the history of the area; the most popular motif was that of a wild west/Victorian saloon. Postwar resorts like Benjamin Siegal's Flamingo adopted the flamboyent modernist style characteristic of Palm Springs or Miami Beach resorts. Caesars was the first in Las Vegas to adopt a non-contextual historical theme that was fully woven into the hotel, with details like art, costumes, and actors impersonating historical characters (see Hess, 1993).
2 For an expanded discussion of the urban politics of theming, see article by Salmon in this volume.
3 See also industry newsletters like "The Entertainment Zone Real Estate Report," published by Ecklein Communications <www.eci-global.com>; and "The Ezone," published by The Urban Land Institute *www.uli.org*. Both are devoted to urban entertainment centers.
4 It is worth noting that gambling is not about luck. The average take in Las Vegas casinos is 17 percent of the wagers, a percentage called "the hold," and is always a known quantity. The advent of debit-style cards used by gamblers allows casinos to keep track of exactly who plays what and for how much in the same way the supermarket buyer's cards allow markets to keep track of shopping habits. Nothing about casino gambling is left to chance (see Bowden, 1998).
5 Findlay (1986) cites a 1976 study by Robert D. Herman, *Gamblers and Gambling: Motives, Institutions, and Controls*.
6 Casino surveillance takes many forms, from security in mufti to high-tech "eye-in-the-sky" camera systems.
7 Caesars Palace, media information, Deborah Munch.
8 See Braun (1995) for comparisons with other themed retail/entertainment centers.
9 In 1968, Nevada's laws were changed and with them, the financing of casinos. Prior to 1968, only individuals were permitted to hold gambling licenses, which limited casino ownerships to the mega-rich like Kirk Kerkorian and Howard Hughes. After 1968, corporations could own casinos.
10 Caesars has gone through a series of owners, from Jay Sarno to ITT-Sheraton to Starwood to its acquisition by Park Place Entertainment in April 1999.
11 Comdex is no longer owned by Adelson but was bought by a Japanese consortium (McKee, 1997).
12 Even Yasser Arafat has jumped onto the themed casino resort bandwagon, in partnership with an Australian casino developer (see Lee in *The Entertainment Zone*, Urban Land Institute, September 1998).

References

Apple, R. W.: "In Las Vegas, top restaurants are the hot new game," *New York Times* (February 18, 1998), pp. F1, F6.

Binkley, Christina: "Vegas's merchandising of Venice brings ire from the real thing," *The Wall Street Journal* (May 4, 1999), p. B1.

Binkley, Christina: "Gambling on culture: Casinos invest in fine art," *The Wall Street Journal* (April 6, 1998), p. B1, B2.

Bobrow, A. Scott: "Casino execs bite branding bug," The Entertainment Real Estate Report, IV (January 1998), 1–9.

Bowden, Charles: "Crapshoot nation," *GQ* (April 1998), pp. 131–45.

Boyer, M. Christine: "Cities for sale: Merchandising history at South Street Seaport," *Variations on a Theme Park*, ed. Michael Sorkin (New York: Hill and Wang, 1992).

Bragg, Rick: "Las Vegas is booming after city reinvention," *The New York Times* (May 4, 1997), A22.

Braun, Raymond E.: "Exploring the urban entertainment center universe," *Urban Land* (Supplement to August 1995 issue), 11–15.

The Emperors Guide (with Caesars Palace, Las Vegas: ITT, 1997).

The Entertainment Real Estate Report: "Get a lifestyle, Part II," The Entertainment Real Estate Report, III (June 1998), 1, 16–17.

The Entertainment Zone: "What the museum people are thinking – sound familiar?," (The Urban Land Institute, 1997), p. 5.

Findlay, John M.: *People of Chance: Gambling in American Society from Jamestown to Las Vegas* (New York: Oxford University Press, 1986).

Goldberger, Paul: "New York–New York, it's a casino's replica town," *The New York Times* (January 15, 1997), pp. B1, B6.

Hess, Alan: *Viva Las Vegas: After-Hours Architecture* (San Francisco, CA: Chronicle Books, 1993).

Jameson, Frederic: "Postmodernism and consumer society," *The Anti-Aesthetic*, ed. Hal Foster (Seattle, WA: Baypress, 1983), pp. 111–25.

Lee, Nora: "Reality check: Experience economic principles," *The Entertainment Zone* (The Urban Land Institute, September 1998), p. 2.

McKee, Jamie: "Venice in Las Vegas," *Casino Journal*, 10 (1997), unpaginated reprint.

Menzies, Neal: telephone interview (July 29, 1999).

Passeron, Jean-Claude and Bourdieu, Pierre: *Reproduction in Education, Society and Culture*, trans. Richard Nice (London: Sage Publications, 1977).

Part II

Cultural Production/Commodification

6 Art as Collective Action

Howard S. Becker

A distinguished sociological tradition holds that art is social in character, this being a specific instance of the more general proposition that knowledge and cultural products are social in character or have a social base. A variety of language has been used to describe the relations between art works and their social context. Studies have ranged from those that attempted to correlate various artistic styles and the cultural emphases of the societies they were found in to those that investigated the circumstances surrounding the production of particular works. Both social scientists and humanistic scholars have contributed to this literature. (A representative sample of work can be found in Albrecht, Barnett and Griff, 1970).

Much sociological writing speaks of organizations or systems without reference to the people whose collective actions constitute the organization or system. Much of the literature on art as a social product does the same, demonstrating relations or congruences without reference to the collective activities by which they came about, or speaking of social structures without reference to the actions of people doing things together which create those structures. My admittedly scattered reading of materials on the arts, the available sociological literature, (especially Blumer, 1966, and Strauss et al., 1964) and personal experience and participation in several art worlds have led me to a conception of art as a form of collective action.

In arriving at this conception, I have relied on earlier work by social scientists and humanists in the traditions I have just criticized. Neither the examples I use nor the specific points are novel; but I do not believe they have been used in connection with the conception of collective activity here proposed. None of the examples stands as evidence for the theory. Rather, they illustrate the kinds of materials a theory about this area of human life must take account of. Applying such a conception to the area of art generates some broader ideas about social organization in general, which I consider in conclusion. They are evidence that a theory of the kind proposed is necessary.

Cooperation and Cooperative Links

Think, with respect to any work of art, of all the activities that must be carried on for that work to appear as it finally does. For a symphony orchestra to give a concert, for instance, instruments must have been invented, manufactured and maintained, a notation must have been devised and music composed using that notation, people must have learned to play the notated notes on the instruments, times and places for rehearsal must have been provided, ads for the concert must have been placed, publicity arranged and tickets sold, and an audience capable of listening to and in

Original publication: Becker, Howard S. "Art as Collective Action" *American Sociological Review*, 39 (December 1974).

some way understanding and responding to the performance must have been recruited. A similar list can be compiled for any of the performing arts. With minor variations (substitute materials for instruments and exhibition for performance), the list applies to the visual and (substituting language and print for materials and publication for exhibition) literary arts. Generally speaking, the necessary activities typically include conceiving the idea for the work, making the necessary physical artifacts, creating a conventional language of expression, training artistic personnel and audiences to use the conventional language to create and experience, and providing the necessary mixture of those ingredients for a particular work or performance.

Imagine, as an extreme case, one person who did all these things: made everything, invented everything, performed, created and experienced the result, all without the assistance or cooperation of anyone else. In fact, we can barely imagine such a thing, for all the arts we know about involve elaborate networks of cooperation. A division of the labor required takes place. Typically, many people participate in the work without which the performance or artifact could not be produced. A sociological analysis of any art therefore looks for that division of labor. How are the various tasks divided among the people who do them?

Nothing in the technology of any art makes one division of tasks more "natural" than another. Consider the relations between the composition and performance of music. In conventional symphonic and chamber music, the two activities occur separately; although many composers perform, and many performers compose, we recognize no necessary connection between the two and see them as two separate roles which may occasionally coincide in one person. In jazz, composition is not important, the standard tune merely furnishing a framework on which the performer builds the improvisation listeners consider important. In contemporary rock music, the performer ideally composes his own music; rock groups who play other people's music (Bennett, 1972) carry the derogatory title of "copy bands." Similarly, some art photographers always make their own prints; others seldom do. Poets writing in the Western tradition do not think it necessary to incorporate their handwriting into the work, leaving it to printers to put the material in readable form, but Oriental calligraphers count the actual writing an integral part of the poetry. In no case does the character of the art impose a natural division of labor; the division always results from a consensual definition of the situation. Once that has been achieved, of course, participants in the world of art[1] regard it as natural and resist attempts to change it as unnatural, unwise or immoral.

Participants in an art world regard some of the activities necessary to the production of that form of art as "artistic," requiring the special gift or sensibility of an artist. The remaining activities seem to them a matter of craft, business acumen or some other ability less rare, less characteristic of art, less necessary to the success of the work, and less worthy of respect. They define the people who perform these special activities as artists, and everyone else as (to borrow a military term) support personnel. Art worlds differ in how they allocate the honorific title of artist and in the mechanisms by which they choose who gets it and who doesn't. At one extreme, a guild or academy (Pevsner, 1940) may require long apprenticeship and prevent those it does not license from practicing. At the other, the choice may be left to the lay public that consumes the work, whoever they accept being ipso facto an artist.

An activity's status as art or non-art may change, in either direction. Kealy (1974) notes that the recording engineer has, when new technical possibilities arose that artists could use expressively, been regarded as something of an artist. When the effects he can produce become commonplace, capable of being produced on demand by any competent worker, he loses that status.

How little of the activity necessary for the art can a person do and still claim the title of artist? The amount the composer contributes to the material contained in the final work has varied greatly. Virtuoso performers from the Renaissance through the nineteenth century embellished and improvised on the score the composer provided (Dart, 1967, and Reese, 1959), so it is not unprecedented for contemporary composers to prepare scores which give only the sketchiest directions to the performer (though the counter-tendency, for composers to restrict the interpretative freedom of the performer by giving increasingly detailed directions, has until recently been more prominent). John Cage and Karlheinz Stockhausen (Wörner, 1973) are regarded as composers in the world of contemporary music, though many of their scores leave much of the material to be played to the decision of the player. Artists need not handle the materials from which the art work is made to remain artists; architects seldom build what they design. The same practice raises questions, however, when sculptors construct a piece by sending a set of specifications to a machine shop; and many people balk at awarding the title of artist to authors of conceptual works consisting of specifications which are never actually embodied in an artifact. Marcel Duchamp outraged many people by insisting that he created a valid work of art when he signed a commercially produced snowshovel or signed a reproduction of the Mona Lisa on which he had drawn a mustache, thus classifying Leonardo as support personnel along with the snowshovel's designer and manufacturer. Outrageous as that idea may seem, something like it is standard in making collages, in which the entire work may be constructed of things made by other people. The point of these examples is that what is taken, in any world of art, to be the quintessential artistic act, the act whose performance marks one as an artist, is a matter of consensual definition.

Whatever the artist, so defined, does not do himself must be done by someone else. The artist thus works in the center of a large network of cooperating people, all of whose work is essential to the final outcome. Wherever he depends on others, a cooperative link exists. The people with whom he cooperates may share in every particular his idea of how their work is to be done. This consensus is likely when everyone involved can perform any of the necessary activities, so that while a division of labor exists, no specialized functional groups develop. This situation might occur in simple communally shared art forms like the square dance or in segments of a society whose ordinary members are trained in artistic activities. A well-bred nineteenth century American, for instance, knew enough music to take part in performing the parlor songs of Stephen Foster just as his Renaissance counterpart could participate in performing madrigal. In such cases, cooperation occurs simply and readily.

When specialized professional groups take over the performance of the activities necessary to an art work's production, however, their members tend to develop specialized aesthetic, financial and career interests which differ substantially from the artist's. Orchestral musicians, for instance, are notoriously more concerned with how they sound in performance than with the success of a particular work; with good reason, for their own success depends in part on impressing those who hire them with their competence (Faulkner, 1973a, 1973b). They may sabotage a new work which can make them sound bad because of its difficulty, their career interests lying at cross-purposes to the composer's.

Aesthetic conflicts between support personnel and the artist also occur. A sculptor friend of mine was invited to use the services of a group of master lithographic printers. Knowing little of the technique of lithography, he was glad to have these master craftsmen do the actual printing, this division of labor being customary and having generated a highly specialized craft of printing. He drew designs containing large areas of solid colors, thinking to simplify the printer's job. Instead, he made it more difficult. When the printer rolls ink onto the stone, a large area will require more than one rolling to be fully inked and may thus exhibit roller marks. The printers, who prided themselves on being the greatest in the world, explained to my friend that while they could print his designs, the areas of solid color could cause difficulty with roller marks. He had not known about roller marks and talked of using them as part of his design. The printers said, no, he could not do that, because roller marks were an obvious sign (to other printers) of poor craftsmanship and no print exhibiting roller marks was allowed to leave their shop. His artistic curiosity fell victim to the printers' craft standards, a neat example of how specialized support groups develop their own standards and interests.[2]

My friend was at the mercy of the printers because he did not know how to print lithographs himself. His experience exemplified the choice that faces the artist at every cooperative link. He can do things the way established groups of support personnel are prepared to do them; he can try to make them do it his way: he can train others to do it his way; or he can do it himself. Any choice but the first requires an additional investment of time and energy to do what could be done less expensively if done the standard way. The artist's involvement with and dependence on cooperative links thus constrains the kind of art he can produce.

Similar examples can be found in any field of art. e.e. cummings had trouble getting his first book of poetry published because printers were afraid to set his bizarre layouts (Norman, 1958). Producing a motion picture involves multiple difficulties of this kind: actors who will only be photographed in flattering ways, writers who don't want a word changed, cameramen who will not use unfamiliar processes.

Artists often create works which existing facilities for production or exhibition cannot accommodate. Sculptors build constructions too large and heavy for existing museums. Composers write music which requires more performers than existing organizations can furnish. Playwrights write plays too long for their audience's taste. When they go beyond the capacities of existing institutions, their works are not exhibited or performed: that reminds us that most artists make sculptures which are not too big or heavy, compose music which uses a comfortable number of players, or write plays which run a reasonable length of time. By accommodating their conceptions to available resources, conventional artists accept the constraints arising from their dependence on the cooperation of members of the existing art world. Wherever the artist depends on others for some necessary component he must either accept the constraints they impose or expend the time and energy necessary to provide it some other way.

To say that the artist must have the cooperation of others *for the art work to occur as it finally does* does not mean that he cannot work without that cooperation. The art work, after all, need not occur as it does, but can take many other forms, including those which allow it to be done without others' help. Thus, though poets do depend on printers and publishers (as cummings' example indicates), one can produce poetry without them. Russian poets whose work circulates in privately copied typescripts do that, as did Emily Dickinson (Johnson, 1955). In both cases, the poetry does not circulate in conventional print because the artist would not accept the censorship or rewriting imposed by those who would publish the work. The poet either has to reproduce and circulate his work himself or not have it circulated. But he can still write poetry. My argument thus differs from a functionalism that asserts that the artist must have cooperation, ignoring the possibility that the cooperation can be foregone, though at a price.

The examples given so far emphasize matters more or less external to the art work – exhibition space, printing or musical notation. Relations of cooperation and constraint, however, penetrate the entire process of artistic creation and composition, as will become clear in looking at the nature and function of artistic conventions.

Conventions

Producing art works requires elaborate modes of cooperation among specialized personnel. How do these people arrive at the terms on which they will cooperate? They could, of course, decide everything fresh on each occasion. A group of musicians could discuss and agree on such matters as which sounds would be used as tonal resources, what instruments might be constructed to make those sounds, how those sounds would be combined to create a musical language, how the language would be used to create works of a particular length requiring a given number of instruments and playable for audiences of a certain size recruited in a certain way. Something like that sometimes happens in, for instance, the creation of a new theatrical group, although in most cases only a small number of the questions to be decided are actually considered anew.

People who cooperate to produce a work of art usually do not decide things afresh. Instead, they rely on earlier agreements now become customary, agreements that have become part of the conventional way of doing things in that art. Artistic conventions cover all the decisions that must be made with respect to works produced in a given art world, even though a particular convention may be revised for a given work. Thus, conventions dictate the materials to be used, as when musicians agree to base their music on the notes contained in a set of modes, or on the diatonic, pentatonic or chromatic scales with their associated harmonies. Conventions dictate the abstractions to be used to convey particular ideas or experiences, as when painters use the laws of perspective to convey the illusion of three dimensions or photographers use black, white and shades of gray to convey the interplay of light and color. Conventions dictate the form in which materials and abstractions will be combined, as in the musical use of the sonata form or the poetic use of the sonnet. Conventions suggest the appropriate dimensions of a work, the proper length for a musical or dramatic event, the proper size and shape of a painting or sculpture. Conventions regulate the relations between artists and audience, specifying the rights and obligations of both.

Humanistic scholars – art historians, musicologists and literary critics – have found the concept of the artistic convention useful in accounting for artists' ability to produce art works which produce an emotional response in audiences. By using such a conventional organization of tones as a scale, the composer can create and manipulate the listener's expectations as to what sounds will follow. He can then delay and frustrate the satisfaction of those expectations, generating tension and release as the expectation is ultimately satisfied (Meyer, 1956, 1973; Cooper and Meyer, 1960). Only because artist and audience share knowledge of and experience with the conventions invoked does the art work produce an emotional effect. Smith (1968) has shown how poets manipulate conventional means embodied in poetic forms and diction to bring poems to a clear and satisfying conclusion, in which the expectations produced early in the lyric are simultaneously and satisfactorily resolved. Gombrich (1960) has analyzed the visual conventions artists use to create the illusion for viewers that they are seeing a realistic depiction of some aspect of the world. In all these cases (and in others like stage design, dance, and film), the possibility of artistic experience arises from the existence of a body of conventions that artists and audiences can refer to in making sense of the work.

Conventions make art possible in another sense. Because decisions can be made quickly, because plans can be made simply by referring to a conventional way of doing things, artists can devote more time to actually doing their work. Conventions thus make possible the easy and efficient coordination of activity among artists and support personnel. Ivins (1953), for instance, shows how, by using a conventionalized scheme for rendering shadows, modeling and other effects, several graphic artists could collaborate in producing a single plate. The same conventions made it possible for viewers to read what were essentially arbitrary marks as shadows and modeling. Seen this way, the concept of convention provides a point of contact between humanists and sociologists, being interchangeable with such familiar sociological ideas as norm, rule, shared understanding, custom or folkway, all referring in one way or another to the ideas and understandings people hold in common and through which they effect cooperative activity. Burlesque comedians could stage elaborate three man skits without rehearsal because they had only to refer to a conventional body of skits they all knew, pick one and assign the parts. Dance musicians who are total strangers can play all night with no more prearrangement than to mention a title ("Sunny Side of the Street," in C) and count off four beats to give the tempo; the title indicates a melody, its accompanying harmony and perhaps even customary background figures. The conventions of character and dramatic structure, in the one case, and of melody, harmony and tempo, in the other, are familiar enough that audiences have no difficulty in responding appropriately.

Though standardized, conventions are seldom rigid and unchanging. They do not specify an inviolate set of rules everyone must refer to in settling questions of what to do. Even where the directions seem quite specific, they leave much unsettled which gets resolved by reference to customary modes of interpretation on the one hand and by negotiation on the other. A tradition of performance practice, often codified in book form, tells performers how to interpret the musical scores or dramatic scripts they perform. Seventeenth century scores, for instance, contained relatively little information; but contemporary books explained how to deal with questions of instrumentation, note values, extemporization and the realization of embellishments and ornaments. Performers read their music in the light of all these customary styles of interpretation and thus were able to coordinate their activities (Dart, 1967). The same thing occurs in the visual arts. Much of the content, symbolism and coloring of Italian Renaissance religious painting was conventionally given; but a multitude of decisions remained for the artist, so that even within those strict conventions different works could be produced. Adhering to the conventional materials, however, allowed viewers to read much emotion and meaning into the picture. Even where customary interpretations of conventions exist, having become conventions themselves, artists can agree to do things differently, negotiation making change possible.

Conventions place strong constraints on the artist. They are particularly constraining because they do not exist in isolation, but come in complexly interdependent systems, so that making one small change often requires making changes in a variety of other activities. A system of conventions gets embodied in equipment, materials, training, available facilities and sites, systems of notation and the like, all of which must be changed if any one segment is.

Consider what a change from the conventional western chromatic musical scale of twelve tones to one including forty-two tones between the octaves entails. Such a change characterizes the compositions of Harry Partch (1949). Western musical instruments cannot produce these microtones easily and some cannot produce them at all, so conventional instruments must be reconstructed (as Partch does) or new instruments must be invented and built. Since the instruments are new, no one knows how to play them, and players must train themselves. Conventional Western notation is inadequate to score forty-two tone music, so a new notation must be devised, and players must learn to read it. (Comparable resources can be taken as given by anyone who writes for the conventional twelve chromatic tones). Consequently, whereas a performance of music scored for the conventional set of tones can be performed adequately after relatively few hours of rehearsal, forty-two tone music requires much more work, time, effort and resources. Partch's music has typically come to be performed in the following way: a university invites him to spend a year. In the fall, he recruits a group of interested students, who build the instruments (which he has already invented) under his direction. In the winter, they learn to play the instruments and read the notation he has devised. In the spring, they rehearse several works and finally give a performance. Seven or eight months of work finally result in two hours of music, hours which could have been filled with other music after eight to ten hours of rehearsal by trained symphonic musicians playing the standard repertoire. The difference in the resources required measures the strength of the constraint imposed by the conventional system.

Similarly, conventions specifying what a good photograph should look like are embodied not only in an aesthetic more or less accepted in the world of art photography (Rosenblum, 1973), but also in the acceptance of the constraints built into the neatly interwoven complex of standardized equipment and materials made by major manufacturers. Available lenses, camera bodies, shutter speeds, apertures, films, and printing paper all constitute a tiny fraction of the things that could be made, a selection that can be used together to produce acceptable prints; with ingenuity they can also be used to produce effects their purveyors did not have in mind. But some kinds of prints, once common, can now only be produced with great difficulty because the materials are no longer available. Specifically, the photosensitive material in conventional papers is a silver salt, which produces a characteristic look. Photographers once printed on paper sensitized with platinum salts, until it went off the market in 1937 (Newhall, 1964, p. 117). You can still make platinum prints, which have a distinctively softer look, but only by making your own paper. Not surprisingly, most photographers accept the constraint and learn to maximize the effects that can be obtained from available silver-based materials. They likewise prize the standardization and dependability of mass-produced materials; a roll of Kodak Tri-X film purchased anywhere in the world has approximately the same characteristics and will produce the same results as any other roll, that being the opportunity that is the obverse of the constraint.

The limitations of conventional practice, clearly, are not total. One can always do things differently if one is prepared to pay the price in increased effort or decreased circulation of one's work. The experience of composer Charles Ives exemplifies the latter possibility. He experimented with polytonality and polyrhythms before they became part of the ordinary performer's competence. The New York players who tried to play his chamber and orchestral music told him that it was unplayable, that their instruments could not make those sounds, that the scores could not be played in any practical way. Ives finally accepted their judgment, but continued to compose such music. What makes his case interesting is that, according to his biographers (Cowell and Cowell, 1954), though he was also bitter about it, he experienced this as a great liberation. If no one could play his music, then he no longer had to write music that musicians could play, no longer had to accept the constraints imposed by the conventions that regulated cooperation between contemporary composer and player. Since, for instance, his music would not be played, he never needed to finish it; he was quite unwilling to confirm John Kirkpatrick's pioneer reading of the *Concord Sonata* as a correct one because that would mean that he could no longer change it. Nor did he have to accommodate his writing to the practical constraints of what could be financed by conventional means, and so he wrote his Fourth Symphony for three orchestras. (That impracticality lessened with time; Leonard Bernstein premiered the work in 1958 and it has been played many times since.)

In general, breaking with existing conventions and their manifestations in social structure and material artifacts increases the artist's trouble and decreases the circulation of his work, on the one hand, but at the same time increases his freedom to choose unconventional alternatives and to depart substantially from customary practice. If that is true, we can understand any work as the product of a choice between conventional ease and success and unconventional trouble and lack of recognition, looking for the experiences and situational and structural elements that dispose artists in one direction or the other.

Interdependent systems of conventions and structures of cooperative links appear very stable and difficult to change. In fact, though arts sometimes experience periods of stasis, that does not mean that no change or innovation occurs (Meyer, 1967). Small innovations occur constantly, as conventional means of creating expectations and delaying their satisfaction become so well-known as to become conventional expectations in their own right. Meyer (1956) analyzes this process and gives a nice example in the use of vibrato by string instrument players. At one time, string players used no vibrato, introducing it on rare occasions as a deviation from convention which heightened tension and created emotional response by virtue of its rarity. String players who wished to excite such an emotional response began using vibrato more and more often until the way to excite the emotional response it had once produced was to play without vibrato, a device that Bartok and other composers exploited. Meyer describes the process by which deviations from convention become accepted conventions in their own right as a common one.

Such changes are a kind of gradualist reform in a persisting artistic tradition. Broader, more disruptive changes also occur, bearing a marked resemblance to political and scientific revolutions (Kuhn, 1962). Any major change necessarily attacks some of the existing conventions of the art directly, as when the Impressionists or Cubists changed the existing visual language of painting, the way one read paint on canvas as a representation of something. An attack on convention does not merely mean an attack on the particular item to be changed. Every convention carries with it an aesthetic, according to which what is conventional becomes the standard by which artistic beauty and effectiveness is judged. A play which violates the classical unities is not merely different, it is distasteful, barbaric and ugly to those for whom the classical unities represent a fixed criterion of dramatic worth. An attack on a convention becomes an attack on the aesthetic related to it. But people do not experience their aesthetic beliefs as merely arbitrary and conventional; they feel that they are natural, proper and moral. An attack on a convention and an aesthetic is also an attack on a morality. The regularity with which audiences greet major changes in dramatic, musical and visual conventions with vituperative hostility indicates the close relation between aesthetic and moral belief (Kubler, 1962).

An attack on sacred aesthetic beliefs as embodied in particular conventions is, finally, an attack on an existing arrangement of ranked statuses, a stratification system.[3] Remember that the conventional way of doing things in any art utilizes an existing cooperative network, an organized art world which rewards those who manipulate the existing conventions appropriately in light of the associated sacred aesthetic. Suppose that a dance world is organized around the conventions and skills embodied in classical ballet. If I then learn those conventions and skills, I become eligible for positions in the best ballet companies; the finest choreographers will create ballets for me that are just the kind I know how to dance and will look good in; the best composers will write scores for me; theaters will be available; I will earn as good a living as a dancer can earn; audiences will love me and I will be famous. Anyone who successfully promotes a new convention in which he is skilled and I am not attacks not only my aesthetic but also my high position in the world of dance. So the resistance to the new expresses the anger of those who will lose materially by the change, in the form of aesthetic outrage.

Others than the artist have something invested in the status quo which a change in accepted conventions will lose them. Consider earthworks made, for instance, by a bulldozer in a square mile of pasture. Such a sculpture cannot be collected (though a patron can pay for its construction and receive signed plans or photographs as a document of his patronage), or put in museums (though the mementos the collector receives can be displayed). If earthworks become an important art form, the museum personnel whose evaluations of museum-collectable art have had important consequences for the careers of artists and art movements lose the power to choose which works will be displayed, for their museums are unnecessary for displaying those works. Everyone involved in the museum-collectable kind of art (collectors, museum curators, galleries, dealers, artists) loses something. We might say that every cooperative network that constitutes an art world creates value by the agreement of its members as to what is valuable (Levine, 1972; Christopherson, 1974). When new people successfully create a new world which defines other conventions as embodying artistic value, all the participants in the old world who cannot make a place in the new one lose out.

Every art world develops standardized modes of support and artists who support their work through those conventional means develop an aesthetic which accepts the constraints embedded in those forms of cooperation. Rosenblum (1973) has shown that the aesthetic of photographers varies with the economic channels through which their work is distributed in the same way that their customary work styles do, and Lyon (1974) has analyzed the interdependence of aesthetic decisions and the means by which resources are gathered in a semi-professional theater group. One example will illustrate the nature of the dependence. The group depended on volunteer help to get necessary work done. But people volunteered for non-artistic kinds of work largely because they hoped eventually to get a part in a play and gain some acting experience. The people who ran the company soon accumulated many such debts and were constrained to choose plays with relatively large casts to pay them off.[4]

Conclusion

If we focus on a specific art work, it proves useful to think of social organization as a network of people who cooperate to produce that work. We see that the same people often cooperate repeatedly, even routinely, in similar ways to produce similar works. They organize their cooperation by referring to the conventions current among those who participate in the production and consumption of such works. If the same people do not actually act together in every case, their replacements are also familiar with and proficient in the use of the same conventions, so that the cooperation can go on without difficulty. Conventions make collective action simpler and less costly in time, energy and other resources; but they do not make unconventional work impossible, only more costly and more difficult. Change can occur, as it often does, whenever someone devises a way to gather the greater resources required. Thus, the conventional modes of cooperation and collective action need not recur because people constantly devise new modes of action and discover the resources necessary to put them into practice.

To say all this goes beyond the assertion that art is social and beyond demonstrations of the congruence between forms of social organization and artistic styles or subjects. It shows that art is social in the sense that it is created by networks of people acting together, and proposes a framework in which differing modes of collective action, mediated by accepted or newly developed conventions, can be studied. It places a number of traditional questions in the field in a context in which their similarity to other forms of collective action can be used for comparative theoretical work.

The discussion of art as collective action suggests a general approach to the analysis of social organization. We can focus on any event (the more general term which encompasses the production of an art work as a special case) and look for the network of people, however large or extended, whose collective activity made it possible for the event to occur as it did. We can look for networks whose cooperative activity recurs or has become routine and specify the conventions by which their constituent members coordinate their separate lines of action.

We might want to use such terms as social organization or social structure as a metaphorical way of referring to those recurring networks and their activities. In doing so, however, we should not forget their metaphorical character and inadvertently assert as a fact implied in the metaphor what can only be discovered through research. When sociologists speak of social structure or social systems, the metaphor implies (though its user neither proves nor argues the point) that the collective action involved occurs "regularly" or "often" (the quantifier, being implicit, is non-specific) and, further, that the people involved act together to produce a large variety of events. But we should recognize generally, as the empirical materials require us to do in the study of the arts, that whether a mode of collective action is recurrent or routine enough to warrant such description must be decided by investigation, not by definition. Some forms of collective action recur often, others occasionally, some very seldom. Similarly, people who participate in the network that produces one event or kind of event may not act together in art works producing other events. That question, too, must be decided by investigation.

Collective actions and the events they produce are the basic unit of sociological investigation. Social organization consists of the special case in which the same people act together to produce a variety of different events in a recurring way. Social organization (and its cognates) are not only concepts, then, but also empirical findings. Whether we speak of the collective acts of a few people – a family or a friendship – or of a much larger number – a profession or a class system – we need always to ask exactly who is joining together to produce what events. To pursue the generalization from the theory developed for artistic activities, we can study social organizations of all kinds by looking for the networks responsible for producing specific events, the overlaps among such cooperative networks, the way participants use conventions to coordinate their activities, how existing conventions simultaneously make coordinated action possible and limit the forms it can take, and how the development of new forms of acquiring resources makes change possible. (I should point out that, while this point of view is not exactly commonplace, neither is it novel. It can be found in the writings of among others, Simmel [1898], Park [1950, 1952, 1955 passim], Blumer [1966] and Hughes [1971, esp. pp 5–13 and 52–64]).

Notes

1 The concept of an art world has recently been used as a central idea in the analysis of key issues in aesthetics. (See Dickie, 1971, Danto, 1964, and Blizek, n.d.). I have used the term

in a relatively unanalyzed way here, letting its meaning become clear in context, but intend a fuller analysis in another paper.

2 The arrangements between artists, printers and publishers described in Kase (1973).

3 I am indebted to an unpublished paper by Everett C. Hughes (n.d.) for the argument that an attack on the mores is an attack on social structure. He develops the argument by combining two points in Sumner's *Folkways*, that (1) the folkways create status, and (2) sects (whether religious, political, or artistic) are at war with the mores.

4 The problem of financial and other resources and the institutions which have grown up to provide them for artists deserves much more extended consideration than I give it here, and some sociological and social-historical literature is available (see, for instance, White and White, 1965; Hirsch, 1972; Grana, 1964; Coser, 1965; Haskell, 1963).

References

Albrecht, Milton C., James H. Barnett and Mason Griff (eds) 1970. *The Sociology of Art and Literature: A Reader*. New York: Praeger Publishers.

Bennett, H.S. 1972. Other People's Music. Unpublished doctoral dissertation, Northwestern University.

Blizek, William. n.d. "An institutional theory of art." Unpublished paper.

Blumer, Herbert. 1966. "Sociological implications of the thought of George Herbert Mead." *American Journal of Sociology* 71: 535–44.

Christopherson, Richard 1974 "Making art with machines: photography's institutional inadequacies." *Urban Life and Culture* 3(1): 3–34.

Cooper, Grosvenor W. and Leonard B. Meyer 1960 *The Rhythmic Structure of Music*. Chicago: University of Chicago Press.

Coser, Lewis 1965 *Men of Ideas*. New York: Free Press.

Cowell, Henry and Sidney Cowell 1954 *Charles Ives and His Music*. New York: Oxford University Press.

Danto, Arthur 1964 "The art world." *Journal of Philosophy*, LXI: 571–84.

Dart, Thurston 1967 *The Interpretation of Music*. 4th ed. London: Hutchinson.

Dickie, George 1971 *Aesthetics: An Introduction*. New York: Pegasus.

Faulkner, Robert R. 1973a "Orchestra interaction: some features of communication and authority in an artistic organization." *Sociological Quarterly* 14: 147–57.

Faulkner, Robert R. 1973b "Career concerns and mobility motivations of orchestra musicians." *Sociological Quarterly* 14: 334–49.

Gombrich, E. H. 1960 *Art and Illusion*. New York: Bollingen.

Grana, Cesar 1964 *Bohemian Versus Bourgeois*. New York: Basic Books.

Haskell, Francis 1963 *Patrons and Painters*. New York: Knopf.

Hirsch, Paul M. 1972 "Processing fads and fashions: an organization-set analysis of cultural industry systems." *American Journal of Sociology* 77: 639–59.

Hughes, Everett C. 1971 "Action Catholique and nationalism: a memorandum on church and society in French Canada." *The Sociological Eye*. New York: Aldine Atherton.

Ivins, W. 1953 *Prints and Visual Communication*. Cambridge: MIT Press.

Johnson, Thomas 1955 *Emily Dickinson*. Cambridge, MA: Harvard University Press.

Kase, Thelma 1973 The Artist, the Printer and the Publisher. Unpublished master's thesis. University of Missouri–Kansas City.

Kealy, Edward 1974 The Real Rock Revolution: Sound Mixers, their Work, and the Aesthetics of Popular Music Production. Unpublished doctoral dissertation, Northwestern University.

Kealy, Edward 1974 The Recording Engineer. Doctoral dissertation in progress, Northwestern University.

Kubler, George 1962 *The Shape of Time*. New Haven: Yale University Press.

Kuhn, Thomas 1962 *The Structure of Scientific Revolution*. Chicago: University of Chicago Press.

Levine, Edward M. 1972 "Chicago's art world." *Urban Life and Culture* 1: 292–322.

Lyon, Eleanor 1974 "Work and play: resource constraints in a small theater." *Urban Life and Culture* 3(1): 71–97.

Meyer, L. B. 1956 *Emotion and Meaning in Music*. Chicago: University of Chicago.

Meyer, L. B. 1967 *Music, the Arts and Ideas*. Chicago: University of Chicago.

Meyer, L. B. 1973 *Explaining Music*. Berkeley: University of California.

Newhall, Beaumont 1964 *The History of Photography*. New York: Museum of Modern Art.

Norman, Charles 1958 *The Magic-maker, e. e. cummings*. New York: MacMillan.

Park, Robert E. 1950 *Race and Culture*. New York: Free Press.

Park, Robert E. 1952 *Human Communities*. New York: Free Press.

Park, Robert E. 1955 *Society*. New York: Free Press.

Partch, Harry 1949 *Genesis of a Music*. Madison: University of Wisconsin Press.

Pevsner, Nikolaus 1940 *Academies of Art: Past and Present*. Cambridge: Cambridge University Press.

Reese, Gustave 1959 *Music in the Renaissance*. Revised ed. New York: W. W. Norton.

Rosenblum, Barbara 1973 Photographers and their Photographs. Unpublished doctoral dissertation, Northwestern University.

Simmel, Georg 1898 "The persistence of social groups." *American Journal of Sociology* 3: 662–69 and 829–36; 4: 35–50.

Smith, B. H. 1968 *Poetic Closure*. Chicago: University of Chicago Press.

Strauss, Anselm L. et al. 1964 *Psychiatric Ideologies and Institutions*. New York: Free Press.

White, Harrison C. and Cynthia A. 1965 *Canvasses and Careers*. New York: John Wiley.

Wörner, Karl H. 1973 *Stockhausen: Life and Work*. Berkeley: University of California Press.

7 Commodity Lesbianism

Danae Clark

> A commodity appears, at first sight, a very trivial thing, and easily understood. Its analysis
> shows that it is, in reality, *a very queer thing*.   (*Karl Marx, Capital*)[1]

In an effort to articulate the historical and social formation of female subjectivity
under capitalism, feminist investigations of consumer culture have addressed a
variety of complex and interrelated issues, including the construction of femininity
and desire, the role of consumption in media texts, and the paradox of the woman/
commodity relation. Implicit in these investigations, however, has been an underlying concern for the heterosexual woman as consuming subject.[2] Perhaps because,
as Jane Gaines notes, "consumer culture thrives on heterosexuality and its institutions by taking its cues from heterosexual 'norms,'"[3] theories *about* consumerism
fall prey to the same normalizing tendencies. In any event, analyses of female
consumerism join a substantial body of other feminist work that "assumes, but
leaves unwritten, a heterosexual context for the subject" and thus contributes to
the continued invisibility of lesbians.[4]

But lesbians too are consumers. Like heterosexual women they are major purcha-
sers of clothing, household goods, and media products. Lesbians have not, however,
been targeted as a separate consumer group within the dominant configuration of
capitalism, either directly through the mechanism of advertising or indirectly
through fictional media representations; their relation to consumerism is thus necessarily different. This "difference" requires a careful look at the relation between
lesbians and consumer culture, representations of lesbianism and consumption in
media texts, and the role of the lesbian spectator as consuming subject. Such an
investigation is especially timely since current trends in both advertising and commercial television show that lesbian viewers (or at least some segments of the lesbian
population) are enjoying a certain pleasure as consumers that was not available to
them in the past. An analysis of these pleasures should therefore shed light not only
on the place that lesbians occupy within consumer culture, but on the identificatory
processes involved in lesbian reading formations.

Dividing the Consumer Pie

Lesbians have not been targeted as consumers by the advertising industry for several
historical reasons. First, lesbians as a social group have not been economically
powerful; thus, like other social groups who lack substantial purchasing power
(e.g., the elderly), they have not been attractive to advertisers. Second, lesbians

Original publication: Clark, Danae, "Commodity Lesbianism," from Corey K. Creekmur and Alexander
Doty (eds.), *Out in Culture: Gay, Lesbian and Queer Essays on Popular Culture* (Duke University Press,
Durham, NC, 1995).

have not been easily identifiable as a social group anyway. According to the market strategies commonly used by advertisers to develop target consumer groups, four criteria must be met. A group must be (1) identifiable, (2) accessible, (3) measurable, and (4) profitable.[5] In other words, a particular group must be "knowable" to advertisers in concrete ways. Lesbians present a problem here because they exist across race, income, and age (three determinants used by advertisers to segment and distinguish target groups within the female population). To the extent that lesbians are not identifiable or accessible, they are not measurable and, therefore, not profitable. The fact that many lesbians prefer not to be identified because they fear discrimination poses an additional obstacle to targeting them. Finally, most advertisers have had no desire to identify a viable lesbian consumer group. Advertisers fear that by openly appealing to a homosexual market their products will be negatively associated with homosexuality and will be avoided by heterosexual consumers. Thus, although homosexuals (lesbians and gay men) reputedly compose 10 percent of the overall US market population – and up to 20–22 percent in major urban centers such as New York and San Francisco – advertisers have traditionally stayed in the closet when it comes to peddling their wares.[6]

Recently, however, this trend has undergone a visible shift – especially for gay men. According to a 1982 review in the *New York Times Magazine* called "Tapping the Homosexual Market," several of today's top advertisers are interested in "wooing...the white, single, well-educated, well-paid man who happens to be homosexual." This interest, prompted by surveys conducted by the *Advocate* between 1977 and 1980 that indicated that 70 percent of their readers aged twenty to forty earned incomes well above the national median, has led companies such as Paramount, Seagram, Perrier, and Harper and Row to advertise in gay male publications like *Christopher Street* and the *Advocate*. Their ads are tailored specifically for the gay male audience. Seagram, for example, ran a "famous men of history" campaign for Boodles Gin that pictured men "purported to be gay."[7]

A more common and more discreet means of reaching the gay male consumer, however, is achieved through the mainstream (predominately print) media. As one marketing director has pointed out, advertisers "really want to reach a bigger market than just gays, but [they] don't want to alienate them" either. Thus, advertisers are increasingly striving to create a dual marketing approach that will "speak to the homosexual consumer in a way that the straight consumer will not notice." As one observer explains, "It used to be that gay people could communicate to one another, in a public place, if they didn't know one another, only by glances and a sort of *code behavior*...to indicate to the other person, but not to anybody else, that you, too, were gay. Advertisers, if they're smart, can do that too" (emphasis added). One early example of this approach was the Calvin Klein jeans series that featured "a young, shirtless blond man lying on his stomach" and, in another ad, "a young, shirtless blond man lying on his side, holding a blue-jeans jacket." According to Peter Frisch, a gay marketing consultant, one would "have to be comatose not to realize that it appeals to gay men" (I presume he is referring to the photographs' iconographic resemblance to gay pornography). Calvin Klein marketing directors, however, denied any explicit gay element: "We did not try *not* to appeal to gays. We try to appeal, period. With healthy, beautiful people. If there's an awareness in that community of health and grooming, they'll respond to the ads."[8]

This dual marketing strategy has been referred to as "gay window advertising." Generally, gay window ads avoid explicit references to heterosexuality by depicting only one individual or same-sexed individuals within the representational frame. In addition, these models bear the signifiers of sexual ambiguity or androgynous style. But "gayness" remains in the eye of the beholder: gays and lesbians can read into an ad certain subtextual elements that correspond to experiences with or representations of gay/lesbian subculture. If heterosexual consumers do not notice these subtexts or subcultural codes, then advertisers are able to reach the homosexual market along with the heterosexual market without ever revealing their aim.

The metaphor of the window used by the advertising industry to describe gay marketing techniques is strikingly similar to feminist descriptions of women's relation to consumer culture and film representation. Mary Ann Doane, for example, remarks that "the film frame is a kind of display window and spectatorship consequently a form of window shopping."[9] Jane Gaines likewise suggests that cinema going is "analogous to the browsing-without-obligation-to-buy pioneered by the turn-of-the-century department store, where one could, with no offense to the merchant, enter to peruse the goods, exercising a kind of *visual connoisseurship*, and leave without purchase" (emphasis added). Gaines further argues that the show window itself is "a medium of circulation" and that "commodification seems to facilitate circulation by multiplying the number of possible contexts."[10] The metaphor of the window, in other words, posits an active reader as well as a multiple, shifting context of display.

The notion of duality that characterizes gay window advertising's marketing strategy is also embodied in various theoretical descriptions and approaches to consumer culture in general. Within the Frankfurt School, for example, Adorno speaks of the dual character or dialectic of luxury that "opens up consumer culture to be read as its opposite," and Benjamin suggests that consumer culture is a dual system of meaning whereby "the economic life of the commodity imping[es] upon its life as an object of cultural significance."[11] More recently, a duality has been located in feminist responses to consumer culture and fashion culture in particular. As Gaines notes, the beginning of the Second Wave of feminist politics and scholarship was marked by a hostility toward fashion, perceiving it as a patriarchal codification and commodification of femininity that enslaved women and placed their bodies on display. But this "antifashion" position is now joined by a feminist perspective that sees fashion culture as a site of female resistance, masquerade, and self-representation.[12] At the heart of this "fabrication," says Gaines, is a gender confusion and ambiguity that disrupts and confounds patriarchal culture.[13]

Lesbians have an uneasy relation to this dual perspective on fashion. First of all, lesbians have a long tradition of resisting dominant cultural definitions of female beauty and fashion as a way of separating themselves from heterosexual culture politically and as a way of signaling their lesbianism to other women in their subcultural group. This resistance to or reformulation of fashion codes thus distinguished lesbians from straight women at the same time that it challenged patriarchal structures. As Arlene Stein explains in an article on style in the lesbian community, "Lesbian-feminist anti-style was an emblem of refusal, an attempt to strike a blow against the twin evils of capitalism and patriarchy, the fashion industry and the female objectification that fueled it. The flannel-and-denim look was not so much a style as it was anti-style – an attempt to replace the artifice of fashion with a supposed naturalness, free of gender roles and commercialized pretense."[14] Today, however, many lesbians, particularly younger, urban lesbians, are challenging this look, exposing the constructedness of "natural" fashion, and finding a great deal of pleasure in playing with the possibilities of fashion and beauty.

This shift, which is not total and certainly not without controversy, can be attributed to a number of factors. First of all, many lesbians are rebelling against a lesbian-feminist credo of political correctness that they perceive as stifling. As a *Village Voice* writer observes, "A lesbian can wag her fingers as righteously as any patriarchal puritan, defining what's acceptable according to what must be ingested, worn, and especially desired. . . . In a climate where a senator who doesn't like a couple of photographs tries to do away with the National Endowment for the Arts, censorious attacks within the lesbian community begin to sound a lot like fundamentalism. . . . They amount to a policing of the lesbian libido."[15] Stein thus notes that while the old-style, politically correct(ing) strain of lesbian feminism is on the wane, "lifestyle" lesbianism is on the rise. Lifestyle lesbianism is a recognition of the "diverse subcultural pockets and cliques – corporate dykes, arty dykes, dykes of color, clean and sober dykes – of which political lesbians are but one among many."[16] But it may also be a response to the marketing strategies of consumer culture.

The predominate research trend in U.S. advertising for the past two decades has been VALS (values and lifestyles) research. By combining information on demographics (sex, income, educational level), buying habits, self-image, and aspirations, VALS research targets and, in the case of yuppies, effectively *creates* consumer lifestyles that are profitable to advertisers.[17] Given lesbian-feminism's countercultural, anticapitalist roots, it is not surprising that lesbians who "wear" their lifestyles or flaunt themselves as "material girls" are often criticized for trading in their politics for a self-absorbed materialism. But there is more to "lipstick lesbians" or "style nomads" than a freewheeling attitude toward their status as consumers or a boredom with the relatively static nature of the "natural look" (fashion, after all, implies change). Fashion-conscious dykes are rebelling against the idea that there is a clear one-to-one correspondence between fashion and identity. As Stein explains, "You can dress as a femme one day and a butch the next. You can wear a crew-cut along with a skirt. Wearing high heels during the day does not mean you're a femme at night, passive in bed, or closeted on the job."[18] Seen in this light, fashion becomes an assertion of personal freedom as well as political choice.

The new attitudes of openness toward fashion, sexuality, and lifestyle would not have been possible, of course, without the lesbian-feminist movement of recent decades. Its emergence may also have an economic explanation. According to a recent survey in *Out/look*, a national gay and lesbian quarterly, the average annual income for individual lesbians (who read *Out/look*) is $30,181; the average lesbian household income is approximately $58,000.[19] Since lesbians as a group are beginning to raise their incomes and class standing, they are now in a position to afford more of the clothing and "body maintenance" that was once beyond their financial capabilities. Finally, some credit for the changing perspectives on fashion might also be given to the recent emphasis on masquerade and fabrication in feminist criticism and to the more prominent role of camp in lesbian criticism. At least within academic circles these factors seem to affect, or to be the effect of, lesbian theorists' fashion sensibilities.

But regardless of what has *caused* this shift, or where one stands on the issue of fashion, advertisers in the fashion industry have begun to capitalize on it. Given the increasing affluence and visibility of one segment of the lesbian population – the predominantly white, predominantly childless, middle-class, educated lesbian with disposable income – it appears that advertisers are now interested in promoting "lesbian window advertising." (Even while recognizing the highly problematic political implications of such a choice, I will continue to use the term *gay* instead of *lesbian* when referring to this marketing strategy since *gay window advertising* is the discursive phrase currently employed by the advertising industry.) In fashion magazines such as *Elle* and *Mirabella*, and in mail-order catalogs such as *Tweeds, J. Crew*, and *Victoria's Secret*, advertisers (whether knowingly or not) are capitalizing on a dual market strategy that packages gender ambiguity and speaks, at least indirectly, to the lesbian consumer market. The representational strategies of gay window advertising thus offer what John Fiske calls "points of purchase" or points of identification that allow readers to make sense of cultural forms in ways that are meaningful or pleasurable to them.[20] The important question here is how these consumer points of purchase become involved in lesbian notions of identity, community, politics, and fashion.

When Dykes Go Shopping...

In a recent issue of *Elle*, a fashion layout entitled "Male Order" shows us a model who, in the words of the accompanying ad copy, represents "the zenith of masculine allure." In one photograph the handsome, short-haired model leans against the handlebars of a motorcycle, an icon associated with bike dyke culture. Her man-styled jacket, tie, and jewelry suggest a butch lesbian style that offers additional points of purchase for the lesbian spectator. In another photograph from the series, the model is placed in a more neutral setting, a café, that is devoid of lesbian iconography. But because she is still dressed in masculine attire and, more important, exhibits the "swaggering" style recommended by the advertisers, the model incorporates aspects of lesbian style. Here, the traditional "come-on" look of advertising can be read as the look or pose of a cruising dyke. Thus, part of the pleasure that lesbians find in these ads might be what Elizabeth Ellsworth calls "lesbian verisimilitude," or the representation of body language, facial expression, and general appearance that can be claimed and coded as "lesbian" according to current standards of style within lesbian communities.[21]

A fashion layout from *Mirabella*, entitled "Spectator," offers additional possibilities for lesbian readings. In this series of photographs by Deborah Turbeville, two women (not always the same two in each photograph) strike poses in a fashionable, sparsely decorated apartment. The woman who is most prominently featured has very short, slicked-back hair, and, in three of the photographs, she is wearing a tank top (styled like a man's undershirt) and baggy trousers. With her confident poses, her broad shoulders, and strong arms (she obviously pumps iron), this fashion model can easily be read as "high-style butch." The other women in the series are consistently more "femme" in appearance, though they occasionally wear masculine–style apparel as well. The lesbian subtext in this fashion layout, however, is not limited to the models' appearances. The adoption of butch and femme *roles* suggests the possibility of interaction or a "playing out" of a lesbian narrative. Thus, while the women are physically separated and do not interact in the photographs,[22] their stylistic role-playing invites the lesbian spectator to construct a variety of (butch–femme) scenarios in which the two women come together. The eroticism of these imaginary scenes is enhanced by compositional details such as soft lighting and a rumpled bedsheet draped over the apartment window to suggest a romantic encounter. The variation of poses and the different combination of models also invites endless possibilities for narrative construction. Have these two women just met? Are they already lovers? Is there a love triangle going on here? and so on.

Much of what gets negotiated, then, is not so much the contradictions between so-called dominant and oppositional readings, but the details of the subcultural reading itself. Even so, because lesbians (as members of a heterosexist culture) have been taught to read the heterosexual possibilities of representations, the "straight" reading is never entirely erased or replaced. Lesbian readers, in other words, know that they are not the primary audience for mainstream advertising, that androgyny is a fashionable and profitable commodity, and that the fashion models in these ads are quite probably heterosexual. In this sense, the dual approach of gay window advertising can refer not only to the two sets of readings formulated by homosexuals and heterosexuals, but to the dual or multiple interpretations that exist *within* lesbian reading formations. The straight readings, however, do not simply exist alongside alternative readings, nor do they necessarily diminish the pleasure found in the alternate readings. As "visual connoisseurs" lesbians privilege certain readings (styles) over others, or, in the case of camp readings, the straight reading itself forms the basis of (as it becomes twisted into) a pleasurable interpretation.

Here, as Sue-Ellen Case might argue, is the locus of a true masquerade of readership.[23] Lesbians are accustomed to playing out multiple styles and sexual roles as a tactic of survival and thus have learned the artifice of invention in defeating heterosexual codes of naturalism: "The closet has given us the lie; and the lie has given camp – the style, the discourse, the mise-en-scène of butch–femme roles. The survival tactic of hiding and lying [has] produced a camp discourse...in which gender referents are suppressed, or slip into one another, fictional lovers are constructed, [and] metaphors substitute for literal descriptions." I would not argue, as Case does, that "the butch-femme couple inhabit the [lesbian] subject position together"[24] since the butch-femme aesthetic is a historically specific (and even community and lifestyle specific) construct that ranges from the rigid butch-femme roles of the fifties to the campy renaissance of today's butch-femme role-playing, and thus cannot represent a consistent subject position. But a lesbian subject's recognition of the butch-femme binarism, as it has been historically styled by lesbian communities, is an essential component of a reading practice that distances, subverts, and plays with both heterosexist representations and images of sexual indeterminacy. Another aspect of reading that must be considered is the pleasure derived from seeing the dominant media "attempt, but fail, to colonize 'real' lesbian space." Even in representations that capitalize on sexual ambiguity there are certain aspects of lesbian subculture that remain (as yet) inaccessible or unappropriated. By claiming this unarticulated space as something distinct and separable from heterosexual (or heterosexist) culture, lesbian readers are no longer outsiders, but insiders privy to the inside jokes that create an experience of pleasure and solidarity with other lesbians "in the know." Thus, as Ellsworth notes, lesbians "have responded to the marginalization, silencing, and debasement" found in dominant discourse "by moving the field of social pleasures...to the center of their interpretive activities" and reinforcing their sense of identity and community.[25]

This idea assumed concrete dimensions for me during the course of researching and presenting various versions of this paper. Lesbians across the country were eager to talk about or send copies of advertisements that had *dyke appeal* (and there was a good deal of consensus over how that term was interpreted). A number of lesbians admitted to having an interest in *J. Crew* catalogs because of a certain model they looked forward to seeing each month. Another woman told me of several lesbians who work for a major fashion publication as if to reassure me that gay window fashion photography is not an academic hallucination or a mere coincidence. Gossip, hearsay, and confessions are activities that reside at the center of lesbian interpretive communities and add an important discursive dimension to lesbians' pleasure in looking.

This conception of readership is a far cry from earlier (heterosexist) feminist analyses of advertising that argued that "advertisements help to endorse the powerful male attitude that women are passive bodies to be endlessly looked at, waiting to have their sexual attractiveness matched with *active* male sexual desire", or that women's relation to advertisements can only be explained in terms of anxiety or "narcissistic damage."[26] These conclusions were based on a conspiracy theory that placed ultimate power in the hands of corporate patriarchy and relegated no power or sense of agency to the female spectator. Attempts to modify this position, however, have created yet another set of obstacles around which we must maneuver with caution. For in our desire and haste to attribute agency to the spectator and a means of empowerment to marginal or oppressed social groups, we risk losing sight of the interrelation between reading practices and the political economy of media institutions.

In the case of gay window advertising, for example, appropriation cuts both ways. While lesbians find pleasure (and even validation) in that which is both accessible and unarticulated, the advertising industry is playing on a material and ideological tension that simultaneously appropriates aspects of lesbian subculture and positions lesbian reading practices in relation to consumerism. As John D'Emilio explains, "This dialectic – the constant interplay between exploitation and some measure of autonomy – informs all of the history of those who have lived under capitalism." According to D'Emilio's argument that capitalism and the institution of wage labor have created the material conditions for homosexual desire and identity, gay window advertising is a logical outgrowth of capitalist development, one that presumably will lead to more direct forms of marketing in the future. But the reasons behind this development can hardly be attributed to a growing acceptance of homosexuality as a legitimate lifestyle. Capitalist enterprise creates a tension: materially it "weakens the bonds that once kept families together," but ideologically it "drives people into

heterosexual families." Thus, "while capitalism has knocked the material founda-
tions away from family life, lesbians, gay men, and heterosexual feminists have
become the scapegoats for the social instability of the system."[27] The result of this
tension is that capitalists welcome homosexuals as consuming subjects but not as
social subjects. Or, as David Ehrenstein remarks, "the market is there for the picking,
and questions of 'morality' yield ever so briefly to the quest for capital."[28]

The sexual indeterminacy of gay window advertising's dual market approach
thus allows a space for lesbian identification, but must necessarily deny the representation of lesbian identity politics. This is a point that has so far been overlooked
in the ongoing feminist and lesbian/gay debates over the issue of identity politics.[29]
At the core of these debates is the poststructuralist challenge to essentialist definitions of identity. While theorists and activists alike agree that some shared sense of
identity is necessary to build a cohesive and visible political community, some
theorists argue that any unified conception of gay/lesbian identity is reductive and
ahistorical. They thus opt for a historically constructed notion of *identities* that is
contradictory, socially contingent, and rooted in progressive sexual politics. But
while the controversies are raging over whether gay/lesbian identity is essential or
constructed, media industries are producing texts that deny the very politics feminists and lesbians are busy theorizing.

Mainstream media texts employ representational strategies that generally refer to
gays and lesbians in *anti-essentialist* terms. That is, homosexuals are not depicted as
inherently different from heterosexuals; neither does there exist a unified or authentic "gay sensibility." As Mark Finch observes, "The most recuperable part of the gay
movement's message is that gay people are individuals."[30] The result is a liberal gay
discourse that embraces humanism while rejecting any notion of a separate and
authentic lesbian/gay subject. The homosexual, says John Leo, is thus "put together
from disarticulating bits and pieces of the historical discourse on homosexual desire,
which become a narrative pastiche for middle-class 'entertainment.'"[31] As a mode of
representation that lacks any clear positioning toward what it shows, pastiche
embodies "the popular" in the sense that people are free to make their own meanings
out of the cultural bits and ideological pieces that are presented to them.

But this postmodern, anti–essentialist (indeed, democratic) discourse could also be
interpreted as a homophobic response. As Jeffrey Weeks ironically points out, "The
essentialist view lends itself most effectively to the defense of minority status."[32] (For
example, if homosexuality were to be classified by the courts as biologically innate,
discrimination would be more difficult to justify. By contrast, when a sense of lesbian
or gay identity is lost, the straight world finds it easier to ignore social and political
issues that directly affect gays and lesbians as a group.) The constructionist strategies
of the media are thus not as progressive as antiessentialist theorists (or media
executives) might have us believe. The issue is not a matter of choosing between
constructionism or essentialism, but a matter of examining the political motivations
involved in each of these approaches – whether they appear in theory or media texts.

If we take politics as our starting point, then media and advertising texts can be
analyzed in terms of their (un)willingness or (in)ability to represent the identity
politics of current lesbian communities. Gay window advertising, as suggested earlier, consciously disavows any explicit connection to lesbianism for fear of offending
or losing potential customers. At the same time, an appropriation of lesbian styles or

appeal to lesbian desires can also assure a lesbian market. This dual approach is effective because it is based on two key ingredients of marketing success: style and choice. As Dick Hebdige has noted, "It is the subculture's stylistic innovations which first attract the media's attention."[33] Because style is a cultural construction, it is easily appropriated, reconstructed, and divested of its original political or subcultural signification. Style as resistance becomes commodifiable as chic when it leaves the political realm and enters the fashion world. This simultaneously diffuses the political edge of style. Resistant trends (such as wearing men's oversized jackets or oxford shoes – which, as a form of masquerade, is done in part for fun, but also in protest against the fashion world's insistence on dressing women in tightly fitted garments and dangerously unstable footwear) become restyled as high-priced fashions.

In an era of "outing" (the practice of forcing gay and lesbian public figures to come out of the closet as a way to confront heterosexuals with our ubiquity as well as our competence, creativity, or civic-mindedness), gay window advertising can be described as a practice of "ining." In other words, this type of advertising invites us to look *into* the ad to identify with elements of style, invites us *in* as consumers, invites us to be part of a fashionable "*in* crowd," but negates an identity politics based on the act of "coming out." Indeed, within the world of gay window advertising, there is no lesbian community to come out to, no lesbian community to identity with, no indication that lesbianism or "lesbian style" is a political issue. This stylization furthermore promotes a liberal discourse of choice that separates sexuality from politics and connects them both with consumerism. Historically, this advertising technique dates back to the twenties, as Roland Marchand explains: "The compulsion of advertising men to relegate women's modernity to the realm of consumption and dependence found expression not only in pictorial styles but also in tableaux that sought to link products with the social and political freedoms of the new woman. Expansive rhetoric that heralded women's march toward freedom and equality often concluded by proclaiming their victory only in the narrower realm of consumer products."[34] Just as early twentieth-century advertisers were more concerned about women's votes in the marketplace than their decisions in the voting booth, contemporary advertisers are more interested in lesbian consumers than lesbian politics. Once stripped of its political underpinnings, lesbianism can be represented as a style of consumption linked to sexual preference. Lesbianism, in other words, is treated as merely a sexual style that can be chosen – or not chosen – just as one chooses a particular mode of fashion for self-expression.

But within the context of consumerism and the historical weight of heterosexist advertising techniques, "choice" is regulated in determinate ways. For example, gay window advertising appropriates lesbian subcultural style, incorporates its features into commodified representations, and offers it back to lesbian consumers in a packaged form cleansed of identity politics. In this way, it offers lesbians the opportunity to solve the "problem" of lesbianism: by choosing to clothe oneself in fashionable ambiguity, one can pass as "straight" (in certain milieux) while still choosing lesbianism as a sexual preference; by wearing the privilege of straight culture, one can avoid political oppression. Ironically, these ads also offer heterosexual women an alternative as well. As Judith Williamson notes, "The bourgeois always wants to be in disguise, and the customs and habits of the oppressed seem so much more fascinating than his [sic] own."[35] Thus, according to Michael Bronski,

"When gay sensibility is used as a sales pitch, the strategy is that gay images imply distinction and non-conformity, granting straight consumers a longed-for place outside the humdrum mainstream."[36] The seamless connections that have traditionally been made between heterosexuality and consumerism are broken apart to allow straight and lesbian women alternative choices. But these choices, which result in a rearticulated homogenized style, deny the differences among women as well as the potential antagonisms that exist between straight and lesbian women over issues of style, politics and sexuality. As Williamson might explain, "Femininity needs the 'other' in order to function...even as politically [it] seek[s] to eliminate it."[37]

Similar contradictions and attempts at containment occur within the discourses surrounding women's bodybuilding. As Laurie Schulze notes, "The deliberately muscular woman disturbs dominant notions of sex, gender, and sexuality, and any discursive field that includes her risks opening up a site of contest and conflict, anxiety and ambiguity." Thus, within women's fashion magazines, bodybuilding has been recuperated as a normative ideal of female beauty that promotes self-improvement and ensures attractiveness to men. This discourse "also assures women who are thinking about working out with weights that they need not fear a loss of privilege or social power; despite any differences that may result from lifting weights, they will still be able to 'pass.'" The assurances in this case are directed toward heterosexual women who fear that bodybuilding will bring the taint of lesbianism. The connection between body-building and lesbianism is not surprising, says Schulze, for "the ways in which female bodybuilders and lesbians disturb patriarchy and heterosexism... draw very similar responses from dominant culture."[38] Both the muscular female and the butch lesbian are accused of looking like men or wanting to be men. As Annette Kuhn puts it, "Muscles are rather like drag."[39] Lesbian style, too, tends toward drag, masquerade, and the confusion of gender. Thus, both are subjected to various forms of control that either refuse to accept their physical or sexual "excesses" or otherwise attempt to domesticate their threat and fit them into the dominant constructions of feminine appearances and roles.

Both bodybuilders and lesbians, in other words, are given opportunities to "pass" in straight feminine culture. For bodybuilders, this means not flexing one's muscles while walking down the street or, in the case of competitive body-builders, exhibiting the signs of conventional style (e.g., makeup, coiffed hair, and string bikinis) while flexing on stage.[40] For lesbians, as discussed earlier, this means adopting more traditionally feminine apparel or the trendy accoutrements of gender ambiguity. But within these passing strategies are embodied the very seeds of resistance. As Schulze argues, muscle culture is a "terrain of resistance/refusal" as well as a "terrain of control."[41] It's simply a matter of how much muscle a woman chooses to flex. Within bodybuilding subculture, flexing is encouraged and admired; physical strength is valorized as a new form of femininity. Lesbians engage in their own form of "flexing" within lesbian subcultures (literally so for those lesbians who also pump iron) by refusing to pass as straight.

This physical and political flexing calls the contradictions of women's fashion culture into question and forces them out of the closet. It thus joins a long history of women's subversive and resistant responses to consumer culture in general. Although consumer culture has historically positioned women in ways that benefit heterosexist, capitalist patriarchy, women have always found ways to exert their agency and create their own pleasures and spaces. Fiske, for example, discusses the way that shopping has become a "terrain of guerrilla warfare" where women change price tags, shoplift, or try on expensive clothing without the intent of purchase.[42] The cultural phenomenon of shopping has also provided a homosocial space for women (e.g., mothers and daughters, married and single adult women, teenage girls) to interact and bond. Lesbians have been able to extend this pleasure by shopping with their female lovers or partners, sharing the physical and erotic space of the dressing room, and, afterward, wearing/exchanging the fashion commodities they purchase. Within this realm, the static images of advertising have even less control over their potential consumers. Gay window advertising, for example, may commodify lesbian masquerade as legitimate high-style fashion, but lesbians are free to politicize these products or reappropriate them in combination with other products/fashions to act as new signifiers for lesbian identification or ironic commentaries on heterosexual culture.

This is not to suggest that there exists an authentic "lesbian sensibility" or that all lesbians construct the same, inherently progressive, meanings in the realm of consumption. One must be wary of the "affirmative character" of a cultural studies that leans toward essentialist notions of identity at the same time as it tends to overestimate the freedom of audience reception.[43] Since lesbians are never simply lesbians but also members of racial groups, classes, and so on, their consumption patterns and reading practices always overlap and intersect those of other groups. In addition, there is no agreement within lesbian communities on the "proper" response or relation to consumer culture. This is precisely why the lesbian "style wars" have become a topic of such heated debate. Arlene Stein pinpoints the questions and fears that underlie this debate: "Are today's lesbian style wars skin-deep, or do they reflect a changed conception of what it means to be a dyke? If a new lesbian has in fact emerged, is she all flash and no substance, or is she at work busily carving out new lesbian politics that strike at the heart of dominant notions of gender and sexuality?"[44] The answers are not simple, not a matter of binary logic. Some lesbians choose to mainstream. Others experience the discourse of fashion as an ambivalence – toward power, social investment, and representation itself.[45] Still others engage a camp discourse or masquerade that plays on the lesbian's ambivalent position within straight culture. These responses, reading practices, interpretive activities – whatever one might call them – are as varied as the notions of lesbian identity and lesbian community.

Given the conflicts that lesbians frequently experience within their communities over issues of race, class, and lifestyle, lesbians are only too aware that a single, authentic identity does not exist. But, in the face of these contradictions, lesbians are attempting to forge what Stuart Hall calls an *articulation*, "a connection, a linkage that can establish a unity among different elements within a culture, under certain conditions."[46] For lesbians, the conditions are *political*. Lesbian identity politics must therefore be concerned with constructing political agendas and articulating collective identities that take into account our various needs and differences as well as our common experiences and oppressions *as a social group*. So too a theory of lesbian reading practices rooted in identity politics must stretch beyond analyses of textual contradictions to address the history of struggle, invisibility, and ambivalence that positions the lesbian subject in relation to cultural practices.

Ironically, now that our visibility is growing, lesbians have become the target of "capitalism's constant search for new areas to colonize."[47] This consideration must remain central to the style debates. For lesbians are not simply forming a new relation with the fashion industry, *it* is attempting to forge a relation with us. This imposition challenges us and is forcing us to renegotiate certain aspects of identity politics. (I can't help but think, e.g., that the fashion controversy may not be about "fashion" at all but has more to do with the fact that it is the femmes who are finally asserting themselves.) In the midst of this challenge, the butch-femme aesthetic will undoubtedly undergo realignment. We may also be forced to reconsider the ways in which camp can function as a form of resistance. For once "camp" is commodified by the culture industry, how do we continue to camp it up?

The only assurance we have in the shadow of colonization is that lesbians *as lesbians* have developed strategies of selection, (re)appropriation, resistance, and subversion in order to realign consumer culture according to the desires and needs of lesbian sexuality, subcultural identification, and political action. Lesbian reading/ social practices, in other words, are informed by an identity politics, however that politics may be formulated historically by individuals or by larger communities. This does not mean that the readings lesbians construct are always "political" in the strictest sense of the term (e.g., one could argue that erotic identification is not political, and there is also the possibility that lesbians will identify with mainstreaming). Nonetheless, the discourses of identity politics – which arise out of the lesbian's marginal and ambivalent social position – have *made it possible* for lesbians to consider certain contradictions in style, sexual object choice, and cultural representation that inform their reading practices, challenge the reading practices of straight culture, and potentially create more empowered, or at least pleasurable, subject positions as lesbians. Because identities are always provisional, lesbians must also constantly assert themselves. They must replace liberal discourse with camp discourse, make themselves visible, foreground their political agendas and their politicized subjectivities.

This may explain why feminists have avoided the issue of lesbian consumerism. Lesbians may present too great a challenge to the heterosexual economy in which they are invested, or lesbians may be colonizing the theoretical and social spaces they wish to inhabit. As long as straight women focus on the relation between consumer culture and women in general, lesbians remain invisible, or are forced to pass as straight, while heterosexual women can claim for themselves the oppression of patriarchal culture or the pleasure of masquerade that offers them "a longed for place outside the humdrum mainstream." On the other hand, straight feminists may simply fear that lesbians are better shoppers. When dykes go shopping in order to "go camping," they not only subvert the mix 'n' match aesthetic promoted by dominant fashion culture, they do it with very little credit.

Notes

1 Karl Marx, *Capital*, vol. I (London: Lawrence & Wishart, 1970), 71.
2 For a recent overview of the literature, see Lynn Spigel and Denise Mann, "Women and Consumer Culture: A Selective Bibliography," *Quarterly Review of Film and Video* 11, no. I

(1989): 85–105. Spigel and Mann's compilation does not so much reproduce as *reflect* the heterosexual bias of scholarship in this field.

3 Jane Gaines, "The Queen Christina Tie-Ups: Convergence of Show Window and Screen," *Quarterly Review of Film and Video*, 11, no. I (1989): 50. Gaines is one of the few feminist critics who acknowledge gays and lesbians as consuming subjects.

4 Sue-Ellen Case, "Toward a Butch-Femme Aesthetic," *Discourse* II, no. I (1988–9): 56.

5 Roberta Astroff, "Commodifying Cultures: Latino Ad Specialists as Cultural Brokers" (paper presented at the Seventh International Conference on Culture and Communication, Philadelphia, 1989).

6 Karen Stabiner, "Tapping the Homosexual Market," *New York Times Magazine*, 2 May 1982, 79, 80.

7 Ibid., 75.

8 Ibid., 80, 81.

9 Mary Ann Doane, "The Economy of Desire: The Commodity Form in/of the Cinema," *Quarterly Review of Film and Video* II, no. I (1989): 27.

10 Gaines, "The Queen Christina Tie-Ups," 35, 56.

11 Jane Gaines, "Introduction: Fabricating the Female Body," in *Fabrications: Costume and the Female Body*, ed. Jane Gaines and Charlotte Herzog (New York: Routledge, 1990), 12–13.

12 Ibid., 3–9. Also see Kaja Silverman, "Fragments of a Fashionable Discourse," in *Studies in Entertainment: Critical Approaches to Mass Culture*, ed. Tania Modleski (Bloomington: Indiana University Press, 1986), 139–52.

13 Gaines, "Fabricating the Female Body," 27.

14 Arlene Stein, "All Dressed Up, But No Place to Go? Style Wars and the New Lesbianism," *Out/look* I, no. 4 (1989): 37.

15 Alisa Solomon, "Dykotomies: Scents and Sensibility in the Lesbian Community," *Village Voice*, 26 June 1990, 40.

16 Stein, "All Dressed Up," 39.

17 Stan LeRoy Wilson, *Mass Media/Mass Culture* (New York: Random House, 1989), 279.

18 Stein, "All Dressed Up," 38.

19 "*Out/look* Survey Tabulations," Queery 10, Fall 1990.

20 John Fiske, "Critical Response: Meaningful Moments," *Critical Studies in Mass Communication* 5 (1988): 247.

21 Elizabeth Ellsworth, "Illicit Pleasures: Feminist Spectators and *Personal Best*," *Wide Angle* 8, no. 2 (1986): 54.

22 Cathy Griggers, "A Certain Tension in the Visual/Cultural Field: Helmut Newton, Deborah Turbeville and the *Vogue* Fashion Layout," *differences* 2, no. 2 (1990): 87–90. Griggers notes that Turbeville's trademark is photographing women (often in pairs or groups) who "stand or sit like pieces of sculpture in interiors from the past in [a] grainy, nostalgic soft-focused finish."

23 Case, "Butch-Femme Aesthetic," 64.

24 Case, 60, 58.

25 Ellsworth, "Illicit Pleasures," 54.

26 Jane Root, *Pictures of Women* (London: Pandora, 1984), 68; Rosalind Coward, *Female Desires* (New York: Grove, 1985), 80.

27 John D'Emilio, "Capitalism and Gay Identity," in *Powers of Desire: The Politics of Sexuality*, ed. Ann Snitow, Christine Stansell, and Sharon Thompson (New York: Monthly Review Press, 1983), 102, 109.

28 David Ehrenstein, "Within the Pleasure Principle or Irresponsible Homosexual Propaganda," *Wide Angle* 4, no. I (1980): 62.

29 See, e.g., Teresa de Lauretis, "The Essence of the Triangle or, Taking the Risk of Essentialism Seriously: Feminist Theory in Italy, the U.S., and Britain," *differences* I, no. 2 (1989):

3–37; Diana Fuss, *Essentially Speaking* (New York: Routledge, 1989); Diana Fuss, "Reading Like a Feminist," *differences* I, no. 2 (1989): 72–92; Carol Vance, "Social Construction Theory: Problems in the History of Sexuality," in *Which Homosexuality?* (London: GMP, 1989), 13–34; Jeffrey Weeks, "Against Nature," in *Which Homosexuality?* 99–213, and *Sexuality and Its Discontents* (London: Routledge, 1985).

30 Mark Finch, "Sex and Address in 'Dynasty,'" *Screen* 27, no. 6 (1986): 36.

31 John R. Leo, "The Familialism of 'Man' in American Television Melodrama," *South Atlantic Quarterly* 88, no. 1 (1989): 42.

32 Weeks, *Sexuality*, 200.

33 Dick Hebdige, *Subculture: The Meaning of Style* (London: Methuen, 1979), 93.

34 Roland Marchand, *Advertising the American Dream* (Berkeley and Los Angeles: University of California Press, 1985), 186.

35 Judith Williamson, "Woman Is an Island: Femininity and Colonization," in *Studies in Entertainment*, 116.

36 Michael Bronski, *Culture Clash: The Making of Gay Sensibility* (Boston: South End, 1984), 187.

37 Williamson, "Woman Is an Island," 109, 112.

38 Laurie Schulze, "On the Muscle," in *Fabrications*, 59, 63, 73.

39 Annette Kuhn, "The Body and Cinema: Some Problems for Feminism," *Wide Angle* II, no. 4 (1989): 56.

40 Schulze, "On the Muscle," 68.

41 Ibid., 67.

42 John Fiske, *Reading the Popular* (Boston: Unwin Hyman, 1989), 14–17. Fiske cites the research of M. Pressdee, "Agony or Ecstasy: Broken Transitions and the New Social State of Working-Class Youth in Australia," Occasional Papers, S. Australian Centre for Youth Studies, S. A. College of A. E., Magill, S. Australia, 1986.

43 Mike Budd, Robert M. Entman, and Clay Steinman, "The Affirmative Character of U.S. Cultural Studies," *Critical Studies in Mass Communication* 7, no. 2 (1990): 169–84.

44 Stein, "All Dressed Up", 37.

45 Griggers, "A Certain Tension," 101.

46 Jacqueline Bobo, "*The Color Purple*: Black Women as Cultural Readers," in *Female Spectators*, ed. E. Deidre Pribram (London: Verso, 1988), 104–5. See also Stuart Hall, "Race, Articulation and Societies Structured in Dominance," in *Sociological Theories: Race and Colonialism* (Unesco, 1980), 305–45.

47 Williamson, "Woman Is an Island," 116.

8 Alternative to What?

Tom Frank

It's Not Your Father's Youth Movement.

There are few spectacles corporate America enjoys more than a good counterculture, complete with hairdos of defiance, dark complaints about the stifling "mainstream," and expensive accessories of all kinds. So now that the culture industry has nailed down the twenty-somethings, it comes as little surprise to learn that it has also uncovered a new youth movement abroad in the land, sporting all-new looks, a new crop of rock 'n' roll bands, and an angry new 'tude harsher than any we've seen before. Best of all, along with the media's Columbus-like discovery of this new "underground" skulking around exotic places like Seattle, consumers have been treated to what has undoubtedly been the swiftest and most profound shift of imagery to come across their screens since the 1960s. New soundtracks, new product design, new stars, new ads. "Alternative," they call it. Out with the old, in with the new.

Before this revelation, punk rock and its descendants had long been considered commercially unviable in responsible business circles because of their incorrigible angriness, their implacable hostility to the cultural climate that the major record labels had labored so long to build, as well as because of their difficult sound. Everyone knows pop music is supposed to be simple and mass-producible, an easy matter of conforming to simple genres, of acting out the standard and instantly recognizable cultural tropes of mass society: I love love, I'm sad sometimes, I like America, I like cars, I'm my own person, I'm something of a rebel, I'm a cowboy, on a steel horse I ride. And all through the '80s the culture industry knew instinctively that the music that inhabited the margins couldn't fit, didn't even merit consideration. So at the dawn of punk the American media, whose primary role has long been the uncritical promotion of whatever it is that Hollywood, the record labels, or the networks are offering at the time, lashed out at this strange, almost unfathomable movement. "Rock Is Sick," declared the cover of *Rolling Stone*. The national news magazines pronounced the uprising to be degeneracy of the worst variety, then proceeded to ignore it all through the following decade. Its listeners were invisible people, unmentionable on TV, film, and radio except as quasi-criminals. And in the official channels of music-industry discourse – radio, MTV, music magazines – this music and the tiny independent labels that supported it simply didn't exist.

But now, it seems, the turning of generations and the inexorable logic of the market have forced the industry to reconsider, and it has descended in a ravenous frenzy on what it believes to be the natural habitats of those it once shunned. Now we watch with interest as high-powered executives offer contracts to bands they have

Original publication: Frank, Tom, "Alternative to What?" from Ron Sakolsky and Fred Wei-han (eds.), *Sounding Off! Music as Subversion/Resistance/Revolution* (Autonomedia, Brooklyn, New York, 1995).

seen only once, college radio playlists become the objects of intense corporate scrutiny, and longstanding independent labels are swallowed whole in a colossal belch of dollars and receptions. Now *Rolling Stone* magazine makes pious reference to the pioneering influence of defunct bands like Big Black and Mission of Burma whose records they ignored when new. Now we enjoy a revitalized MTV that has hastily abandoned its pop origins to push "alternative" bands round the clock, a 50-million-watt radio station in every city that calls out to us from what is cleverly called "the cutting edge of rock." And now, after lengthy consultation with its "twenty-something" experts, the mass media rises as one and proclaims itself in solidarity with the rebels, anxious to head out to Lollapalooza on the weekend and 'mosh' with the kids, don flannel, wave their fists in the air, and chant lyrics that challenge parental authority.

Time magazine has finally smelled green in the music of what it longingly calls "the hippest venues going," and, in its issue of October 25, 1993, flings itself head-long into the kind of reckless celebrationism usually reserved only for the biggest-budget movies and the most successful TV shows. Salivating over the "anxious rebels" of "a young, vibrant alternative scene," it is all *Time* can do to avoid falling over itself in a delirious pirouette of steadily escalating praise. The magazine breathlessly details every aspect of the youngsters' deliciously ingenuous insurrection: they're "defiant," they're concerned with "purity and anticommercialism," they sing about "homes breaking," and – tastiest of all – they're upset about "being copied or co-opted by the mainstream." But for all this, *Time's* story on "alternative" rock never once mentions a band that is not a "co-optation," that still produces records on an actual independent label. As per the usual dictates of American culture, only money counts, and indie labels don't advertise in *Time*. So Pearl Jam, a major-label band that has made a career out of imitating the indie sounds of the late eighties, wins the magazine's accolades as the "demigod" of the new "underground," leading the struggle for "authenticity" and against "selling out."

Of course this is poor reporting, but journals like *Time* have always been more concerned with industry boosterism and the hard, profitable facts of making credible the latest packaging of youth culture than with a vague undefinable like "news." Thus while we read almost nothing about the still unmentionable world of independent rock, we are bombarded with insistences that Pearl Jam is the real rebel thing, the maximum leaders of America's new youth counterculture – assertions that are driven home by endless descriptions of the band going through all the varieties of insurgent posturing. They have a "keen sense of angst," and singer Eddie Vedder feels bad about the family problems of his youth. He rose to success from nowhere, too: he was a regular guy with a taste for living on the edge (much like the people in ads for sneakers and cars and jeans), a "gas station attendant and high school dropout," who thought up the band's lyrics while surfing. But Eddie's real sensitive also, a true Dionysian like Mick Jagger, with a "mesmerizing stage presence" that "reminded fans of an animal trying to escape from a leash." In fact, he's so sensitive that certain of the band's lyrics aren't included with the others on the album sleeve because "the subject matter is too painful for Vedder to see in print."

The gushing of official voices like *Time* make necessary a clarification that would ordinarily go without saying: among the indie-rock circles which they mimic and from which they pretend to draw their credibility, bands like Pearl Jam are universally recognized to suck. Almost without exception, the groups and music that are celebrated as "alternative" are watery, derivative, and strictly second-rate; so uniformly bad, in fact, that one begins to believe that stupid shallowness is a precondition of their marketability. Most of them, like Pearl Jam, play pre-digested and predictable versions of formulaic heavy guitar rock, complete with moronic solos and hoarse masculine poutings. There is certainly nothing even remotely "alternative" about this sound, since music like this has long been the favorite of teenage boys everywhere; it's just the usual synthetic product, repackaged in a wardrobe of brand new imagery made up of thousands of fawning articles and videos depicting them as "rebels" this or "twenty-something" that. A band called the Stone Temple Pilots, who grace the cover of other national magazines, have distinguished themselves as the movement's bargain boys, offering renditions of all the various "alternative" poses currently fashionable: all in one package the consumer gets sullen angst, sexual menace, and angry pseudo-protest with imitation punk thrown in for no extra charge. Another group called Paw is exalted by their handlers and a compliant media as the premier product of the ever-so-authentic Kansas "scene," complete with album-cover photographs of farms and animals; their lukewarm mimicry of Nirvana hailed as a sort of mid-western "grunge." Never mind that the band's founders come from a privileged Chicago background and that they have long since alienated most of Lawrence's really good bands by publicly crowing that one of their number killed himself out of jealousy over Paw's major-label success. The sole remarkable feature of these otherwise stunningly mediocre bands is their singers' astonishing ability to warble the shallowest of platitudes with such earnestness, as though they have actually internalized their maudlin, Hallmark-worthy sentimentality. But we aren't supposed to be concerned with all this: the only thing that matters is that the latest product be praised to the skies; that new rebels triumph happily ever after over old.

As ever, the most interesting aspect of the industry's noisy clamoring and its self-proclaimed naughtiness is not the relative merits of the "alternative" culture products themselves, but the shift of imagery they connote. Forget the music; what we are seeing is just another overhaul of the rebel ideology that has fueled business culture ever since the 1960s, a new entrant in the long, silly parade of "counter-cultural" entrepreneurship. Look back at the ads and the records and the artists of the pre-Nirvana period: all the same militant protestations of non-conformity are there, just as they are in the ads and records and artists of the '70s and the '60s. Color Me Badd and Wham! once claimed to be as existentially individualist, as persecuted a group of "anxious rebels" as Rage Against the Machine now does. But by the years immediately preceding 1992, these figures' claims to rebel leadership had evaporated, and American business faced a serious imagery crisis. People had at long last tired of such obvious fakery, grown unconvinced and bored. No one except the most guileless teeny-boppers and the most insecure boomers fell for the defiant posturing of Duran Duran or Vanilla Ice or M.C. Hammer or Bon Jovi; especially when the ghettos began to burn, especially when the genuinely disturbing sounds of music that was produced without benefit of corporate auspices were finding ever wider audiences.

By the beginning of the new decade, the patina of daring had begun to wear thin on the eighties' chosen crop of celebrity-rebels. Entire new lines of insolent shoes would have to be designed and marketed; entire new looks and emblems of protest would have to be found somewhere. Consumerism's traditional claim to be the spokesman for our inchoate disgust with consumerism was hemorrhaging credibility, and independent rock, with its Jacobin "authenticity" obsession, had just the things capital required.

Out went the call for an "alternative" from a thousand executive suites, and overnight everyone even remotely associated with independent rock in Seattle – and Minneapolis, Chapel Hill, Champaign, Lawrence, and finally Chicago – found themselves the recipients of unsolicited corporate attention. Only small adjustments were required to bring the whole universe of corporate-sponsored rebellion up to date, to give us Blind Melon instead of Frankie Goes to Hollywood; 10,000 Maniacs instead of Sigue Sigue Sputnik. And suddenly we were propelled into an entirely new hip paradigm, a new universe of cool, with all new stars and all new relationships between the consumer, his celebrities, and his hair.

And now Pepsi is no longer content to cast itself as the beverage of Michael Jackson or Ray Charles or even Madonna: these figures' hip has been obsoleted suddenly, convincingly, and irreparably. Instead we watch a new and improved, an even more anti-establishment Pepsi Generation, cavorting about to what sounds like "grunge" rock; engaged in what appears to be a sort of oceanside slam dance. *Vanity Fair*, a magazine devoted strictly to the great American pastime of celebrating celebrity, hires the editors of a noted "alternative" zine to overhaul its hipness; *Interview*, the great, stupid voice of art as fashion, runs a lengthy feature on college radio, the site of the juiciest, most ingenuously "alternative" lifestyle innovations in the land. Ad agencies and record labels compete with each other in a frenzied scramble to hire leading specimens of the "alternative" scene they have ignored for fifteen years. Even commercial radio stations have seen the demographic writing on the wall and now every city has one that purports to offer an "alternative" format, featuring musical hymns to the various rebellious poses available to consumers at malls everywhere.

In the same spirit the Gap has enlisted members of Sonic Youth and the cloying pop band Belly to demonstrate their products' continuing street-cred; Virginia Slims has updated its vision of rebel femininity with images of a woman in flannel sitting astride a motorcycle and having vaguely '60s designs painted on her arm. Ralph Lauren promotes its astoundingly expensive new line of pre-weathered blue jeans and flannel shirts with models done up in "dreadlocks" and staring insolently at the camera. The United Colors of Benetton hone their subversive image by providing the costume for indie-rock figure "Lois." Another firm offers "Disorder Alternative Clothing" for the rebellious grungy "few who are tired of the mainstream." Quite sensibly, the makers of Guess clothing prefer imagery of an idealized "alternative" band, played by models, to the real thing, since actual rock 'n' rollers rarely state the company's larger obsession with human beauty. So there they stand, in a pose that just screams "authentic": four carefully unshaven guys in sunglasses, grimaces, and flannel shirts, each with a bandana or necklace suspended carefully from their neck, holding guitar cases and trying to look as hardened, menacing, and hip as possible, with a lone blonde babe clinging off to one side. In another ad the Guess Clothing fantasy band are pictured "in concert," a flannel-clad guitarist spotlit with eyes closed, stretching one hand out to the heavens in an anthemic consumer epiphany.

But the most revealing manifestation of the new dispensation is something you aren't supposed to see: an ad for MTV that ran in the business sections of a number of newspapers. "Buy this 24-year-old and get all his friends absolutely free," its headline reads. Just above these words is a picture of the 24-year-old referred to, a quintessential "alternative" boy decked out in the rebel garb that the executives who read this ad will instantly recognize from their market reports to be the costume of the "twenty-somethings": beads and bracelets, a vest and T-shirt, torn jeans, Doc Martens and a sideways haircut like the Jesus and Mary Chain wore in 1985. His pose: insolent, sprawled insouciantly in an armchair, watching TV of course. His occupation: consumer. "He watches MTV," continues the ad, "Which means he knows a lot. More than just what CDs to buy and what movies to see. He knows what car to drive and what credit cards to use. And he's no loner. What he eats, his friends eat. What he wears, they wear. What he likes, they like."

Thus with the "alternative" face-lift, "rebellion" continues to perform its traditional function of justifying the economy's ever-accelerating cycles of obsolescence with admirable efficiency. Since our willingness to load up our closets with purchases depends upon an eternal shifting of the products paraded before us, upon our being endlessly convinced that the new stuff is better than the old, we must be persuaded over and over again that the "alternatives" are more valuable than the existing or the previous. Ever since the 1960s hip has been the native tongue of advertising, "anti-establishment" the vocabulary by which we are taught to cast off our old possessions and buy whatever they have decided to offer this year. And over the years the rebel has naturally become the central image of this culture of consumption, symbolizing endless, directionless change, an eternal restlessness with "the establishment" – or, more correctly, with the stuff "the establishment" convinced him to buy last year.

Not only did the invention of "alternative" provide capital with a new and more convincing generation of rebels, but in one stroke it has obsoleted all the rebellions of the past ten years, rendered our acid-washed jeans, our Nikes, our DKNYs meaningless. Are you vaguely pissed off at the world? Well, now you get to start proving it all over again, with flannel shirts, a different brand of jeans, and big clunky boots. And in a year or two there will be an "alternative" to that as well, and you'll get to do it yet again.

It's not only the lure of another big Nirvana-like lucre-glut that brings label execs out in droves to places like Seattle, or hopes of uncovering the new slang that prompts admen to buy journals like *The Baffler*. The culture industry is drawn to "alternative" by the more general promise of finding the eternal new, of tapping the very source of the fuel that powers the great machine. As *Interview* affirms, "What still makes the genre so cool is not its cash potential or hype factor but the attendant drive and freedom to create and discover fresh, new music." Fresh new music, fresh new cars, fresh new haircuts, fresh new imagery.

Thus do capital's new dancing flunkeys appear not in boater hat and ingratiating smile, but in cartoonish postures of sullen angst or teen frustration: dyed hair, pierced appendages, flannel shirt around the waist. Everyone in advertising remembers how frightening and enigmatic such displays were ten years ago when they encountered them in TV stories about punk rock, and now their time has come to be deployed as the latest signifiers of lifestyle savvy. Now it's executives themselves on their days off, appearing in their weekend roles as kings of the consumer hill, who flaunt such garb, donning motorcycle jackets and lounging around the coffeehouses they imagine to be frequented by the latest generation of angry young men. Of course every other persecuted-looking customer is also an advertising account exec or a junior vice president of something-or-other; of course nobody would ever show up to see a band like, say, the New Bomb Turks or Prisonshake in a costume like this. As ever, *Interview* magazine, the proudest exponent of the commercialization of dissent, explains the thinking of the corporate mandarin who has now decided to dude himself up in a Sid Vicious leather jacket and noticeable tattoo. Punk, as the magazine triumphantly announces in a recent issue, has been successfully revived as a look only, happily stripped of any problematic ideological baggage: maybe '90s punk is just a great high style. Some will slash their own clothes, and others will clamor after the fashions of rule-slashing designers. (Are there ever any designers who don't claim to "slash rules?") If your mother doesn't like it, who cares? If your kid is embarrassed, stand proud. If your bosses fire you for it, screw 'em. And if people stare at you in the street, isn't that the point?

So on we plod through the mallways of our lives, lured into an endless progression of shops by an ever-changing chorus of manic shaman-rebels, promising existential freedom – sex! ecstasy! liberation! – from the endless trudge. All we ever get, of course, are some more or less baggy trousers or a hat that we can wear sideways. Nothing works, we are still entwined in vast coils of tawdriness and idiocy, and we resolve not to be tricked again. But lo! Down the way is a new rebel-leader, doing handstands this time, screaming about his untrammelled impertinence in an accent that we know could never be co-opted, and beckoning us into a shoe store. Marx's quip that the capitalist will sell the rope with which he is hanged begins to seem ironically incomplete. In fact, with its endless ranks of beautifully coiffed, fist-waving rebel boys to act as barker, business is amassing great sums by charging admission to the ritual simulation of its own lynching.

Interlude: Come Around to My Way of Thinking

Perhaps the only good thing about the commodification of "alternative" is that it will render obsolete, suddenly, cleanly, and inexorably, that whole flatulent corpus of "cultural studies" that seeks to appreciate Madonna as some sort of political subversive. Even though the first few anthologies of writings on the subject only appeared in 1993, the rise of a far more threatening generation of rock stars has ensured that this singularly annoying pedagogy will never become a full-fledged "discipline," with its own lengthy quarterly issued by some university press, with annual conferences where the "subaltern articulations" of "Truth or Dare" are endlessly dissected and debated.

Looking back from the sudden vantage point that only this kind of image-revolution affords, the scholarship of academia's Madonna fans now appears as predictable in its conclusions as it was entertaining in its theoretical pyrotechnics. After careful study of the singer's lyrics and choreography, the professors breathlessly insisted, they had come upon a crucial discovery: Madonna was a gender-questioning revolutionary of explosive potential, a rule-breaking avatar of female empowerment, a person who disliked racism! One group of gaping academics hailed her "ability to tap into and disturb established hierarchies of gender and sexuality." Another celebrated her video

"Vogue" as an "attempt to enlist us in a performance that, in its kinetics, deconstructs gender and race," an amusing interpretation, to be sure, but also one which could easily have been translated into academese directly from a Madonna press kit.

The problem is not that academics have abandoned their sacred high-culture responsibilities for a channel changer and a night at the disco, but that in so doing they have uncritically reaffirmed the mass media's favorite myths about itself. Discovering, after much intellectual twisting and turning, that Madonna is exactly the rebel that she and her handlers imagine her to be, is more an act of blithe intellectual complicity than of the "radicalism" to which the Madonna analysts believe they are contributing. After all, it was Madonna's chosen image as liberator from established mores that made her so valuable to the culture industry in the first place. It doesn't take a genius to realize that singing the glories of pseudo-rebellion remains to this day the monotone anthem of advertising, film, and TV sitcom, or that the pseudo-rebel himself – the defier of repressive tradition, ever overturning established ways to make way for the new; the self-righteous pleasure-monad, changing identity, gender, hair color, costume, and shoes on a whim – is more a symbol of the machine's authority than an agent of resistance. But academics seem to have missed the point. For years the culture industry has held up for our admiration an unending parade of such self-proclaimed subverters of middle-class tastes, and certain scholars have been only too glad to play their part in the strange charade, studying the minutiae of the various artists' rock videos and deciding, after long and careful deliberation, that yes, each one is, in fact, a bona fide subversive. How thoroughly had they come around to the Industry's way of thinking; how desperately did they want to, want to get along!

But thanks to the rise of "alternative," with its new and vastly improved street "cred," sneers, and menacing hairdos, the various postmodern courses by which each scribbler arrived at his or her conclusion that Madonna is "subverting" from within, and the particular costly academic volume in which they presented their "findings" are now, thankfully, finally, and irresistibly made irrelevant. Just as Madonna's claims to rebel authenticity have been made suddenly laughable by an entirely new package of much more rebellious rebel imagery, so their works are consigned to the same fate. Academia's Madonna fans have built their careers by performing virtually the same task, with a nice intellectual finish, as the toothy hosts of "Entertainment Tonight," and now they are condemned to the same rubbish bin of instant forgetting. Their embrace of corporate culture has brought them face to face with its unarguable conclusions, the steel logic of its unprotestable workings: obsolescence.

In at least one sense, then, the triumph of Urge Overkill is a liberation. At least we will never, ever have to hear this favorite Paglian (or, should we say, all-American) platitude chanted for the thousand-and-first time: "I admire Madonna because she's a woman who's totally in control of her career." And since it will take at least three years for the first close readings of the "Sister Havana" video to appear in assigned texts, let us enjoy the respite and ponder the strange twists of history that brought academia so closely into line with the imperatives of mass culture.

In this spirit, I offer the following observation.

Perhaps the saddest aspect of all this is not scholars' gullible swallowing of some industry publicist's line, or even their naïve inability to discern Madonna's obvious labor-fakery. The real disappointment lies in their abject inability to recognize "popular culture" anywhere but in the officially-sanctioned showplaces of corporate

America; their utter dependence on television to provide them with an imagery of rebellion. Even as they delved deeper and deeper into the esoterica of poststructuralist theory, investing countless hours scrutinizing bad rock videos frame by frame, they remained hopelessly ignorant of the actual insurgent culture that has gone on all around them for fifteen years, for the simple reason that it's never made MTV. And academics, the wide-eyed, well-scrubbed sons and daughters of the suburbs, cannot imagine a "counterculture" that exists outside of their full-color, 36-inch screens. So in TV-land as well as the academy, Madonna was as "radical" as it got. Thus did the role of criticism become identical to that of the glossy puff magazines, with their well-practiced slavering over the latest products of the Culture Industry: to celebrate celebrity, to find an epiphany in shopping, a happy heteroglossia in planned obsolescence. As for their interpretations, the professorial class might just as well have been proclaiming the counter-hegemonic undercurrents of "Match Game" or the patriarchy-resisting profundity of Virginia Slims advertising.

Imagine what they could do if they only knew about Borbetomagus or Merzbow!

Fuck You and Your Underground

At the center of the academics' intricate webs of Madonna-theories lay the rarely articulated but crucial faith that the workings of the culture industry, the stuff that comes over our TV screens and through our stereos, are profoundly normal. The culture-products that so unavoidably define our daily lives, it is believed, are a given – a natural expression of the tastes of "the people." This has long been a favorite sophistry of the industry's paid publicity flacks as well: mass culture is fundamentally democratic. The workings of the market ensure that the people get what the people want; that sitcoms and Schwarzenegger and each of the various sneering pop stars are the embodiment of the general will. Thus, as the academic celebrators of Madonna were always careful to assert, those who insist on criticizing Madonna are deeply suspicious, affected adherents of an elitist and old-fashioned aesthetic that unfairly dismisses "low" culture in favor of such insufferably stuffy pastimes as ballet and opera.

This anti-elitist theme is, quite naturally, also a favorite in sitcoms and movies, which establish their hegemony over the public mind by routinely bashing various stock snobs and hapless highbrow figures. Advertising repeatedly strikes the same note: a drink called "Somers" is to gin, one ad asserts, as a bright green electric guitar, implement of transgressive cool, is to an old brown violin, squeaky symbol of the slow-moving. A Pizza Hut commercial similarly juxtaposes a moralizing, old-fashioned stuffed-shirt man who is filmed in black and white, with a full-color, rock 'n' roll rendition of the restaurant of revolt. And when the straw man of "cultural elitism" is conjured up by the academics for its ritual stomping, the feeling is exactly the same. There is only the dry, spare, highbrow of the privileged and the lusty, liberated lowbrow of the masses, and between these two the choice is clear.

This, then, is the culture of "the people." Never mind all the openly conducted machinations of the culture industry – the mergers and acquisitions, the "synergy," the admen's calculations of "penetration" and "usage pull," the dismantling of venerable publishing operations for reasons of fiscal whimsy. What the corporations have decided we will watch and read and listen to is somehow passed off as the grass-roots expressions of the nation. And this is a crucial financial distinction, since the primary business of business is no longer, say, making things or exploiting labor, but manufacturing culture, finding the means to make you buy and consume as much as you possibly can, convincing you of the endless superiority of the new over the old, that the solution to whatever your unhappiness may be lies in a few new purchases. It is a truism of the business world that Coke and Pepsi don't make soda pop; they make advertising. Nike may pay Asian laborers starvation wages, but their most important concern is convincing us that it is meaningful, daring, and fulfilling to spend over one hundred dollars for a pair of sneakers. If you feel a burning need to understand "culture," get out of the coffee house and buy yourself a subscription to *Advertising Age*.

The media-flurry over the definition of the "twenty-somethings" provides an interesting example of the ways in which "popular culture" is made, not born. Between the multitude of small presses and independent record labels that were founded, produced, and distributed by young people over the last decade, we have been a remarkably articulate, expressive group. But this is not what was meant when the various lifestyle journalists and ad agency hacks went looking for "Generation X." The only youth culture that concerned them was the kind that's pre-fabricated for us in suites on the Sunset Strip and Madison Avenue, and the only question that mattered was how to refine this stuff so that we, too, could be lured into the great American consumer maelstrom. Take a look at the book *13th Gen* by Neil Howe and Bill Strauss, the most baldfaced attempt to exploit the culture industry's confusion about how to pigeonhole us. As with the *Time* article on Pearl Jam, the book's lengthy cataloguing of "twenty-something" culture never once even mentions an actual indie-label band or a magazine produced by young people; all that matters are the movies, the TV sitcoms, the major-label records that are targeted our way. The book's press kit (which, again, you aren't supposed to see) explicitly cast *13th Gen* as a useful guide for executives in the advertising, public-relations, and election-winning industries. We are to be sold, not heard.

Under no condition is "popular culture" something that we make ourselves, in the garage with electric guitars and second-hand amplifiers, on the office photocopier when nobody's looking. It is, strictly and exclusively, the stuff produced for us in a thousand corporate board rooms and demographic studies. "Popular culture" doesn't enlighten, doesn't seek to express meaning or shared aspects of our existence; on the contrary, it aims to make people stupid and complacent. "Popular culture" sells us stuff, convinces us to buy more soap or a different kind of shirt, assures us of the correctness of business paternalism, offers us a rebel fantasy world in which to drown our never-to-be-realized frustration with lives that have become little more than endless shopping trips, marathon filing sessions.

"Popular Culture" is the Enemy; Rock 'n' Roll is the Health of the State

In such a climate, the old highbrow/lowbrow categorization becomes utterly irrelevant: who cares about the intricacies of Brahms when the world is being made and unmade anew every day by the power-tie and mobile-phone wielding commissars of public awareness? The great American cultural conflict has nothing to do with the clever *pas de deux* of affected outrage acted out by sputtering right-wingers and their blustering counterparts in Soho and Hollywood. It is not concerned with twaddle like "family values" or "cultural elitism," but with a much more basic issue: the power of each person to make his own life without the droning, quotidian dictation of business interests. If we must have grand, sweeping cultural judgments, only one category matters anymore: the adversarial. The business of business is our minds, and the only great divide that counts in music, art, or literature, is whether or not they give us the tools to comprehend, to resist, to evade the all-invasive embrace.

But between the virtual monopoly of business interests over the stuff you spend all day staring at and the decision of the academics to join the burgeoning and noisy legion of culture industry cheerleaders, very little that is adversarial is allowed to filter through. Our culture has been hijacked without a single cry of outrage. However we may fantasize about Madonna's challenging of "oppressive tonal hierarchies," however we may drool over Pearl Jam's rebel anger, there is, quite simply, almost no dissent from the great cultural project of corporate America, no voice to challenge television's overpowering din. You may get a different variety of shoes this year, but there is no "alternative," ever.

And yet it is not for nothing that the rebel is the paramount marketing symbol of the age. Beneath all the tawdry consumer goods through which we are supposed to declare our individuality – the earrings, the sunglasses, the cigarettes, the jackets, the shoes; beneath the obvious cultural necessities of an obsolescence-driven business regime, we find something deeply meaningful in the image of the free-spirit. We need the rebel because we know that there is something fundamentally wrong.

"Something fundamentally wrong." So ubiquitous is this feeling, so deeply entrenched is this unspoken but omnipresent malaise, that it almost seems trite as soon as the words are set on the page. And yet only the simplest, least aware, and most blithely comfortable among us retain any sort of faith in the basic promises of our civilization. Violence, fear, deterioration, and disorder are the omnipresent daily experiences of one class; meaninglessness, mandatory servility, and fundamental dishonesty inform every minute in the lives of another. Conrad's horror and Eliot's futility have become the common language of everyday life. We want out, and the rebel, whether of the "artistic," beatnik variety, the inner-city gangster type, or the liberated star-figures of "alternative" rock, has become the embodiment of our longings.

It is due only to the genius of the market that these desires have been so effectively prevented from achieving any sort of articulation, so cleverly and so imperceptibly channeled into dumb politics and simple acts of consuming, into just more and more and more of the same.

We may never be able to dismantle the culture of consumption and we will almost surely never achieve any sort of political solution to the problems of this botched civilization. Quite simply, no platform exists from which the monomessage of the media might be countered. The traditional organs of resistance, enfeebled by decades of legislative attack and a cultural onslaught they do not comprehend, have either made their peace with consumerism or cling to outdated political goals.

But through the deafening mechanical yammering of a culture long since departed from the rails of meaning or democracy, through the excited hum of the congregation gathered for mandatory celebrity-worship, there is one sound that insists on making sense, that speaks piercingly through the fog of fakery, the airy, detached formulas of official America. Punk rock, hardcore, indie rock, the particular name that's applied is not important: but through its noise comes the scream of torment that is this country's only mark of health; the sweet shriek of outrage that is the only sign that sanity survives amid the stripmalls and hazy clouds of Hollywood desire. That just beyond the silence of suburban stupidity, the confusion of the parking lots, the aggression, display, and desperate supplication of the city streets, the possibility of a worthy, well-screamed no survives. Just behind the stupefying smokescreens of authorized "popular culture" seethes something real, thriving on the margins, condemned to happy obscurity both by the marketplace, to whose masters (and consumers) its violent negation will be forever incomprehensible, and by the academic arbiters of "radicalism," by whom the "culture of the people" is strictly understood to be whatever the corporate donors say it is. Unauthorized and unauthorizable, it clamors in tones forbidden amid the pseudo-rebel propriety of the cultural avenues of the empire: complete, overriding disgust; routine degradation under the tutelage of the machine; a thousand mundane unmentionables like the sheer exhausting idiocy of shopping, the dark and not at all amusing vacancy of celebrity (because no matter what skillful postmodern maneuvers of ironic rationalization they make, the institution of celebrity requires, at its base, the unironic, and very real, mental surrender of millions of people in such places as Toledo and Detroit and Kansas City), the grinding inescapable ruination of the everyday, the mind-numbing boredom, the You're All Twisted, violence, distrust, anger. It is the frenzied transgression of the TV mandatory, the sudden giggling realization that something has finally come close, confronted the electronic fist with such forceful extremist honesty, with an openness so utterly foreign to the "realistic" violence of the Hollywood blockbuster, the scopophilia of the sex drama. For them it's fantasies of the comfortable *cul-de-sac* with state-of-the-art security equipment, the fine car, the airborne curfew enforcement unit, the Lake Forest estate, the Westchester commute; for us it's the secession, the internal exile, the purging clean pure no; the unnuanced thrashing release, the glorious never never never, the Won't Fit the Big Picture, the self-losing refusal to ever submit, the I'm not not not not not not not your academy.

For this expression of dissent there has been no Armory show, no naughty embrace by aesthetes or editors. The only recognition it has garnered is the siege equipment of the consumer age, a corporate-sponsored shadow movement that seeks to mine it for marketable looks, imitable sounds, menacing poses. A travelling youth circus patterned, of course, after the familiar boomer originals of Woodstock and Dead shows, is invented to showcase the new industry dispensations. But so strange, so foreign to the executive are our "punk rock" rantings that they are forced to hire "youth consultants" to explain us to them, to pay marketing specialists vast sums to do nothing but decode our puzzling signifiers. For while we were discovering paths of resistance, the people who are now manufacturing, marketing, and consuming "alternative" product were busily transforming themselves into mandarins at business school, were honing themselves dumber and dumber at the college paper, were practicing their professional skills in the bathrooms of the frat houses. Only lately have they discovered that we're "hip," that our look has "potential," that our music "rocks."

So now, with their bottomless appetite for new territory to colonize, they've finally come around to us. For years they were too busy working their way up the corporate ladder to be bothered, but now what we have been building has begun to look usable, even marketable. But they won't find it easy. Ours is a difficult country, with all sorts of arcane pitfalls that will require an ever-mounting payroll of expensive consultant-guides, many of whom will lead them astray just for the sheer joy of seeing the machine seize up, of watching suburbanities wander about clad in ridiculous slang and hairdos. (Who was it that foisted Paw on A&M?)

We will not be devoured easily. Few among us are foolish enough to believe that "the music industry" is just a bigger version of the nextdoor indie label, just a collection of simple record companies gifted mysteriously with gargantuan budgets and strange powers to silence criticism. Few consider the glorified publicity apparatus that we call media as anything other than an ongoing attack by the nation's owners on the addled minds of the great automaton audience. We inhabit an entirely different world, intend entirely different outcomes. Their culture-products aim explicitly for enervated complacency; we call for resistance. They seek fresh cultural fuel so that the machinery of stupidity may run incessantly; we cry out from under that machine's wheels. They manufacture lifestyle; we live lives.

So as they venture into the dark new world of hip, they should beware: the natives in these parts are hostile, and we're armed with flame-throwers. We will refuse to do their market research for them, to provide them amiably with helpful lifestyle hints and insider trend know-how. We are not a convenient resource available for exploitation whenever they require a new transfusion of rebel street cred; a test-market for "acts" they can someday unleash on the general public. And as they canvass the college radio stations for tips on how many earrings and in which nostril, or for the names of the "coolest" up-and-coming acts, they will find themselves being increasingly misled, embarrassed by bogus slang, deceived by phantom blips on the youth-culture futures index, anticipating releases from nonexistent groups. It has taken years to win the tiny degree of autonomy we now enjoy. No matter which way they cut their hair or how weepily Eddie Vedder reminisces about his childhood, we aren't about to throw it open to a process that in just a few years would leave us, too, jaded and spent, discarded for yet a newer breed of rebels, an even more insolent crop of imagery, looks, and ads. Sanity isn't that cheap.

9 Imagineering the Inner City? Landscapes of Pleasure and the Commodification of Cultural Spectacle in the Postmodern City

Scott Salmon

> With cities it is as with dreams: everything imaginable can be dreamed, but even the most unexpected dream is a rebus that conceals a desire, or its reverse, a fear. Cities, like dreams, are made of desires and fears, even if the thread of their discourse is secret, their rules are absurd, their perspective deceitful, and everything conceals something else.
>
> *(Italo Calvino, Invisible Cities, 1974)*

For hundreds of years, visual representations of cities have "sold" urban growth. Images, from early maps to paintings and picture postcards, have not simply mirrored "real" city spaces; rather they have been imaginative reconstructions – from quite selective viewpoints – of a city's built environment. The rapid development of different visual media in the twentieth century saw the rise of photography and cinematography as the most significant cultural means of framing and (re)presenting urban space. More recently still, as the surrealist modernism of Fritz Lang's 1926 film "Metropolis" has given way to the postmodernism of Ridley Scott's 1982 film "Blade Runner," there has been a clear shift in the locus of this representation. In recent decades, as the redevelopment of cities has been increasingly driven by the activities of consumption rather than production, there has been a growing recognition of the role of culture in framing and shaping urban space (see, for example, Harvey, 1989a; Jencks, 1984, 1986; Knox, 1993; Zukin, 1989, 1995). Indeed, according to some observers, the rise of this new urban order has been reflected in a "crisis of representation" as old (industrial) images are cast aside and new post-industrial images are presented in their place (Short and Kim, 1998, p. 57). In the process, the urban landscape itself – its built form, parks, and streets – has become the city's most important visual representation.

This shift has been reflected in the rise of the new practice of "theming" urban space – particularly that of the inner city – in order to orchestrate an appealing urban imagery. This, for many cities, has entailed the deliberate (re)construction of the built environment in an attempt to transform the landscape of the central city from a space of crime, poverty, and decay into a sanitized space dedicated to entertainment, upscale consumption and the (legitimate) pursuit of pleasure. Appropriating a term

This chapter was specifically commissioned for this volume.

from Walt Disney, I refer to this coordinated making and marketing of image as urban "imagineering."[1] In this context my use of the term is more expansive than Disney's original application, which primarily referred to "blending creative imagination with technical know-how" in the "theming" of goods and services (Beard, 1982, p. 25). In the urban context, the process of imagineering involves "making place" through "themed" urban design, the material and discursive (re)presentation of space coupled with aggressive marketing and promotion strategies in order to "sell" cities (cf. Ashworth and Vogt, 1990; Kearns and Philo, 1993). Downtown growth agendas have long been a feature of urban politics in the US (e.g. Molotch, 1976; Logan and Molotch, 1987), but this new emphasis on image and cultural representation marks the period of urban development since the late 1980s as unique.

However, as I argue in this chapter, this new emphasis on "culture" in urban design is not what it appears to be. The "city of dreams" can indeed be imagineered, but, like the dreams they spring from, this process conceals both desires and fears. In this article, I argue that the real significance of the post-modern city lies beneath its glittering surface – on the level of an underlying terrain where these landscapes represent a space, a symbol, and a site under contention by major political-economic forces. The imagineering of US cities[2] must be understood within the context of the changing geographies of contemporary capitalism and the transformation of urban governance – reflected, as I argue in the following section, in the rise of entrepreneurial "city-states." Utilizing this framework I examine the role of culture-based urban regeneration as a localized growth strategy, arguing that it can be read as a symptom of global uncertainty and disorder. If the postmodern urban landscape is both a material and a symbolic construction (Zukin, 1995), the economies of US cities are increasing tied to the process of symbolic production and the commodification of cultural spectacle. The practice of theming must be understood as both a consequence and a component of the new global geographies of contemporary capitalism. I trace the origin of these strategies to specific developments in the cities of Baltimore and Cleveland, and conclude with some reflections on the popularity of these strategies and their implications for the future of U.S. urbanism.

"Glocalization," Restructuring, and the Rise of the Entrepreneurial City-State

There is widespread agreement that something dramatic has been happening in the world economy over the past two decades. For many "advanced" capitalist nations, like the US, the 1980s were a troubled period of economic restructuring and social readjustment, during which formerly propulsive mass production industries increasingly lost their place as the leading source of growth within the economy. At the same time, as the American position in the world economy began to change, the nation-state, which had orchestrated post-war prosperity, began to unravel in significant ways. Accompanied by the rhetoric of deregulation and fiscal responsibility, power and decision-making responsibilities were displaced "upwards" to supra-national and global entities and "downwards" to regional and local states (Jessop, 1994). In fact, one of the most characteristic features of this current period of crisis and readjustment is the extent to which it has led to a restructuring of the spatial scale at which political and economic activity takes place. This re-articulation of spatial scale, or "glocalization" implies "a double movement of globalization on the one hand and devolution, decentralization or localization on the other" (Swyngedouw, 1992, p. 40). Thus, in recent years local and regional economies have become much more involved in the global economy while, at the same time, the relative dominance of the nation-state has given way to new configurations where both local and transnational scales have assumed a greater prominence.[3]

Geographically, the impacts of this reorganization have led to a dramatic series of role reversals and a marked widening of spatial inequalities at all scales. During the 1990s the growing tendency towards globalization, driven by the rise of new foot-loose industries (especially in the finance, high technology and information fields) has been manifest in a greater locational flexibility within the world economy. Impermanence and change characterize the new global economic order, as jobs and investment move quickly and often around the world, from city to city, up and down the urban hierarchy. Amidst these chaotic and restless geographies, cities have been forced to continuously reposition themselves, flinging themselves into the competitive process of attracting jobs and investment (Peck and Tickell, 1994). In the vacuum created by the demise of the "interventionist" national state, "city-states" have emerged as the most salient unit of policy formation, accepting growing responsibility for the competitiveness of their local economies in the new global environment (Eisinger, 1999; Gaffikin and Warf, 1993; Jessop, 1998).

The outcome of this growing mobilization of local politics in support of economic development has been dubbed the "entrepreneurial city" (e.g. Hall and Hubbard, 1998; Jewson and MacGregor, 1997). These new city-states entail an expanded sphere of urban govenance that includes not only the traditional municipal actors but also a range of private actors in all stages of the policy-making process. To coordinate these expanded spheres of interest, new governing systems have emerged. These are dominated by new forms of public-private partnership in which the role of the local authority in respect to business and real estate interests is becoming redefined. In this way, the rise of the entrepreneurial city-state heralds what is, in many respects, a new concept of the local state which involves an unprecedented degree of participation in the global market economy.

Nowhere has the rise of entrepreneurialism and imagineering been more obvious, or more instrumental, than in the fields of urban planning and design. One of the most fundamental shifts is the way in which planning has been reorganized away from comprehensive planning serving the abstract ideal of the "public good" to a more fragmented approach designed to meet the demands of developers.[4] In practice, this has moved planners away from a concern with long term solutions and the provision of citywide services or investments (in health care, education, or housing, for example) towards a new focus on competitiveness and market viability. The new role assumed by local government as partner of the private sector has brought with it changes in decision-making styles characterized by greater emphasis on flexibility and efficiency. Proponents of the partnership argue that locating decision-making outside bureaucratic government structures enables the process to become more market driven, developer initiated, and project specific, making the whole development process more efficient (see Friedan and Sagalyn, 1989; Judd and

Parkinson, 1990). In contrast, critics argue that these partnerships typically operate behind closed doors, effectively removing the decision-making process from the public arena and thus insulating it from normal political accountability (see Squires, 1989; Stephenson, 1991).

This trend towards privatization has also been reflected in the practice of architecture. Jencks (1986) argues that modern architecture, which once self-consciously regarded itself as an agent of social redemption, failed the test of reality. The democratic desire to produce inexpensive, functional buildings accessible to the masses was co-opted by commercial imperatives, and translated into cheapness, conformity, and anonymity. Post-modern architecture has rejected the social object-ives and lofty claims of the modernists in favor of much less grandiose and more playful aesthetic concerns (Jencks, 1984, 1986). Once again, these changes can be traced to broader economic shifts, notably the desire for differentiation in an era of growing global competition for capital. At the same time, cutbacks in public spending mean that the majority of architects now work directly in an increasingly competitive private sector. As a result, architecture has become overwhelmingly market driven (Jencks, 1984) and, as Boyer (1993, p. 112) suggests, architects are regarded as scene-makers, no longer concerned with the difference between public or private space in the city and with little concern for social accountability. Although the challenge to traditional architectural practice has not met with universal acclaim, the profession has become fragmented, "flexible," and increasingly commercial, retreating into a pragmatic project-by-project approach (Boyer, 1993; Sorkin, 1991).

Urban Regeneration: Cultural Spectacle as an Accumulation Strategy?

The uncertainty and turbulence of the recent period has been reflected in the pro-liferation of a number of institutional experiments at the local level (cf. Peck and Tickell, 1994). In this context, I am particularly concerned with one extremely popular variant driven by the demands of inter-urban competition and linked to the practice of urban imagineering. These initiatives can be considered "post-indus-trial" in that they are rarely oriented towards attracting industrial and manufactur-ing employment, the traditional targets of growth promotion strategies, but are overwhelmingly oriented towards increasingly sophisticated and specialized cultures of consumption. Despite the desire to project an appropriately local flavor, urban regeneration efforts throughout the US and beyond now exhibit a growing conform-ity, as ever more cities attempt to imagineer their own urban renaissance through the replication of these technologies. I argue that this conformity reflects the existence of an identifiable *growth strategy*, based around a specific model of urban regeneration that has emerged as a localized response to the economic and institutional crises of advanced capitalism. I refer to these as "localized" rather than "local" because I interpret the uniformity of these strategies as an outcome of the new global context in which they are being formulated (cf. Cox, 1993). Thus, the frantic search for a "local fix" has found expression in an ever-expanding number of cities in the form of a clearly identifiable "model" of urban regeneration rooted in the commodification of cultural spectacle, and can be understood as a symptom of the broader global political-economic disorder.

In many centers this has entailed attempts to "theme" the inner city through the construction of symbolically encoded urban spaces and the more or less permanent institutionalization of cultural spectacle in the built environment. In sharp contrast to the austere modernism that dominated downtown renewal efforts during the 1960s and 1970s, the "architecture of spectacle, with its sense of surface glitter and transitory participatory pleasure, of display and ephemerality, of *jouissance*," has become essential to projects of this sort (Harvey, 1989a, p. 91). In recent years the continued growth of cultural consumption (arts, theater, fashion, music, and "heritage") has propelled the commodification and marketing of culture to the forefront of the regeneration industry. In this way, the symbolic and cultural economies have become increasingly important in representing and selling cities as sites for consumption and leisure (Zukin, 1995). In the course of this process we have witnessed urban development strategies move from a reliance on the culture of consumption towards the commodification and consumption of culture.

According to this rationality, the selling of the city as location for activity (and investment) entails the (re)creation and marketing of an appropriately appealing image. Thus, in centers throughout the country, we have witnessed the attempt to build physical and social imagery of cities suited for that competitive purpose. This kind of imagineering relies heavily on the production of the appropriate visual aesthetics and the creation of an appealing ambiance to achieve the desired impression. Following the lead established by the successful projects of the early 1980s, this usually involves the (re)use or (re)creation of old infrastructure, preferably on the waterfront,[5] wharves, warehouses, ports, factories, historic districts and so on, suitably rehabilitated, gentrified and, where necessary, sanitized for their new roles.

Debord (1983) has argued that the spectacle is capital accumulated to such a degree that it becomes an image. By creating simulated tradition, the commodified spectacle, studded with all available artifacts and relics, obscures the city's real history as well as its contemporary reality. As Christine Boyer suggests:

> The spectacle is always part of a show, and going to the theater part of leisure-time experience. Devoted to entertainment and wish fulfillment, city tableaux on the margins of reality are designed explicitly for escape and gratification... These tableaux separate pleasure from necessity, escape from reality. They widen the gap between the city on display and the city beyond our view.   (1992, p. 192)[6]

The transformation of what were once working waterfronts into "walking water-fronts" (Thaler, 1988, p. 35) means that "the middle-classes can now leisurely stroll where working classes historically labored" (Goss, 1996, p. 238). The port, water-front, mill or festival marketplace of the imagineered inner-city "aestheticizes dead maritime labor in the restored built environment; and where it remains alive in the fishing boats, tugboats, barges, and ferries, observation decks and coin-operated binoculars are provided for its visual appropriation" (Goss, 1996, p. 238).

Perhaps not surprisingly, the actual implementation of these "technologies" is characteristically privatized, market-based, and often involves exposing public funds to speculative risk to an unprecedented extent. Indeed, although many of these schemes convey the impression of operating on private funding, they are usually heavily dependent on public funding and the participation of public authorities (Leitner, 1990). As Leitner and Garner have argued, it is important to recognize that at the center of this strategy, beneath the rhetoric of negotiated development and public private partnerships, is public subsidy for private real estate development (1993, p. 60). The distinction between public and private sector interests is often blurred or concealed by the use of non-profit, quasi-public development organizations which legitimate, orchestrate, and manage these alliances and sustain their institutional embeddedness.

In practice, this strategy is commonly anchored by a single, spectacular set-piece project, often involving the conservation of selected fragments or the recreation of idealized tableaux of past development to present a "packaged landscape" (Boyer, 1992). The involvement of conglomerate corporations and large financial institutions has made it possible to put together large-scale highly visible projects involving several mutually supporting revenue-producing uses.[7] Likewise, private developers often insist that revitalization projects be distinctive, singular in form, or at least attention grabbing, as such qualities define a clearly identifiable image which is advantageous in the sale of floor space, and, not insignificantly, provide a justification for higher rents (Knox, 1993, p. 15). Under this model of urban regeneration, the commodification of culture in the built environment through the construction of waterfront developments, festival market places, sports stadia, theme parks, museums, and conference centers is seen as having the greatest capacity to enhance property values, and generate retail turnover and employment growth. In the mind's eye of the imagineer, they have the potential to cast a beneficial glow over the whole city; even in the face of poor performance they can be regarded as a "loss-leader" that has the capacity to bolster the image of a city and pull in other forms of development (Fainstein, 1991).

Projects developed according to this strategy are typically advocated and justified with reference to a characteristic "rationality" which emphasizes nostalgia and the virtues of localism (see Goss, 1996; Boyer, 1992). This is true not only in the sense that such projects frequently seek to exploit some aspect of local culture or history to generate a distinctive, even parochial, image, but also in the sense that they explicitly seek to advance the interests and well being of one locality and its residents at the expense of others. This results in the somewhat paradoxical situation whereby cities across the nation are pursuing virtually identical strategies that are premised on the notion that each locality is culturally unique. In effect, these local strategies serve to heighten the destructive competition for new capital investment among local governments, and further undermine strained state and local tax bases. Thus, while these schemes are characterized by a discourse of local empowerment, it is ultimately destructive in that it explicitly seeks to privilege one locality at the expense of others.

Baltimore and Cleveland: Archetypal Cities?

No two cities in the United States have become more emblematically associated with the success of this growth strategy than Baltimore and Cleveland. I single them out here not solely because they have been widely hailed as success stories, but because in many respects they have served as exemplars, both discursively and symbolically, for the diffusion of these strategies. The success of Baltimore's leisure-led "revival" set off a wave of similar schemes in declining industrial centers during the 1980s, just as the widely publicized cultural "rebirth" of Cleveland's central city sparked a further diffusion of these strategies into the 1990s.

According to popular narrative, the Baltimore revival was primarily imagineered through a partnership between then-Mayor William Schaeffer and renown developer James Rouse. In fact, the Baltimore project was initially undertaken on a piecemeal basis through the replication of projects that had been successful in other settings. Once the institutional framework for regeneration was established, these projects were integrated into a single vision that eventually expanded to encompass the greater part of downtown Baltimore in a regeneration strategy of unprecedented scale and scope. The process began with the Charles Center, a mixed-use develop-ment in the central business district which was completed in 1973. This project was implemented by the first of Baltimore's highly effective non-profit, quasi-public development agencies and involved public expenditures of nearly $39 million, which were largely devoted to site clearance, infrastructure development, landscap-ing, and the construction of plazas and walkways. But the symbolic centerpiece of Baltimore's regeneration remains the sprawling Inner Harbor Project. Fueled by the success of the Charles Center, the Inner Harbor project was proposed as a "regional playground" centered on the city's deteriorating waterfront. A truly impressive example of theming, the project's recreational, cultural, entertainment and convention facilities encompass 240 acres.

The focal point of this ambitious undertaking was an expanded version of the concept that had proved so successful for Rouse in his renovation of Boston's Faneuil Hall – the "festival marketplace." While Faneuil Hall, which opened in 1976, entailed the adaptive reuse of the historic building, the $22 million "festival mall" Harborplace opened in 1980 with the construction of new buildings evocative of a historic market. Both were developed by Rouse Co. and designed by Benjamin Thompson and Associates, and this partnership effectively created the model on which hundreds of replicas have been based. Described as a regionally sensitive adaptation of an "ideal market form," the festival marketplace combines indoor and outdoor spaces to provide a context for social interaction and the re-integration of the city and the market ("Roundtable on Rouse," 1981, p. 101). Unlike conven-tional shopping malls, festival marketplaces lack a conventional anchor store, relying instead on a nostalgic representation of historic public life, articulated through architecture, cultural exhibits, concert programs and ethnic festivals, to attract customers to specialty retail outlets, produce markets, restaurants, and entertain-ment facilities (Goss, 1996; Sawicki, 1989).

The immediate commercial success of Harborplace, which drew unforeseen hordes to the inner city, probably did the most to advance the idea that Baltimore had broken out of its downward economic spiral and inspired liberal commentaries celebrating the return of public life to the city (e.g. Kostoff, 1987, pp. 260–2). Since that time the city has continued to innovate, competitively positioning itself within the tourism and convention market. The ever-expanding Inner Harbor Project, reputed to attract more visitors than Disneyland,[8] now includes a Convention Center, an Aquarium, a Science Center, a marina, "neo-traditional" baseball and football stadiums, countless hotels and "innumerable...pleasure citadels of all kinds" (Harvey, 1989a, p. 90).

In many ways the Baltimore project represents a clear, concrete, example of the way in which the local becomes global. In a few short decades the city ostensibly engineered the transformation from "armpit of the East Coast" to "Cinderella city of the 1980s" (Levine, 1987, p. 105). The Inner Harbor Project, and indeed the city itself, serve as the prototype for the growth strategy outlined in the previous section, a strategy which has arguably become one of the most characteristic features of urban politics in the current period. The institutional innovations imagineered in the relatively unique mix of circumstances prevailing in Baltimore have been imitated and adapted in cities throughout the US and beyond. By the mid-1980s, according to one syndicated columnist, Baltimore had become "the town other cities unabashedly seek to copy to revive their own decaying downtowns" (Pierce, 1986, p. 69).

In the process, the "festival marketplace" effectively became public policy during the 1980s as the cornerstone of numerous downtown regeneration efforts undertaken in partnership between public and private interests (Sawicki, 1989). Ironically, given that he had made his fortune developing suburban shopping malls, Rouse has been variously hailed as an "urban visionary" (Demerest, 1981, p. 42) and the savior of downtown (Fulton, 1985; James, 1985). Baltimore itself, widely heralded as *the* city of the 80s, did much to advance its image as an innovator of urban recovery strategies. The city conducted tours for other city administrators in order that they should understand how to "copy Baltimore's recovery act" (Pierce, 1986, p. 70). After leaving office, Baltimore's former Mayor took his message on the road, preaching revitalization and sharing the lessons of Baltimore's success with developers and politicians throughout the country. By the close of the decade Baltimore had become the "model of how Frostbelt cities can be turned around" (Levine, 1987, p. 105).

More recently, the city of Cleveland, Ohio, has emerged as the latest and brightest model of urban regeneration, adapting the formula originally forged in Baltimore to create its own urban regeneration model. While Baltimore's "renaissance" was initially orchestrated around the festival marketplace and mixed-use office and retail centers, combining traditional downtown office developments with a strong pitch for the tourism and convention industries, by the time the Cleveland project was initiated there were indications that this formula had begun to lose its magic in other locales. Rouse's Portside development in nearby Toledo and the Water Street Pavilion project in Flint, Michigan, both fairly formulaic attempts to replicate the Harbor Place recipe, were already colorful failures by the late 1980s (Weber and Phillips, 1988). While Baltimore was able to capitalize on its early advantage, adding a marina and a "neo-traditional" baseball stadium, other smaller centers with thinner market areas and a paucity of tourists were evidently finding the road to riches more rocky.

In light of these difficulties, the Cleveland strategy emphasized a quite different mix of projects, according entertainment and cultural spectacle an even more central role in the redevelopment process. At the center of Cleveland's revival effort is the $425 million Gateway project, a 28 acre downtown entertainment and sports complex which encompasses a 42,000 seat baseball stadium and a 20,750 seat basketball arena. Associated with this are a number of other mixed-used retail and entertainment projects, such as the Playhouse Square complex of restored 1920s theaters and ower City, a renovated landmark railroad center which now serves as a downtown shopping magnet, anchored by the new Ritz Carlton-Cleveland.

At the other end of downtown, linked by a series of pedestrian walkways and plazas, the Lake Erie waterfront is the setting for "a cluster of architectural gems surrounded by airy greenspace" (The New Cleveland Campaign, 1998, p. 2). Here the glass pyramid of the striking I. M. Pei designed, $92 million, Rock and Roll Hall of Fame provides another eye-arresting feature in the urban panorama of "New Cleveland." Elsewhere on the newly sanitized lakefront are the Great Lakes Science Center and the William S. Mather Museum, which occupies a 66-year-old ore-boat. Just west of the science center, and very much in keeping with the downtown's recreated atmosphere, the new $200 million Cleveland Browns stadium is rising. The "neo-traditional" stadium is part of a deal struck between the mayor and the National Football League to replace the original Cleveland Browns, who were, ironically, lured to Baltimore amid a frenzy of inter-urban competition for professional sports franchises.[9] The Flats, a low-lying riverside industrial district which has emerged as a hot-spot for nightlife, and the nineteenth Century Warehouse District, a rapidly gentrifying residential area, serve to extend and enhance Cleveland's downtown culture and entertainment spectacle.

Accompanying this new emphasis on the "cultural economy" there have also been significant shifts in the mechanisms of finance employed in the Cleveland model. While projects of the earlier era relied heavily on tax write-offs and increment financing schemes, the Cleveland project, and those following in its wake, involve more direct forms of public financing. This trend is reflected in the growing use of city bond issues and direct tax levies to fund regeneration projects. Most of the funding for the Gateway project, for example, was raised through a special 15 year "sin tax" on alcoholic beverages and cigarettes sold in Cuyahoga County, estimated to bring in $275 million (Keating, 1997, p. 199).[10] Once this tax was approved, the Gateway Economic Development Corporation (GEDC), a quasi-public non-profit entity, was formed to oversee the construction out of the public limelight, operating with minimal accountability or oversight (Keating, 1997, p. 200). Likewise, after a hard fought bidding war with a number of other potential sites, much of the funding for the Rock and Roll Hall of Fame had to be raised locally from public sources. This was achieved by diverting property tax revenue, draining much needed funds from an already deficit ridden school district in the process (Keating, 1997). More recently, revelations of cost overruns totaling $28 million on the Gateway project, which the GEDC was unable to pay, ultimately forced the county to offer the corporation an interest-free $11.5 million loan and to guarantee a private loan to cover the remainder (Keating, 1997, p. 202). At the time of this writing, the Gateway Corporation remains insolvent.

Accompanying the almost wholesale reconstruction of the inner city, the New Cleveland Campaign, "an independent, nonprofit organization dedicated to championing and enhancing Greater Cleveland's image," was remarkably successful in mobilizing public support and ensuring that the city's "renaissance" was given due attention in the national media (see also Holcomb, 1993). Cleveland has effectively replaced Baltimore as the success story du jour; from Fortune magazine (1997) to MTV the city has been heralded as the "New American City" of the 90s.[11] Like Baltimore in the previous decade, Cleveland has actively assumed the mantle of exemplar and advocate. The Chairman of the New Cleveland Campaign, Jim Biggar, proudly boasted that record numbers of officials from cities across the country had come to study Cleveland as a model for their own communities. Mayor Michael White, who was elected to a fourth term in 1998, has also become a media celebrity and was featured in a recent *Time* spread on the "new pragmatist mayors" (cited in Knack, 1999, p. 13). Just as in Baltimore, the discourse of regeneration employed in the promotion of the Cleveland "rebirth" engenders the diffusion of a set of relatively specific strategies, developed in that setting, for more widespread adoption and adaptation.

Conclusion

In this chapter I have suggested that a set of "cultural" strategies for urban regeneration have emerged as a response to new geographies created by the current period of globalization. At the regional scale, the popularity of this growth strategy is readily apparent. If the prototypes for this pattern of development are to be found in cities like Baltimore and Cleveland, it is by no means confined to them. Throughout the 1980s and into the 1990s these urban regeneration strategies have been adopted by numerous cities, large and small, throughout the US and beyond. The timing and diffusion of these strategies reflects their popularity amongst older industrial centers, most notably those in the nation's aging manufacturing belt, where the realities of globalization and state restructuring at the federal level have been most keenly felt.

At the level of the locality, the appeal of this strategy can be seen in terms of its apparent potential to offer a "local fix" in the vacuum created by the collapse of the old order. In many cities the combination of rapid economic change, heightened inter-urban competition for capital investment and the demise of federal urban aid have dramatically narrowed the range of policy options available to planners and politicians seeking to rejuvenate depressed local economies (e.g. Fainstein, 1991; Harvey, 1989b; Leitner and Garner, 1993). In the competitive environment of the current era, "style-of-life" and image, visualized and represented in spaces of conspicuous consumption, have become important urban assets (Boyer, 1992). The rise of the cultural and symbolic economies as a force in urban development must be interpreted as a product of the new global geographies from which they have emerged. Epochal changes in the world economy have evoked new needs and tensions, alliances and uncertainties, that have quickly been inscribed in the urban landscape.

To return to the Italo Calvino epigram that opened this piece; dreaming – and creating – the imaginable city is born of both desires and fears. But the practice of imagineering conceals more than the fear of change or the desire for prosperity. Despite the apparent appeal of this growth strategy there were clear and early indications, even in the widely touted exemplars of Baltimore and Cleveland, that at best these projects may have achieved no more than a triumph of image over substance (Hula, 1990; Keating et al., 1989; Levine, 1987). A critical point often overlooked in the popular celebration of America's urban renaissance is that success as defined by the private sector does not necessarily equate to benefits for wider civic partners (Sawicki, 1989; Squires, 1989). Thus, despite Baltimore's glittering harbor, there is now ample evidence that conditions in the city's poorest neighborhoods continue to deteriorate. Likewise, in Cleveland, its new reputation as "Comeback City" notwithstanding, 40 percent of residents live below the poverty line and the city remains one of the most segregated in the nation (see Holcomb, 1993; Keating, 1997; Warf and Holly, 1997). Despite massive investment in the inner city, the majority of the population remains impoverished and half of Cleveland's high school students fail to graduate. This burden is disproportionately borne by the city's minority population (Warf and Holly, 1997, p. 219).

Such disturbing realities beg the question of whether this growth strategy really has the potential to contribute to the formation of a stable period of prosperity, or whether it is just a relatively fleeting moment in the restless reformation of capitalism's ever-changing landscapes (Harvey, 1989a). By way of epilogue I want to very briefly consider the implications of my argument for the emergence, if indeed there is one, of a new path to urban prosperity for America's increasingly beleaguered industrial centers. At this point the prospect seems unlikely. Alliances between public and private interests, such as those which form the basis of regeneration projects at the local level, are both unequal and inherently unstable, and tend to be forged only on a project-by-project basis. The combination of internal divisions and external pressures make it extremely difficult to maintain a productive long-term alliance between public and private interests in the face of contesting forces. Secondly, the heightened inter-urban competition which is such a feature of these regeneration strategies suggests that, far from providing the basis for a stable institutional ensemble, such projects are likely only to increase the vulnerability of regional and national economies. In the face of rapid globalization, strategies such as the one I have described in this article are by themselves unlikely to sustain long-term or equitable growth. The ability of this model of regeneration to serve as a vehicle for economic growth in ever more – ever smaller – urban centers is increasingly threatened. Local strategies such as the one I have described are unlikely to sustain long-term growth if they are simply reduced to unfettered, beggar-thy-neighbor competition. Attracting growth has proved difficult; keeping it may prove harder still.

Notes

1 The term imagineering has recently been used to refer to the aestheticization of urban development (e.g. Archer, 1997; Rutheiser, 1996; Warren, 1994), but in this essay I develop the notion in a more systematic way to refer specifically to the politics of theming, place-making, and place promotion in the contemporary context of aggressive inter-urban competition.

2 This paper focuses upon the experience of two US cities, Baltimore and Cleveland. This is not to imply that the practice of theming has been confined to the US, but simply that Baltimore and Cleveland have served as "hearths" for the dissemination of these strategies, nationally and globally. Perhaps as a result, imagineering has been an integral and important feature of urban development and change in the US.

3 These processes are highly interrelated, and are embedded in the institutional and economic crisis of the industrial core and the "hollowing out" of the nation state (cf. Clark and Gaile, 1997; Jessop, 1994; Mayer, 1994).

4 As Eisinger (1989) points out, the rise of urban entrepreneurialism is the product of a decisive shift from a reliance on "supply side" philosophies and practices to an approach which emphasizes the "demand" factors in the market as a guide to the design or invention of economic and social policy.

5 The waterfront imperative is apparently so strong that some cities have resorted to creating waterfronts where none existed. Breen and Rigby (1991) cite the example of Lubbock, Texas, where recycled water was introduced into a dry creek bed in order to provide the justification for a river walk.

6 For an analysis of the theming of Las Vegas as "spectacle," please see the article by McCombie in this collection.

7 The typical mixed-use development of the late 1980s required an investment of about $200 million spread over 10 years or more before any return could be expected (Knox, 1993, p. 6).

8 According to the Baltimore Development Corporation, seven million people visited the Inner Harbor in 1990 and spent over $800 million. The Charles Center and the Inner Harbor collectively generate $25–$35 million per year in real estate tax revenues, and have produced 30,000 new jobs (cited in Kelly and Lewis, 1992, p. 30).

9 In return for building a new stadium and an undertaking not to take the NFL and the former Browns organization to court, the city has received a new professional football franchise. Even though the team, the organization, and owners, are entirely new, the city retains the Browns name, colors, and "history" (see article by Schimmel in this volume).

10 This was passed by public referendum, in May 1995, avoiding potential opposition to blanket increases in either property or sales taxes. The Gateway "sin tax" passed by only 51.7 percent of the 383,000 votes cast. The tax was favored by suburban voters by a margin of 55 percent to 45 percent but opposed in all but one of the city wards, losing by an overall margin of 56 percent to 44 percent (figures cited in Keating, 1997, p. 200).

11 In fact, Cleveland was singled out as a success story by special features aired on all three of the national television networks during the last six months of 1994.

References

Archer, K.: "The limits to the imagineered city: Sociospatial polarization in Orlando," *Economic Geography*, 73 (1997), 322–36.

Ashworth, G. and Vogt, H., eds.: *Selling the City: Marketing Approaches in Public Sector Urban Planning* (London: Belhaven, 1990).

Beard, R.: *Walt Disney's Epcot* (New York: Abrahams Publishers, 1982).

Boyer, C.: "Cities for sale: Merchandising history at South Street Seaport," *Variations on a Theme Park: The New American City and the End of Public Space*, ed. M. Sorkin (New York: Hill and Wang, 1992), pp. 181–204.

Boyer, C.: "The city of illusion: New York's public places," *The Restless Urban Landscape*, ed. P. Knox (Englewood Cliffs, NJ: Prentice Hall, 1993), pp. 111–26.

Breen A. and Rigby, D.: "The urban waterfront phenomenon: Cities reclaim their edge," *Waterfront World*, 10 (1991), 7–14.

Calvino, I.: *Invisible Cities* (London: Picador, 1974).

Clarke, S. and Gaile, G.: "Local politics in a global era: Thinking locally, acting globally," Annals, *AAPSS*, 551 (1997), 28–43.

"Cleveland, the new American city," *Fortune Magazine*, 136 (November 24, 1997), 186.

Cox, K.: "The local and the global in the new urban politics: A critical view," *Environment and Planning D: Society and Space*, 11 (1993), 433–48.

Debord, G.: *Society of the Spectacle* (Detroit: Black and Red, 1983).

Demerest, M.: "He digs downtown: For master planner James Rouse, urban life is a festival," *Time* (August 24, 1981), 42–53.

Eisinger, P.: *The Rise of the Entrepreneurial State* (Madison WI: University of Wisconsin Press, 1989).

Eisinger, P.: "City politics in an era of federal devolution," *Urban Affairs Annual Review*, 33 (1999), 308–25.

Fainstein, S.: "Promoting economic development," *Journal of the American Planning Association*, 57 (1991), 22–33.

Friedan, B. and Sagalyn, L.: *Downtown, Inc.* (Cambridge, MA: MIT Press, 1989).

Fulton, W.: "The Robin Hood of real estate planning," *Planning*, 51 (1985), 4–10.

Gaffikin F. and Warf, B.: "Urban policy and the post-Keynesian state in United Kingdom and the United States," *International Journal of Urban and Regional Research*, 17 (1993), 67–84.

Goss, J.: "Disquiet on the waterfront: Reflections on nostalgia and utopia in the urban archetypes of festival marketplaces," *Urban Geography*, 17 (1996), 221–47.

Hall, T. and Hubbard, P. eds.: *The Entrepreneurial City: Geographies of Politics, Regime, and Representation* (New York: Wiley, 1998).

Harvey, D.: *The Condition of Postmodernity: An Inquiry into the Origins of Cultural Change* (Oxford: Basil Blackwell, 1989a).

Harvey, D.: "From managerialism to entrepreneurialism: The transformation in urban governance in late capitalism," *Geografiska Annaler*, 71B (1989b), 3–17.

Holcomb, B.: "Revisioning place: De-and re-constructing the image of the industrial city," *Selling Places*, ed. G. Kearns and C. Philo (New York: Pergamon Press, 1993), pp. 133–44.

Hula, R.: "The two Baltimores," *Leadership and Urban Regeneration*, ed. D. Judd and M. Parkinson (Newbury Park, CA: Sage, 1990), pp. 191–215.

James, E.: "The sure touch of the Rouse Company," *Financial World*, 154 (1985), 44–6.

Jencks, C.: *Late Modern Architecture* (New York: Rizzoli, 1984).

Jencks, C.: *What is Postmodernism?* (New York: St. Martin's Press, 1986).

Jessop, B.: "Post-Fordism and the state," *Post-Fordism: A Reader*, ed. A. Amin (Cambridge, MA: Blackwell, 1994), pp. 251–79.

Jessop, B.: "The narrative of enterprise and the enterprise of narrative: Place marketing and the entrepreneurial city," *The Entrepreneurial City: Geographies of Politics, Regime, and Representation*, ed. T. Hall and P. Hubbard (New York: Wiley, 1998), pp. 77–106.

Jewson, N. and MacGregor, S., eds.: *Transforming Cities: Contested governance and new spatial divisions* (New York: Routledge, 1997).

Judd, D. and Parkinson, M., eds.: *Leadership and Urban Regeneration*, Vol. 57, Urban Affairs Annual Reviews (Newbury Park CA: Sage, 1990).

Kearns, G., and Philo, C., eds.: *Selling Places: The City as Cultural Capital, Past and Present* (New York: Pergamon Press, 1993).

Keating, D.: "Cleveland: The 'comeback city': The politics of redevelopment and sports stadiums amidst urban decline," *Reconstructing Urban Regime Theory*, ed. M. Lauria (Thousand Oaks, CA: Sage, 1997), pp. 189–205.

Keating, D., Krumholz, N., and Metzger, J.: "Cleveland: Post-populist public private partnerships," *Unequal Partnerships: The Political Economy of Urban Redevelopment in Postwar America*, ed. G. Squires (New Brunswick, NJ: Rutgers University Press, 1989), pp. 121–41.

Kelly, B. and Lewis, R.: "What's right (and wrong) about the Inner Harbor," *Planning (APA)*, 58 (1992), 28–32.

Knack, R.: "Cleveland: the morning after," *Planning (APA)*, 65 (1999), 12–15.

Knox, P.: "Capital, material culture and socio-spatial differentiation," *The Restless Urban Landscape*, ed. P. Knox (Englewood Cliffs, NJ: Prentice Hall, 1993), pp. 1–32.

Kostoff, S.: *America by Design* (New York: Oxford University Press, 1987).

Leitner, H.: "Cities in pursuit of economic growth: The local state as entrepreneur," *Political Geography Quarterly*, 9 (1990), 146–70.

Leitner, H., and Garner, M.: "The limits of local initiatives," *Urban Geography*, 14 (1993), 57–77.

Levine, M.: "Downtown redevelopment as an urban growth strategy: A critical appraisal of the Baltimore renaissance," *Journal of Urban Affairs*, 9 (1987), 103–23.

Logan, J., and Molotch, H.: *Urban Fortunes: The Political Economy of Place* (Berkeley and Los Angeles, CA: University of California Press, 1987).

Mayer, M.: "Post-Fordist city politics," *Post-Fordism: A Reader*, ed. A. Amin (Cambridge, MA: Blackwell, 1994), pp. 316–37.

Molotch, H.: "The city as a growth machine: Toward a political economy of place," *American Journal of Sociology*, 82 (1976), 309–32.

The New Cleveland Campaign: "Cleveland: Is this heaven?," *The New Cleveland Campaign* (Cleveland, Ohio, 1988), pp. 1–20.

Peck, J. and Tickell, A.: "Searching for a new institutional fix: The after-Fordist crisis and the global-local disorder," *Post-Fordism: A Reader*, ed. A. Amin (Cambridge, MA: Blackwell, 1994), pp. 280–315.

Pierce, N.: "Is Baltimore unique?," *Baltimore Magazine* (October, 1986), 69–71.

"Roundtable on Rouse," *Progressive Architecture*, 7 (1981), 100–6.

Rutheiser, C.: *Imagineering Atlanta: The politics of place in the city of dreams* (New York: Verso, 1996).

Sawicki, D.: "The festival market place as public policy," *Journal of the American Planning Association*, Summer (1989), 347–61.

Short, J. and Kim, Y-H.: "Urban crises/urban representations: Selling the city in difficult times," *The Entrepreneurial City: Geographies of Politics, Regime, and Representation*, ed. T. Hall and P. Hubbard (New York: Wiley, 1998), pp. 55–76.

Sorkin, M.: *The Exquisite Corpse* (New York: Verso, 1991).

Sorkin, M., ed.: *Variations on a Theme Park: The New American City and the End of Public Space* (New York: Hill and Wang, 1992).

Squires, G., ed.: *Unequal Partnerships: The Political Economy of Urban Redevelopment in Postwar America* (New Brunswick, NJ: Rutgers University Press, 1989).

Stephenson, M.: "Whither the public private partnership? A critical overview," *Urban Affairs Quarterly*, 27 (1991), 109–27.

Swyngedouw, E.: "The Mammon quest: 'Glocalisation', interspatial competition and the monetary order: the construction of new scales," *Cities and Regions in the New Europe*, ed. M. Dunford and G. Kafkalas (London: Belhaven Press, 1992), pp. 39–67.

Swyngedouw, E.: "Neither global nor local: 'Glocalization' and the politics of scale," *Spaces of Globalization: Reasserting the Power of the Local*, ed. K. Cox (New York: Guilford), pp. 137–66.

Thaler, R.: "Water: The ultimate amenity," Urban Waterfronts '87 (Washington DC: Waterfront Press, 1988).

Warf, B., and Holly, B.: "The rise and fall and rise of Cleveland," Annals, AAPS, 551 (May 1997), 208–21.

Warren S.: "Disneyfication of the metropolis: Popular resistance in Seattle," *Journal of Urban Affairs*, 16 (1994), 89–107.

Weber, J. and Phillips, S.: "Jim Rouse may be losing his touch," *Business Week*, (April 4, 1988), 33–4.

Zukin, S.: *Loft Living: Culture and Capital in Urban Change*, 2nd ed. (New Brunswick, NJ: Rutgers University Press, 1989).

Zukin, S.: *The Cultures of Cities* (Cambridge, MA: Blackwell, 1995).

Part III

Taste, Reception, and Resistance

10 Encoding/Decoding

Stuart Hall

Traditionally, mass-communications research has conceptualized the process of communication in terms of a circulation circuit or loop. This model has been criticized for its linearity – sender/message/receiver – for its concentration on the level of message exchange and for the absence of a structured conception of the different moments as a complex structure of relations. But it is also possible (and useful) to think of this process in terms of a structure produced and sustained through the articulation of linked but distinctive moments – production, circulation, distribution/consumption, reproduction. This would be to think of the process as a "complex structure in dominance", sustained through the articulation of connected practices, each of which, however, retains its distinctiveness and has its own specific modality, its own forms and conditions of existence. This second approach, homologous to that which forms the skeleton of commodity production offered in Marx's *Grundrisse* and in *Capital*, has the added advantage of bringing out more sharply how a continuous circuit – production – distribution – production – can be sustained through a "passage of forms". It also highlights the specificity of the forms in which the product of the process "appears" in each moment, and thus what distinguishes discursive "production" from other types of production in our society and in modern media systems.

The "object" of these practices is meanings and messages in the form of sign-vehicles of a specific kind organized, like any form of communication or language, through the operation of codes within the syntagmatic chain of a discourse. The apparatuses, relations and practices of production thus issue, at a certain moment (the moment of "production/circulation") in the form of symbolic vehicles constituted within the rules of "language". It is in this discursive form that the circulation of the "product" takes place. The process thus requires, at the production end, its material instruments – its "means" – as well as its own sets of social (production) relations – the organization and combination of practices within media apparatuses. But it is in the *discursive* form that the circulation of the product takes place, as well as its distribution to different audiences. Once accomplished, the discourse must then be translated – transformed, again – into social practices if the circuit is to be both completed and effective. If no "meaning" is taken, there can be no "consumption". If the meaning is not articulated in practice, it has no effect. The value of this approach is that while each of the moments, in articulation, is necessary to the circuit as a whole, no one moment can fully guarantee the next moment with which it is articulated. Since each has its specific modality and conditions of existence, each can constitute its own break or interruption of the "passage of forms" on whose continuity the flow of effective production (that is, "reproduction") depends.

Original publication: Hall, Stuart, "Encoding/Decoding," from S. Hall, D. Hobson, A. Lowe, and P. Willis (eds.), *Culture, Media, Language: Working Papers in Cultural Studies* (Hutchinson Publishing, London, 1980).

Thus while in no way wanting to limit research to "following only those leads which emerge from content analysis",[1] we must recognize that the discursive form of the message has a privileged position in the communicative exchange (from the viewpoint of circulation), and that the moments of "encoding" and "decoding", though only "relatively autonomous" in relation to the communicative process as a whole, are *determinate* moments. A "raw" historical event cannot, *in that form*, be transmitted by, say, a television newscast. Events can only be signified within the aural-visual forms of the televisual discourse. In the moment when a historical event passes under the sign of discourse, it is subject to all the complex formal "rules" by which language signifies. To put it paradoxically, the event must become a "story" before it can become a *communicative event*. In that moment the formal sub-rules of discourse are "in dominance", without, of course, subordinating out of existence the historical event so signified, the social relations in which the rules are set to work or the social and political consequences of the event having been signified in this way. The "message form" is the necessary "form of appearance" of the event in its passage from source to receiver. Thus the transposition into and out of the "message form" (or the mode of symbolic exchange) is not a random "moment", which we can take up or ignore at our convenience. The "message form" is a determinate moment; though, at another level, it comprises the surface movements of the communications system only and requires, at another stage, to be integrated into the social relations of the communication process as a whole, of which it forms only a part.

From this general perspective, we may crudely characterize the television communicative process as follows. The institutional structures of broadcasting, with their practices and networks of production, their organized relations and technical infrastructures, are required to produce a programme. Using the analogy of *Capital*, this is the "labour process" in the discursive mode. Production, here, constructs the message. In one sense, then, the circuit begins here. Of course, the production process is not without its "discursive" aspect: it, too, is framed throughout by meanings and ideas: knowledge-in-use concerning the routines of production, historically defined technical skills, professional ideologies, institutional knowledge, definitions and assumptions, assumptions about the audience and so on frame the constitution of the programme through this production structure. Further, though the production structures of television originate the television discourse, they do not constitute a closed system. They draw topics, treatments, agendas, events, personnel, images of the audience, "definitions of the situation" from other sources and other discursive formations within the wider socio-cultural and political structure of which they are a differentiated part. Philip Elliott has expressed this point succinctly, within a more traditional framework, in his discussion of the way in which the audience is both the "source" and the "receiver" of the television message. Thus – to borrow Marx's terms – circulation and reception are, indeed, "moments" of the production process in television and are reincorporated, via a number of skewed and structured "feedbacks", into the production process itself. The consumption or reception of the television message is thus also itself a "moment" of the production process in its larger sense, though the latter is "predominant" because it is the "point of departure for the realization" of the message. Production and reception of the television message are not, therefore, identical, but they are related: they are differentiated moments within the totality formed by the social relations of the communicative process as a whole (figure 10.1)

At a certain point, however, the broadcasting structures must yield encoded messages in the form of a meaningful discourse. The institution-societal relations of production must pass under the discursive rules of language for its product to be "realized". This initiates a further differentiated moment, in which the formal rules of discourse and language are in dominance. Before this message can have an "effect" (however defined), satisfy a "need" or be put to a "use", it must first be appropriated as a meaningful discourse and be meaningfully decoded. It is this set of decoded meanings which "have an effect", influence, entertain, instruct or persuade, with very complex perceptual, cognitive, emotional, ideological or behavioural consequences. In a "determinate" moment the structure employs a code and yields a "message": at another determinate moment the "message", via its decodings, issues into the structure of social practices. We are now fully aware that this re-entry into the practices of audience reception and "use" cannot be understood in simple behavioural terms. The typical processes identified in positivistic research on isolated elements – effects, uses, "gratifications" – are themselves framed by structures of understanding, as well as being produced by social and economic relations, which shape their "realization" at the reception end of the chain and which permit the meanings signified in the discourse to be transposed into practice or consciousness (to acquire social use value or political effectivity).

Clearly, what we have labelled in figure 10.1 "meaning structures 1" and "meaning structures 2" may not be the same. They do not constitute an "immediate identity". The codes of encoding and decoding may not be perfectly symmetrical. The degrees of symmetry – that is, the degrees of "understanding" and "misunderstanding" in the communicative exchange – depend on the degrees of symmetry/asymmetry (relations of equivalence) established between the positions of the "personifications", encoder-producer and decoder-receiver. But this in turn depends on the degrees of identity/non-identity between the codes which perfectly or imperfectly transmit, interrupt or systematically distort what has been transmitted. The lack of fit between the codes has a great deal to do with the structural differences of relation and position between broadcasters and audiences, but it also has something to do with the asymmetry between the codes of "source" and "receiver" at the moment of transformation into

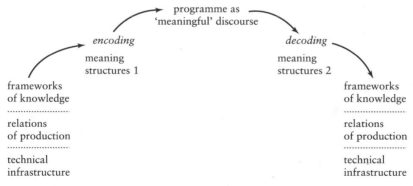

Figure 10.1   The television communicative process.

and out of the discursive form. What are called "distortions" or "misunderstandings" arise precisely from the *lack of equivalence* between the two sides in the communicative exchange. Once again, this defines the "relative autonomy", but "determinateness", of the entry and exit of the message in its discursive moments.

The application of this rudimentary paradigm has already begun to transform our understanding of the older term, television "content". We are just beginning to see how it might also transform our understanding of audience reception, "reading" and response as well. Beginnings and endings have been announced in communications research before, so we must be cautious. But there seems some ground for thinking that a new and exciting phase in so-called audience research, of a quite new kind, may be opening up. At either end of the communicative chain the use of the semiotic paradigm promises to dispel the lingering behaviourism which has dogged mass-media research for so long, especially in its approach to content. Though we know the television programme is not a behavioural input, like a tap on the knee cap, it seems to have been almost impossible for traditional researchers to conceptualize the communicative process without lapsing into one or other variant of low-flying behaviourism. We know, as Gerbner has remarked, that representations of violence on the TV screen "are not violence but messages about violence":[2] but we have continued to research the question of violence, for example, as if we were unable to comprehend this epistemological distinction.

The televisual sign is a complex one. It is itself constituted by the combination of two types of discourse, visual and aural. Moreover, it is an iconic sign, in Peirce's terminology, because "it possesses some of the properties of the thing represented".[3] This is a point which has led to a great deal of confusion and has provided the site of intense controversy in the study of visual language. Since the visual discourse translates a three-dimensional world into two-dimensional planes, it cannot, of course, *be* the referent or concept it signifies. The dog in the film can bark but it cannot bite! Reality exists outside language, but it is constantly mediated by and through language: and what we can know and say has to be produced in and through discourse. Discursive "knowledge" is the product not of the transparent representation of the "real" in language but of the articulation of language on real relations and conditions. Thus there is no intelligible discourse without the operation of a code. Iconic signs are therefore coded signs too – even if the codes here work differently from those of other signs. There is no degree zero in language. Naturalism and "realism" – the apparent fidelity of the representation to the thing or concept represented – is the result, the effect, of a certain specific articulation of language on the "real". It is the result of a discursive practice.

Certain codes may, of course, be so widely distributed in a specific language community or culture, and be learned at so early an age, that they appear not to be constructed – the effect of an articulation between sign and referent – but to be "naturally" given. Simple visual signs appear to have achieved a "near-universality" in this sense: though evidence remains that even apparently "natural" visual codes are culture-specific. However, this does not mean that no codes have intervened; rather, that the codes have been profoundly *naturalized*. The operation of naturalized codes reveals not the transparency and "naturalness" of language but the depth, the habituation and the near-universality of the codes in use. They produce apparently "natural" recognitions. This has the (ideological) effect of concealing the practices of coding which are present. But we must not be fooled by appearances. Actually, what naturalized codes demonstrate is the degree of habituation produced when there is a fundamental alignment and reciprocity – an achieved equivalence – between the encoding and decoding sides of an exchange of meanings. The functioning of the codes on the decoding side will frequently assume the status of naturalized perceptions. This leads us to think that the visual sign for "cow" actually *is* (rather than *represents*) the animal, cow. But if we think of the visual representation of a cow in a manual on animal husbandry – and, even more, of the linguistic sign "cow" – we can see that both, in different degrees, are *arbitrary* with respect to the concept of the animal they represent. The articulation of an arbitrary sign – whether visual or verbal – with the concept of a referent is the product not of nature but of convention, and the conventionalism of discourses requires the intervention, the support, of codes. Thus Eco has argued that iconic signs "look like objects in the real world because they reproduce the conditions (that is, the codes) of perception in the viewer".[4] These "conditions of perception" are, however, the result of a highly coded, even if virtually unconscious, set of operations – decodings. This is as true of the photographic or televisual image as it is of any other sign. Iconic signs are, however, particularly vulnerable to being "read" as natural because visual codes of perception are very widely distributed and because this type of sign is less arbitrary than a linguistic sign: the linguistic sign, "cow" possesses *none* of the properties of the thing represented, whereas the visual sign appears to possess *some* of those properties.

This may help us to clarify a confusion in current linguistic theory and to define precisely how some key terms are being used in this article. Linguistic theory frequently employs the distinction "denotation" and "connotation". The term "denotation" is widely equated with the literal meaning of a sign: because this literal meaning is almost universally recognized, especially when visual discourse is being employed, "denotation" has often been confused with a literal transcription of "reality" in language – and thus with a "natural sign", one produced without the intervention of a code. "Connotation", on the other hand, is employed simply to refer to less fixed and therefore more conventionalized and changeable, associative meanings, which clearly vary from instance to instance and therefore must depend on the intervention of codes.

We do *not* use the distinction – denotation/connotation – in this way. From our point of view, the distinction is an *analytic* one only. It is useful, in analysis, to be able to apply a rough rule of thumb which distinguishes those aspects of a sign which appear to be taken, in any language community at any point in time, as its "literal" meaning (denotation) from the more associative meanings for the sign which it is possible to generate (connotation). But analytic distinctions must not be confused with distinctions in the real world. There will be very few instances in which signs organized in a discourse signify *only* their "literal" (that is, near-universally consensualized) meaning. In actual discourse most signs will combine both the denotative and the connotative *aspects* (as redefined above). It may, then, be asked why we retain the distinction at all. It is largely a matter of analytic value. It is because signs appear to acquire their full ideological value – appear to be open to articulation with wider ideological discourses and meanings – at the level of their "associative" meanings (that is, at the connotative level) – for here "meanings" are *not* apparently fixed in natural perception (that is, they are not fully naturalized), and their fluidity of meaning and association can be more fully exploited and transformed. So it is at the connotative *level* of the sign that situational ideologies alter and transform signification. At this level we can see more clearly the active intervention of ideologies in and on discourse: here, the sign is open to new accentuations and, in Vološinov's terms, enters fully into the struggle over meanings – the class struggle in language.[5] This does not mean that the denotative or "literal" meaning is outside ideology. Indeed, we could say that its ideological value is strongly *fixed* – because it has become so fully universal and "natural". The terms "denotation" and "connotation", then, are merely useful analytic tools for distinguishing, in particular contexts, between not the presence/absence of ideology in language but the different levels at which ideologies and discourses intersect.

The level of connotation of the visual sign, of its contextual reference and positioning in different discursive fields of meaning and association, is the point where *already coded* signs intersect with the deep semantic codes of a culture and take on additional, more active ideological dimensions. We might take an example from advertising discourse. Here, too, there is no "purely denotative", and certainly no "natural", representation. Every visual sign in advertising connotes a quality, situation, value or inference, which is present as an implication or implied meaning, depending on the connotational positioning. In Barthes's example, the sweater always signifies a "warm garment" (denotation) and thus the activity/value of "keeping warm". But it is also possible, at its more connotative levels, to signify "the coming of winter" or "a cold day". And, in the specialized sub-codes of fashion, sweater may also connote a fashionable style of *haute couture* or, alternatively, an informal style of dress. But set against the right visual background and positioned by the romantic sub-code, it may connote "long autumn walk in the woods".[6] Codes of this order clearly contract relations for the sign with the wider universe of ideologies in a society. These codes are the means by which power and ideology are made to signify in particular discourses. They refer signs to the "maps of meaning" into which any culture is classified; and those "maps of social reality" have the whole range of social meanings, practices, and usages, power and interest "written in" to them. The connotative levels of signifiers. Barthes remarked, "have a close communication with culture, knowledge, history, and it is through them, so to speak, that the environmental world invades the linguistic and semantic system. They are, if you like, the fragments of ideology".[7]

The so-called denotative *level* of the televisual sign is fixed by certain, very complex (but limited or "closed") codes. But its connotative *level*, though also bounded, is more open, subject to more active *transformations*, which exploit its polysemic values. Any such already constituted sign is potentially transformable into more than one connotative configuration. Polysemy must not, however, be confused with pluralism. Connotative codes are *not* equal among themselves. Any society/ culture tends, with varying degrees of closure, to impose its classifications of the social and cultural and political world. These constitute a *dominant cultural order*, though, it is neither univocal nor uncontested. This question of the "structure of discourses in dominance" is a crucial point. The different areas of social life appear to be mapped out into discursive domains, hierarchically organized into *dominant or preferred meanings*. New, problematic or troubling events, which breach our expectancies and run counter to our "common-sense constructs", to our "taken-for-granted" knowledge of social structures, must be assigned to their discursive domains before they can be said to "make sense". The most common way of "mapping" them is to assign the new to some domain or other of the existing "maps of problematic social reality". We say *dominant*, not "determined", because it is always possible to order, classify, assign and decode an event within more than one "mapping". But we say "dominant" because there exists a pattern of "preferred readings"; and these both have the institutional/political/ideological order imprinted in them and have themselves become institutionalized. The domains of "preferred meanings" have the whole social order embedded in them as a set of meanings, practices and beliefs: the everyday knowledge of social structures, of "how things work for all practical purposes in this culture", the rank order of power and interest and the structure of legitimations, limits and sanctions. Thus to clarify a "misunder-standing" at the connotative level, we must refer, *through* the codes, to the orders of social life, of economic and political power and of ideology. Further, since these mappings are "structured in dominance" but not closed, the communicative process consists not in the unproblematic assignment of every visual item to its given position within a set of prearranged codes, but of *performative rules* – rules of competence and use, of logics-in-use – which seek actively to *enforce* or *pre-fer* one semantic domain over another and rule items into and out of their appropriate meaning-sets. Formal semiology has too often neglected this practice of *interpretative work*, though this constitutes, in fact, the real relations of broadcast practices in television.

In speaking of *dominant meanings*, then, we are not talking about a one-sided process which governs how all events will be signified. It consists of the "work" required to enforce, win plausibility for and command as legitimate a *decoding* of the event within the limit of dominant definitions in which it has been connotatively signified. Terni has remarked:

> By the word *reading* we mean not only the capacity to identify and decode a certain number of signs, but also the subjective capacity to put them into a creative relation between themselves and with other signs: a capacity which is, by itself, the condition for a complete awareness of one's total environment.[8]

Our quarrel here is with the notion of "subjective capacity", as if the referent of a televisional discourse were an objective fact but the interpretative level were an individualized and private matter. Quite the opposite seems to be the case. The televisual practice takes "objective" (that is, systemic) responsibility precisely for the relations which disparate signs contract with one another in any discursive instance, and thus continually rearranges, delimits and prescribes into what "aware-ness of one's total environment" these items are arranged.

This brings us to the question of misunderstandings. Television producers who find their message "failing to get across" are frequently concerned to straighten out the kinks in the communication chain, thus facilitating the "effectiveness" of their communication. Much research which claims the objectivity of "policy-oriented analysis" reproduces this administrative goal by attempting to discover how much of a message the audience recalls and to improve the extent of understanding. No doubt misunderstandings of a literal kind do exist. The viewer does not know the terms employed, cannot follow the complex logic of argument or exposition, is unfamiliar with the language, finds the concepts too alien or difficult or is foxed by the expository narrative. But more often broadcasters are concerned that the audience has failed to take the meaning as they – the broadcasters – intended. What they really mean to say is that viewers are not operating within the "dominant" or "preferred" code. Their ideal is "perfectly transparent communication". Instead, what they have to confront is "systematically distorted communication".[9]

In recent years discrepancies of this kind have usually been explained by reference to "selective perception". This is the door via which a residual pluralism evades the compulsions of a highly structured, asymmetrical and non-equivalent process. Of course, there will always be private, individual, variant readings. But "selective perception" is almost never as selective, random or privatized as the concept suggests. The patterns exhibit, across individual variants, significant clusterings. Any new approach to audience studies will therefore have to begin with a critique of "selective perception" theory.

It was argued earlier that since there is no necessary correspondence between encoding and decoding, the former can attempt to "pre-fer" but cannot prescribe or guarantee the latter, which has its own conditions of existence. Unless they are wildly aberrant, encoding will have the effect of constructing some of the limits and parameters within which decodings will operate. If there were no limits, audiences could simply read whatever they liked into any message. No doubt some total misunderstandings of this kind do exist. But the vast range must contain *some* degree of reciprocity between encoding and decoding moments, otherwise we could not speak of an effective communicative exchange at all. Nevertheless, this "correspondence" is not given but constructed. It is not "natural" but the product of an articulation between two distinct moments. And the former cannot determine or guarantee, in a simple sense, which decoding codes will be employed. Otherwise communication would be a perfectly equivalent circuit, and every message would be an instance of "perfectly transparent communication". We must think, then, of the variant articulations in which encoding/decoding can be combined. To elaborate on this, we offer a hypothetical analysis of some possible decoding positions, in order to reinforce the point of "no necessary correspondence".

We identify *three* hypothetical positions from which decodings of a televisual discourse may be constructed. These need to be empirically tested and refined. But the argument that decodings do not follow inevitably from encodings, that they are not identical, reinforces the argument of "no necessary correspondence". It also helps to deconstruct the common-sense meaning of "misunderstanding" in terms of a theory of "systematically distorted communication".

The first hypothetical position is that of the *dominant-hegemonic position*. When the viewer takes the connoted meaning from, say, a television newscast or current affairs programme full and straight, and decodes the message in terms of the reference code in which it has been encoded, we might say that the viewer *is operating inside the dominant code*. This is the ideal-typical case of "perfectly transparent communication" – or as close as we are likely to come to it "for all practical purposes". Within this we can distinguish the positions produced by the *professional code*. This is the position (produced by what we perhaps ought to identify as the operation of a "metacode") which the professional broadcasters assume when encoding a message which has *already* been signified in a hegemonic manner. The professional code is "relatively independent" of the dominant code, in that it applies criteria and transformational operations of its own, especially those of a technico-practical nature. The professional code, however, operates *within* the "hegemony" of the dominant code. Indeed, it serves to reproduce the dominant definitions precisely by bracketing their hegemonic quality and operating instead with displaced professional codings which foreground such apparently neutral-technical questions as visual quality, news and presentational values, televisual quality, "professionalism" and so on. The hegemonic interpretations of, say, the politics of Northern Ireland, or the Chilean *coup* or the Industrial Relations Bill are principally generated by political and military elites: the particular choice of presentational occasions and formats, the selection of personnel, the choice of images, the staging of debates are selected and combined through the operation of the professional code. How the broadcasting professionals are able *both* to operate with "relatively autonomous" codes of their own *and* to act in such a way as to reproduce (not without contradiction) the hegemonic signification of events is a complex matter which cannot be further spelled out here. It must suffice to say that the professionals are linked with the defining elites not only by the institutional position of broadcasting itself as an "ideological apparatus",[10] but also by the structure of *access* (that is, the systematic "over-accessing" of selective elite personnel and their "definition of the situation" in television). It may even be said that the professional codes serve to reproduce hegemonic definitions specifically by *not overtly* biasing their operations in a dominant direction: ideological reproduction therefore takes place here inadvertently, unconsciously, "behind men's backs". Of course, conflicts, contradictions and even misunderstandings regularly arise between the dominant and the professional significations and their signifying agencies.

The second position we would identify is that of the *negotiated code* or position. Majority audiences probably understand quite adequately what has been dominantly defined and professionally signified. The dominant definitions, however, are hegemonic precisely because they represent definitions of situations and events which are "in dominance" (*global*). Dominant definitions connect events, implicitly or explicitly, to grand totalizations, to the great syntagmatic views-of-the-world: they take "large views" of issues: they relate events to the "national interest" or to the level of geo-politics, even if they make these connections in truncated, inverted or mystified ways. The definition of a hegemonic viewpoint is (a) that it defines within its terms the mental horizon, the universe, of possible meanings, of a whole sector of relations in a society or culture; and (b) that it carries with it the stamp of legitimacy – it appears coterminous with what is "natural", "inevitable", "taken for granted" about the social order. Decoding within the *negotiated version* contains a mixture of adaptive and oppositional elements: it acknowledges the legitimacy of the hegemonic definitions to make the grand significations (abstract), while, at a more restricted, situational (situated) level, it makes its own ground rules – it operates with exceptions to the rule. It accords the privileged position to the dominant definitions of events while reserving the right to make a more negotiated application to "local conditions", to its own more *corporate* positions. This negotiated version of the dominant ideology is thus shot through with contradictions, though these are only on certain occasions brought to full visibility. Negotiated codes operate through what we might call particular or situated logics: and these logics are sustained by their differential and unequal relation to the discourses and logics of power. The simplest example of a negotiated code is that which governs the response of a worker to the notion of an Industrial Relations Bill limiting the right to strike or to arguments for a wages freeze. At the level of the "national interest" economic debate the decoder may adopt the hegemonic definition, agreeing that "we must all pay ourselves less in order to combat inflation". This, however, may have little or no relation to his/her willingness to go on strike for better pay and conditions or to oppose the Industrial Relations Bill at the level of shop-floor or union organization. We suspect that the great majority of so-called "misunderstandings" arise from the contradictions and disjunctures between hegemonic-dominant encodings and negotiated-corporate decodings. It is just these mismatches in the levels which most provoke defining elites and professionals to identify a "failure in communications".

Finally, it is possible for a viewer perfectly to understand both the literal and the connotative inflection given by a discourse but to decode the message in a *globally* contrary way. He/she detotalizes the message in the preferred code in order to retotalize the message within some alternative framework of reference. This is the case of the viewer who listens to a debate on the need to limit wages but "reads" every mention of the "national interest" as "class interest". He/she is operating with what we must call an *oppositional code*. One of the most significant political moments (they also coincide with crisis points within the broadcasting organizations themselves, for obvious reasons) is the point when events which are normally signified and decoded in a negotiated way begin to be given an oppositional reading. Here the "politics of signification" – the struggle in discourse – is joined.

Notes

1 J.D. Halloran, 'Understanding television', paper for the Council of Europe Colloquy on 'Understanding Television' (University of Leicester 1973).
2 G. Gerbner et al., *Violence in TV Drama: A Study of Trends and Symbolic Functions* (The Annenberg School, University of Pennsylvania 1970).
3 Charles Peirce, *Speculative Grammar*, in *Collected Papers* (Cambridge, Mass.: Harvard University Press 1931–58).
4 Umberto Eco, 'Articulations of the cinematic code', in *Cinemantics*, no. 1.
5 Vološinov, *Marxism And The Philosophy of Language* (The Seminar Press 1973).
6 Roland Barthes, 'Rhetoric of the image', in *WPCS* 1 (1971).
7 Roland Barthes, *Elements of Semiology* (Cape 1967).
8 P. Terni, 'Memorandum', Council of Europe Colloquy on 'Understanding Television' (University of Leicester 1973).
9 The phrase is Habermas's, in 'Systematically distorted communications', in P. Dretzel (ed.), *Recent Sociology 2* (Collier-Macmillan 1970). It is used here, however, in a different way.
10 See Louis Althusser, 'Ideology and ideological state apparatuses', in *Lenin and Philosophy and Other Essays* (New Left Books 1971).

11 (Male) Desire and (Female) Disgust: Reading *Hustler*

Laura Kipnis

Let's begin with two images. The first is of feminist author-poet Robin Morgan as she appears in the anti-pornography documentary *Not a Love Story*. Posed in her large book-lined living room, poet-husband Kenneth Pitchford at her side, she inveighs against a number of sexualities and sexual practices: masturbation – on the grounds that it promotes political quietism – as well as "superficial sex, kinky sex, appurtenances and [sex] toys" for benumbing "normal human sensuality." She then breaks into tears as she describes the experience of living in a society where pornographic media thrives.[1] The second image is the one conjured by a recent letter to *Hustler* magazine from E.C., a reader who introduces an account of an erotic experience involving a cruel-eyed, high-heeled dominatrix with this vivid vocational self-description: "One night, trudging home from work – I gut chickens, put their guts in a plastic bag and stuff them back in the chicken's asshole – I varied my routine by stopping at a small pub...."[2] Let's say that these two images, however hyperbolically (the insistent tears, the insistent vulgarity), however inadvertently, offer a route toward a consideration of the relation between discourses on sexuality and the social division of labor, between sexual representation and class. On one side we have Morgan, laboring for the filmmakers and audience as a feminist intellectual, who constructs, from a particular social locus, a normative theory of sexuality. And while "feminist intellectual" is not necessarily the highest paying job category, it is a markedly different class location – and one definitively up the social hierarchy – from that of E.C., whose work is of a character which tends to be relegated to the lower rungs within a social division of labor that categorizes jobs dealing with things that smell, or that for other reasons we prefer to hide from view – garbage, sewerage, dirt, animal corpses – as of low status, both monetarily and socially. E.C.'s letter, carefully (certainly more carefully than Morgan) framing his sexuality in relation to his material circumstances and to actual conditions of production, is fairly typical of the discourse of *Hustler* – in its vulgarity, its explicitness about "kinky" sex, and in its imbrication of sexuality and class. So as opposed to the set of norms Morgan attempts to put into circulation (a "normal human sensuality" far removed from E.C.'s night of bliss with his Mistress, who incidentally, "mans" herself with just the kind of appurtenances Morgan seems to be referring to), *Hustler* also offers a theory of sexuality – a "low theory." Like Morgan's radical feminism, it too offers an explicitly political and counter-hegemonic analysis of power and the body; unlike Morgan it is also explicit about its own class location.

Original publication: Kipnis, Laura, "(Male) Desire and (Female) Disgust: Reading *Hustler*," from Law rence Grosserg, Cary Nelson and Paula A. Treichler (eds.) *Cultural Studies* (Routledge, New York, 1991).

The feminist anti-porn movement has achieved at least temporary hegemony over the terms in which debates on pornography take place: current discourses on porn on the left and within feminism are faced with the task of framing themselves in relation to a set of arguments now firmly established as discursive landmarks: pornography is defined as a discourse about male domination, is theorized as the determining instance in gender oppression – if not a direct cause of rape – and its pleasures, to the extent that pleasure is not simply conflated with misogyny, are confined to the male sphere of activity. "Pro-sex" feminists have developed arguments against these positions on a number of grounds, but invariably in response to the terms set by their opponents: those classed by the discourse as sexual deviants (or worse, as "not feminists") – S/M lesbians, women who enjoy porn – have countered on the basis of experience, often in first person, asserting both that women *do* "look" and arguing the compatibility of feminism and alternative sexual practice – while condemning anti-porn forces for their universalizing abandon in claiming to speak for all women. There have been numerous arguments about the use and misuse of data from media effects research by the anti-porn movement and charges of misinterpretation and misrepresentation of data made by pro-porn feminists (as well as some of the researchers). On the gendered pleasure front, psychoanalytic feminists have argued that identification and pleasure don't necessarily immediately follow assigned gender: for instance, straight women may get turned on by gay male porn or may identify with the male in a heterosexual coupling. Others have protested the abrogation of hard-won sexual liberties implicit in any restrictions on sexual expression, further questioning the politics of the alliance of the anti-porn movement and the radical right.[3] Gayle Rubin (1984) has come closest to undermining the terms of the anti-porn discourse itself: she points out, heretically, that feminism, a discourse whose object is the organization of gendered oppression, may in fact not be the most appropriate or adequate discourse to analyze sexuality, in relation to which it becomes "irrelevant and often misleading." Rubin paves the way for a re-examination of received truths about porn: is pornography, in fact, so obviously and so simply a discourse about gender? Has feminism, in arrogating porn as its own privileged object, foreclosed on other questions? If feminism, as Rubin goes on, "lacks angles of vision which can encompass the social organization of sexuality," it seems clear that at least one of these angles of vision is a theory of class, which has been routinely under-theorized and undetermined within the anti-porn movement in favor of a totalizing theory of misogyny. While class stratification, and the economic and profit motives of those in the porn industry have been exhaustively covered, we have no theory of how class plays itself out in nuances of representation.

The extent of misogyny is certainly monumental, so monumental as to be not only tragic, but banal in its everyday omnipresence. If it appears as superficially more evident in the heightened and exaggerated realms of fantasy, pleasure, and projection – the world of pornography – then this is certainly only a localized appearance, and an appearance which may be operating under other codes than those of gender alone. So if the question of misogyny is momentarily displaced here to allow consideration of questions of class, it isn't because one supersedes the other but because bringing issues of class into the porn debates may offer a way of breaking down the theoretical monolith of misogyny – and in a manner that doesn't involve jumping on the reassuring bandwagon of repression and policing the image world or the false catharsis of taking symptoms for causes. The recent tradition of cultural studies work on the body might pose some difficult questions for feminism (and thus might contribute to the kind of revamped critical discourse on sexuality that Rubin calls for): questions such as whether anti-porn feminists, in abjuring questions of class in analyzing representation, are constructing (and attempting to enforce) a theory and politics of the body on the wrong side of struggles against bourgeois hegemony, and ultimately complicit in its enforcement. But at the same time, in taking on porn as an object, US cultural studies – or at least that tendency to locate resistance, agency, and micro-political struggle just about everywhere in mass cultural reception – might have difficulty finding good news as it takes on the fixity of sexuality and power.

Hustler is certainly the most reviled instance of mass circulation porn, and at the same time probably one of the most explicitly class-antagonistic mass circulation periodicals of any genre. Although it's been the tendency among writers on porn to lump it together into an unholy triad with *Penthouse* and *Playboy*, the other two top circulating men's magazines, *Hustler* is a different beast in any number of respects, even in conventional men's magazine terms. *Hustler* set itself apart from its inception through its explicitness, and its crusade *for* explicitness, accusing *Playboy* and *Penthouse* of hypocrisy, veiling the body, and basically not delivering the goods. The strategy paid off – *Hustler* captured a third of the men's market with its entree into the field in 1974 by being the first to reveal pubic hair – with *Penthouse* swiftly following suit (in response to which a *Hustler* pictorial presented its model shaved),[4] then upping the explicitness ante and creating a publishing scandal by displaying a glimpse of pubic hair on its cover in July 1976 (this a typically *Hustler* commemoration of the Bicentennial: the model wore stars and stripes, although not enough of them). Throughout these early years *Hustler*'s pictorials persisted in showing more and more of the forbidden zone (the "pink" in *Hustler* speak) with *Penthouse* struggling to keep up and *Playboy* – whose focus was always above the waist anyway – keeping a discreet distance. *Hustler* then introduced penises, first limp ones, currently hefty erect-appearing ones, a sight verboten in traditional men's magazines where the strict prohibition on the erect male sexual organ impels the question of what traumas it might provoke in the male viewer. *Hustler*, from its inception, made it its mission to disturb and unsettle its readers, both psycho-sexually and socio-sexually, interrogating, as it were, the typical men's magazine codes and conventions of sexual representation: *Hustler*'s early pictorials included pregnant women, middle-aged women (horrified news commentaries referred to "geriatric pictorials"), overweight women, hermaphrodites, amputees, and in a moment of true frisson for your typical heterosexual male, a photo spread of a pre-operative transsexual, doubly well-endowed. *Hustler* continued to provoke reader outrage with a 1975 interracial pictorial (black male, white female) which according to *Hustler* was protested by both the KKK and the NAACP. It's been known to picture explicit photo spreads on the consequences of venereal disease, the most graphic war carnage... None of these your typical, unproblematic turn-on.

And even more so than in its explicitness, *Hustler*'s difference from *Playboy* and *Penthouse* is in the sort of body it produces. Its pictorials, far more than other magazines, emphasize gaping orifices, as well as a consistent sharp focus on *other* orifices. *Hustler* sexuality is far from normative. It speaks openly of sexual preferences as "fetishes" and its letters and columns are full of the most specific and wide-ranging practices and sexualities, which don't appear to be hierarchized, and many of which have little to do with the standard heterosexual telos of penetration. (Male-male sexuality is sometimes raised as a possibility as well, along with the men's magazine standard woman-woman scenario.) The *Hustler* body is an unromanticized body – no vaselined lenses or soft focus: this is neither the airbrushed top-heavy fantasy body of *Playboy*, nor the ersatz opulence, the lingeried and sensitive crotch shots of *Penthouse*, transforming female genitals into *objets d'art*. It's a body, not a surface or a suntan: insistently material, defiantly vulgar, corporeal. In fact, the *Hustler* body is often a gaseous, fluid-emitting, *embarrassing* body, one continually defying the strictures of bourgeois manners and mores and instead governed by its lower intestinal tract – a body threatening to erupt at any moment. *Hustler*'s favorite joke is someone accidentally defecating in church.

Particularly in its cartoons, but also in its editorials and political humor, *Hustler* devotes itself to what tends to be called "grossness": an obsessive focus on the lower stratum, humor animated by a downward movement, representational techniques of exaggeration and inversion. *Hustler*'s bodily topography is straight out of Rabelais, as even a partial inventory of the subjects it finds of interest indicates: fat women, assholes, monstrous and gigantic sexual organs, body odors (the notorious Scratch and Sniff centerfold, which due to "the limits of the technology," publisher Larry Flynt apologized, smelled definitively of lilacs); and anything that exudes from the body: piss, shit, semen, menstrual blood, particularly when it sullies a sanitary or public site; and most especially, farts: farting in public, farting loudly, Barbara Bush farting, priests and nuns farting, politicians farting, the professional classes farting, the rich farting...(see Bakhtin, 1984). Certainly a far remove from your sleek, overlaminated *Playboy/Penthouse* body. As *Newsweek* complained, "The contents of an average issue read like something Krafft-Ebing might have whispered to the Marquis de Sade... *Hustler* is into erotic fantasies involving excrement, dismemberment, and the sexual longings of rodents... where other skin slicks are merely kinky, *Hustler* can be downright frightful... The net effect is to transform the erotic into the emetic."[5]

It's not clear if what sets *Newsweek* to crabbing is that *Hustler* transgresses bourgeois mores of the proper or that *Hustler* violates men's magazine conventions of sexuality. On both fronts its discourse is transgressive – in fact on *every* front *Hustler* devotes itself to producing generalized transgression. Given that control over the body has long been associated with the bourgeois political project, with both the "ability and the right to control and dominate others" (Davidoff, 1979, p. 97), *Hustler*'s insistent and repetitious return to the iconography of the body out of control, rampantly transgressing bourgeois norms and sullying bourgeois property and proprieties, raises certain political questions. On the politics of such social transgressions, for example, Peter Stallybrass and Allon White (1986), following Bakhtin, write of a transcoding between bodily and social topography, a transcoding which sets up an homology between the lower bodily stratum and the lower social classes – the reference to the body being invariably a reference to the social.

Here perhaps is a clue to *Newsweek*'s pique, as well as a way to think about why it is that the repressive apparatuses of the dominant social order return so invariably to the body and to somatic symbols. (And I should say that I write this during the Cincinnati Mapplethorpe obscenity trial, so this tactic is excessively visible at this particular conjuncture.) It's not only because these bodily symbols "are the ultimate elements of social classification itself" but because the transcoding between the body and the social sets up the mechanisms through which the body is a privileged political trope of lower social classes, and through which bodily grossness operates as a critique of dominant ideology. The power of grossness is predicated on its opposition from *and to* high discourses, themselves prophylactic against the debasements of the low (the lower classes, vernacular discourses, low culture, shit . . .). And it is dominant ideology itself that works to enforce and reproduce this opposition – whether in producing class differences, somatic symbols, or culture. The very highness of high culture is structured through the obsessive banishment of the low, and through the labor of suppressing the grotesque body (which is, in fact, simply the material body, gross as that can be) in favor of what Bakhtin refers to as "the classical body." This classical body – a refined, orifice-less, laminated surface – is homologous to the forms of official high culture which legitimate their authority by reference to the values – the highness – inherent in this classical body. According to low-theoretician Larry Flynt: "Tastelessness is a necessary tool in challenging preconceived notions in an uptight world where people are afraid to discuss their attitudes, prejudices and misconceptions." This is not so far from Bakhtin on Rabelais:

> Things are tested and reevaluated in the dimensions of laughter, which has defeated fear and all gloomy seriousness. This is why the material bodily lower stratum is needed, for it gaily and simultaneously materializes and unburdens. It liberates objects from the snares of false seriousness, from illusions and sublimations inspired by fear.   *(p. 376)*

So in mapping social topography against bodily topography, it becomes apparent how the unsettling effects of grossness and erupting bodies condense all the unsettling effects (to those in power) of a class hierarchy tenuously held in place through symbolic (and less symbolic) policing of the threats posed by bodies, by lower classes, by angry mobs.

Bakhtin and others have noted that the invention of the classical body and the formation of this new bodily canon have their inception in the sixteenth-century rise of individualism and the attendant formation and consolidation of bourgeois subjectivity and bourgeois political hegemony, setting off, at the representational level, the struggle of grotesque and classical concepts (Bakhtin, 1984, p. 320; see also F. Barker, 1984). A similar historical argument is made by Norbert Elias (1978) in his study *The History of Manners*, which traces the effects of this social process on the structure of individual affect. The invention of Bakhtin's classical body entails and is part of a social transformation within which thresholds of sensitivity and refinement in the individual psyche become heightened. Initially this reform of affect takes place in the upper classes, within whom increasingly refined manners and habits – initially a mechanism of class distinction – are progressively restructuring standards of privacy, disgust, shame, and embarrassment. These affect-reforms are gradually, although incompletely, disseminated downward through the social hierarchy (and finally to other nations whose lack of "civilization" might reasonably necessitate colonial etiquette lessons). These new standards of delicacy and refinement become the very substance of bourgeois subjectivity: constraints that were originally socially generated gradually become reproduced in individuals as habits, reflexes, as the structure of the modern psyche. And as Elias reminds us, the foundational Freudian distinction between id and ego corresponds to historically specific demands placed on public behavior in which certain instinctual behaviors and impulses – primarily bodily ones like sex and elimination – are relegated to the private sphere, behind closed doors, or in the case of the most shameful and most socially prohibited drives and desires, warehoused as the contents of the unconscious.

So we can see, returning to our two opening images, how Morgan's tears, her sentiment, might be constructed *against* E.C.'s vulgarity, how her desire to distance herself from and if possible banish from existence the cause of her distress – the sexual expression of people unlike herself – has a sort of structural imperative: as Stallybrass and White (1986) put it, the bourgeois subject has "continuously defined and redefined itself through the exclusion of what it marked out as low – as dirty, repulsive, noisy, contaminating... [the] very act of exclusion was constitutive of its identity" (p. 191). So disgust has a long and complicated history, the context within which should be placed the increasingly strong tendency of the bourgeois to want to remove the distasteful from the sight of society (including, of course, dead animals, which might interest E.C. – as "people in the course of the civilizing process seek to suppress in themselves every characteristic they feel to be animal..." [Elias, 1978, p. 120]). These gestures of disgust are crucial in the production of the bourgeois body, now so rigidly split into higher and lower stratum that tears will become the only publicly permissible display of bodily fluid. So the bodies and bodily effluences start to stack up into neat oppositions: on the one side upper bodily productions, a heightened sense of delicacy, and the project of removing the distasteful from sight (and sight, of course, at the top of the hierarchization of the senses central to bourgeois identity and rationality); and on the other hand, the lower body and *its* productions, the insistence on vulgarity and violations of the bourgeois body. To the extent that, in Morgan's project, discourse and tears are devoted to concealing the counter-bourgeois body from view by regulating its representation and reforming its pleasures into ones more consequent with refined sensibilities, they can be understood, at least in part, as the product of a centuries-long socio-historical process, a process that has been a primary mechanism of class distinction, and one that has played an important role as an ongoing tool in class hegemony. So perhaps it becomes a bit more difficult to see feminist disgust in isolation, and disgust at pornography as strictly a gender issue, for any gesture of disgust is not without a history and not without a class character. And whatever else we may say about feminist arguments about the proper or improper representation of women's bodies – and I don't intend to imply that my discussion is exhaustive of the issue – bourgeois disgust, even as mobilized against a sense of violation and violence to the female body, is not without a function in relation to class hegemony, and more than problematic in the context of what purports to be a radical social movement.

Perhaps this is the moment to say that a large part of what impels me to write this essay is my own disgust in reading *Hustler*. In fact, I have wanted to write this essay for several years, but every time I trudge out and buy the latest issue, open it and begin to try to bring analytical powers to bear upon it, I'm just so disgusted that I give up, never quite sure whether this almost automatic response is one of feminist disgust or bourgeois disgust. Of course, whether as feminist, bourgeois, or academic, I and most likely you, are what could be called *Hustler*'s implied target, rather than its implied reader. The discourse of *Hustler* is quite specifically *constructed against* – not only the classical body, a bourgeois hold-over of the aristocracy, but against all the paraphernalia of petit-bourgeoisiehood as well. At the most manifest level *Hustler* is simply against any form of social or intellectual pretention: it is against the pretensions (and the social power) of the professional classes – doctors, optometrists, dentists are favored targets; it is against liberals, and particularly cruel to academics who are invariably prissy and uptight. (An academic to his wife: "Eat your pussy? You forget Gladys, I have a Ph.D.") It is against the power of government – which is by definition corrupt, as are elected officials, the permanent government, even foreign governments. Of course, it is against the rich, particularly rich women, down on the Chicago Cubs, and devotes many pages to the hypocrisy of organized religion – with a multiplication of jokes on the sexual instincts of the clergy, the sexual possibilities of the crucifixion, the scam of the virgin birth – and, as mentioned previously, the plethora of jokes involving farting/shitting/fucking in church and the bodily functions of nuns, priests, and ministers. In *Hustler* any form of social power is fundamentally crooked and illegitimate.

These are just *Hustler*'s more manifest targets. Reading a bit deeper, its offenses provide a detailed road map of a cultural psyche. Its favored tactic is to zero in on a subject, an issue, which the bourgeois imagination prefers to be unknowing about, which a culture has founded itself upon suppressing, and prohibits irreverent speech about. Things we would call "tasteless" at best, or might even become physically revulsed by: the materiality of aborted fetuses,[6] where homeless people go to the bathroom, cancer, the proximity of sexual organs to those of elimination – any aspect of the material body, in fact. A case in point, one which again subjected *Hustler* to national outrage: its two cartoons about Betty Ford's mastectomy. If one can distance oneself from one's automatic indignation for a moment, *Hustler* might be seen as posing, through the strategy of transgression, an interesting metadiscursive question: which are the subjects that are taboo ones for even sick humor? Consider for a moment that while, for example, it was not uncommon, following the Challenger explosion, to hear the sickest jokes about scattered body parts, while jokes about amputees and paraplegics are not entirely unknown even on broadcast TV (and, of course, abound on the pages of *Hustler*), while jokes about blindness are considered so benign that one involving Ray Charles features in a current "blind taste test" soda pop commercial, mastectomy is one subject that appears to be completely off limits as a humorous topic. But back to amputees for a moment, perhaps a better comparison: apparently a man without a limb is considered less tragic by the culture at large, less mutilated, and less of a cultural problem it seems, than a woman without a breast. A mastectomy more of a tragedy than the deaths of the seven astronauts. This, as I say, provides some clues into the deep structure of a cultural psyche – as does our outrage. After all, what *is* a woman without a breast in a culture that measures breasts as the measure of the woman? Not a fit subject for comment. Its subject so veiled that it's not even available to the "working through" of the joke. (And again a case where *Hustler* seems to be deconstructing the codes of the men's magazine: where *Playboy* creates a fetish of the breast, and whose *raison d'être* is, in fact, very much the cultural obsession with them, *Hustler* perversely points out that they are, after all, materially, merely tissue – another limb.)[7]

Hustler's uncanny knack for finding and attacking the jugular of a culture's sensitivity might more aptly be regarded as intellectual work on the order of the classic anthropological studies which translate a culture into a set of structural oppositions (obsession with the breast/prohibition of mastectomy jokes), laying bare the structure of its taboos and arcane superstitions. (Or do only "primitive" cultures have irrational taboos?) *Hustler*, in fact, performs a similar cultural mapping to that of anthropologist Mary Douglas, whose study *Purity and Danger* (1966) produces a very similar social blueprint. The vast majority of *Hustler* humor seems to be animated by the desire to violate what Douglas describes as "pollution" taboos and rituals – these being a society's set of beliefs, rituals, and practices having to do with dirt, order, and hygiene (and by extension, the pornographic). As to the pleasure produced by such cultural violations as *Hustler*'s, Douglas cheerily informs us, "It is not always an unpleasant experience to confront ambiguity," and while it is clearly more tolerable in some areas than in others, "there is a whole gradient on which laughter, revulsion and shock belong at different points and intensities" (p. 37).

The sense of both pleasure and danger that violation of pollution taboos can invoke is clearly dependent on the existence of symbolic codes, codes that are for the most part only semi-conscious. Defilement can't be an isolated event, it can only engage our interest or provoke our anxiety to the extent that our ideas about such things are systematically ordered, and that this ordering matters deeply – in our culture, in our subjectivity. As Freud (1963a) notes, "Only jokes that have a purpose run the risk of meeting with people who do not want to listen to them."

Of course, a confrontation with ambiguity and violation can be profoundly dis-pleasurable as well, as the many opponents of *Hustler* might attest. And for Freud this displeasure has to do with both gender and class (p. 9a).[8] One of the most interesting things about Freud's discussion of jokes is the theory of humor and gender he elaborates in the course of his discussion of them, with class almost inadvertently intervening as a third term. He first endeavors to produce a typology of jokes according to their gender effects. For example, in regard to excremental jokes (a staple of *Hustler* humor) Freud tells us that this is material *common to both sexes*, as both experience a common sense of shame surrounding bodily functions. And it's true that *Hustler*'s numerous jokes on the proximity of the sexual organs to elimination functions, the confusion of assholes and vaginas, turds and penises, shit and sex – i.e., a couple fucking in a hospital room while someone in the next bed is getting an enema, all get covered with shit – can't really be said to have a gender basis or target (unless, that is, we women put ourselves, more so than men, in the position of upholders of "good taste").

But obscene humor, whose purpose is to expose sexual facts and relations verbally, is, for Freud, a consequence of male and female sexual incommensurability, and the dirty joke is something like a seduction gone awry. The motive for (men's) dirty jokes is "in reality nothing more than women's incapacity to tolerate undisguised sexuality, an incapacity correspondingly increased with a rise in the educational and social level." Whereas both men and women are subject to sexual inhibition or repression, apparently upper-class women are the more seriously afflicted in the Freudian world, and dirty jokes thus function as a sign for both sexual difference ("smut is like an exposure of the sexually different person to whom it is directed . . . it compels the person who is assailed to imagine the part of the body or the procedure in question"), and class difference. So apparently, if it weren't for women's lack of sexual willingness and class refinement the joke would be not a joke, but a proposition: "If the woman's readiness emerges quickly the obscene speech has a short life; it yields at once to a sexual action," hypothesizes Freud. While there are some fairly crude gender and class stereotypes in circulation here – the figure of the lusty barmaid standing in for the lower-class woman – it's also true that obscene jokes and pornographic images *are* perceived by *some* women as an act of aggression against women. But these images and jokes are aggressive only insofar as they're capable of causing the woman discomfort, and they're capable of causing discomfort *only* insofar as there *are* differing levels of sexual inhibition between at least some men and some women. So Freud's view would seem to hold out: the obscene joke is directed originally toward women; it presupposes not only the presence of a woman, but that women are sexually constituted differently than men; and upper classness or upper-class identification – as Morgan's discourse also indicates – exacerbates this difference.

But if there are differing levels of inhibition, displeasure, or interest between some men and some women (although *Hustler*'s readership is primarily male, it's not exclusively male), the origins of this pleasure/displeasure disjunction are also a site of controversy in the porn debates. For Freud it's part of the process of *differentiation* between the sexes, not originative – little girls are just as "interested" as little boys. Anti-porn forces tend to reject a constructionist argument such as Freud's in favor of a description of female sexuality as inborn and biologically based – something akin to the "normal human sensuality" Morgan refers to.[9] Women's discomfiture at the dirty joke, from this vantage point, would appear to be twofold. There is the discomfort at the intended violation – at being assailed "with the part of the body or the procedure in question." But there is the further discomfort at being addressed as a subject of repression – as a subject with a history – and the rejection of porn can be seen as a defense erected against representations which mean to unsettle her in her subjectivity. In other words, there is a violation of the *idea* of the "naturalness" of female sexuality and subjectivity, which is exacerbated by the social fact that not all women *do* experience male pornography in the same way. That "pro-sex" feminists, who tend to follow some version of a constructionist position on female sexuality, seem to feel less violated by porn is some indication that these questions of subjectivity are central to porn's address, misaddress, and violations. To the extent that pornography's discourse engages in setting up disturbances around questions of subjectivity and sexual difference – after all, what does *Hustler*-variety porn consist of but the male fantasy of women whose sexual desires are in concert with men's – and that this fantasy of undifferentiation is perceived as doing violence to female subjectivity by some women but not others, the perception of this violence is an issue of difference between women.[10] But the violence here is that of misaddress, of having one's desire misfigured as the male's desire. It is the violence of being absent from the scene. The differentiation between female spectators as to how this address or misaddress is perceived appears to be bound up with the degree to which a certain version of female sexuality is hypostatized as natural, versus a sense of mobility of sexuality, at least at the level of fantasy. But hypostatizing female sexuality and assigning it to all women involves universalizing an historically specific class position as well, not as something acquired and constructed through difference, privilege, and hierarchy, but as also somehow inborn – as identical to this natural female sexuality. Insisting that all women are violated by pornography insists that class or class identification doesn't figure as a difference between women, that "normal human sensuality" erases all difference between women.

For Freud, even the form of the joke is classed, with a focus on joke technique associated with higher social classes and education levels. In this light it's interesting to note how little *Hustler* actually engages in the technique of the joke – even to find a pun is rare. But then as far as obscene humor, we're subject to glaring errors of judgment about the "goodness" of jokes insofar as we judge them on formal terms, according to Freud – the technique of these jokes is often "quite wretched, but they have immense success in provoking laughter." Particularly in regard to obscene jokes, we aren't "in a position to distinguish by our feelings what part of the pleasure arises from the sources of their technique and what part from those of their purpose. Thus, strictly speaking, we do not know what we are laughing at" (p. 102). And so too with displeasure – it would seem we can't be entirely sure what we're *not* laughing at either, and this would be particularly true of both the bourgeois and the anti-pornography feminist, to the extent that both seem likely to displace or disavow pleasure or interest in smut, one in favor of technique – like disgust, a mechanism of class distinction – and the other against perceived violations against female subjectivity. So for both, the act of rejection takes on far more significance than the terrains of pleasure; for both, the nuances and micro-logics of *displeasure* are defining practices.

Yet at the same time, there does seem to be an awful lot of interest in porn among both, albeit a negative sort of interest. It's something of a Freudian cliche that shame, disgust, and morality are reaction-formations to an original interest in what is not "clean." One defining characteristic of a classic reaction-formation is that the subject actually comes close to "satisfying the demands of the opposing instinct while actually engaged in the pursuit of the virtue which he affects," the classic example being the housewife obsessed with cleanliness who ends up "concentrating her whole existence on dust and dirt" (Laplanche and Pontalis, 1973, pp. 376–8). And it does seem to be the case that a crusader against porn will end up making pornography the center of her existence. Theorizing it as central to women's oppression means, in practical terms, devoting one's time to reading it, thinking about it, and talking about it. It also means simultaneously conferring this *interest*, this subject-effect, onto others – predicting tragic consequences arising from such dirty pursuits, unvaryingly dire and uniform effects, as if the will and individuality of consumers of porn are suddenly seized by some (projected) all-controlling force, a force which becomes – or already is – the substance of a monotonic male sexuality. Thusly summing up male sexuality, Andrea Dworkin (1987) writes: "Any violation of a woman's body can become sex for men; this is the essential truth of pornography" (p. 138).

The belief in these sorts of essential truths seem close to what Mary Douglas (1966) calls "danger-beliefs" –

> [A] strong language of mutual exhortation. At this level the laws of nature are dragged in to sanction the moral code: this kind of disease is caused by adultery, that by incest...the whole universe is harnessed to men's attempts to force one another into

good citizenship. Thus we find that certain moral values are upheld and certain social rules defined by beliefs in dangerous contagion. *(p. 3)*

And Douglas, like Freud, also speaks directly about the relation of gender to the "gradient" where laughter, revulsion, and shock collide: her discussion of danger beliefs also opens onto questions of class and hierarchy as well. For her, gender is something of a trope in the realm of purity rituals and pollution violations: it functions as a displacement from issues of social hierarchy.

> I believe that some pollutions are used as analogies for expressing a general view of the social order. For example, there are beliefs that each sex is a danger to the other... Such patterns of sexual danger can be seen to express symmetry or hierarchy. It is implausible to interpret them as expressing something about the actual relation of the sexes. I suggest that many ideas about sexual dangers are better interpreted as symbols of the relation between parts of society, as mirroring designs of hierarchy or symmetry which apply in the larger social system. *(p. 3)*[11]

To put a feminist spin on Douglas's pre-feminist passage, while men do certainly pose actual sexual danger to women, the content of pollution beliefs expresses that danger symbolically at best: it would be implausible to take the content of these beliefs literally. So while, for Douglas, gender is a trope for social hierarchy, a feminist might interpret the above passage to mean that *danger* is a trope for gender hierarchy. Douglas's observations on the series of displacements between defilement, danger, gender, and class puts an interesting cast on female displeasure in pornography in relation to class hierarchies and "the larger social system" – in relation to *Hustler*'s low-class tendentiousness and its production of bourgeois displeasure, and why it might happen that the feminist response to pornography ends up reinscribing the feminist into the position of enforcer of class distinctions.

But historically, female reformism aimed at bettering the position of women has often had an unfortunately conservative social thrust, as in the case of the temperance movement. The local interests of women in reforming male behavior can easily dovetail with the interests of capital in producing and reproducing an orderly, obedient, and sober workforce. In social history terms we might note that *Hustler* galumphs onto the social stage at the height of the feminist second wave, and while the usual way to phrase this relation would be the term "backlash," it can also be seen as a retort – even a political response – to feminist calls for reform of the male imagination. There's no doubt that *Hustler* sees itself as doing battle with feminists: ur-feminist Gloria Steinem makes frequent appearances in the pages of the magazine as an uptight, and predictably, upper-class, bitch. It's fairly clear that from *Hustler*'s point of view, feminism is a class-based discourse. So *Hustler*'s production of sexual differences are also the production of a form of class consciousness – to accede to feminist reforms would be to identify upward on the social hierarchy.

But any automatic assumptions about *Hustler*-variety porn aiding and abetting the entrenchment of male power might be put into question by actually reading the magazine. Whereas Freud's observations on dirty jokes are phallocentric in the precise sense of the word – phallic sexuality is made central – *Hustler* itself seems much less certain about the place of the phallus, much more wry and often troubled about male and female sexual incommensurability. On the one hand it offers the standard men's magazine fantasy babe – always ready, always horny, willing to do anything, and who finds the *Hustler* male inexplicably irresistible. But just as often there is her flip side: the woman who is disgusted by the *Hustler* male's desires and sexuality, a superior, rejecting, often upper-class woman. It becomes clear how class resentment is modulated through resentment of what is seen as the power of women to humiliate and reject: "Beauty isn't everything, except to the bitch who's got it. You see her stalking the aisles of Cartier, stuffing her perfect face at exorbitant cuisineries, tooling her Jag along private-access coastline roads. . . . " Doesn't this reek of a sense of disenfranchisement rather than any sort of certainty about male power over women? The fantasy life here is animated by cultural disempowerment in relation to a sexual caste system and a social class system. This magazine is tinged with frustrated desire and rejection: *Hustler* gives vent to a vision of sex in which sex is an arena for failure and humiliation rather than domination and power. There are numerous ads addressed to male anxieties and sense of inadequacy: various sorts of penis enlargers ("Here is your chance to overcome the problems and insecurities of a penis that is too small. Gain self-confidence and your ability to satisfy women will sky rocket" reads a typical ad), penis extenders, and erection aids (Stay-Up, Stay-Hard . . .).[12] One of the problems with most porn from even a pro-porn feminist point of view is that men seize the power and privilege to have public fantasies about women's bodies, to imagine and represent women's bodies without any risk, without any concomitant problematization of the male body – which is invariably produced as powerful and inviolable. But *Hustler* does put the male body at risk, representing and never completely alleviating male anxiety (and for what it's worth, there is a surprising amount of castration humor in *Hustler* as well). Rejecting the sort of compensatory fantasy life mobilized by *Playboy* and *Penthouse* in which all women are willing and all men are studs – as long as its readers fantasize and identify upward, with money, power, good looks, and consumer durables – *Hustler* pulls the window dressing off the market/ exchange nature of sexual romance: the market in attractiveness, the exchange basis of male-female relations in patriarchy. Sexual exchange is a frequent subject of humor: women students are coerced into having sex with professors for grades, women are fooled into having sex by various ruses, lies, or barters usually engineered by males in power positions: bosses, doctors, and the like. All this is probably truer than not true, but problematic from the standpoint of male fantasy: power, money, and prestige are represented as essential to sexual success, but the magazine works to disparage and counter identification with these sorts of class attributes on every other front. The intersections of sex, gender, class, and power here are complex, contradictory, and political.

Much of *Hustler*'s humor *is*, in fact, manifestly political, and much of it would even get a warm welcome in left-leaning circles, although its strategies of conveying those sentiments might give some of the flock pause. A 1989 satirical photo feature titled "Farewell to Reagan: Ronnie's Last Bash" demonstrates how the magazine's standard repertoire of aesthetic techniques – nudity, grossness, and offensiveness – can be directly translated into scathingly effective political language. It further shows how the pornographic idiom can work as a form of political speech that refuses to buy into the pompously serious and highminded language in which official culture conducts its political discourse: *Hustler* refuses the language of high culture along with its political forms. The photospread, laid out like a series of black and white surveillance photos, begins with this no-words-minced introduction:

It's been a great eight years – for the power elite, that is. You can bet Nancy planned long and hard how to celebrate Ron Reagan's successful term of filling special-interest coffers while fucking John Q. Citizen right up the yazoo. A radical tax plan that more than halved taxes for the rich while doubling the working man's load; detaxation of industries, who trickled down their windfalls into mergers, takeovers, and investments in foreign lands; crooked deals with enemies of U.S. allies in return for dirty money for right wing killers to reclaim former U.S. business territories overseas; more than 100 appointees who resigned in disgrace over ethics or outright criminal charges . . . are all the legacies of the Reagan years . . . and we'll still get whiffs of bullyboy Ed Meese's sexual intimidation policies for years to come, particularly with conservative whores posing as Supreme Court justices.

The photos that follow are of an elaborately staged orgiastic White House farewell party as imagined by the *Hustler* editors, with the appropriate motley faces of the political elite photomontaged onto naked and semi-naked bodies doing fairly obscene and polymorphously perverse things to each other. (The warning "Parody: Not to be taken seriously. Celebrity heads stripped onto our model's bodies," accompanies each and every photo – more about *Hustler*'s legal travails further on.) That more of the naked bodies are female and that many are in what could be described as a service relation to male bodies clearly opens up the possibility of a reading limited to its misogynistic tendencies. But what becomes problematic for such a singular reading is that within these parodic representations, this staging of the rituals of male hegemony also works in favor of an overtly counter-hegemonic political treatise. The style is something like a *Mad* magazine cartoon come to life with a multiplication of detail in every shot (the Ted Kennedy dartboard in one corner, in another stickers that exhort "Invest in South Africa," the plaque over Reagan's bed announcing "Joseph McCarthy slept here"). The main room of the party: various half-naked women cavort, Edwin Meese is glimpsed filching a candelabra. Reagan greets a hooded Ku Klux Klanner at the door, and a helpful caption translates the action: "Ron tells an embarrassed Jesse Helms it wasn't a come-as-you-are party," while in the background the corpse of Bill Casey watches benignly over the proceedings (his gaping mouth doubles as an ashtray), as does former press secretary James Brady – victim of John Hinckley's attempted assassination and Reagan's no-gun control policy – who, propped in a wheelchair, wears a sign bluntly announcing "Vegetable Dip" around his neck. In the next room Ollie North as a well-built male stripper gyrates on top of a table while a fawning Poindexter, Secord, and Weinberger gathered at his feet stuff dollar bills into his holster/g-string in homoerotic reverie. In the next room Jerry Falwell's masturbating to a copy of *Hustler* concealed in the Bible, a bottle of Campari at his bedside and an "I love Mom" button pinned to his jacket (this a triumphant *Hustler* pouring salt on the wound – more on the Falwell Supreme Court case further on). In another room "former Democrat and supreme skagbait Jeanne Kirkpatrick demonstrates why she switched to the Republican Party," as, grinning and topless, we find her on the verge of anally penetrating a bespectacled George Bush with the dildo attached to her ammunition belt. A whiny Elliott Abrams, pants around his ankles and dick in hand, tries unsuccessfully to pay off a prostitute who won't have him; and a naked Pat Robertson, doggie style on the bed, is being disciplined by a naked angel with a cat-o-nine-tails. And on the last page the invoice to the American Citizens: $283,000,000.

While the anti-establishment politics of the photospread are fairly clear, *Hustler* can also be maddeningly incoherent, all over what we usually think of as the political spectrum. Its incoherence as well as its low-rent tendentiousness can be laid at the door of publisher Larry Flynt as much as anywhere, as Flynt, in the early days of the magazine, maintained such iron control over the day-to-day operations that he had to approve even the pull quotes. Flynt is a man apparently both determined and destined to play out the content of his obsessions as psychodrama on our public stage; if he weren't so widely considered such a disgusting pariah, his life could probably supply the material for many epic dramas. The very public nature of Flynt's blazing trail through the civil and criminal justice system and his one-man campaign for the first amendment justify a brief descent into the murkiness of the biographical, not to make a case for singular authorship, but because Flynt himself has had a decisive historical and political impact in the realpolitik of state power. In the end it has been porn king Larry Flynt – not the left, not the avant-garde – who has decisively expanded the perimeters of political speech.

Larry Flynt is very much of the class he appears to address – his story is like a pornographic Horatio Alger. He was born in Magoffin County, Kentucky, in the Appalachians – the poorest county in America. The son of a pipe welder, he quit school in the eighth grade, joined the Navy at fourteen with a forged birth certificate, got out, worked in a G. M. auto assembly plant, and turned $1,500 in savings into a chain of go-go bars in Ohio named the Hustler Clubs. The magazine originated as a 2-page newsletter for the bars, and the rest was rags to riches: Flynt's income was as high as $30 million a year when *Hustler* was at its peak circulation of over 2 million (he then built himself a scale replica of the cabin he grew up in in the basement of his mansion to, he says, remind him where he came from, one replete with chickenwire and hay, and a three-foot lifelike statue of the chicken he claims to have lost his virginity to at age eight).

Since the magazine's inception Flynt has spent much of his time in and out of the nations courtrooms on various obscenity and libel charges as well as an array of contempt charges and other bizarre legal entanglements – notably his somehow becoming entangled in the government's prosecution of automaker John DeLorean. All proceeded as normal (for Flynt) until his well-publicized 1978 conversion to evangelical Christianity at the hands of presidential sister Ruth Carter Stapleton. The two were pictured chastely hand in hand as Flynt announced plans to turn *Hustler* into a *religious* skin magazine and told a Pentecostal congregation in Houston (where he was attending the National Women's Conference) "I owe every woman in America an apology." Ironically, it was this religious conversion that led to the notorious *Hustler* cover of a woman being ground up in a meat grinder, which was, in fact, another sheepish and flat-footed attempt at apologia by Flynt. "We will no longer hang women up as pieces of meat," was actually the widely ignored caption to the photo. (Recall here Freud's observation on the sophistication of the joke form as a class trait.)[13]

In 1978, shortly after the religious conversion, during another of his obscenity trials in Lawrenceville, Georgia, Flynt was shot three times by an unknown assassin with a 44 magnum. His spinal nerves were severed, leaving him paralyzed from the waist down and in constant pain. He became a recluse, barricading himself in his Bel Air mansion, surrounded by bodyguards. His wife Althea, then 27, a former go-go dancer in the Hustler clubs, took over control of the corporation and the magazine, and returned the magazine to its former focus. Flynt became addicted to morphine and Dilaudid, finally detoxing to methadone. (He repudiated the religious conversion after the shooting.) Now confined to a wheelchair, he continued to be hauled into court by the government for obscenity and in various civil suits. He was sued by *Penthouse* publisher Bob Guccione and a female *Penthouse* executive who claimed *Hustler* had libeled her by printing that she had contracted VD from Guccione. He was sued by author Jackie Collins after the magazine published nude photos it incorrectly identified as the nude author. He was fined $10,000 a day – increased to $20,000 a day – when he refused to turn over to the feds tapes he claimed he possessed documenting a government frame of DeLorean. Flynt's public behavior was becoming increasingly bizarre. He appeared in court wearing an American flag as a diaper and was arrested. At another 1984 Los Angeles trial, described by a local paper as "legal surrealism," his own attorney asked for permission to gag his client and after an "obscene outburst" Flynt, like Black Panther Bobby Seale, was bound and gagged at his own trial.

The same year the FCC was forced to issue an opinion on Flynt's threat to force television stations to show his X-rated presidential campaign commercials. Flynt, whose compulsion it was to find loopholes in the nation's obscenity laws, vowed to use his presidential campaign(!) to test those laws by insisting that TV stations show his campaign commercials featuring hard core sex acts. (The equal time provision of the Federal Communications Act prohibits censorship of any ad in which a candidate's voice or picture appears – while the U.S. Criminal Code prohibited dissemination of obscene material.) He had begun to make it his one-man mission to exploit every loophole in the first amendment as well. In 1986 a federal judge ruled that the U.S. Postal Service could not constitutionally prohibit *Hustler* and Flynt from sending free copies of the magazine to members of Congress, a ruling stemming from Flynt's decision to mail free copies of *Hustler* to members of Congress, so they could be "well informed on all social issues and trends." Flynt's next appearance, ensconced in a gold-plated wheelchair, was at the $45 million federal libel suit brought by the Reverend Jerry Falwell over the notorious Campari ad parody, in which the head of the Moral Majority describes his "first time" as having occurred with his mother behind an outhouse. A Virginia jury dismissed the libel charge but awarded Falwell $200,000 for intentional infliction of emotional distress. A federal district court upheld the verdict, but when it landed in the Rehnquist Supreme Court the judgment was reversed by a unanimous Rehnquist-written decision that the Falwell parody was not reasonably believable, and thus fell into category of satire – an art form often "slashing and one-sided." This Supreme Court decision significantly extended the freedom of the press won in the 1964 New York Times vs. Sullivan ruling (which mandated that libel could only be founded in cases of "reckless disregard"), and "handed the press one of its most significant legal triumphs in recent years," was "an endorsement of robust political debate," and ended the influx of "pseudo-libel suits" by celebrities with hurt feelings, crowed the grateful national press, amidst stories generally concluding that the existence of excrescences like *Hustler* are the price of freedom of the press.

Flynt and wife Althea had over the years elaborated various charges and conspiracy theories about the shooting, including charges of a CIA-sponsored plot (Flynt claimed to have been about to publish the names of JFK's assassins – conspiracy theories being another repeating feature of the *Hustler mentalité*). Further speculation about the shooting focused on the mob, magazine distribution wars, and even various disgruntled family members. The shooting was finally acknowledged by white supremacist Joseph Paul Franklin, currently serving two life sentences for racially motivated killings. No charges were ever brought in the Flynt shooting. That Flynt, who has been regularly accused of racism, should be shot by a white supremacist is only one of the many ironies of his story. In another – one which would seem absurd in the most hackneyed morality tale – this man who made millions on the fantasy of endlessly available fucking is now left impotent. And in 1982, after four years of constant and reportedly unbearable pain, the nerves leading to his legs were cauterized to stop all sensation – Flynt, who built an empire on offending bourgeois sensibilities with their horror of errant bodily functions, is now left with no bowel or urinary control.

Flynt, in his obsessional one-man war against state power's viselike grip on the body of its citizenry, seized as his *matériel* the very pornographic idioms from which he had constructed his *Hustler* empire. The exhibitionism, the desire to shock, the deployment of the body – these are the very affronts that have made him the personification of evil to both the state and anti-porn feminists. Yet willingly or not, Flynt's own body has been very much on the line as well – the pornographer's body has borne the violence of the political and private enforcement of the norms of the bourgeois body. If *Hustler*'s development of the pornographic idiom as a political form seems – as with other new cultural political forms – politically incoherent to traditional political readings based on traditional political alliances and political oppositions – right-left, misogynist-feminist – then it is those very political meanings that *Hustler* throws into question. It is *Hustler*'s very political incoherence – in conventional political terms – that makes it so available to counter-hegemonic readings, to opening up new political alliances and strategies. And this is where I want to return to the question of *Hustler*'s misogyny, another political category *Hustler* puts into question. Do I feel assaulted and affronted by *Hustler*'s images, as do so many other women? Yes. Is that a necessary and sufficient condition on which to base the charge of its misogyny? Given my own gender and class position I'm not sure that I'm exactly in a position to trust my immediate response.

Take, for example, *Hustler*'s clearly political use of nudity. It's unmistakable from the "Reagan's Farewell Party" photospread that *Hustler* uses nudity as a leveling device, a deflating technique following in a long tradition of political satire. And perhaps this is the subversive force behind another of *Hustler*'s scandals (or publishing coups from its point of view), its notorious nude photospread of Jackie Onassis, captured sunbathing on her Greek island, Skorpios. Was this simply another case of misogyny? The strategic uses of nudity we've seen elsewhere in the magazine might provoke a conceptual transition in thinking through the Onassis photos: from Onassis as unwilling sexual object to Onassis as political target. Given that nudity is used throughout the magazine as an offensive against the rich and powerful – Reagan, North, Falwell, Abrams, as well as Kirkpatrick, and in another feature, Thatcher, all, unfortunately for the squeamish, through the magic of photomontage, nude – it would be difficult to argue that the nudity of Onassis functions strictly in relation to her sex, exploiting women's vulnerability as a class, or that its message can be reduced to a genericizing one like "you may be rich but you're just a cunt like any other cunt." Onassis's appearance on the pages of *Hustler* does raise questions of sex and gender insofar as we're willing to recognize what might be referred to as a sexual caste system, and the ways in which the imbrication of sex and caste make it difficult to come to any easy moral conclusions about *Hustler*'s violation of Onassis and her right to control and restrict how her body is portrayed. As recent pulp biographies inform us, the Bouvier sisters, Jacqueline and Princess Lee, were more or less bred to take up positions as consorts of rich and powerful men, to, one could put it bluntly, professionally deploy their femininity. This is not so entirely dissimilar from *Hustler*'s quotidian and consenting models, who while engaged in a similar activity are confined to very different social sites. Such social sites as those pictured in a regular *Hustler* feature, "The Beaver Hunt," a photo gallery of snapshots of non-professional models sent in by readers.[14] Posed in paneled rec rooms, on plaid Sears sofas or chenille bedspreads, amidst the kind of matching bedroom suites seen on late night easy credit furniture ads, nude or in polyester lingerie, they are identified as secretaries, waitresses, housewives, nurses, bank tellers, cosmetology students, cashiers, factory workers, sales women, data processors, nurse's aides.... Without generalizing from this insufficiency of data about any kind of *typical* class-based notions about the body and its appropriate display,[15] we can simply ask, where are the doctors, lawyers, corporate execs, and college professors? Or moving up the hierarchy, where are the socialites, the jet-setters, the wives of the chairmen of the board? Absent because of their fervent feminism? Or merely because they've struck a better deal? Simply placing the snapshots of Onassis in the place of the cashier, the secretary, the waitress, violates the rigid social distinctions of place and hardened spatial boundaries (boundaries most often purchased precisely as protection from the hordes) intrinsic to class hierarchy. These are precisely the distinctions that would make us code differently the deployment of femininity that achieves marriage to a billionaire shipping magnate from those that land you a spot in this month's Beaver Hunt. These political implications of the Onassis photospread indicate, I believe, the necessity of a more nuanced theory of misogyny than those currently in circulation. If any symbolic exposure or violation of *any* woman's body is automatically aggregated to the transhistorical misogyny machine that is the male imagination, it overlooks the fact that *all* women, simply by virtue of being women, are not necessarily political allies, that women can both symbolize and exercise class power and privilege, not to mention oppressive political power.

Feminist anti-pornography arguments, attempting to reify the feminine as an a priori privileged vantage point against pornographic male desires work on two fronts: apotropaic against the reality of male violence they simultaneously work to construct a singular version of (a politically correct) femininity against other "unreconstructed" versions. Their reification of femininity defends against any position that might suggest that femininity is not an inherent virtue, an inborn condition, or in itself a moral position from which to speak – positions such as those held by pro-sex feminists, psychoanalytic theory, and the discourse of pornography itself. But among the myraid theoretical problems which the reification of femininity gives rise to,[16] there are the contradictions of utilizing class disgust as a vehicle of the truly feminine. A theory of representation that automatically conflates bodily representations with real women's bodies, and symbolic or staged sex or violence as equivalent to real sex or violence, clearly acts to restrict political expression and narrow the forms of political struggle by ignoring differences between women – and the class nature of feminist reformism. The fact that real violence against women is so pervasive as to be almost unlocalizable may lead us to want to localize it within something so easily at hand as representation; but the political consequences for feminism – to reduce it to another variety of bourgeois reformism – make this not a sufficient tactic.

However, having said this, I must add that *Hustler* is certainly not politically unproblematic. If *Hustler* is counter-hegemonic in its refusal of bourgeois proprieties, its transgressiveness has real limits. It is often only incoherent and banal where it means to be alarming and confrontational. Its banality can be seen in its politics of race, an area where its refusal of polite speech has little countercultural force. *Hustler* has been frequently accused of racism, but *Hustler* basically just wants to offend – anyone, of any race, any ethnic group. Not content merely to offend the right, it makes doubly sure to offend liberal and left sensibilities too, not content merely to taunt whites, it hectors blacks. Its favored tactic in regard to race is to simply reproduce the stupidest stereotype it can think of – the subject of any *Hustler* cartoon featuring blacks will invariably be huge sexual organs which every women lusts after, or alternately, black watermelon-eating lawbreakers. *Hustler*'s letter columns carry out a raging debate on the subject of race, with black readers writing both that they find *Hustler*'s irreverence funny or resent its stereotypes, whites both applauding and protesting. It should also be noted that in the area of ugly stereotypes *Hustler* is hardly alone these days. The most explicitly political forms of popular culture recently are ones which also refuse to have proper representations – as any number of examples from the world of rap, which has also been widely accused of misogyny, as well as anti-Semitism, would attest. What this seems to imply is that there is no guarantee that counter-hegemonic or even specifically anti-bourgeois cultural forms are necessarily also going to be progressive. And as one of the suppositions in recent American cultural studies seems to have been that there is something hopeful to find in popular culture this might demand some rethinking.[17] *Hustler* is against government, against authority, against the bourgeoisie, diffident on male power – but its anti-liberalism, anti-feminism, anti-communism, and anti-progressivism leave little space for envisioning any alternative kind of political organization.

Hustler does powerfully articulate class resentment, and to the extent that anti-porn feminism lapses into bourgeois reformism, and that we devote ourselves to sanitizing representation, we are legitimately a target of that resentment. Leninism is on the wane around the world. The model of a vanguard party who will lead the rest of us to true consciousness holds little appeal these days. The policing of popular representation seems like only a path to more domination, and I despair for the future of a feminist politics that seems dedicated to following other vanguard parties into dogma and domination.

Acknowledgments

I'd like to thank Lauren Berlant for her extensive and exhaustive aid and comfort on this paper, and Lynn Spigel for many helpful suggestions.

Notes

1 For an interesting and far more extensive analysis of the politics of *Not a Love Story* see B. Ruby Rich (1986), "Anti-Porn: Soft Issue, Hard World" in *Films For Women*, ed. Charlotte Brunsdon, pp. 31–43.

2 Several writers who have visited the *Hustler* offices testify that to their surprise these letters *are* sent by actual readers, and *Hustler* receives well over 1000 letters a month. As to whether this particular letter is genuine in its authorship I have no way of knowing, but I'm happy enough to simply consider it as part of the overall discourse of *Hustler*.

3 Central anti-anti-porn texts are *Pleasure and Danger*, ed. Carole S. Vance (1984); *Caught Looking: Feminism, Pornography and Censorship*, ed. Kate Ellis, et al. (1988); *Powers of Desire: The Politics of Sexuality*, ed. Ann Snitow, Christine Stansell, and Sharon Thompson (1983), especially section VI on "Current Controversies." Also see Linda Williams (1989), *Hard Core: Power, Pleasure and the Frenzy of the Visible*, and Andrew Ross (1989b), "The Popularity of Pornography" in *No Respect: Intellectuals and Popular Culture* (1989), pp. 171–208 for a thorough summation of anti-pornography arguments.

4 This corresponds to Linda Williams's analysis of pornography as a "machine of the visible" devoted to intensifying the visibility of all aspects of sexuality, but most particularly, to conducting detailed investigations of female bodies. Williams (1989), pp. 34–57.

5 *Newsweek* (February 16, 1976), p. 69.

6 And there are ongoing attempts to regulate this sort of imagery. In the current NEA controversies, a Republican representative plans to introduce amendments that would prohibit funding of art that depicts aborted fetuses, the *New York Times* reports (October 10, 1990, p. B6). This would seem to be something of a shortsighted strategy for anti-abortion forces, as the aborted fetus has been the favored incendiary image of anti-abortion forces, including anti-abortion artists. See Laura Kipnis (1986), "Refunctioning Reconsidered: Toward a Left Popular Culture," *High Culture/Low Theory*, ed. Colin MacCabe, pp. 29–31.

7 Of course, the counter-argument could be made that such a cartoon really indicates the murderous male desire to see a woman mutilated, and that the cartoon thus stands in for the actual male desire to do violence to women. This was, of course, a widespread interpretation of the infamous *Hustler* "woman in the meat grinder" cover, about which more later. This sort of interpretation would hinge on essentializing the male imagination and male sexuality as, a priori, violent and murderous, and on a fairly literal view of humor and representation, one that envisions a straight leap from the image to the social practice rather than the series of mediations between the two I'm describing here.

8 Freud's observations on jokes, particularly on obscene humor, might be extended to the entirety of *Hustler* as so much of its discourse, even aside from its cartoons and humor, is couched in the joke form.

9 For an interesting deconstruction of the essentialist/anti-essentialism debate see Diana Fuss (1989a), *Essentially Speaking: Feminism, Nature and Difference*.

10 By violence here I mean specifically violence to subjectivity. On the issue of representations of actual physical violence to women's bodies that is represented as non-consensual – as

opposed to the sort of tame consensual S/M occasionally found in *Hustler* – my view is that this sort of representation should be analyzed as a subgenre of mainstream violent imagery, not only in relation to pornography. I find the continual conflation of sexual pornography and violence a deliberate roadblock to thinking through issues of porn – only abetted by a theorist like Andrea Dworkin for whom *all* heterosexuality is violence. The vast majority of porn represents sex, not physical violence, and while sexuality generally undoubtedly contains elements of aggression and violence, it's important to make these distinctions.

11 The passage in the ellipsis reads "For example, there are beliefs that each sex is a danger to the other through contact with sexual fluids." Compare Douglas to this passage by Andrea Dworkin, "... in literary pornography, to ejaculate is to *pollute* the woman" [her emphasis]. Dworkin goes on to discuss, in a lengthy excursus on semen, the collaboration of women-hating women's magazines, which "sometimes recommend spreading semen on the face to enhance the complexion" and pornography, where ejaculation often occurs on the woman's body or face [see Linda Williams, pp. 93–119, on another reading of the "money shot"], to accept semen and eroticize it. Her point seems to be that men prefer that semen be a violation of the woman by the man, as the only way they can get sexual pleasure is through violation. Thus semen is "driven into [the woman] to dirty her or make her more dirty or make her dirty by him." But at the same time semen has to be eroticized to get the woman to comply in her own violation. Andrea Dworkin (1987), p. 187. In any case, that Dworkin sees contact with male "sexual fluids" as harmful to women seems clear, as does the relation of this pollution (Dworkin's word) danger to Douglas's analysis.

12 *Hustler*'s advertising consists almost entirely of ads for sex toys, sex aids, porn movies, and phone sex services, as the automobile makers, liquor companies and manufacturers of other upscale items that comprise the financial backbone of *Playboy* and *Penthouse* refuse to hawk their wares in the pages of *Hustler*. In order to survive financially, *Hustler* began, among other enterprises, a successful and extensive magazine distribution company which distributes, among other periodicals, the *New York Review of Books*.

13 The story of the cover was related by Paul Krassner (1984) who worked for *Hustler* in 1978. Recall also that this cover was instrumental in the founding the following year of Women Against Pornography. The meat grinder joke seems to encapsulate many of the aforementioned issues of class, humor, vulgarity, and gender.

14 Recently *Hustler*, after yet another legal entanglement, began threatening in its model release form to prosecute anyone who sent in a photo without the model's release. They now demand photocopies of two forms of ID for both age and identity purposes; they also stopped paying the photographer and began paying only the model (currently $250 and the promise of consideration for higher paying photospreads).

15 Throughout this essay, my intent has not been to associate a particular class with particular or typical standards of the body, but rather to discuss how *Hustler* opposes hegemonic, historically bourgeois, conceptions of the body. Whether the *Hustler* bodily idiom represents a particular class or class fraction is not readily ascertainable without extensive audience studies of the sort difficult to carry out with a privatized form like porn magazines. The demographics that are available aren't current (because the magazine doesn't subsist on advertising, its demographics aren't made public, and *Hustler* is notoriously unwilling to release even circulation figures). The only readership demographics I've been able to find were published in *Mother Jones* magazine in 1976, and were made available to them because publisher Larry Flynt desired, for some reason, to add *Mother Jones* to his distribution roster. Jeffrey Klein (1978) writes: "Originally it was thought that *Hustler* appealed to a blue collar audience yet... demographics indicate that except for their gender (85 percent male), *Hustler* readers can't be so easily categorized. About 40 percent attended college; 23 percent are professionals; 59 percent have household incomes of $15,000 or more a year [about $29,000 in 1989 dollars], which is above the national

mean, given the median reader age of 30." His analysis of these figures is: "Probably it's more accurate to say that *Hustler* appeals to what people would like to label a blue-collar urge, an urge most American men seem to share."

16 For an analysis of the structuring contradictions in the discourse of Catharine MacKinnon, who along with Dworkin, is the leading theorist of the anti-pornography movement, see William Beatty Warner (1989), "Treating Me Like an Object: Reading Catharine MacKinnon's Feminism."

17 For a critique of this tendency see Mike Budd, Robert M. Entman, and Clay Steinman (1990), "The Affirmative Character of U.S. Cultural Studies."

References

Bakhtin, M. (1984) *Rabelais and His World.* Bloomington: Indiana University Press.

Barker, Francis (1984) *The Tremulous Private Body.* New York: Methuen.

Budd, Mike, Robert Entman and Clay Steinman (1990) "The affirmative character of U.S. cultural studies." *Critical Studies in Mass Communication*, 7, pp. 169–84.

Davidoff, Leonore (1979) "Class and gender in Victorian England." *Feminist Studies*, 5.

Douglas, Mary (1966) *Purity and Danger: An Analysis of the Concepts of Pollution and Taboo.* London: Routledge.

Dworkin, Andrea (1987) *Intercourse.* New York: Macmillan.

Elias, Norbert (1978) *The History of Manners.* New York: Urizen Books.

Ellis, Kate et. al (eds.) (1988) *Caught Looking: Feminism, Pornography, and Censorship.* Seattle: The Real Comet Press.

Freud, S. (1963a) *Jokes and Their Relation to the Unconscious.* New York: Norton.

Fuss, Diana (1989a) *Essentially Speaking: Feminism, Nature and Difference.* New York: Routledge.

Kipnis, Laura (1986) "Refunctioning reconsidered: Toward a left popular culture." In C. MacCabe (ed.) *High Culture/Low Theory.* New York: St. Martin's Press, pp. 29–31.

Klein, Jeffrey (1978) "Born against porn." *Mother Jones*, Feb./Mar., p. 18.

Krassner, Paul (1984) "Is this the real message of pornography?" *Harpers*, Nov., p. 35.

Laplanche, J. and J. B. Pontalis (1973) *The Language of Psychoanalysis.* New York: Norton.

Rich, B. Ruby (1986) "Anti-porn: Soft issue, hard world." In C. Brunsdon (ed.) *Films for Women.* London: BFI, pp. 31–43.

Ross, A. (1989a) *No Respect: Intellectuals and Popular Culture.* London: Routledge.

Ross, A. (1989b) "The popularity of pornography." In A. Ross (1989a), pp. 171–208.

Rubin, Gayle (1984) "Thinking sex: Notes for a radical theory of the politics of sexuality." In C. Vance (ed.) (1984), pp. 267–319.

Snitow, Ann, Christine Stansell and Sharon Thompson (eds.) (1983) *Powers of Desire: The Politics of Sexuality.* New York: Monthly Review Press.

Stallybrass, Peter and Allon White (1986) *The Politics and Poetics of Transgression.* Ithaca: Cornell University Press.

Vance, Carole (ed.) (1984) *Pleasure and Danger.* Boston: Routledge.

Warner, William (1989) "Treating me like an object: Reading Catharine MacKinnon's Feminism." In L. Kauffman (ed.) *Feminism and Institutions: Dialogues on Feminist Theory.* Cambridge: Basil Blackwell.

Williams, L. (1989) *Hard Core: Power, Pleasure and the Frenzy of the Visible*, Berkeley: University of California Press.

12 "Hang Up My Rock and Roll Shoes": The Cultural Production of Rock and Roll

Harris Friedberg

My title comes from a song by Chuck Willis recorded on Atlantic, the premier independent rhythm and blues label out of New York. Written by Willis and released in April of 1958, it is an example of the important but overlooked rock and roll genre, an anthem not so much of defiance as annoyance, that treats the predictable skirmishes over dating or chores within the family that occur when one member is an adolescent. The genre includes songs like Eddie Cochran's "Summertime Blues" or the Coasters' "Yakety Yak," with their classic refrains: "There ain't no cure for the summertime blues" and "Yakety yak. Don't talk back." And its laureate is certainly Chuck Berry, author of such plaints as "Too Much Monkey Business," "School Days," and my favorite, "Almost Grown."

But Chuck Willis's song is different. It locates the rift over rock and roll itself and describes how rock and roll became the field on which teens and parents battled. In the first verse and chorus, the singer promises his mother, who doesn't like rock and roll, "Yes, I will do my homework, clean the yard every day, Yes, I will wipe those dishes, I'll do anything you say" (Willis 1958), just to keep from hanging up his rock and roll shoes. Rather than give up that ecstatic release, this teen plea bargains away his resistance to work, all to save his precious rock and roll.

In "Hang Up My Rock and Roll Shoes," rock and roll becomes the very icon of teen freedom and teen constraint. It represents that very bliss, that literally ecstatic moment when, by strapping on his dancing shoes, like Bobby Darin in "Splish Splash," the teen escapes adult servitude into pure joy. In all of these songs the singer speaks as a teen, articulating teen frustrations out of teen experience; he testifies. But except for Cochran, then twenty, none was even a recent teen. Willis himself was born in Atlanta in 1928. After a string of rhythm-and- blues hits on Okeh, Columbia's "race" label, his publicists dubbed him "The Sheik of the Shake," and he started appearing garbed in one of a collection of turbans that eventually numbered fifty-four. But his hits on Okeh dried up, and in 1956 he signed with Atlantic, just coming into its own as the top independent rhythm-and-blues label. For his third Atlantic date Willis, along with Atlantic's crack producer, Jerry Wexler, and band leader and arranger, Jesse Stone, took an old folk blues recorded by Malisa "Ma" Rainey, "C. C. Rider," retooled the melody, added a great, even tasteful, tenor solo by Gene "Daddy G" Barge, and rode it to number 12 on the pop charts and number three, rhythm-and-blues. Halfway

This chapter was specifically commissioned for this volume.

between a slow song – called a "grind," which, like "rock" and "roll" and even "rider" itself, was slang for sex – and a fast song – called a "workout" – the song went ballistic when teens discovered that they could do the stroll to it, a dance invented by black teens in 1952 to dance to Lloyd Price's "Lawdy Miss Clawdy." "The Sheik of the Shake" promptly became "the King of the Stroll," although thankfully he kept the turbans. "Hang Up My Rock and Roll Shoes" was cut on Valentine's Day, 1958, and released as the B side of a grind called "What Am I Living For?" A double-sided hit, the record rocketed up the pop charts to number nine, but by that time Willis, two months past his thirtieth birthday, was dead, of peritonitis from a burst appendix.

I tell Willis's story not just out of affection for his music – had he lived he might have become as big as Chuck Berry, Ray Charles, or Sam Cooke, the other black men who had also crossed over from rhythm and blues to the white pop charts – but because his story poses a central question about the culture industry and pop culture in particular: who produces it? Where does it come from? Is it imposed from above by a monolithic culture industry ramming a dominant ideology down our throats or is it an authentic voice of the people resisting hegemony? Does it, in the debased coinage of politics, trickle down or bubble up? The question may be particularly interesting when asked about rock and roll, an institution that is pushing forty-five and has significantly scaled back its plan of revolution and world dominion since it ceased to be a teenager itself.

In this essay I'll be asking, where does rock and roll come from, and who, specifically, sings or speaks in rock and roll? In "Hang Up My Rock and Roll Shoes" the singer speaks self-consciously of representing a generation: "The kids are rock and rollin' from eight to twenty-five," Willis sings. He purports to speak for teenagers as a teenager, to articulate their complaints and to voice their grievances with a world of power and authority that demeans them. How does rock and roll acquire the authority to speak for teens, a tribe whose emergence into popular consciousness, whose social construction, is roughly contemporaneous with rock and roll itself? In that construction does rock and roll function as rallying cry or background music, aural wallpaper? Is rock and roll the authentic voice of teen anguish and teen rage or is it itself mere ventriloquism, a trick of throwing the voice by which an older and more powerful interest, which we might loosely call ideology, speaks? Does rock and roll speak *for* teens, or merely *to* them?

In posing the question, I look at the years in which rock and roll begins. And I'll be looking simultaneously both at the production and consumption of rock and roll during that period. In recent years it has become fashionable to argue that neither "supply," "the arrival of creative individuals" like Elvis, nor "demand," a "changing audience preference," but changes in the commercial culture industry account for the emergence of rock and roll:

[B]ecause of its oligopolistic control of the production, distribution and marketing of new music, [it] was able to thwart the marketing of alternative styles. Then with the transfer of network radio programming to television, radio turned to playing records as the cheapest effective form of programming. The arrival of cheap transistor radios and the development of the Top Forty radio-as-jukebox format meant that a much larger number and far wider range of music was exposed to the audience. Using the new durable 45 rpm records, and taking advantage of the developing network of

independent record distributors, numerous independent record companies experimented with a wide range of new sounds in an effort to tap the unsatiated market demand.
In a matter of two dozen months between late 1954 and early 1957 rock was forged in
this cauldron of entrepreneurial creativity.   *(Peterson, 1990, pp. 113–14)*

The problems with this account, though, are many. For one thing, these changes were
in motion long before the explosion of rock and roll. The broadcasting and record
industries were clearly trying to expand and differentiate their markets long before
the mid-1950s; the 45 rpm "single" and the cheap plastic record player retailing for
$12.95, for example, date from 1948 (Ennis, 1992, pp. 132–5). The cheap transistor
radio, however, only arrived in the waning years of the 1950s (Schiffer, 1991, pp.
181–2). Disc jockeys started to appear in the 1930s; by the 1940s many, like Arthur
Godfrey and Henry Morgan, were household names (Ennis, 1992, pp. 131–60). The
growth of the small independent radio station without access to expensive network
programming occurred between 1945 and 1949, when the number of radio stations
doubled. By 1948 these poorly capitalized small indies outnumbered the network
affiliates and the large indies combined; thereafter their growth slowed (Ennis, 1992,
p. 136). Clearly disc jockeys had been playing records on the radio for years before
the advent of rock and roll.

Similarly, small independent record companies had been experimenting with new
kinds of music for at least as long. The indie record labels began forming in the early-
to mid-1940s: Savoy in 1942; Apollo in 1943; King, 1944; Modern/Aladdin, 1945;
Specialty, 1946; Atlantic and Aristocrat/Chess, 1947; Dot, Peacock, Capitol, and
Imperial, 1949. By 1952 Memphis alone had three: Duke, Meteor, and Sun. None of
them had any real ethnic or aesthetic identity; they all released whatever they
thought would sell. Aladdin, Specialty, Mercury, Chess, Apollo, and Sun all released
hillbilly records as well as "race" records. King Records had both Wynonie Harris,
"Mr. Blues," and Grampa Jones, staple of the Opry; Atlantic, Bill Haley and the
Saddlemen as well as Big Joe Turner (Tosches, 1991, p. 6).

The major record labels *did* dominate country and western: less than five per cent
of the best-selling country records from 1946 to 1953 were released by indie labels,
but all but one were on indie labels, like King, that also had strong rhythm-and-blues
rosters (Ennis, 1992, p. 171). On the other hand, only 8 per cent of the best-selling
rhythm-and-blues records from 1949 and 1953 were from major labels. By 1949
fewer than ten indies dominated the rhythm-and-blues field, and almost two-thirds
of the rhythm-and-blues chart toppers came from the seven indies – Aladdin, Atlantic, Chess, King, Modern, Savoy, and Specialty – capable of finding talent and selling
records coast to coast. The explosion of hits from mom-and-pop labels is really a
consequence of the coming of rock and roll; it begins to gather steam in 1956 and
1957, with labels like Josie, Herald, Flip, Ace, Keen, Cadence, and Coral challenging
both the majors and the established indies, but it is really only in 1958 that, joined by
Junior, Ember, Falcon, Jamie, Dore, Del-Fi, Fury, Gone, End, Ebb, Challenge, Apt,
Argo, Class, Laurie, Cameo and others, they threaten to crowd the major and
established indie labels off the charts (Gillet, 1983, pp. 67–118).

At best, then, changes in the music industry only set the stage for the advent of
rock and roll; they cannot account for the music that was actually played on the new
record players and transistors. And the evidence suggests that rock and roll itself

changed the industry. For one thing, record sales were essentially flat from 1946 to 1954, although the sale of phonographs grew steadily. But starting in 1954, record sales took off, doubling by 1956, the very years in which the first black rock and roll greats – Chuck Berry, Little Richard, Fats Domino – the black vocal groups – the Chords, the Penguins, the Crows, the Five Satins, Frankie Lymon and the Teenagers – and the white rockabilly "cats" – Bill Haley, Carl Perkins, Jerry Lee Lewis, and Elvis – cracked the pop charts. Suddenly a new audience wanted to buy records, lots of records, of a new kind of music.

And the music was new. Rock and roll was not waiting around to be discovered; it did not so much emerge full grown as it was assembled, cobbled up. It appeared when black rhythm and bluesmen and white purveyors of country boogie began to mingle on the jukeboxes and airwaves. But what emerged from this largely virtual encounter was neither black nor white, blues nor country.

According to Muddy Waters, perhaps the greatest of the Mississippi Delta bluesmen to make the migration to Chicago, "the blues had a baby and they called it rock and roll." But if rock and roll was born of the blues it was sired by country and western, the music white people made out of Appalachian folk music and elements of boogie-woogie and swing. Rock and roll was neither, although it contained elements of both. And when blues and country were brought together – if only on the radio – and marketed to predominantly white teenagers, blues and country were ideologically processed and refracted in the vain hope of winning the parental approval that Chuck Willis's teen narrator bargains for in "Hang Up My Rock and Roll Shoes."

First, what happened to rhythm and blues as it turned into rock and roll? Let me demonstrate by comparing two songs, Big Joe Turner's 1952 rhythm-and-blues hit, "Sweet Sixteen," and Chuck Berry's rock-and-roll anthem, "Sweet Little Sixteen," cut five years later. Born in Kansas City in 1911, Turner was singing on the streets and hanging out at the Backbiters' Club in his home town when he joined up with boogie-woogie pianist Pete Johnson in 1929. Turner worked clubs in the Midwest with Johnson, never getting far from Kansas City until he electrified the audience at John Hammond's "Spirituals to Swing" concert at Carnegie Hall on Christmas Eve, 1938, with a shouting style that won him recognition as "Boss of the Blues" and perhaps the loudest singer of all time (Tosches, 1991, p. 23). "I've been called a lot of things in my life," Turner has said, "Blues shouter, Jumpin' Joe, Howlin' Joe Turner, Barkin' Joe Turner, 'cause my voice is so loud. I used to sing without a mike in the old days; you had to have a strong voice to get over to the people, they'd drown out the music" (Dawson and Propes, 1992, p. 119). Turner credited himself with inventing the style of blues shouting: "Everybody was singin' slow blues when I was young and I thought I'd put a beat to it and sing it up-tempo. Pete Johnson and I . . . got pretty good at it." With Johnson Turner cut the hits "Roll 'Em Pete" and "Cherry Red" and began a five-year engagement with pianists Albert Ammons and Meade "Lux" Lewis at New York's Café Society that started the boogie-woogie craze. By the time Atlantic Records impresario Ahmet Ertegun caught up with Turner in 1951, though, the hits had stopped, and Turner was reduced to subbing for a sick Jimmy Rushing with Count Basie at the Apollo; poorly rehearsed, he flubbed the chart, coming in at the wrong place and finishing before the band. His first session for Atlantic, in front of a band recruited from Lionel Hampton's and led by Harry Van "Piano Man" Walls, yielded "Chains of Love," a slow twelve-bar blues with music by Walls and words by the mysterious Nugetre (Ertegun spelled backwards). Released in the new 45 rpm format in April, 1951, it rocketed to number 2 on Billboard's newly renamed "Rhythm and Blues" chart and became the first record cut by a black vocalist for the "race" market to cross over to the white Pop charts – it reached number thirty – since Louis Jordan's party record, "Saturday Night Fish Fry" of 1949.

Turner was pushing forty from the wrong direction in February of 1952, when Atlantic released "Sweet Sixteen"; it went to number three on the rhythm and blues charts, although it failed to crack the pop charts. A mid-tempo eight-bar blues, slower than the up-tempo tunes Turner specialized in when he roared out of Kansas City, it featured classic rhythm and blues instrumentation: a rhythm section made up of a pianist (Harry Van Walls again) playing a bass phrase in double time, a string bass played on the beats, and a snare drums stressing the four beat, and riffing horns (again from the Lionel Hampton band) repeating the same rhythmic phrases in unison. The inventive fills – instrumental responses to the vocalist's calls – were played by piano, not guitars, and Walls's development in his fills from two-fisted bass licks – short phrases in a distinctive style – to right-handed (and sometimes one-fingered) treble ones was a real departure from long-time partner Pete Johnson's boogie-woogie rhythmic attack. Turner's singing style, though, had not changed. Always a shouter, he made little use of dynamics, maintaining the same level of intensity and loudness throughout: he slurred and growled the lyrics with the same rough, country intonation of the Kansas City blues shouter of the nineteen-thirties.

Despite their reference to Korea, the lyrics, too, belonged to an earlier time. They lament the singer's imminent loss of his lover, only sixteen-years old when they met, who has renounced parental authority and now threatens to run away from the singer, too. She is no innocent but an inconstant woman with knowledge and sexual experience well beyond her years. This the singer merely accepts; her fault is not her sexuality, which the singer only cites, but her perverse refusal to submit to his will: "You would not do anything I asked you to/You run away from home, baby, now you gonna run away from me, too" (Nugetre, 1952). The song's title is ironic; there's nothing sweet about this woman except for her sexuality, but the singer never condemns her for her sexual experience – she is no devil (like the woman in Turner's other big hit, "Shake, Rattle and Roll," who is "the devil in nylon hose") – and challenges neither her reasons for leaving him nor her home.

Chuck Berry's "Sweet Little Sixteen" shows how rock and roll differs from rhythm and blues. Berry was one of rock's founding fathers, the first singer-songwriter-guitarist and the first to successfully merge rhythm and blues with country and western, and in many ways he defined early rock and roll. In 1955, when country-blues great Muddy Waters hauled him into Leonard Chess's office in Chicago, Berry was a few months shy of thirty, a mostly black and part Native American, country-and-western singing, blues-guitar playing cosmetician from East St. Louis who had done three years for armed robbery. His first record, "Maybellene," named for the cosmetics, was "a western tune," his piano player Johnny Johnson recalled (Dawson and Propes, 1992, p. 183). Based on an old country hit, "Ida Red," recorded by fiddler Bob Wills and the Texas Playboys, the progenitors of western swing, and then by hot-licks practitioner Lloyd "Cowboy" Copas, who died in the plane crash that killed country singer Patsy Cline, "Maybellene" put a rechristened Ida Red in the front seat of a speeding Cadillac, her spurned lover chasing her in his V-8 Ford. Thus

Berry managed to cash in as well on the fad for hot rod songs started by Arkie Shibley and His Mountain Dew Boys, whose country boogie tune, "Hot Rod Race," went to number five on the country charts in 1950. Hot rods were a real draw for better-off white teens, but Berry was the first black performer to show any interest in them.

"Maybellene" was the first pop hit – it stayed at number 1 on the rhythm and blues charts for eleven weeks and hit number 5 on the pop charts – by a black singer that systematically mixed country with rhythm and blues. Berry took the chords of his songs from the blues. He showcased his guitar playing, borrowed the slurs and bent notes (notes flatted by "bending" or pushing on the strings with the left hand) of urban-blues master T-Bone Walker, and added the stop-time of his mentor Muddy Waters to shuffle rhythms. But he then threw in the sturdy, steady beat of country boogie – a guitar style that owes as much to Western Swing like Bill Haley's as to urban blues. He added a brighter, faster, double-stringed twang more reminiscent of country guitar to his blues licks. He also dropped the microtones, the vocal slurs, swoops, and howls, of a Muddy Waters. "When I played hillbilly songs," Berry recounted in his autobiography, "I stressed my diction so that it was harder and whiter" (Berry, 1987, p. 90–1).

Berry also envisioned a different audience from that of his rhythm and blues peers. "I was trying to shoot for the entire population instead of, shall we say, the 'neighborhood,'" he explained in the documentary, "Hail, Hail, Rock and Roll" (1987). "Why can't I . . . play good music for the white people and sell as well there as I could in the neighborhood. That's what I shot for, writing 'School Days'." Starting in 1956 with "School Days," and then in a series of pop hits ending only with a racially-motivated conviction for transporting a minor across state lines in 1959, Berry took on the persona of the teens who were buying his records, crafting his lyrics to echo their themes and frustrations.

"Sweet Little Sixteen" was his fourth top-ten hit. A sixteen-bar blues, the song opens with a tribal anthem detailing the conquests made by rock and roll itself. All over the country teens rock to the same backbeat, united into a single tribe defined not by region or ethnicity but by age. This world is a male one. Berry's epic catalogue ends not with rock and roll's triumph but with male desire: the "cats," whites who emulated the styles of blacks, who desire to "dance" – the word was already a euphemism in Etta James's "Dance with Me, Henry" – with her. But in the first verse we see that Sweet Little Sixteen herself is blissfully ignorant of the male desire she arouses. She only lusts after autographs, the visible signs of her communion with the singers whose records she collects. She herself embodies rock and roll's largest market, the junior and senior high school girls who bought most of the $75 million dollars' worth of 45s sold in 1957. She inhabits an entirely different world, the middle-class world of "Father Knows Best," where girls still listen to their mommies and obey their daddies. This sweet sixteen is "little" – infantilized, submissive, white and obedient.

But in the last verse the veil drops, and Berry reveals glimpses of a very different world, the "grown up blues." Now Sweet Little Sixteen courts the male gaze, offers herself up as a sexualized object of desire in tight dresses, lipstick, and high-heeled shoes. This woman threatens the rule of parental authority to govern and restrain her sexuality. But at this point Berry, having broached the problem of the teen's troubled passage from child to woman, aligns himself with the authority of the father: her one night of sexual display over, "she'll have to change her trend,/And be sweet sixteen and back in class again" (Berry 1958). This brief flirtation with sexuality is contained; the woman returns to become the little girl all over again.

To become rock and roll, then, rhythm and blues censored itself, purging itself of its frank acknowledgement of sexuality and its power. This was the strategy of most of Chuck Berry's avowedly teen songs. In "School Days" Berry speaks to teens in the second person: delivered from the bondage of school, the teens surge into the juke joint: "All day long you've been wanting to dance" (Berry 1957). The song is an exercise in empathy; the singer shares the frustration of the teen. In "Almost Grown" the singer becomes a teen, asking only to be left alone. Here instead of speaking with the parental voice, Berry speaks for the teen, answering a wave of accusations parents hurl at teens: he's never been "in dutch," his grades are decent, he doesn't "browse around" or hang out with gangs. He pays for his car with a "little job" and he and his girlfriend drive around in his car instead of parking. And the song ends with the speaker having made the difficult transit to adulthood, "married and settled down." Berry's songs are not anthems of defiance, the barbarous yawps of a generation of rebels and delinquents, but comedies of accommodation crafted by a black man passing for a white teen.

Many other performers make the same accommodation when they turn to rock and roll, not so much restraining sexuality as exculpating that other demon of nineteen-fifties' youth, the rebel without a cause. Frankie Lymon and the Teenagers, a New York doo-wop group featuring both blacks and Puerto Ricans, followed their transcendent hit, "Why Do Fools Fall in Love?" with "(NO, NO, NO) I'm Not a Juvenile Delinquent." And the Coasters speak for all good teens when they rat on "Charlie Brown:" "That's him. Who, me? Yeah, you." Purporting to speak for teens, songs like these reflect an anxiety that rock and roll must voice parental ideology to justify teens to their parents.

The same uncertainty dogged that part of rock and roll that emerged out of country music. Take the Everly Brothers, for example. Teens themselves – Don was eighteen and Phil, sixteen when they cut their first records – they had grown up in Mullenberg County, Kentucky, home of the guitar-picking style later named for Merle Travis, singing country music in pure Appalachian close harmony on their parents' radio show, "The Little Donnie Show," broadcast on KMA in Shenandoah, Iowa. Recommended by country picker Chet Atkins, a friend of their father, they cut some sides for Columbia in 1955 that went nowhere. Signed to Cadence Records by its impresario, Archie Bleyer, former music director for a tart-tongued former disc jockey and ukulele-player named Arthur Godfrey, they were turned over to song writers Boudleaux and Felice Bryant, who had become the first professional country-and-western songwriters when they set up shop in Nashville in 1950 (Ward, 1986, pp. 63, 145). Their second release with the Bryants was "Wake Up, Little Susie." (You might note the ideological function of "little" in this song as well as "Sweet Little Sixteen.")

"Wake Up, Little Susie" is constructed around the familiar I–IV–V chord progression of the blues, but the Everlys sing in the traditional close harmony of the Appalachian hills, and the story they tell – of teen "steadies" who have goofed up again by nodding off at the drive-in and missing her curfew – applies as much to

Beverly Hills. Their male teen narrator is horrified at the prospect not only of facing Little Susie's ma and pa but, more tellingly, the couples' peers: "What are we going to tell our friends when they go 'Ooh, la la'," he asks (Bryant and Bryant, 1957).

"Wake Up, Little Susie" imagines a perfect world in which teens and their parents agree on the contractual limits of dating. The dating system appeared in the 1920s among middle-class kids. It replaced the system of calling on, in which the boy called upon and was entertained by the girl in her parents' house and under their watchful eye, with the system of going out, a system organized and run by teens themselves, in which teens leave the girl's house and parents' authority to go somewhere, often in cars, where they are alone and unchaperoned. Once parents lost the ability to control teen courtship under their roof, they campaigned to exert as much control over dating, and the sexual opportunities dating offers. They organized dances, record "hops" in the 1950s, where they bargained for their position as chaperones by offering to pay for and play the kind of music teens liked. But they were never able to gain complete control over the date outside of the house or dance.

In many ways dating is a prelude to, a simulacrum of, patriarchal marriage, a system in which men control and exchange the sexuality of women in order to provide themselves with a pure blood line, purchasing virginal wives to perpetuate their lineages. Dating, in a sense, is a contract that anticipates the marriage contract; in both the male exchanges money for sexual intimacy with females. Just as the male pays for a single date, he receives a temporary sexual intimacy that need not be consummated, even with a kiss, but that is sexual (Bailey, 1988, p. 22).

Parents quickly realized the economic basis of dating and struggled to limit the amount of time and money spent on dates. The more the boy spent, the more sexual intimacy he could argue he had purchased; the longer and later the couple stayed out, the more likely, their parents reasoned, that they would go "all the way." Parents especially feared cars and movies; joined, as in drive-ins, they were sexual dynamite. Girls who parked in cars risked their reputations; reputation is a gauge of economic worth in the economy of dating. A girl had a good reputation when she was considered to be a virgin, undefiled and therefore able to provide a man with children that were entirely his own. During the 1940s, '50s, and '60s parents fought to control their daughters' reputations. In "Are You Popular?," a short film made for high schools by Coronet Films in 1947, for example, an authoritative patriarchal voiceover intones, "No. Girls who park in cars are not popular."

"Wake Up, Little Susie" makes sense only in this context. In this imagined world teens and their parents agree on the limits of dating; Susie and the singer have to answer not only to her mama and pa but also to their peers, who "Ooh, la la" in disapproval. Teens and parents alike agree to regulate sexuality, to police reputation, to define what it means to be popular.

What's fascinating about these attempts to accept and voice parental authority and restraint in rock and roll are how unsuccessful they were. Despite rock and roll's attempt to capitulate, its voicings of essentially parental and patriarchal ideologies, its willingness to barter good grades and hateful chores to keep its rock and roll shoes, its offer is never accepted. Parents and pundits see through its lip service. And all they have to do is to feel the beat. Even a song like "Susie" undoes its pious acceptance of the sanctity of reputation with its pulsing rhythmic drive, an open-tuning power-chording riff traditionally associated with the Delta blues tune,

"Highway 51." (Such cross-pollination was not uncommon. Sanford Clark's country-based hit, "The Fool," which went to number 7 on the pop charts in 1956, borrows its opening riff from Howling Wolf's "Smokestack Lightning," recorded the same year.) Whatever the ideology of the song text, the ideology of the beat is profoundly sexual.

Rock's white detractors and censors were quick to see that. Take, for example, Elvis's recording of "Hound Dog." The song, a mid-to slow-tempo twelve-bar blues, was originally written by two white teenagers immersed in black culture, Jerry Leiber and Mike Stoller, and recorded in 1952 by Willie Mae "Big Mama" Thornton, a three-hundred pound, black, lesbian blues shouter from Montgomery, fronting Johnny Otis's band. In black slang, a hound dog was a man who has outlived his sexual powers, and Big Mama Thornton's singer shooes him away with a dismissive double entendre: "You can wag your tail, but I ain't gone feed you no more."

Thorton growled the lyrics, and Otis's band backed her in a rough-hewn, already dated style. Louisiana guitarist Pete Lewis answered her vocals with guitar fills mixing single-stringed, quarter-note licks full of bent notes and slurred chords in T-Bone Walker's style but without Walker's fluency, and Otis played a strong backbeat on the shell of the drums underscored by hand claps. Singer and guitar lagged slightly behind the beat, and Thornton accompanied Lewis's guitar solo with growled encouragement – "listen to that old hound dog howl" – and howls. As the song ended, the singer and band erupted in more howls, barks, and yelps. Big Mama's "Hound Dog" sold half a million copies, topping the rhythm-and-blues charts for five weeks in 1953 and whelping four covers, inexplicably by male country singers.

Elvis's cover, released in September, 1956, was another story. His version is much faster than Big Mama Thornton's, and he sings in an urbane, polished style; for most of the record he is in tune, and he avoids the slurred microtones of Thornton's country-blues vocalizing. You can understand all the words. The production is more country than country blues. Whereas Thornton's record is essentially a duet between voice and guitar, the production on Elvis's is slicker. The rhythm section contains a bass playing riffs like Bill Haley's sax player's, and the drums provide a heavy backbeat under Elvis's vocals and jackhammer fills after each verse. The guitar fills are country-styled, with few bent notes, and the back-up vocals are by country gospel singers.

But most importantly Elvis's lyrics don't make any sense. Elvis's hound dog has been released from its meaning in black slang: gone is his phallic tail. It's hard to tell whether Elvis's hound dog is a literal dog that won't hunt – "you never caught a rabbit" – or a metaphoric one, perhaps a woman, who claims to be "high class" but can't perform some simple function – something that TV host and rock-and-roll detractor Steve Allen grasped when he put Elvis on his variety show in tails and made him sing "Hound Dog" to a live basset hound with improbably pendulous ears propped on a pedestal. And it's very possible that Elvis didn't understand the words either. He modeled his version of "Hound Dog" not on Thornton's but on a spoof of Thornton's recorded by a lounge act, Freddy Bell and the Bell Boys, whose act he had caught in Vegas (Dawson and Propes, 1992, pp. 117–18). But, of course, it doesn't matter. All that counts is the ferocity of Elvis's performance, its searing intensity, burned indelibly into parental consciousness when Elvis first performed "Hound Dog" on Milton Berle's TV show on June 5, 1956. Taking the band by surprise, Elvis tacked two half-tempo choruses onto the song, accentuating the beat with bumps and grinds that the New York *Herald-American*'s Jack O'Brien called "the weirdest and plainly planned suggestive animation short of an aborigine's mating dance"; WNEW disc jockey Jerry Marshall dubbed him "Pelvis Presley" (Ward, 1986, p. 121). They reacted not to the words but to the music, the speech of the body.

And what they heard there was the adoption of a rhythmic drive that they saw, incorrectly, as an expression of the hypersexuality of black men and women. Explicitly racist in the South, veiled in the North as a concern for public safety, rock and roll's white censors saw it as a reversion to a primitive savagery. In April, 1956, Asa Carter, leader of the North Alabama Citizen's Council, a feared bulwark against desegregation, denounced rock and roll as an attempt to force "Negro culture" on whites: "The obscenity and vulgarity of the rock and roll is obviously a means by which the white man and his children can be driven to the level of the nigger" (Schiffer, 1991, p. 179; Solt, 1995). To white supremacists like Carter, black sexuality – through miscegenation and racial degeneration, through congress with the primitive other – was a threat to civilization itself, and rock and roll was proof that America had failed – through animalistic sex – to maintain the social and personal restraints which were the very stuff of civilization. No amount of accommodation to parental ideology in the lyrics of rock and roll could convince the parents of 1950s' America into admitting rock and roll into their homes. And so a battle was joined to force American teens to hang up their rock and roll shoes.

References

Bailey, Beth L.: *From Front Porch to Back Seat: Courtship in Twentieth-Century America* (Baltimore and London: Johns Hopkins University Press, 1988).

Berry, Chuck: "Almost Grown" (Arc Music: BMI, 1959).

Berry, Chuck: *Chuck Berry, the Autobiography* (New York: Crown, 1987).

Berry, Chuck: "School Days" (Arc Music: BMI, 1957).

Berry, Chuck: "Sweet Little Sixteen" (Arc Music: BMI, 1958).

Bryant, Boudleaux and Felice, "Wake Up, Little Susie" (House of Bryant Publications: BMI, 1957).

Dawson, Jim and Propes, Steve: *What Was the First Rock'n' Roll Record?* (Boston and London: Faber and Faber, 1992).

Ennis, Philip H.: The Seventh Stream: *The Emergence of Rocknroll in American Popular Music* (Hanover and London: Wesleyan University Press/University Press of New England, 1992).

Gillett, Charlie: *The Sound of the City: The Rise of Rock and Roll*, revised edn. (New York: Pantheon, 1983).

"Hail, Hail, Rock and Roll!": Director Taylor Hackforth (Delilah Films, 1987).

Solt, Andrew: "The History of Rock 'n' Roll, 1: Rock 'n' Roll Explodes" (Time-Life, 1995).

Leiber, Jerry and Stoller, Mike: "Hound Dog" (Gladys Music/MCA Music: ASCAP, 1953).

Nugetre, A. [Ahmet Ertegun]: "Sweet Sixteen" (Hill and Range Music: BMI, 1952).

Peterson, Richard A.: "Why 1955? Explaining the advent of rock music," *Popular Music*, 9 (1990), 97–116.

Schiffer, Michael Brian: *The Portable Radio in American Life* (Tucson and London: University of Arizona Press, 1991).

Tosches, Nick: *Unsung Heroes of Rock'n' Roll: The Birth of Rock in the Wild Years before Elvis*, revised edn. (New York: Harmony, 1991).

Ward, Ed: *Rock of Ages: The Rolling Stone History of Rock & Roll* (New York: Summit Books, 1986).

Willis, Chuck: "Hang Up My Rock and Roll Shoes" (Tideland Music/Hill & Range Music: BMI, 1958).

13 Site Reading?: Globalization, Identity, and the Consumption of Place in Popular Music

Minelle Mahtani and Scott Salmon

> If someone were to ask me what it meant to be Canadian, I would sit them down in a big comfy chair with a Canadian brew in one hand and a hockey stick in the other, play a Hip CD and watch them experience one of the most intellectual and musically talented ensembles produced this side of the border. (*a fan of The Tragically Hip*)[1]

National identity is notoriously hard to define. It is at once an intensely unique and personal experience and, at the same time, a collective entity that is constantly being re-negotiated, contested, re-defined and re-imagined in relation to changing conditions. For the young Canadian quoted above, the experience of national identity is inextricably bound up with the consumption of the music of a particular local rock band, The Tragically Hip. As a multi-cultural society in an increasingly interconnected world, contemporary Canada is grappling with issues of identity and nationhood, striving to maintain an international identity while simultaneously attempting to reconcile major internal conflict over the very nature of that identity (Taylor, 1993). Perhaps better than anything else, popular music exemplifies this new post-colonial context and the conflicts within it, for the very malleability of music makes possible local appropriations and alterations, resulting in all kinds of syncretisms and hybridities. In the Canadian context, the music of The Tragically Hip has provided a vehicle for the expression and assertion of national identity among many of their fans. In this chapter we examine the music of the Hip as a site for the intersection of globalizing forces and local cultures.

Like many other fields, cultural studies has recently been infused with the discourse of globalization. Unfortunately, as elsewhere in the social sciences, the concept remains opaque, contested and subject to a variety of often competing interpretations. Typically, however, the globalization narrative refers to a process involving the transcending of national borders and the internationalization of the production and consumption of commodities (Walters, 1995). In the cultural realm attention has thus been focused on the processes of transculturation, the interchange of cultural elements and the breaking down of distinctive cultural identities, and the loss of national sovereignty (see Bird et al., 1993; Featherstone, 1990).

This chapter was specifically commissioned for this volume.

These themes have been echoed in the literature on popular music; writers have focused on the impacts of commercialization, suggesting they have led to a process of cultural homogenization associated with conditions of placelessness and timelessness (e.g. Adorno, 1992; Meyrowitz, 1985; Wallis and Malm, 1984). For many this equates to a process of "cultural imperialism" whereby local forms of musical expression in societies around the world are being replaced by mass-produced and mass-marketed western (American) ones, or being diluted into a cheap imitation of western pop. More recently, Tomlinson has argued that by the end of the 1980s, the term "imperialism" needed to be replaced by "globalization," indicating a far more disorganized, random process involving "interconnection and interdependence of all global areas which happens in a far less purposeful way" and which "weaken[s] the cultural coherence of all individual nation states, including the economically powerful ones – the 'imperialist powers' of previous era" (Tomlinson, 1991, pp. 175, 178). This means that while the cultural and social identities of small nations are still dominated by the larger forces of information technology, these forces operate in a remote global sphere where notions of identity cannot be articulated (Mitchell, 1996, p. 50).

In this chapter we contest this reading of the globalization of popular music. We focus on the relationship between globalization, popular music, and the expression of national identity. We argue that the cultural homogeneity interpretation is a misconception of the process of globalization as it has unfolded in the music industry, and is based on a static and rigid opposition of the spheres of the "global" and the "local." The notion of impending homogenization rests on a reductionist understanding of the creative and reflexive nature of the production and consumption of popular music. Drawing on a geographic perspective, we argue that the growing ascendance of globalizing processes actually accentuates the importance of localized processes of consumption and the identification with place as represented through unique musical forms. While we acknowledge that many musical groups have taken advantage of the internationalization of the music industry, deliberately marketing themselves within the global context (e.g. "The Spice Girls" and "The Backstreet Boys"), many other "local" bands, like The Tragically Hip, have capitalized instead on the importance of inserting their own place-based, hybridized sense of national identity into their singing and songwriting styles.

The impossibility of defining any real sense of a global identity in popular music means that local practices and musical idiosyncrasies are increasingly important, not just in terms of providing a expression for notions of national musical identity but as agents of the "repatriation of difference" which adapt homogenized global musical forms into "heterogeneous dialogues of national sovereignty" (Appadurai, 1990, p. 16). Global musical forms may well be (mis)interpreted in creative and idiosyncratic ways in different localities which invest them with new significance. The reception of local musicians in local contexts is even more idiosyncratic, involving an insider field of reference and interpretation that is often impenetrable to the outsider. Despite the existence of globalizing forces, distinctive musical forms and differentiated identities have evolved in distinct "local musical spaces."

Musical Futures: Globalization and Homogeneity or a Reassertion of the Local?

In the conclusion to their book *Big Sounds from Small Peoples*, Wallis and Malm (1984) suggest two possible future directions for the ongoing processes of globalization and transculturation in music: the interaction of global and local musical cultures will increase to the extent that more and more musical features will become common to an increasing range of musical cultures, and global homogeneity will ensue; or, a variety of different types of music from different cultural contexts and musical practices will emerge, adapting traditional musical forms to new environments (Wallis and Malm, 1984, pp. 323–4). Since the mid-1980s a number of writers have considered the impact of globalization on the music industry, variously emphasizing either the internationalization of the musical production industry or the consequences of globalization for the process of music consumption (e.g. Burnett, 1996; Kong, 1997; Lovering, 1998; Negus, 1992; Shuker, 1994).

In the sphere of production, the focus on globalization emphasizes the increasing internationalization of music production and trade accompanying the rise of transnational corporations (TNCs) (Burnett, 1996; Negus, 1992; Shuker, 1994). Yet a closer inspection of the reality behind this representation reveals a pattern of investment that is still significantly less than global. An ongoing process of global restructuring over the past decade has actually resulted in the increasing concentration of the industry as a whole. On the eve of the millennium, the "global" music industry remains remarkably concentrated both in terms of control and sales (Leyshon, et al., 1998; Negus, 1992).

In 1992 the music industry generated around $36 billion from the sale of recorded music worldwide, yet over three-quarters of this went to a handful of TNCs (Negus, 1992). Following a series of international mergers in the early 1990s, the music industry was dominated by just five corporations headquartered in Europe, the U.S., and Japan.[2] This process of concentration is not limited to music. All five of these TNCs are currently positioning themselves for the anticipated overlap of global markets for information and entertainment – reflected, for example, in the rapid integration of the personal computer, telephone, and video into a single product (Askoy and Robins, 1992). Although these corporations are undoubtedly searching the globe for new or as yet untapped markets, over seventy percent of world record sales are generated in just five national markets. The music industry is undoubtedly globalizing, but its current pattern of ownership and sales remains remarkably concentrated.

According to a number of observers, "globalization" has also transformed the processes of consumption. Once again, interpretations of the consequences vary but the recurring motifs are those of homogeneity and placeless-ness. Perhaps the most well cited reading is that of Theodore Adorno (1976; 1992), who presents a gloomy vision of the future where globalization simply accelerates the widespread commercialization and commodification of cultural expression, leading to homogenization and uniformity dominated by the lowest common denominator. For Negus (1992), the increasingly global production and consumption of popular music in the 1990s is "defined by the North Atlantic Anglo-American cultural movements of sounds and images and European, USA and Japanese dominance of financial capital and hardware" (1992, p. 14). This new "global cultural imperialism" is a "true melange of disparate components drawn from everywhere and nowhere, borne upon the modern chariots of global telecommunications systems" (Smith, 1990, p. 177).

However, we believe the processes of globalization are more complex than many of these accounts allow. In particular, the spheres of the "local" and the "global" are more intertwined than these studies lead us to believe. In the realm of commercial production, the globalization of the music industry clearly involves a qualitative – global – reorganization which has involved the concentration of capital in a small number of key corporations and the centralization of production and control within a relatively small number of global sites (Leyshon, et al., 1998; Lovering, 1998; Negus, 1992). However, while these companies certainly have a "global reach," the industry as a whole still exhibits strong tendencies towards localization. This suggests that the global/local interplay embodied in the recent restructuring of the music industry might be better conceptualized as a set of combined processes within which the tendencies of globalization and localization coexist. In a similar way it is possible to see that in the sphere of consumption "globalization" implies a complex recombination of cultural forms in different places. Far from producing a single homogeneous cultural space, we believe globalization has in fact heightened "localization" of musical tastes and the appreciation of musical diversity (cf. Featherstone, 1993; Harvey, 1989).

Recent marketing trends within the music industry have certainly encouraged the production of a "global sound" which sells equally across national and international cultural boundaries. This, for Adorno and others, suggests a future of global uniformity where local differences are flattened beneath the dominance of a bad Western pop universal. It is also possible that particular rock bands have achieved worldwide success by downplaying their national or local styles in favor of a standardized and homogenized production or "look." Indeed, artists such as Madonna, Mariah Carey, Michael Jackson, and the Rolling Stones may have originally been the products of Anglo-American culture, but in a real sense they have become virtually placeless as their product ceaselessly circulates the globe via performance or replication. The consequence of these developments, in the eyes of some observers, is a situation where the sense of collective memory, context and sense of place is effectively erased in favor of a predictable, monolithic global culture (Meyrowitz, 1985; Smith, 1990).

Whatever the judgmental nature of these predictions,[3] they are based on a passive and rather limited conception of processes of cultural production and consumption. It is surely possible to package sound and image and diffuse this product through global media and entertainment networks. It is a challenge of quite a different order to ensure that such products have the capacity to move and inspire audiences, with their own national, ethnic, and personal tastes, to purchase them. In other words, to paraphrase Smith (1990, p. 179), these sounds and images do not descend upon mute (or deaf!) and passive populations on whose tabula rasa they inscribe themselves. If the global sound is to survive and flourish as part of the repertoire of any national culture, it must be successfully integrated with existing tastes. The major music corporations may indeed strive to produce and market a seamless global sound but this fact alone does not guarantee that we will consume it or that, even if we do, that it will constitute the majority of our musical diet.[4]

Place, Popular Music, and National Identity

> The experience of pop music is an experience of placing: in responding to a song, we are drawn, haphazardly, into affective and emotional alliances with the performers and with the performers' other fans.
> *(Frith, 1988, p. 139)*

The narratives of globalization have called into question our traditional conception of the nation. Indeed, in the last decade, many cultural theorists have declared that the nation, rather than a "real" category, is an invention (Eisenstein, 1996, p. 43). Stuart Hall insists that the "relationship between a national-cultural identity and a nation-state is now beginning...to disappear" (1986, p. 46). Mohanty further declares that "the nation-state is no longer an appropriate socioeconomic unit for analysis" (1991, p. 2). Yet the experience of popular music suggests such declarations are misleading. Despite the global reach of transnational recording companies, the landscape of popular music is characterized by the continued existence of alternative spaces of production and resistance. These sites reflect local forms of cultural expression and give rise to "local sounds" – however intangible – produced in particular localities and specific to certain contexts.

Cultural geographers have recently begun to explore these connections between place, nation, and popular music (see Leyshon, et al., eds., 1998; Kong, 1997). Halfacree and Kitchen (1996), for example, discuss the evolution of "Manchester sounds" emanating from the United Kingdom. Outlining geography's role in forging a specific distinctiveness to the city's independent music scene, they suggest that postmodern "neo-tribes" (see Maffesoli, 1989) are produced when fragments of popular music are formed and sustained through specific geographical contexts. Although the authors are careful to explain that popular music does not "spring unproblematically...from place and should not be over-romanticized," they emphasize the need for an analytical approach sensitive to the constitutive role of place in the production of musical forms (Halfacree and Kitchen, 1996, p. 54).

In a similar way, Lovering (1998) suggests that "local music spaces" can be thought of as territories in which a "community of musical taste," identifiable to its participants, emerges and is sustained, reproduced and disseminated through a place-based network of creation, production and consumption (1998, p. 47). In this way distinctive "soundscapes" are formed, nurtured and diffused. These soundscapes can be interpreted as both the product and expression of place-based identities. As is now well documented, rock and roll developed out of styles nurtured in local music spaces in black, and subsequently white, communities mobilized by local entrepreneurs. Likewise, the British pop invasion of the 1960s emerged from a local music space, as did ska, reggae and punk. The subsequent diffusion of these styles and their imitation and adaptation in other music spaces gave rise to the development of distinct recognizable – and commodified – genres. For the listener, these musical forms create an embodied but imaginary space that mediates our feelings, dreams, desires – our internal space – with the social, external space (Berland, 1998, p. 131). In this way music gives us a sense of place, sometimes in connection with coherent spaces, sometimes in their stead. The production – and consumption – of musical forms is thus an expression of place and identity. This reflexivity is vibrant and unpredictable.

Considering the National Context: The Case of Canada

Living in the shadow of a dominant neighbor, questions of national identity and distinctiveness understandably loom large in the Canadian consciousness (Hutcheon, 1991). But anxiety over national identity is more pronounced in Canada than in many post-colonial countries. This is clearly reflected in the case of the music industry by a public discourse that positions it within the political problematic of Canada itself. Far from "disappearing" or being the passive recipient of global forces, the Canadian nation-state has been active in shaping the context in which music is produced and consumed. In the early 1930s the Canadian Parliament, following popular public sentiment, decreed that communication technologies were a central element for the development of national identity and that their content should therefore be qualitatively different than that produced by American commerce. Canada's national broadcasting system was developed with the mandate to "create national community, to resist foreign hegemony, and to advance public interest in contradistinction to commercial (American) media" (Berland, 1998, p. 136). As a result of this official demarcation of a marginalized national space, the Canadian media and arts have been infused with anxiety about cultural and economic sovereignty.

This is particularly pronounced in the case of the music industry, largely through its connection with radio. As Straw (1993) argues, the bond between music and listeners became inextricably linked to government cultural policy. Government agencies currently defend "Canadian culture" through a complex combination of protective regulations, such as Canadian content quotas for broadcasters, and financial subsidy for recording and publishing, such as those supporting recording projects by local musicians. However, as Berland (1998) points out, the results of this policy have effectively served the interests of multinational capital. The quota system has become so arcane and complex that its effectiveness in promoting truly indigenous product is questionable[5] and the subsidies for recording are strongly shaped by the demands of commercial airplay and export potential. As a result, state intervention:

> assists the Canadian music industry to export recordings by deepening and extending the means whereby internal manufacture complements and serves the international industry. By seeking to reconcile citizenship and consumption in a mutual enterprise of privatization and delocalization, the state demonstrates its complicity in the ongoing capitalization of national space.   (*Berland, 1998, p. 137*)

Somewhat suprisingly, Canadians, rather than Americans, rank as the second highest (following the Dutch) music consumers in the world, as measured in per capita expenditure on recorded music (Berland, 1998, pp. 135–6). However, only a small fraction of this revenue is reinvested in Canadian music. Indeed, Berland (1998) asserts that the interest of global corporations in Canadian music is largely restricted to the recording of "global sounds" (such as those of Alanis Morrissette or Shania Twain) that can be marketed across the continent (Berland, 1998, p. 136). As a result, smaller Canadian recording companies produce most Canadian content recordings, bearing the creative and economic risks of making music within the country. However, because the record distribution networks are also owned and controlled by global corporations, most Canadian records manufactured and sold within Canada are actually made from imported master tapes. Given the economies of scale involved, it costs approximately ten times more to produce an indigenous product than to import a similar product from the United States (Berland, 1998; Straw, 1993). This situation is further complicated by the "particularities of the Canadian situation" (see Straw, 1993, p. 58). The geographical expanse of Canada and the existence of two distinct linguistic communities and identities have encouraged the development of distribution operations that are either regional in scope or directed towards dispersed international markets. Thus, despite the existence of Canadian content quota regulations for radio, a recording artist usually needs to succeed in the US to be heard in Canada. In the Canadian context of music production, most bands succeed outside of Canada before they "make it big" in their own country.

In the next section, we will examine the ways in which The Tragically Hip confound this scenario. We deliberately avoid providing exhaustive examination of song lyrics,[6] choosing instead to offer comments from band members concerning their musical intentions and comments from fans, who "read" The Tragically Hip through a particular framework of "quintessential" Canadianness.[7] Rather than treat their audience as a passive, uninscribed mass of individuals (i.e. the traditional mass culture critique), we show how fans evoke a sense of nationalism and patriotism through their interpretation of the music of The Tragically Hip, reflecting the "seductive pleasure of belonging...in nations" (George, 1996, p. 200).

The Tragically Hip

The Tragically Hip formed in Kingston, Ontario, Canada in 1983.[8] Since that time the band has carved out a loyal and steady following in Canada, graduating from underground clubs to become one of the major acts in Canada. The Tragically Hip have achieved widespread acclaim for their ability to wed gritty rock to impressionistic lyrics, penned primarily by their charismatic lead singer, Gordon Downie. Earning a reputation as exciting performers, their shows now consistently sell out throughout the country to the extent that these "legendary live performers are – easily – the biggest Canadian concert draw today" (Ohler, 1996). This massive national success has prompted numerous Canadian music critics to ask, "What's behind our country's love affair with these five shop-worn, Joe-Everyman guys from Kingston, Ont?" (Ohler, 1996). Local fans and industry insiders attribute it to a combination of many factors, including Downie's manic and hypnotizing stage presence and his richly geographical lyrics. Downie's songs are described as "oblique, often esoteric, but never short of poetic" (Ohler, 1996).[9] However, although critics and fans laud the band's live performances and Downie's lyrics, most attribute The Tragically Hip's national following to their status as the quintessential Canadian band.

The band is currently signed to a multinational recording company and has achieved unprecedented sales figures in Canada,[10] but have yet to replicate this success in the United States. Despite the fact that The Tragically Hip tour regularly in the US, the band seems reluctant to compromise their performance for commercial acceptance in the US or for the "global" legitimacy such success would bring at home in Canada. As Gordon Downie told *Musician* magazine:

> You see the road to Los Angeles littered with the corpses of bands seeking American acceptance, as if that would make you a legitimate success story back home. The lesson is that it's pointless to do anything differently to attract the American audience.
>
> *(quoted in Rubiner, 1997)*

Ironically, given this refusal to bend to commercial pressure, the band has been dubbed "Canada's Rolling Stones," in large part because of the identifiably Canadian content in the lyrics of their songs. It is this aspect of the band's popularity that we explore below.

The Production of Place: Performing the Nation?

The lyrics of Tragically Hip songs are peppered with local references and imagery of an identifiably Canadian flavor. Their musical style has repeatedly been described as distinctively Canadian, "raw and melodic...straight-ahead yet also strange and strangely inviting, just like the country and the people that it portrays in its songs" (Muretich, 1996a). To the outsider, the identifiably Canadian nature of this sound may be somewhat ephemeral, but lyrically the band has a distinctly local flavor. Evoking a strong sense of place and national identity, contemporary and historical references abound. These range from well-known Canadian places and popular landmarks to regional cuisine and semi-sacred national iconography (canoes, maple leafs and hockey among them). Over the course of several albums, Downie has also ventured into social criticism, addressing a variety of controversial Canadian topics in his songwriting ranging from a highly controversial wrongful murder conviction to the Canadian Broadcasting Corporation.

The sense of place evoked in the songs of The Tragically Hip is, however, often one tinged with an atmosphere of nostalgia. A number of Downie's more place-specific songs present narratives of collective loss, recalling times past and landmark events in Canadian history. The song "Fifty-Mission Cap" (1992), for example, recalls local mythology concerning the mysterious disappearance of a former hockey player and national icon, as well as the Toronto Maple Leaf's landmark Stanley Cup hockey victories. The emergence of a local particularity is explored and mutated in the recovery of a new, national, heritage that remains fluid and flexible. Referring to a collective memory and sense of place, The Tragically Hip contributes to a new re-reading of the past and understanding of Canadian history within a contemporary context. Such representations of national history provide a way to emphasize the local, while continuing to promote Canadian identity in a new, distinctive format which fans obviously find appealing. In working through some of these complicated issues of identity, Downie explores global issues within a local context. The band's sound and style also reveal a search for identity which reconciles various forces, reinterpreting the Canadian tradition of folk singer-songwriters and giving voice to poetic Canadian images. Although Downie is the first to admit that his work is influenced by transcultural elements, a sense of the local remains strong in his performance, where distinctive local contexts are key in creating a sense of place. As guitarist Rob Baker observes, "Every album we've done has reflected who we are and where we come from. We're Canadians who live in a border town in the shadow of the big neighbor" (quoted in Doole, 1991).

Hip Fans: The Consumption of National Identity?

The Tragically Hip's loyal Canadian following enthusiastically embraces the identifiably national aspects of the band's recordings and live performances. Given the accessible and democratic nature of the Internet, much of this is represented in websites created by fans to celebrate and share their enthusiasm for the band and its music.[11] At the time of writing there were well over a hundred websites devoted exclusively to The Tragically Hip (most of which appear to be based in Canada).[12] Many of these explicitly celebrate the band's Canadian roots and the sense of national identity they represent for their audience. One website, for example, has been created for "all the Hip fans who want to know what Canadian References are in the Hip songs."[13] This site contains a lengthy list of the specifically Canadian references made in the band's lyrics which, in turn, leads to links which explain their significance in further detail. Apart from a number of specific Canadian geographical locations the list also includes a number of (only) locally famous events, such as the 1972 Summit Hockey Series between Canada and Russia, the 1998 ice storm in Eastern Canada and Quebec, Highway 401 and Bobby Orr (a famous Canadian hockey player – who played his professional career in the US). Visitors are also invited to cast their vote for the "most Canadian" Tragically Hip song. Another interesting site in this genre is that of The Tragically Hip Roadtrip Club, established by a group of fans who "visit various places that the Hip have wrote about [sic] or have special meaning about them in relation to the Tragically Hip." At the time of writing all the locations listed on this site were in Canada.[14]

Websites like these illustrate that, for many fans, appreciation of The Tragically Hip centers on the band's ability to evoke a popular and accessible representation of Canadian identity. This is manifest in the band's distinctively Canadian image, not least of which is the reference to local place names and "Canadiana" in their songs. Arguably, for many young Canadians these signifiers resonate more eloquently than many more traditional symbols of nationalism (such as the flag or coat of arms). Indeed, many fans tend to equate The Tragically Hip with an essential, if somewhat ephemeral, "Canadianness." "A big part of the Tragically Hip's appeal is that they're Canadian, they're homegrown...they speak to the Canadian in me" (quoted in

Muretich, 1996b). Music critics compare the group with historical Canadian popular culture icons:

> Just like Hockey Night in Canada and Don Cherry, The Tragically Hip have always been there. The band also reflects our image of ourselves as down-to-earth yet intelligent, from its practical attire to its concerts.   (*Muretich, 1996b*)

The Tragically Hip are somehow interpreted as holding a mirror to national life, articulating through their music the essence of what it means to be Canadian, reflecting a unique interpretation of the fans' response to the band's lyrics and sound.

Repatriating the Global? The Tragically Hip's Interpretation

Clearly many of The Tragically Hip's fans are attracted by the sense of identification the band's music stirs in them, fueled by Downie's tendency to employ specific Canadian references in his lyrics. However, band members themselves insist that they do not intentionally stress nationalism in their music. According to guitarist Rob Baker:

> I think there's a certain Canadian content in the songs which stirs Canadians up and doesn't have the same effect on American audiences...[O]ur doing that is a reaction to those bands from 15 years ago that were singing about going to high school in Hollywood. It just seemed natural to sing about what you know, your hometown. But we never considered it nationalism when we were doing it. It was just being honest.
>   (*quoted in Ostroff, 1999*)

While fans and music critics in Canada equate The Tragically Hip with a certain reading of Canadian identity, band members' own reading of nationalism suggests a less static and far more fluid conception which is informed by a sense of global context. For lead singer/lyricist Downie, questions of personal identity, motivated primarily by his interest in exploring who he was and where he came from, inspired his articulation of these subjects in his songwriting. In an interview in 1996 he responded to a question from a fan concerning the band's tendency to evoke a strong sense of patriotism in their fans:

> We've never tried consciously to elicit a patriotic response from our fans, nor have we tried to embody that in our lyrics...Over the years, we have written some songs that refer to Canadian events specifically, and others that reflect our response as Canadians to other themes and issues, because of who we are and how we've been raised. If some of our fans can only identify with us on a nationalistic level, instead of a musical one, then I think that reflects more on them than it does on us. Travelling abroad as much as we do has led us to appreciate where we live and who we are and I think our work reflects that; but we have definitely learned that there is no one distinct Canadian voice.[15]

Indeed, it would be unjust to claim that The Tragically Hip's lyrics deal exclusively with Canadian places and events. In scanning for Canadian references on their album "Day for Night" (1994), for example, out of a total of fourteen songs, only three make explicit reference to a Canadian place, event or moment in history. There are also references to other places and times, including El Paso, war-time Russia and coastal France. Elsewhere, the band has dedicated entire songs to places as diverse as Vienna, New Orleans and Chagrin Falls, Ohio. Nevertheless, these allusions tend to be either forgotten or ignored by the fans. Despite the band's attempts to introduce or "repatriate" global themes within their music, their fans' appreciation seems to center on the band's Canadianness and their ability to evoke a particular experience or sense of what it means to be Canadian.

There are also indications that the band is not entirely comfortable with their role as national symbols or the response that their performances elicit from Canadian fans. Downie recalled one particularly uncomfortable situation which brought this contradiction, between the band's conception of themselves and their audience's reception, into sharp focus:

> The closest I've come to feeling entirely strange about what I do was in Europe. We were attracting a lot of Canadians, mostly students abroad. In Scotland, these two guys came out, decked out in Canadian flags, Canadian sweatshirts, Bluejays caps. That's just not what we're about. Nationalism in the textbook definition is a chauvinistic belief.
>
> *(quoted in Littlejohn, 1993, p. 13)*

In turn, in acknowledging that many fans identify with them as sonic symbols of nationalism, Downie also recognizes that The Tragically Hip's music is being consumed in a particularized way by their fans. Although the band freely admits that their music is strongly influenced by their appreciation of place, it is the fans themselves who focus on issues of nationalism and patriotism. Downie insists that because of the band's experiences of the global, their understanding of nationalism and the local is altered and mutated accordingly. Their own hybrid forms of identity are expressed in their musical performances, which demonstrate how, in the context of a shifting and changing world where borders and boundaries are effortlessly crossed, their comprehension of the local and differentiated expression of hybrid identities becomes even more appealing.

Conclusion

In this chapter we have addressed various consequences of the "globalization" of music. In contrast to some of the rather blanket claims made in many recent accounts we believe that, while certainly international in scope, the music industry is, in several crucial respects, still significantly less than truly global. As a result, we have argued that the processes of globalization within the music industry are vastly more complex than many recent accounts allow.

A more appropriate view of the current changes transforming the music industry, we suggest, might be one that viewed the processes of globalization and localization as coexisting in a complex re-articulation of both production and consumption. Thus, in contrast to the dismal predictions of a blight of homogeneity and dullness, we argue that "globalization" has in fact heightened the localization of musical tastes and the appreciation of musical diversity.

The realm of popular music provides a forum for artists to proclaim their various fluid and flexible national hybridized identities through the commodification of creative performance. It does not seem to us that a growing global awareness has brought about the demise of local particularisms in popular music. In fact, the influence of the global has a significant impact upon the ways in which the local and the national are interpreted and, in turn, produced through musical performances. Local particularisms are therefore not simply muted or submerged – rather they are asserted and negotiated through new musical forms.

We examined the way the music of Canadian artists, The Tragically Hip, has been interpreted by their fans as embodying a sense of Canadian identity and nationalism. This reading allows for a closer scrutiny of the connections between the production and consumption of place-based lyrics and images in the Hip's music. In the process of cultural consumption, fans may appropriate popular music as symbols of nationhood and national identity. Some suggest that the growing significance of place in the midst of globalizing forces has been interpreted as a desire for stability and security of identity in the middle of an era of turbulence and change (Massey, 1993, p. 236). We have argued here that a sense of identity is being produced, interpreted and transformed in the reflexive creation of music, where live and recorded performances are interpreted and consumed in unpredictable and often localized ways. In the case of The Tragically Hip, the reception of the band's music in the Canadian context was driven by the idiosyncratic interpretation of local fans who "read" the band almost exclusively through the lens of national identity. Indeed, as we have demonstrated, this took place somewhat independently of the band members' own intentions for their music, in that the fans largely resisted or ignored their attempt to repatriate global themes into the music. In large part this process is conducted through the collective act of creative production and adaptation in particular local musical spaces.

Notes

1 This quote was taken from Lauren Small's review of a concert by The Tragically Hip which took place in Ottowa on February 8, 1999. The review is reproduced at: http://www.canoe.ca/TragicallyHipTour/ottowa2_2.html

2 These corporations include Warner's Music International, US; Bertlesmann Music Group (BMG), Germany; Polygram International Group, the Netherlands; EMI-Virgin, Great Britain; and Sony Music Entertainment, Japan.

3 It must be noted here that there is certainly an element of elitism in some of these accounts. Despite the slick corporate nature of much of the "global sound" it does not compromise our argument to acknowledge that some of it is of very high quality, which may account, at least in part, for a good measure of its popularity.

4 Lovering (1998) quotes one industry observer struck by the irony that, "at a time when the music business has become more international . . . musical taste is increasingly parochial. The American charts are dominated by indigenous genres such as rap and grunge, Germany is awash with thrash metal bands, Britain has Britpop" (1998, p. 46). These impressions are borne out by sales figures that point to changing geographies of consumption within the music industry. Artists from the US accounted for 45% of global sales in the mid-1980s, but for only 35% by the mid-1990s, and during the mid-1980s, non-American artists surpassed American artists in sales volume within the European market. Similarly, the share of the

world market enjoyed by British artists is falling, from 20% in 1989 to 15% in 1993, and sales of English language pop music declined sharply relative to local language artists in Germany, Italy and France among other countries (all figures cited in Lovering, 1998, p. 47).

5 A recent example is the song "American Woman," released by African-American recording artist Lenny Kravitz through a multinational recording label, which was deemed "Canadian" under the current quota system because the original version (of which Kravitz's version is a cover) was co-written by Canadian singer–songwriter Burton Cummings.

6 Apart from our desire to emphasize the creative dialectic of consumption and production, the band's chief lyricist has expressly stated: "I'm not too comfortable with the lyrics being separated from the music. I'm not a poet, I'm a lyric writer, and I just want to make them fit or sound right" (quoted in Doole, 1991).

7 Clearly this interpretation does not extend to all Tragically Hip fans or even all Canadian fans, but is nevertheless a distinctive characteristic of their following in Canada.

8 Current band members include: Robert Baker, guitar; Gordon Downie, vocals; Johnny Fay, drums; Paul Langlois, guitar, vocals; and Gordon Sinclair, bass, vocals.

9 Downie's enigmatic lyrics range from the somber in the song "Inevitability of Death" (1994) where he sings, "But I thought you beat the death of inevitability to death just a little bit/I thought you beat the inevitability of death to death just a little bit," to the tongue-in-cheek humor of the line, "Your imagination's having puppies" in "Something On" (1999).

10 By 1995, combined sales of the Hip catalogue had passed the 2.5 million mark: one for every 10 people in Canada.

11 Obviously, not all Hip followers have created web sites but this is one tangible – and relatively accessible – expression of fan sentiment.

12 At the time of writing the majority of these sites could be accessed from The Tragically Hip Webring located at: http://www.webring.org/cgi-bin/webring?ring=hipring/

13 This site can be found at: http://www.angelfire.com/on/canadianhip/

14 This site can be found at: http://members.home.net/noodles2/tth_club

15 A transcript of this interview can be found at "The fans interview the Hip": http://www.canoe.ca/HipLetter/hip_letter1html

References

Adorno, T.: *Introduction to the Sociology of Music* (New York: Seabury Press, 1976).

Adorno, T.: *Quasi Una Fantasia*. Translated by R. Livingstone. (London: Verso, 1992).

Appadurai, A.: "Disjuncture and difference in the global cultural economy," *Public Culture*, 2 (1990), 1–24.

Askoy, A., and Robins, K.: "Hollywood for the 21st century: global competition for critical mass in image markets," *Cambridge Journal of Economics*, 16 (1992), 1–22.

Berland, J.: "Locating listening: Technological space, popular music and Canadian mediations," *The Place of Music*, ed., A. Leyshon, D. Matless and G. Revill (New York: Guilford, 1998), pp. 129–50.

Bird, J., Curtis, B., Putnam, T., Robertson, G., and Tickner, L., eds.: *Mapping the Futures* (London: Routledge, 1993).

Burnett, R.: *The Global Jukebox: The International Music Industry* (London: Routledge; 1996).

Doole, K.: "A road apple a day…," *HMV Magazine*, June (1991), 1.

Eisenstein, Z.: *Hatreds: Racialized and Sexualized Conflicts in the 21st Century* (London: Routledge, 1996).

Featherstone, M., ed.: *Global Culture: Nationalism, Globalization and Modernity* (London: Sage, 1990).

Featherstone, M.: "Global and local cultures," *Mapping the Futures*, ed., J. Bird, B. Curtis, T. Putnam, G. Robertson, and L. Tickner (London: Routledge, 1993), pp. 169–87.

Frith, S.: *Music For Pleasure* (New York: Routledge, 1988).

George, R.: *The Politics of Home* (Cambridge: Cambridge University Press, 1996).

Halfacree K., and Kitchen R.: "'Madchester rave on': Placing the fragments of popular music," *Area*, 28 (1996), 47–55.

Hall, S.: "On postmodernism and articulation: An interview with Stuart Hall," *Journal of Communication Inquiry*, 10 (1986), 45–60.

Harvey, D.: *The Condition of Postmodernity: An Inquiry into the Origins of Cultural Change* (Oxford: Basil Blackwell, 1989).

Hutcheon, L.: *Splitting Images: Contemporary Canadian Ironies* (Toronto: Oxford University Press, 1991).

Kong, L.: "Popular music in a transnational world: The construction of local identities in Singapore," *Asia Pacific Viewpoint*, 38 (1997), 19–36.

Leyshon, A., Matless D., Revill G., eds.: *The Place of Music* (New York: Guilford, 1998).

Leyshon, A., Matless D., Revill G.: "Introduction: Music, space and the production of place," *The Place of Music*, ed., A. Leyshon, D. Matless and G. Revill (New York: Guilford, 1998), pp. 1–30.

Littlejohn, M.: "Locked in the trunk of Gord Downie's mind: The Tragically Hip story," *HMV Magazine*, June (1993), 12–14.

Lovering, J.: "The global music industry: Contradictions in the commodification of the sublime," *The Place of Music*, ed., A. Leyshon., D. Matless., and G. Revill (New York: Guilford, 1998), pp. 31–56.

Maffesoli, M.: "The sociology of everyday life (epistemological elements)," *Current Sociology*, 37 (1989), 1–16.

Massey D.: "A global sense of place," *Studying Cultures*, ed., A. Gray and J. McGuigan (London: Edward Arnold, 1993), pp. 232–40.

Meyrowitz, J.: *No Sense of Place* (Oxford: Oxford University Press, 1985).

Mitchell, T.: *Popular Music and Local Identity* (Leicester: Leicester University Press, 1996).

Mohanty, C.: "Cartographies of struggle: Third world women and the politics of feminism," *Third World Women and the Politics of Feminism*, ed., C. Mohanty, A. Russo, and L. Torres (Bloomington: Indiana University Press, 1991), pp. 1–51.

Muretich, J.: "Tragically Hip: Band draws the line at Dome," *The Calgary Herald*, November 16 (1996a), p. B8.

Muretich, J.: "When it comes to Hip, these fans know passion," *The Calgary Herald*, November 15 (1996b), p. C1.

Negus, K.: *Producing Pop: Culture and Conflict in the Popular Music Industry* (London: Longman, 1992).

Ohler, S.: "Why do we think the Hip are so hip? Maybe because they're ours," *The Edmonton Journal* (November 12, 1996) p. A1.

Ostroff, J.: "Small steps for Canadian band," *Ottawa Sun* (January 17, 1999), p. B3.

Rubiner, J.: "The Tragically Hip," *Contemporary Musicians*, 18 (1997). Reproduced at: http://members.tripod.com/~ljt/hipbios.html.

Shuker, R.: *Understanding popular music* (London: Routledge, 1994).

Smith, A.: "Towards a Global Culture?," *Theory, Culture and Society*, 7 (1990), 171–91.

Straw, W.: "The English Canadian recording industry since 1970," *Rock and Popular Music: Politics, Policies and Institutions*, ed. T. Bennett, S. Frith, L. Grossberg, J. Shepherd, and G. Turner (London: Routledge, 1993), pp. 52–65.

Taylor, C.: *Reconciling the Solitudes: Essays on Canadian Federalism and Nationalism* (Montreal and Kingston: McGill–Queen's University Press, 1993).

Tomlinson, J.: *Cultural Imperialism* (London: Pinter, 1991).

Wallis, R. and K. Malm: *Big Sounds from Small Peoples* (London: Constable 1984).

Walters, M.: *Globalization* (London: Routledge, 1995).

14 Diasporic Noise: History, Hip Hop, and the Post-colonial Politics of Sound

George Lipsitz

In 1989, a nineteen-year-old African-American woman from Irvington, New Jersey performing under the name Queen Latifah starred in a music video promoting her rap song "Ladies First." At a time when politicians, journalists, and even most male rappers presented few positive images of Black women, Queen Latifah drew upon the diasporic history of Black people around the world to fashion an affirmative representation of women of African descent. Assisted by Monie Love, an Afro-Caribbean rapper from London, as well as Ms. Melody and a chorus of other Black female rappers from the USA, Latifah appeared in a video that interspersed still photos of Angela Davis, Sojourner Truth, and Madame C. J. Walker with newsreel films of women prominent in the struggle against apartheid in South Africa. Uniting Black people across generations and continents, the young rap artist from New Jersey situated claims about her prowess with rap rhythms and rhymes within a broader story of diasporic struggle.

In telling its story about the achievements, ability, and desirability of Black women, "Ladies First" inverted and subverted existing representations with wide circulation in mass media and popular culture. During a decade when politicians and journalists in the USA regularly depicted Black women as unwed mothers and "welfare queens," Latifah's video presented them as "queens of civilization" and "mothers" who "give birth" to political struggle. At a time when "gangsta rap" glamorized the aggression and violence of street criminals, "Ladies First" celebrated the militancy of collective struggles for social change. In an era when some Black nationalists belittled the gains made by Black women as detrimental to the community as a whole and urged them to accept subordinate places behind Black men, Latifah hailed the historic accomplishments of African-American women and emphasized the need for equal dedication and commitment from Black men and Black women in their common struggle against racism. Most important, in an American culture increasingly dismissive of African-American appeals for justice, dignity, and opportunity as "minority" concerns, Latifah's deployment of images from the African diaspora demonstrated that the "minority" populations of the USA are part of the global majority who have been victimized and oppressed by Euro-American racism and imperialism.

Queen Latifah's effort to map out discursive and political space through the trope of the African diaspora builds on historical practices within hip hop culture as well as within the broader history of Afro-America. The first visible manifestations of

Original publication: Lipsitz, George, "Diasporic Noise: History, Hip Hop, and the Post-colonial Politics of Sound," from George Lipsitz, *Dangerous Crossroads: Popular Music, Postmodernism and the Poetics of Place* (Verso, London and New York, 1994).

what we have come to call hip hop culture (rap music, break-dancing, graffiti, B Boy and wild style fashions) appeared in the early 1970s when a member of a New York street gang (The Black Spades) calling himself Afrika Bambaataa organized "The Zulu Nation." Confronted by the ways in which displacement by urban renewal, economic recession, and the fiscal crisis of the state combined to create desperate circumstances for inner-city youths, Bambaataa tried to channel the anger and enthusiasm of young people in the South Bronx away from gang fighting and into music, dance, and graffiti. He attracted African-American, Puerto Rican, Afro-Caribbean, and Euro-American youths into his "nation." He staged dances featuring his estimable talents as a "mixer" and sound system operator capable of providing a non-stop flow of danceable beats from an enormous range of musical styles. In 1982, he recorded "Planet Rock" under the name Afrika Bambaataa and Soulsonic Force, and sold more than a million copies on twelve-inch vinyl of his song "Planet Rock."

Part of a generation of inner-city youths who found themselves unwanted as students by schools facing drastic budget cuts, unwanted as citizens or users of city services by municipalities imposing austerity regimens mandated by private financial institutions, and even unwanted as consumers by merchants increasingly reliant on surveillance and police power to keep urban "have-nots" away from affluent buyers of luxury items, Bambaataa and his Zulu nation used their knowledge as consumers of popular music to become skilled producers of it. They used the conduits of popular culture to bring the expressive forms of their isolated and largely abandoned neighborhoods to an international audience. Hemmed in by urban renewal, crime, and police surveillance, and silenced by neglect from the culture industry, the school system, and city government, they found a way to declare themselves part of a wider world through music. "You can go do anything with rap music," Bambaataa has argued, "you can go from the past to the future to what's happening now."[1]

Bambaataa named his "Zulu Nation" after the 1964 British film *Zulu* directed by Cy Endfield and starring Michael Caine. The motion picture clearly intended to depict the Zulus as predatory savages opposed to the "civilizing mission" of the British empire. But as an American Black whose mother and aunts had migrated to New York from Barbados, Bambaataa saw it another way. In his eyes, the Zulus were heroic warriors resisting oppression. He used their example to inspire his efforts to respond to racism and class oppression in the USA. "Planet Rock" reached a world audience through the same mechanisms of commercial culture that brought *Zulu* from Britain to the Bronx twenty years earlier, but instead of celebrating Western imperialism, the song hailed the utopian potential of Black music to transform the entire world into "a land of master jam."[2]

In lyrics written and rapped by MC Globe, "Planet Rock" celebrated the ability of music to take listeners to the past and to the future, but it also urged them to enjoy the present, to "chase your dreams" and "live it up," because "our world is free." The song located listeners and dancers "on this Mother Earth which is our rock," and combined new styles of rapping with a wide variety of Bambaataa's samples, including the theme music from the film *The Good, the Bad, and the Ugly*, sounds from the German techno band Kraftwerk, and cuts from the British band Babe Ruth over a Roland TR 808 drum synthesizer. Bambaataa and his nation inserted themselves into international commercial culture through "Planet Rock," which one perceptive reviewer described as "an unlikely fusion of bleeping, fizzing, techno-rock, Zulu surrealism, and deep-fried funk."[3]

Afrika Bambaataa's "Planet Rock" and Queen Latifah's "Ladies First" testify to the vitality of what Paul Gilroy calls "diasporic intimacy" in the Black Atlantic world. Their efforts are only a small part of an international dialogue built on the imagination and ingenuity of slum dwellers from around the globe suffering from the effects of the international austerity economy imposed on urban areas by transnational corporations and their concentrated control over capital. In recent recordings, Jamaican toaster Macka B raps an English-language history of Senegal over the singing of Baaba Maal, who speaks the Pulaar language of his native land. Cameroon expatriate Manu Dibango has recorded jazz albums with British rapper MC Mello and Parisian rapper MC Solaar. Solaar appeared on the recent hip hop–jazz fusion recording by Guru of the US rap group Gang Starr, while local rap artists in South Korea, Japan, Germany, France, and New Zealand have found significant popularity imitating the African-American styles mastered by Afrika Bambaataa and Queen Latifah.[4]

The significance of these seemingly ephemeral works of popular culture goes far beyond their role as commodities. The diasporic conversation within hip hop, Afrobeat, jazz and many other Black musical forms provides a powerful illustration of the potential for contemporary commercialized leisure to carry images, ideas, and icons of enormous political importance between cultures. Whatever role they serve in the profit-making calculations of the music industry, these expressions also serve as exemplars of post-colonial culture with direct relevance to the rise of new social movements emerging in response to the imperatives of global capital and its attendant austerity and oppression.

In *Postmodernism, or the Cultural Logic of Late Capitalism*, Fredric Jameson challenges us to imagine a political form suited to "the invention and projection of a global cognitive mapping on a social as well as a spatial scale."[5] That form already exists in hip hop culture as well as in many other forms of global cultural practice. The existence of the African diaspora functions throughout the world as a crucial force for opening up cultural, social, and political space for struggles over identity, autonomy, and power. When properly contextualized as a part of post-colonial culture and of the rise of new social movements, the musical productions of the African diaspora provide one answer to Jameson's challenge with a cultural politics already underway.

Post-colonial Culture

During the great global struggle against colonialism in the years following World War II, national self-determination and anti-colonialist internationalism engaged the attention of intellectuals throughout Africa, Asia, and Latin America. From Che Guevara's *Reminiscences of the Cuban Revolution* to Sembene Ousmane's *God's Bits of Wood*, from Chairman Mao's *Yenan Program* to Frantz Fanon's *The Wretched of the Earth*, nation building occupied center stage as the crucial element in anti-colonial emancipation. Although often somber and self-critical, anti-colonial expressions nonetheless contained an irrepressible optimism about the inevitability of liberation and about the potential achievements of post-colonial nationalism.

Forty years later, a literature of disillusionment and despair calls attention to conditions of austerity and oppression operative everywhere in the Third World. This "post-colonial" literature seems to confirm in the sphere of culture the failure of nationalist anti-colonial movements around the globe to translate national independence into something more than neo-colonial economic, cultural, and even political dependency. Defenders of colonialism point to the pervasive poverty and political problems of post-colonial countries as proof that independence came too soon. Anti-colonialists generally charge that colonialism itself continues to be the problem, that colonial practices did little to prepare people and institutions for independence. Yet both of these arguments hinge on outdated premises with little relevance for the present.

In this debate, anti-colonialists and neo-colonialists both presume that the nation state still holds the key to self-determination, that the "quality" of government officials determines the well-being of the nation. But a combination of political, technological, and cultural changes since the 1970s has undermined the authority of the nation state while making multinational corporations, communications networks, and financial structures more powerful than ever before. In an age when capital, communications, and populations travel across the globe at an accelerated pace, the ability of any one nation state to determine its people's life chances has become greatly constrained. Capitalist transnational corporations have gained great advantages by separating management from production with the aid of computer-generated automation, containerization in shipping, and the new technologies ushered in through fiber optics, computer chips, and satellites. Strategies to extract concessions from capitalists through taxation and regulation fail because of the extraordinary mobility of capital that makes it easy to play one country or region against another. At the same time, the need for capital compels formerly colonized nations to accept the compulsory austerity measures required by the International Monetary Fund and the World Bank as the price of securing loans. In rare cases when these forces fail to bring about desired results, the former imperial powers have shown little reluctance to bring direct or indirect military pressures to bear against nation states deviating from the dictates of this comprehensive world system.[6]

Thus, the failures of newly independent regimes that pervade post-colonial literature stem as much from fundamentally new conditions in world politics, economics, and culture as they do from the legacy of colonialism or the shortcomings of the struggles against it. Without denying the very important critiques of corruption and political oppression that appear in post-colonial culture, it is also important to understand that post-colonial expressions address emerging problems in the present as well as the failures of the past. The post-colonial era is one of displacement and migration, of multi-culturalism and multi-lingualism, of split subjects and divided loyalties. Post-colonial culture exposes the impossibility of *any* national identity incorporating into a unified totality the diverse and diffuse elements that make up a nation. While valuable for its insights into the failures of particular anti-colonial liberation movements, post-colonial art also exposes the inadequacy of national "imagined communities" to monitor, regulate, and remedy the explosive contradictions of global structures of economic, political, and cultural power. Indeed, the popularity of post-colonial writing and film in advanced industrial nations as well as in formerly colonized states stems from its relevance to conditions in metropolitan nations as well to those in the Third World.[7]

The crisis signaled by the emergence of post-colonial literature, art, and music is the crisis confronting movements for progressive social change all around the world. For more than a century, aggrieved populations have pinned their hopes on seizing control of the nation state, or at least on using its mechanisms to extract concessions from capital. But these traditional strategies for social change have been confounded by the emergence of "fast capital" and the equally rapid mobility of ideas, images, and people across national boundaries.

Yet new forms of domination also give rise to new forms of resistance. Rather than viewing post-colonial culture as a product of the *absence* of faith in yesterday's struggles for self-determination, it might be better to view it as product of the *presence* of new sensibilities uniquely suited for contesting the multinational nature of capital. The disillusionment and despair with politics in post-colonial writing may prove extraordinarily relevant beyond the former colonies; it may in fact be a strategically important stance for people around the globe in an age when centralized economic power has rendered many of the traditional functions of the nation state obsolete. As sociologists Harvey Molotch and John Logan argue, "when the state becomes unable to serve as a vehicle for trapping capital (and perhaps redistributing it), it places more than its legitimacy at risk; it loses some of its very meaning."[8] Of course, the state still serves as a source of repression, and still serves as an important instrument for people interested in using politics to address the rampant austerity and injustice of our time. But the state can no longer serve as the sole site of contestation for movements that find they have to be cultural as well as political, global as well as local, transnational as well as national.

One reason for the popularity of post-colonial art among readers in post-imperial countries comes from a shared disillusionment with the nation state and its failed promises. Similarly, stories of exile and return often employ the historical displacement of formerly colonized populations to express a more general sense of cultural displacement engendered everywhere by mass communications, population migrations, and the destructive effects of "fast capital" on traditional communities. Of course consumers of post-colonial cultural artifacts have many different motivations. A search for novelty, boredom with familiar paradigms, and traditional European and American practices of fascination with (but not respect for) the "exotic" also account for the recent "emergence" of post-colonial art in Western consciousness. But while it would be a mistake to ever underestimate the venal intentions and effects of Euro-American appropriations of the cultures of Asia, Africa, and Latin America, it would also be a major error to overlook the strategic importance of post-colonial perspectives for theorizing the present moment in world history.

The strategies of signification and grammars of opposition developed among post-colonial peoples speak powerfully to the paradoxically fragmented and interconnected world created by new structures of commerce culture and technology. The populations best prepared for cultural conflict and political contestation in a globalized world economy may well be the diasporic communities of displaced Africans, Asians, and Latin Americans created by the machinations of world capitalism over the centuries. These populations, long accustomed to code switching, syncretism, and hybridity may prove far more important for what they *possess* in cultural terms than for what they appear to *lack* in the political lexicon of the nation state.

For example, throughout the Black Atlantic world, one function of "Black nationalism" has always been to elide national categories – to turn national minorities into global majorities by affirming solidarity with "people of color" all around the globe. But Black populations have been open to other kinds of internationalism as well. In his excellent book on Black communists in Alabama in the 1930s, Robin D. G. Kelley shows how envisioning themselves as part of an international communist movement emboldened workers who might otherwise have been intimidated by the forbidding equation of power in their own country. They liked to hear that Stalin was on their side, certainly not because of Stalin's actual record on national self-determination or on racism, but because Stalin's existence made the world bigger than Alabama, and it seemed to render the racism in that state relative, provisional, and contingent.[9] Similarly, as Robert A. Hill demonstrates, the emergence of Rastafarianism as an important force within Jamaican politics depended upon antecedents in the "Holy Piby" or "Black Man's Bible" that connected it to the experiences and perspectives of Jamaican migrant workers in diverse sites, from Perth Amboy, New Jersey to Cape Town, South Africa to Colón, Panama. Everywhere, diasporic Africans have used international frames to remedy national frustrations.[10] Their strategies have proved crucial to the success of anti-racist movements on many continents, but they now also hold significance as a model of transnational mobilization for other aggrieved populations.

The present moment in world history is marked by the failure of two grand narratives – the liberal faith in progress, modernization, and the bureaucratic state, and the conservative faith in free trade, de-regulation, and the "free market." The global struggles for democratic change and national independence that reached their apex in the 1960s seriously discredited social theories associated with social democracy and liberal capitalism. There was a rapid unraveling of the post-war "consensus" in industrialized nations that posited a universal stake in the advance of technology, Keynesian economics, and bureaucratic rationality. From "modernization" theory in sociology to "modernism" in the arts, ways of explaining the world that had seemed incontrovertible in the 1950s suddenly seemed totally inadequate for explaining the revolutionary ruptures, clashes, and conflicts of the 1960s. But the inadequacy of existing liberal social theory, coupled with the inability among aggrieved groups to propose or implement credible radical alternatives, created an opportunity for conservatives and plutocrats.

De-industrialization and economic restructuring in capitalist countries in the 1970s and 1980s caused the re-emergence of theories lauding the free market (which themselves had been discredited since the Great Depression) as a frame for interpreting world politics and culture. Neo-conservative policies in all industrialized countries encouraged and subsidized the creation of a world economy under the control of multinational corporations and institutions. The dismantling of social welfare structures in the metropolis and the externalization of class tensions onto unprotected workers and consumers at the periphery served to unite capital while fragmenting its potential opponents. The ideology of free market economics appears to have triumphed all around the world, but rather than prosperity and freedom for all, it has produced extravagant wealth for the few and mostly austerity, corruption, and instability for the many.

Yet the relentlessness of capital in seeking new areas for investment has also led to unexpected emergences and convergences in the field of culture. The reach and scope of commercial mass media unite populations that had previously been divided. The spread of commodities into new areas often creates new economies of prestige and undermines traditional hierarchies. The accelerated flow of commerce, commodities, and people across national boundaries creates new social and political realities that enable some people in colonized countries to create new opportunities and alliances. Moreover, the very obsolescence of previous theories of social organization serves as an impetus for creating new ways of looking at the world.

The contemporary crisis of social theory comes largely from the inability of either the nation state or the free market to address adequately the grim realities of the emerging global economy and culture. Post-colonial culture has emerged in the context of this stalemate between two discredited theories. Important on its own terms as art, it also holds significance because of its potential to become one of the sites where social theory becomes reconstituted on a global scale. Post-colonial cultural expressions are based in the experiences of people and communities, rather than on the master narratives of the nation state. They foreground questions of cultural and social identity, rather than direct struggles for political power. They are pragmatic, immediate, and non-ideological, seeking to change life but putting forth no single blueprint for the future. In short, post-colonial culture contains all of the aspects identified by social theorists as characteristic of the "new social movements."

The New Social Movements

Theorists Manuel Castells and Alain Touraine stress that new social movements are often locally based and territorially defined. Hip hop and other forms of diasporic African music participate in constructing these local identities, but they bring to them a global consciousness.[11] They play out local rivalries (for example between New York and Los Angeles rappers) and speak powerfully to local politics (in the Caribbean, Europe, Africa, and North America), but they also situate themselves within international concerns. They have inverted prestige hierarchies around the world, and established new centers of cultural power from Kingston, Jamaica to Compton, California. But hip hop and reggae have also played roles in political movements opposed to apartheid in South Africa, in struggles for educational and curricular reform, and in battles against police brutality around the globe.

Certain Afro-centric theorists might claim that the extraordinary capacity of African musical systems to "capture" the cultures of their colonizers proves the existence of a trans-cultural trans-historical essential culture within the bodies of Africans. But more accurate is Paul Gilroy's analysis that "the African diaspora's consciousness of itself has been defined in and against constricting national boundaries," – forcing a transnational consciousness. Gilroy notes Ralph Ellison's argument in *Shadow and Act* that the amalgamated cultures formed by the fusion of African identities with European, American, and Asian circumstances mean that "it is not culture which binds the people who are of partially African origin now scattered throughout the world but an identity of passions."[12] The ability to find that identity of passions and turn it into a diasporic conversation informing political struggles in similar but not identical circumstances has enabled peoples of African descent to survive over the centuries; it may now also hold the key to survival for the rest of the world as well.

Like the influence of Central American magic realism on novels by African-American women, like the importance of novels questioning categories of identity by Asian-American and Native American women for feminists from many ethnicities, or like the growing recognition by indigenous populations of congruent realities in diverse national contexts, the music of the African diaspora testifies to the capacity of post-colonial culture to illumine families of resemblance illustrating how diverse populations have had similar although not identical experiences. By virtue of a shared skepticism about the nation state, an identification with the lived experiences of ordinary people, and an imaginative, supple, and strategic reworking of identities and cultures, post-colonial culture holds great significance as a potential site for creating coalitions to pose alternatives to the discredited maxims of conservative free-market capitalism or liberal social democracy.

The terrain of culture has emerged as a privileged site for transnational communication, organization, and mobilization at a time when the parochialism of trade unions and political parties leaves those institutions locked into national identities that seem to render them powerless to confront the inequities and injustices of the new global economy. Jamaican reggae singer Bob Marley's music of the 1970s played an important role in the formation of a "Black Power" movement in Australia, influenced liberation movements in Southern Africa, and formed a focal point of unity between diasporic Blacks and working-class whites in Britain.[13] More recently, Thomas Mapfuzmo's music deployed traditional cultural forms to fuse a new political unity during and after the chimurenga war in Zimbabwe, while Boukman Eksperyans has created music capable of connecting opponents of Haiti's dictatorial governments to popular traditions of slave rebellion and voudou religion. Popular music has also played an important role in movements against police brutality in the United Kingdom and the United States, and in campaigns building pan-ethnic anti-racist alliances in France and Germany.[14]

Among diasporic communities especially, traditional aesthetic, philosophical, moral, and political principles serve as resources in struggles against centralized systems of power. For these populations there have never been any "old social movements," because questions of identity and community always superseded the potential for making claims on the state through ideological coalitions. Their distance from state power and their experiences with cultural exclusion forced upon diasporic communities political practices rooted in the realities of what we have now come to call the "new social movements."[15]

Oppositional practices among diasporic populations emerge from painful experiences of labor migration, cultural imperialism, and political subordination. Yet they are distinguished by an ability to work within these systems. In contemporary culture, artists from aggrieved communities often subvert or invert the very instruments of domination necessary for the creation of the new global economy – its consumer goods, technologies, and images. Post-colonial literature, Third Cinema, and hip hop music all protest against conditions created by the oligopolies who distribute them as commodities for profit. They express painful recognition of cultural displacements, displacements that their very existence accelerates. Yet it is exactly their desire to work *through* rather than *outside* of existing structures that defines their utility as a model for contemporary global politics.

One might conclude that this reliance of post-colonial culture on existing economic and cultural forms can at best lead only to subordinate rather than autonomous reforms. That possibility certainly exists. But the desire to work through existing contradictions rather than stand outside them represents not so much a preference for melioristic reform over revolutionary change, but rather a recognition of the impossibility of standing outside totalitarian systems of domination. Attempts to create liberated zones, cooperatives, "socialism within one country," and counter-cultural communes have all failed because of the hegemonic power of capitalists within the world economic system. Although still useful as a means of raising consciousness, these strategies have been largely superseded by forms of struggle that engage in what Gramsci called the war of position (an effort to build a counter-hegemonic alliance) rather that what he termed the war of maneuver (the effort to seize state power).

Throughout the twentieth century, Leninist vanguard parties and artistic avant-gardes alike have attempted to position themselves outside dominant systems. They sought "free spaces" and "liberated zones" as prerequisites for the kinds of ideological mobilization that they felt would be necessary for radical change. But the Leninist parties always replicated the very structures of hierarchy and exploitation that they presumed to challenge (even after they seized state power), and attempts by artistic avant-gardes to confound the logic of the art market only produced newer and more lucrative objects for collection and exchange.

The cultural politics of post-colonialism flow from experiences resonant with the histories of Leninist parties and artistic avant-gardes, from struggles for independence and autonomy which also proved illusory even when they seemed to have won their goals. Rather than stand outside of society, the new social movements and their cultural corollaries immerse themselves in the contradictions of social life, seeking an immanent rather than a transcendent critique.

Thus, although they seem "new" to theorists of the new social movements, the techniques of immanent critique have a long history among aggrieved populations. People can take action only in the venues that are open to them; oppressed people rarely escape the surveillance and control of domination. Consequently they frequently have to "turn the guns around," to seize the instruments of domination used to oppress them and try to put them to other uses. For example, slave owners in the nineteenth-century South brought the Christian bible to their slaves to teach that true rewards come only in heaven; the slaves inverted their message by embracing Old Testament stories about Moses, Daniel, and Samson who secured deliverance in this world.[16] Similarly, imperialistic oil companies brought forty-five-gallon oil drums to Trinidad in the 1940s and left them discarded and dented; but Black workers discovered that the dents made it possible to turn the barrels into complete melodic and harmonic instruments. By combining rhythmic drumming and systemized pitch into the same instrument, they created a vehicle perfectly suited for expressing their situatedness in both European and African musical traditions.[17] Rastafarians and reggae musicians in Jamaica in the 1960s and 1970s seized the Judeo-Christian bible, English language, and commercial popular music only to reveal them as fabricated artifacts reflective of social hierarchies by "flinging them back rude" through inversions and subversions that de-naturalized religion, language, and music.[18]

The global popularity of hip hop culture – rap music, graffiti, break-dancing, B Boy fashion etc. – has been perhaps the most important recent manifestation of post-colonial culture on a global scale. The "diasporic intimacy" linking cultural production and reception among people of African descent in the Caribbean, the United States, Europe, and Africa has resulted in a cultural formation with extraordinary political implications. Although hip hop circulates as a commodity marketed by highly centralized monopolies from metropolitan countries, it also serves as a conduit for ideas and images articulating subaltern sensitivities. At a time when African people have less power and fewer resources than at almost any previous time in history, African culture has emerged as the single most important subtext within world popular culture. The popularity of hip hop reflects more than cultural compensation for political and economic domination, more than an outlet for energies and emotions repressed by social power relations. Hip hop expresses a form of politics perfectly suited to the post-colonial era. It brings a community into being through performance, and it maps out real and imagined relations between people that speak to the realities of displacement, disillusion, and despair created by the austerity economy of post-industrial capitalism.[19]

Hip Hop and the Politics of Sound

Hip hop culture brings to a world audience the core values of music from most sub-Saharan African cultures.[20] It blends music and life into an integrated totality, uniting performers, dancers, and listeners in a collaborative endeavor. As ethnomusicologist John Miller Chernoff observes, "the model of community articulated in an African musical event is one that is not held together by ideas, by cognitive symbols or by emotional conformity. The community is established through the interaction of individual rhythms and the people who embody them."[21] African music is participatory, collective, and collaborative. Rhythms are layered on top of one another as a dialogue – hearing one enables the others to make sense. The incorporation of these African elements into hip hop raises challenges to Western notions of musical (and social) order. As the great jazz drummer Max Roach explains,

> The thing that frightened people about hip hop was that they heard rhythm – rhythm for rhythm's sake. Hip hop lives in the world of sound – not the world of music – and that's why it's so revolutionary. What we as black people have always done is show that the world of sound is bigger than white people think. There are many areas that fall outside the narrow Western definition of music and hip hop is one of them.[22]

While clearly grounded in the philosophies and techniques of African music, the radical nature of hip hop comes less from its origins than from its uses. The flexibility of African musical forms encourages innovation and adaptation – a blending of old and new forms into dynamic forward-looking totalities. In her important scholarship on rap music, Tricia Rose has argued against reducing hip hop to its origins in African music or African-American oral traditions, but instead calls for an understanding of hip hop as "secondary orality," the deployment of oral traditions in an age of electronic reproduction.[23] As a cultural discourse and political activity, it thus speaks to both residual and emergent realities.

Digital sampling in rap music turns consumers into producers, tapping consumer memories of parts of old songs and redeploying them in the present. It employs advanced technology to reconstruct the human voice, and features robot-like movements and mechanical vocals that simulate machines.[24] Sampling foregrounds the fabricated artifice of machine technologies, calling attention to them through repetition, scratching, and mixing. But at the same time, these tactics humanize the machine by asking it to do the unexpected, and they allow for human imitations of machine sounds – as in the vocals by Doug E. Fresh, "the original human beat box."[25] Hip hop calls into question Western notions of cultural production as property through its evocation, quotation, and outright theft of socially shared musical memories. Yet it also illumines the emancipatory possibilities of new technologies and the readiness of marginalized and oppressed populations to employ them for humane ends – for shedding restricting social identities and embracing new possibilities of a life without hierarchy and exploitation.

Kobena Mercer and others have warned us against the folly of thinking that some cultural forms are innately radical – that the right combination of notes or colors or words can be socially or politically radical by themselves. Culture functions as a social force to the degree that it gets instantiated in social life and connected to the political aspirations and activities of groups.[26] It is here that hip hop holds its greatest significance and its greatest challenge to interpreters.

For example, in the mid-1980s, the New York graffiti artist, style leader, and hip hop entrepreneur Fab Five Freddy learned an important lesson about the politics of sound from Max Roach, the great jazz drummer from the bebop era.[27] Separated by decades and musical styles (Fab Five Freddy's father was once Max Roach's manager), the two men shared a common admiration for the energy and artistry of rap music. But one day Roach baffled his young friend by describing LL Cool J's music as "militant." Freddy later recalled, "I thought it was funny he should say that because I thought LL was an ego rapper, and political rap seemed out of fashion." But Roach persisted, claiming that:

> The rhythm was very militant to me because it was like marching, the sound of an army on the move. We lost Malcolm, we lost King and they thought they had blotted out everybody. But all of a sudden this new art form arises and the militancy is there in the music.

Once Roach had directed his attention away from the lyrics and toward the rhythm, Fab Five Freddy understood the drummer's point. "LL Cool J doesn't seem to like political music," he later explained in describing the incident, "but the politics was in the drums."[28]

The "politics in the drums" that Max Roach disclosed to Fab Five Freddy pervade hip hop. They express the restlessness and energy described by Frantz Fanon in his now classic anti-colonial text, *The Wretched of the Earth*. Speaking about times when desires for radical change permeate popular culture even though no political movement has yet arrived to challenge the established order, Fanon argues:

Well before the political fighting phase of the national movement, an attentive spectator can thus feel and see the manifestation of a new vigor and feel the approaching conflict. He [sic] will note unusual forms of expression and themes which are fresh and imbued with a power which is no longer that of an invocation but rather of the assembling of the people, a summoning together for a precise purpose. Everything works together to awaken the native's sensibility and to make unreal and unacceptable the contemplative attitude or the acceptance of defeat.[29]

Hip hop's energy originates in many sources, but a crucial component of its power comes from its ability to respond to the realities of the African diaspora. Most commentators in the USA. have portrayed diasporic consciousness as essentially a one-way process of preserving African elements in America or maintaining Afro-Caribbean traditions in New York. To be sure, African and Caribbean elements appear prominently in US hip hop, and many of the originators of hip hop in New York during the 1970s had Caribbean backgrounds. (Grandmaster Flash's parents and Afrika Bambaataa's mother and two aunts came to New York from Barbados; Kool DJ Herc aka Clive Campbell was born in Jamaica.)[30] But these claims place a value on origins that distorts the nature of Black Atlantic culture. The flow of information and ideas among diasporic people has not been solely from Africa outward to Europe and the Americas, but rather has been a reciprocal self-renewing dialogue in communities characterized by upheaval and change. The story of the African diaspora is more than an aftershock of the slave trade, it is an ongoing dynamic creation. The radicalism of diasporic African culture comes not only from the contrast between African and Euro-American values, but also from the utility of exploiting diasporic connections as a way of expanding choices everywhere – in Africa as well as in Europe, the Caribbean, and the Americas. Just as American and European Blacks have drawn on African traditions to contest Euro-American power relations, Africans have drawn upon cultures of opposition and strategies of sig-nification developed by diasporic Africans as a form of struggle on the African continent.

For example, Fela Kuti, the founder of Nigeria's radical Afro-beat music subcul-ture, learned part of his political radicalism in Los Angeles. His mother had been an activist, a friend of Ghana's President Kwame Nkrumah, and a founder of the Nigerian Women's Union and a leader in the successful struggle to gain the right to vote for women in her country.[31] For ten months in 1969–1970, Fela played music in Los Angeles at the Citadel de Haiti night club on Sunset Boulevard (owned by Black actor Bernie Hamilton, later featured in the television program "Starsky and Hutch"), but his main focus was on learning about Black nationalism. Sandra Smith (now Sandra Isidore), a woman active in the Black Panther Party, gave Fela a copy of *The Autobiography of Malcolm X* which introduced him to ideas about Pan-Africanism that had been censored in Nigeria.[32] "Sandra gave me the education I wanted to know," he recalled years later. "I swear man! She's the one who spoke to me about . . . Africa! For the first time I heard things I'd never heard before about Africa! Sandra was my adviser."[33]

Fela told friends he learned more about Africa in Los Angeles that he had in Lagos, and insisted that "The whole atmosphere of Black Revolution changed me, my consciousness, my thinking, my perception of things. I was educated."[34] Sandra

Smith recalls that she introduced him to poems by Nikki Giovanni and the spoken-word art of The Last Poets, as well as to writings by Angela Davis, Jesse Jackson, Stokely Carmichael, and Martin Luther King. In addition, she introduced him to music by Nina Simone and Miles Davis, and connected him with a circle of friends that included singer Esther Phillips, actors Melvin van Peebles and Jim Brown, and the comedian Stu Gilliam.[35] "For the first time, I saw the essence of blackism," he later told an interviewer. "I was exposed to awareness. It started me thinking. I saw how everything worked there. I realized that I had no country. I decided to come back and try to make my country African."[36]

Experiences in the USA made Fela Kuti more radical politically, but they also changed his music by informing it with a diasporic consciousness. As he explained, "Most Africans do not really know about life. They think everything from overseas is greater, but they do not know also that everything from overseas could have gone from here to overseas and come back to us. America gave me that line of thought."[37] Kuti has subsequently collaborated with Black American musicians including trumpeter Lester Bowie and vibraphonist Roy Ayers. Bowie went to Nigeria and lived with Fela during a particularly difficult time in his life, and admired both the music and politics that the Nigerian produced. "Fela's stubborn about the right things," Bowie explained to an interviewer. "He wants freedom, he wants to get away from oppression. The inequality of wealth in his country is unbelievable, and he's trying to address that. So did Martin Luther King, Jr., so did Malcolm X and so did the founding fathers of America."[38]

Similarly, Roy Ayers credits Fela for deepening his understanding of Africa during their collaborations. Kuti and Ayers toured Africa and recorded together in 1979. Ayers had been a frequent visitor to Africa, but even in the USA his deep interest in Afro-Cuban jazz gave his music a diasporic flavor. The recordings made by Fela Kuti and Roy Ayers showed traces of the Afro-Cuban influences on North American jazz as well as of Cuban "rhumba" bands on African, especially Congolese, music.[39] In turn, Ayers's 1970s jazz-funk albums (especially his Black nationalist *Red, Black, and Green* from 1973) have been a prime source of samples in recent years for hip hop djs and producers. "I've had about eight hit records on re-releases – rappers who have sampled my music," Ayers told an interviewer recently. "I was very happy because they give you a percentage, but more than that, I was honored that they dig my music. I went from swing to bebop to Latin, disco, funk, and fusion, so I respect all styles of music."[40]

Sojourns in North America and collaborations with African-American artists have been important to other African musicians as well. Aster Aweke sang for exiled Ethiopians in Washington, D.C. during the 1980s, creating a fusion music that turned Ethiopian wind and string parts into horn riffs and vocals in a style clearly influenced by Aretha Franklin and Anita Baker.[41] When Ali Farka Toure of Mali first heard records by Mississippi blues guitarist and singer John Lee Hooker he told a friend, "Listen, this is music that has been taken from here."[42] Toure eventually met Hooker and played music with him in Paris during the 1970s.[43] Expressing a preference for music by Hooker, Albert King, Otis Redding, James Brown, Wilson Pickett, Jimmy Smith, and Ray Charles, Toure explains, "If you listen to them for sixteen hours, you can no longer locate the stars, the sky and the clouds!"[44]

Abdullah Ibrahim left South Africa to tour Europe in 1962 and met Duke Ellington in Zurich. Ellington liked his music and arranged a recording contract for Ibrahim and his trio. When asked by an interviewer if he was surprised to be helped in that way by an American Black, Ibrahim replied that he did not really think of Ellington as an American or as a citizen of any country, but more as "the wise old man in the village – the extended village."[45] James Brown's tour of Zaire in 1969 had a major impact on African music, especially in helping promote the "Congo soul" sound of Trio Madjeski.[46] In the 1970s, songs by US rhythm and blues artists including Harold Melvin and the Blue Notes and the Staples Singers became anthems for township youths in South Africa because the songs enabled them to voice "cries for justice, recognition, and social action" denied them in the rest of their lives.[47]

Diasporic dialogue has also extended far beyond binary exchanges between Africa and North America. For example, Alpha Blondy from Côte d'Ivoire in Africa learned French reading the bible and mastered English from his school lessons and from playing American rock'n'roll in high school.[48] He went to Columbia University in New York in 1976 to study world trade. There he discovered a Jamaican-American reggae band, Monkaya, which he joined, singing his native Mandinka lyrics to the reggae beat. Blondy has become one of the best-selling reggae artists in the world, having recorded reggae songs in English, French, Dioula, and Mandingo. Explaining his interest in what most would consider West Indian music, Blondy argues: "In Africa, the new generation, my generation, is a mixture of Western and African culture. Reggae has succeeded in a musical unification, it's a good therapy to bring people together."[49] As part of this "therapy," Blondy's band includes musicians from Africa and the Caribbean, and he has performed songs in Arabic during concerts in Israel and songs in Hebrew during concerts in Arab countries. He played a concert in 1986 dedicated to encouraging good relations between Mali and Burkina-Faso, and drew 10,000 fans at the Moroccan International Festival of Youth and Music in Marrakech that same year to hear him play reggae.[50]

Reggae itself originated in Afro-Jamaican religious Burru music, especially its bass, funde, and repeater drums, but the form also drew upon African-American soul music, on records smuggled back to the island by Jamaican migrant workers employed to cut sugar cane in the southern USA (including Coxsone Dodd, founder of Kingston's Studio One), as well as on broadcasts by US radio stations including WINZ in Miami.[51] Africans like Alpha Blondy, who were familiar with American soul music, took to reggae in part because it contained elements of music they were already familiar with from America as well as from Africa.

On the other hand, when Jamaican singer Jimmy Cliff first heard the yelle music of Baaba Maal from Senegal, it struck him as structurally connected to the rhythms of reggae. Rap music's popularity in Korea stems in part from the close cultural connections built between the USA and that country since the mass exodus following the Kwangju uprising of the early 1980s, but also from the similarities between rap and traditional Korean sasui lyrics which are recited to the accompaniment of drums.[52]

Manu Dibango, a singer-composer-arranger-reed-piano player from Cameroon, moved to Paris in the 1960s where he started making records, including a tribute to the US rhythm and blues saxophone player King Curtis. In 1972 Dibango's "Soul Makossa" became an international hit. He moved to New York in the early 1970s where he played the Apollo Theatre in Harlem along with the Temptations and Barry White, and he also collaborated there with Afro-Caribbean musicians including Johnny Pacheco and the Fania All-Stars.[53] By the mid-1980s Dibango brought Antillean musicians into his band and expanded his repertoire to include the zouk music of the Francophone West Indies.[54]

Of course Caribbean music had long been familiar in Africa. The British government stationed West Indian regiments in West Africa as early as the 1830s, and their syncopated brass band and gumbey musics gained immediate popularity. The adaba variety of Nigerian highlife bears traces of calypso, while that nation's juju music uses the Brazilian samba drum.[55]

Hip hop employs the legacy of similar instances of diasporic dialogue. Jazzie B of the British group Soul II Soul remembers the lessons he learned in his youth from African American artists. "People like Curtis Mayfield were a very strong part of my life," he remembers. "His songs weren't just songs to me. They were knowledge. I used to carry my records right along with my school books." But at the same time, Jazzie B also credits the "African" community in Britain for having a formative influence on his music. "I don't just remember the music at the Africa Centre [dances], I also remember the people. It was like a religion, all those people sweating and dancing and partying together. It was very inspiring. That's what I tried to put on our album – that same sense of unity and spirit."[56]

The dynamism of diasporic interchanges in music confirms Peter Linebaugh's wry observation that long-playing records have surpassed sea-going vessels as the most important conduits of Pan-African communication.[57] But it is important to understand that diasporic dialogue in music builds on an infrastructure with a long history. For example, in the 1930s, Paul Robeson galvanized the black population of Britain (and other countries) with theatrical performances that complemented his role as a spokesperson for causes like the defense of the Scottsboro boys.[58] His films *King Solomon's Mines* (1937) and *Sanders of the River* (1934, featuring Jomo Kenyatta) brought certain aspects of African culture to world audiences accustomed to only the most caricatured views of the continent. Many Africans encountered Pan-Africanism the way Fela Kuti did, through the writings of diasporic Africans including Malcolm X, Aimé Césaire, Marcus Garvey, George Padmore, and W. E. B. DuBois.[59] As a foreign student, Kwame Nkrumah learned some lessons in politics attending Adam Clayton Powell's activist church in New York City, while Ghanaian activists used the US abolitionist hymn "John Brown's Body" to protest Nkrumah's imprisonment during the struggle for independence.[60] These political connections had deep cultural roots; Manu Dibango remembers how important it was for him to hear Louis Armstrong on the radio when he was growing up in Cameroon. "Here was a black voice singing tunes that reminded me of those that I had learned at the temple. I immediately felt at one with the warmth of that voice and with what it was singing."[61]

More recently, post-colonial writers in Africa have expressed their indebtedness to African-American writers. Ngugi Wa Thiong'o asserts:

> There's a very vibrant connection between Afro-American traditions in literature and those from many parts of the third world. I know that African literature as a whole has borrowed quite heavily from the Afro-American literary tradition, and I hope vice-versa.

Writers like Langston Hughes, Richard Wright, Amiri Baraka, and Alice Walker are quite popular in Africa.[62]

Nigerian writer Buchi Emecheta adds: "To me, the greatest writers who come from ethnic minorities writing in English come from America. I think the deep, the real deep thinkers now writing in the English language are the black women, such as Toni Morrison, Gloria Naylor, Alice Walker, etc."[63]

The dialogue of the African diaspora informs the politics and culture of countries across the globe. It draws upon ancient traditions and modern technologies, on situated knowledge and a nomadic sensibility. Generated from communities often criminally short of resources and institutions, it commands prestige from multi-national corporations and other bastions of privilege. It flows through the circuits of the post-industrial austerity economy, and yet still manages to bring to light inequities and injustices.

From Queen Latifah's "Ladies First" with its images of Africa and the Americas to Thomas Mapfumo's "Hupenyu Wanyu" which appropriates the African-American "Bo Diddley" beat for radical politics in Zimbabwe, diasporic intimacy secures space for oppositional expressions obliterated by much of mass media and electoral politics. In a world coming ever closer together through the machinations of global capital, it displays a situated but not static identity. Rooted in egalitarian and democratic visions of the world, diasporic intimacy nonetheless embraces contradiction, change, and growth. It serves notice of the willingness and ability of millions of people to play a meaningful role in the world that is being constructed around us.

In culture and in politics, diasporic expressions constantly come back to what Frantz Fanon called "the seething pot out of which the learning of the future will emerge."[64] A sense of urgency about the future permeates the practices of popular music. Salif Keita of Mali locates his interest in making popular music as more than a matter of style. In his own performances he blends traditional Malian music with things he learned listening to Western artists ranging from Pink Floyd to Stevie Wonder, from James Brown to Kenny Rogers. Defending his eclecticism, Keita explains, "At home, we are traditionalists. It's an attitude I disapprove of. It's we who make the history, and if we refer only to what has passed, there will be no history. I belong to a century that has little in common with the time of my ancestors. I want society to move."[65]

Manu Dibango sums up the problem with characteristic eloquence (although with unfortunately sexist pronouns) in a statement that might serve as the motto of the post-colonial project. He asserts:

People who are curious search for sounds; they seek out harmony and melody because they are curious. Your curiosity can be limited by your environment, or you can expand it to take in things from outside; a bigger curiosity for a bigger world. The extent of your curiosity should not be determined by the village, or the town, or a city in another continent. The musician moves in these circles, but he moves to break out of his limits.[66]

Notes

1 Mark Dery, "Rap," *Keyboard* (November) 1988, 34.
2 David Toop, *Rap Attack 2: African Rap to Global Hip Hop* (London: Serpent's Tail, 1991), 19, 39, 37, 56–60; Lawrence Stanley, ed., *Rap: The Lyrics* (New York: Penguin, 1992), 8; Joel Whitburn, *Top R & B Singles, 1942–1988* (Menomonee Falls, WI: Record Research, 1988), 33.
3 Mark Dery, "Rap," 46.
4 Larry Birnbaum, "Baaba Maal Sings Blues from the Real Heartland," *Pulse* (September) 1993, 39; Jay Cocks, "Rap Around the Globe," *Time* October 19, 1992, 70; Michael Jarrett, "Guru," *Pulse* (September) 1993, 39.
5 Fredric Jameson, *Postmodernism, or the Cultural Logic of Late Capitalism* (Durham, NC: Duke University Press, 1991), 47.
6 For an eloquent summary of the role played by transnational corporations see Masao Miyoshi, "A Borderless World? From Colonialism to Transnationalism and the Decline of the Nation State," *Critical Inquiry* (Summer) 1993. See also Thomas J. McCormick, *America's Half Century* (Baltimore, MD: Johns Hopkins University Press, 1989).
7 Which, of course, is not to say that messages intended for one purpose in Asia, Africa, and Latin America would not be received with a very different meaning by readers in Europe or North America.
8 Harvey Molotch and John Logan, *Urban Fortunes: The Political Economy of Place* (Berkeley: University of California Press, 1987), 254.
9 Robin D. G. Kelley, *Hammer and Hoe* (Chapel Hill: University of North Carolina Press, 1990).
10 Robert A. Hill, "Dread History: Leonard P. Howell and Millenarian Visions in Early Rastafari Religions in Jamaica," *Epoche: Journal of the History of Religions at UCLA* (1981), 32–4; George Lipsitz, "'How Does It Feel When You've Got no Food?' The Past as Present in Popular Music" in Richard Butsch, ed., *For Fun and Profit* (Philadelphia, PA: Temple University Press, 1990), 195–215; Paul Gilroy, *"There Ain't No Black in the Union Jack": The Cultural Politics of Race and Nation* (Chicago, IL: University of Chicago Press, 1987), 156.
11 Manuel Castells, *The City and the Grass Roots* (London: Edward Arnold, 1983); Alain Touraine, *The Voice and the Eye: An Analysis of Social Movements* (Cambridge: Cambridge University Press, 1981). See Paul Gilroy, *"There Ain't No Black in the Union Jack,"* esp. ch. 6.
12 Paul Gilroy, *"There Ain't No Black in the Union Jack,"* 158, 159.
13 See Marcus Breen, "Desert Dreams, Media, and Interventions in Reality: Australian Aboriginal Music," in Reebee Garofalo, ed., *Rockin' the Boat* (Boston, MA: South End, 1992), 149–70.
14 See for example references to the Newham 7 in Winston James, "Migration, Racism, and Identity: The Caribbean Experience in Britain," *New Left Review* no. 193 (May–June) 1992, 46; Nora Rathzel, "Germany: One Race, One Nation?" *Race and Class* vol. 32 no. 3 (1990). The role of the musical group Boukman Eksperyans and of a wide variety of visual artists in finding new meanings for voudou as part of the Aristide coalition in Haiti provides one of the best examples of these movements. Willie Apollon, "Voodoo and Visual Art," presentation at the University of California, San Diego, April 9, 1993.
15 For "new social movement" activity within old social movements see Robin D. G. Kelley, *Hammer and Hoe* and Vicki Ruiz, *Cannery Women, Cannery Lives* (Albuquerque: University of New Mexico Press, 1987).

16 Lawrence Levine, *Black Culture, Black Consciousness* (Berkeley: University of California Press, 1977); George Lipsitz, "The Struggle for Hegemony," *Journal of American History* vol.75 no.1 (June) 1988, 146–50.

17 Tom Chatburn, "Trinidad All Stars: The Steel Pan Movement in Britain," in Paul Oliver, ed., *Black Music in Britain: Essays on the Afro-Asian Contribution to Popular Music* (Buckingham: Open University Press, 1990), 120–1.

18 Dick Hebdige, "Reggae, Rastas, and Rudies" in Stuart Hall and Tony Jefferson, eds, *Resistance Through Ritual: Youth Subcultures in Post War Britain* (London: Hutchinson, 1976), 138–9; Robert A. Hill, "Dread History: Leonard P. Howell and Millenarian Visions in Early Rastafari Religions in Jamaica," *Epoche: Journal of the History of Religions at UCLA* (1981), 32–4; George Lipsitz, "'How Does it Feel When You've Got No Food?' The Past as Present in Popular Music," 195–214.

19 For discussion of hip hop and the "new social movements" see Paul Gilroy, *"There Ain't No Black in the Union Jack,"* 223–50.

20 It is important not to assume one unified African system of thought, politics, or culture. But especially in comparison to Western music, certain social and stylistic features from West Africa provide a vivid contrast.

21 John Miller Chernoff, "The Rhythmic Medium in African Music," *New Literary History* vol.22 no.4 (Autumn) 1991, 1095. See also J. H. Kwabena Nketia, *The Music of Africa* (New York: Norton, 1974), 21–50.

22 Frank Owen, "Hip Hop Bebop," *Spin* vol.4 (October) 1988, 61.

23 Tricia Rose, "Orality and Technology: Rap Music and Afro-American Cultural Resistance," *Popular Music and Society* vol.14 no.4 (Winter) 1988, 35–44. See also her *Black Noise* (Hanover: Wesleyan/University Press of New England), 1994.

24 High-tech and science-fiction themes played an important role in 1970s African-American music as a way of imagining a space outside of Euro-American racism, especially in the work of George Clinton and Funkadelic.

25 Paul Gilroy, *"There Ain't No Black in the Union Jack,"* 214.

26 I thank Mercer for bringing this to the attention of the Minority Discourse Group at the University of California Humanities Research Institute many times during the Fall of 1992.

27 Fab Five Freddy (Braithwaite) had long known Roach because his father was an attorney who served at one time as Roach's manager. David Toop, *Rap Attack 2*, 140.

28 Frank Owen, "Hip Hop Bebop," 73.

29 Frantz Fanon, *The Wretched of the Earth* (New York: Grove Press, 1968), 243.

30 David Toop, *Rap Attack 2*, 18, 19; Robert Farris Thompson, "Hip Hop 101," *On Campus*, 98.

31 Rob Tannenbaum, "Fela Anikulapao Kuti," *Musician* no. 79 (May) 1985, 30.

32 Born in Arkansas, Sandra Smith met Fela at an NAACP-sponsored performance featuring Fela's band and her own dance troupe that performed what they believed were African dances: Carlos Moore, *Fela, Fela: This Bitch of a Life* (London: Allison & Busby, 1982), 83, 91–2.

33 Carlos Moore, *Fela, Fela*, 85.

34 Tom Cheney, "Sorrow, Tears, and Blood: Q&A with Fela Anikulapo Kuti," *Los Angeles Reader* vol.8 no.41 (August 1, 1986), 1; Labinjog, "Fela Anikulapo Kuti," *Journal of Black Studies* (September) 1982, 126.

35 Carlos Moore, *Fela, Fela*, 95, 100.

36 John Darnton, "Afro-Beat: New Music with a Message," *New York Times*, July 7, 1986, 46.

37 Mabinuori Kayode Idowu, *Fela: Why Blackman Carry Shit* (Kaduna, Nigeria: Opinion Media Limited, 1985), 37.

38 Rob Tannenbaum, "Fela Anikulapao Kuti," 30.

39 Graeme Ewens, *Africa O-Ye! A Celebration of African Music* (New York: Da Capo, 1992), 32, 35; Kuti & Ayers, *Music of Many Colours*, Celluloid CD 6125, 1980, 1986.

40 Larry Birnbaum, "BeBop Meets Hip-Hop: Jazz for the Hip-Hop Nation," *Downbeat* vol.60 no.2 (February 1993), 35–6.

41 Graeme Ewens, *Africa O-Ye!*, 55; Ashenafi Kebede, "Aster Aweke," *Ethnomusicology* vol.35 no.1 (Winter), 1991, 157–9.

42 Ali Farka Toure, *African Blues*, liner notes, Shanachie Records 65002. From an interview with Ian Anderson in *Folk Roots*.

43 Graeme Ewens, *Africa O-Ye!*, 67.

44 Ali Farka Toure, *African Blues*, liner notes.

45 Karen Bennett, "An Audience with Dollar Brand," *Musician* (March) 1990, 41.

46 Graeme Ewens, *Africa O-Ye!*, 127.

47 David B. Coplan, *In Township Tonight! South Africa's Music and Theatre* (London: Longman, 1985), 195.

48 Don Snowden, "Alpha Blondy's Multicultural Universe," *Los Angeles Times*, February 21, 1988, calendar section, 76.

49 Jon Pareles, "African-Style Reggae Crosses the Atlantic," *New York Times*, March 22, 1988, C 13.

50 Stephen Davis, "Alpha Blondy," *The Reggae and African Beat* vol.7 no.1 (1987), 33.

51 Wendell Logan, "Conversation with Marjorie Whylie," *Black Perspective in Music* vol.10 no.1. (n.d.) 86, 88, 89, 92; Dick Hebdige, "Reggae, Rastas, and Rudies," in Stuart Hall and Tony Jefferson eds, *Resistance Through Ritual: Youth Subcultures in Post-war Britain* (London: Hutchinson, 1976), 143; Sebastian Clarke, *Jah Music: The Evolution of the Popular Jamaican Song* (London: Heinemann, 1980), 57–8. Coxsone Dodd, founder of Studio One, got his start as a sound system operator with records he brought back to Jamaica from the USA.

52 Byung Hoo Suh, "An Unexpected Rap Eruption Rocks a Traditional Music Market," *Billboard* vol.104 no.34 (August 22, 1992), S6.

53 Donald Clarke, ed., *The Penguin Encyclopedia of Popular Music* (London: Penguin, 1989), 339–40; Graeme Ewens, *Africa O-Ye!*, 116.

54 Graeme Ewens, *Africa O-Ye!*, 108.

55 John Collins, "Some Anti-Hegemonic Aspects of African Popular Music," in Reebee Garofalo, ed., *Rockin' the Boat*, 188, 189.

56 Robert Hilburn, "Tracing the Caribbean Roots of the New British Pop Invasion," *Los Angeles Times*, calendar section, September 24, 1989, 84. Paul Gilroy's observations about the importance of the USA and the Caribbean to Black Britain are relevant here. See Paul Gilroy, *"There Ain't No Black in the Union Jack,"* 154.

57 Quoted in Paul Gilroy, "Cultural Studies and Ethnic Absolutism," in Lawrence Grossberg, Cary Nelson, and Paula Treichler, *Cultural Studies* (New York: Routledge, 1992), 191.

58 Chris Stapleton, "African Connections: London's Hidden Music Scene," in Paul Oliver, ed., *Black Music in Britain*, 92.

59 John Collins, "Some Anti-Hegemonic Aspects of African Popular Music," in Reebee Garofalo, ed., *Rockin' the Boat*, 189.

60 John Collins, "Some Anti-Hegemonic Aspects of African Popular Music," 191.

61 "Interview with Manu Dibango," *Unesco Courier* (March 1991), 4.

62 Feroza Jussawalla and Reed Way Dasenbrock, eds, *Interviews with Writers of the Post-Colonial World* (Jackson: University Press of Mississippi, 1992), 41.

63 Feroza Jussawalla and Reed Way Dasenbrock, eds, *Interviews with Writers of the Post-Colonial World*, 93.

64 Frantz Fanon, *The Wretched of the Earth*, 225.

65 Banning Eyre, "Routes: The Parallel Paths of Baaba Maal and Salif Keita," *Option* no.53 (November–December, 1993), 48. Quoted in Neil Lazarus, "Unsystematic Fingers at the Conditions of the Times: 'Afropop' and the Paradoxes of Imperialism," in Jonathan White, ed., *Recasting the World: Writing After Colonialism* (Baltimore, MD and London: Johns Hopkins University Press, 1994), 140.

66 Manu Dibango, "Music in Motion," in Graeme Ewens, *Africa O-Ye!*, 7.

Part IV

Authoring Texts/Readers Reading

15 The Concept of Formula in the Study of Popular Literature

John G. Cawelti

The growing interest among humanistic scholars and teachers in popular culture is one of the more exciting academic trends of the present day. This field of study represents a great expansion in the range of human expression and activity subjected to the scrutiny of historians and scholars of the arts. Consequently one of the central problems in giving some shape to our inquiries into popular culture has been the need for analytical concepts which might enable us to find our way through the huge amount of material which is the potential subject-matter of studies in popular culture. Moreover, we badly need some way of relating the various perspectives, historical, psychological, sociological and aesthetic, which are being used in the investigation of such phenomena as the Western, the spy story, pop music, the comic strip, film and TV.

To some extent, students of popular culture have simply applied to a wider range of materials the historical and critical methods of traditional humanistic scholarship. This practice has led to more complex analyses of such popular forms as the detective story and richer, more carefully researched accounts of the development of various popular traditions. Approaching the material of popular culture with the traditional arsenal of humanistic disciplines is certainly a necessary first step. Nonetheless, the analysis of popular culture is somewhat different from that of the fine arts. When we are studying the fine arts, we are essentially interested in the unique achievement of the individual artist, while in the case of popular culture, we are dealing with a product that is in some sense collective. Of course it is possible to study the fine arts as collective products just as it is possible to examine individual works of popular culture as unique artistic creations. In the former case, the present discussion should apply with some qualifications to the fine arts, while in the latter, the traditional methods of humanistic scholarship are obviously the most appropriate, with some allowance for the special aesthetic problems of the popular arts.

Students of popular culture have defined the field in terms of several different concepts. When scholars were first interesting themselves in dime novels, detective stories, etc., they thought of them as subliterature. This concept reflected the traditional qualitative distinction between high culture and mass culture. Unfortunately it was really too vague to be of much analytical use. Even if one could determine where literature left off and subliterature began, a distinction that usually depended on the individual tastes of the inquirer, the term suggested only that the object of study was

Original publication: Cawelti, John G., "The Concept of Formula in the Study of Popular Literature," *Journal of Popular Culture* 3 (Popular Press, Bowling Green University, Ohio, 1969).

a debased form of something better. Like many concepts that have been applied to the study of popular culture, the idea of subliterature inextricably confused normative and descriptive problems.

Four additional concepts have come into fairly wide use in recent work: (a) the analysis of cultural themes; (b) the concept of medium; (c) the idea of myth and (d) the concept of formula. I would like to deal briefly with the first three, mainly by way of getting to a fuller discussion of what I consider the most promising concept of all.

The analysis of cultural, social, or psychological themes is certainly a tried and true method of dealing with popular culture. In essence, what the analyst does is to determine what themes appear most often or most prominently in the works under analysis and to group different works according to the presence or absence of the themes he is interested in. Unfortunately, there is a certain vagueness about the concept of theme. Such various things as the ideal of progress, the oedipal conflict, racism, and innocence have all been treated as themes. In effect, a theme turns out to be any prominent element or characteristic of a group of works which seems to have some relevance to a social or cultural problem. Though the vagueness of the concept can be cleared up when the investigator defines the particular theme or set of themes he is interested in, the concept of theme still seems inadequate because it depends on the isolation of particular elements from a total structure. This not only tends to oversimplify the works under investigation, but to lead to the kind of falsifying reduction that translates one kind of experience into another. Thus, a story of a certain kind becomes a piece of social rhetoric or the revelation of an unconscious urge. No doubt a story is or can be these things and many others, but to treat it as if it were only one or another social or psychological function is too great a reduction. What we need is a concept that will enable us to deal with the total structure of themes and its relationship to the story elements in the complete work.

The concept of medium has become notorious through the fascinating theories of Marshall McLuhan, Walter Ong and others who insist that medium rather than content or form as we have traditionally understood them ought to be the focus of our cultural analyses. This concept seems to have a particular application to studies in popular culture because many of the works we are concerned with are transmitted through the new electric media which McLuhan sees as so different from the Gutenberg galaxy, the media associated with print. The concept of medium is an important one and McLuhan is doubtless correct that it has been insufficiently explored in the past, but I am not persuaded that more sophisticated studies of the nature of media will do away with the need for generalizations about content. I am sure that we will need to revise many of our notions about where medium leaves off and content begins as the new studies in media progress, but for the present, I would like to forget about the idea of medium altogether with the explanation that I'm concerned with a different kind of problem, the exploration of the content of the popular media.

One more distinction along these lines is necessary. In this paper I will be concerned primarily with stories and with understanding the various cultural significances of these stories. While a large proportion of popular culture can be defined as stories of different kinds, this is certainly not an exhaustive way of defining popular culture. Just as there are other arts than fiction, so there are works of popular culture which do not tell stories. With additional qualifications the concepts I am seeking to define are applicable to the analysis of other expressions of popular culture than those embodied in stories, but to keep my task as simple as possible, I have chosen to limit myself to the discussion of stories.

The most important generalizing concept which has been applied to cultural studies in recent years is that of myth. Indeed, it could be argued that the concept of formula which I will develop in the course of this paper is simply another variation on the idea of myth. But if this is the case, I would argue that distinctions between meanings of the concept of myth are worth making and naming, for many different meanings can be ascribed to the term. In fact, the way in which some people use the term myth hardly separates it from the concept of theme, as when we talk about the myth of progress or the myth of success. There is also another common meaning of the term which further obfuscates its use, namely myth as a common belief which is demonstrably false as in the common opposition between myth and reality. Thus, when a critic uses the term myth one must first get clear whether he means to say that the object he is describing is a false belief, or simply a belief, or something still more complicated like an archetypal pattern. Moreover, because of the special connection of the term myth with a group of stories which have survived from ancient cultures, particularly the Greco-Roman, the scholar who uses the concept in the analysis of contemporary popular culture sometimes finds himself drawn into another kind of reductionism which takes the form of statements like the following: "the solution of the paradox of James Bond's popularity may be, not in considering the novels as thrillers, but as something very different, as historic epic and romance, based on the stuff of myth and legend." But if the retelling of myth is what makes something popular why on earth didn't Mr. Fleming simply retell the ancient myths.

Because of this great confusion about the term myth, I propose to develop another concept which I think I can define more clearly and then to differentiate this concept from that of myth, thereby giving us two more clearly defined generalizing concepts to work with. Let me begin with a kind of axiom or assumption which I hope I can persuade you to accept without elaborate argumentation: all cultural products contain a mixture of two kinds of elements: conventions and inventions. Conventions are elements which are known to both the creator and his audience beforehand – they consist of things like favorite plots, stereotyped characters, accepted ideas, commonly known metaphors and other linguistic devices, etc. Inventions, on the other hand, are elements which are uniquely imagined by the creator such as new kinds of characters, ideas, or linguistic forms. Of course it is difficult to distinguish in every case between conventions and inventions because many elements lie somewhere along a continuum between the two poles. Nonetheless, familiarity with a group of literary works will usually soon reveal what the major conventions are and therefore, what in the case of an individual work is unique to that creator.

Convention and invention have quite different cultural functions. Conventions represent familiar shared images and meanings and they assert an ongoing continuity of values; inventions confront us with a new perception or meaning which we have not realized before. Both these functions are important to culture. Conventions help maintain a culture's stability while inventions help it respond to changing circumstances and provide new information about the world. The same thing is true on the individual level. If the individual does not encounter a large number of conventionalized experiences and situations, the strain on his sense of continuity and identity will lead to great tensions and even to neurotic breakdowns. On the other hand, without new information about his world, the individual will be increasingly unable to cope with it and will withdraw behind a barrier of conventions as some people withdraw from life into compulsive reading of detective stories.

Most works of art contain a mixture of convention and invention. Both Homer and Shakespeare show a large proportion of conventional elements mixed with inventions of great genius. Hamlet, for example, depends on a long tradition of stories of revenge, but only Shakespeare could have invented a character who embodies so many complex perceptions of life that every generation is able to find new ways of viewing him. So long as cultures were relatively stable over long periods of time and homogeneous in their structure, the relation between convention and invention in works of literature posed relatively few problems. Since the Renaissance, however, modern cultures have become increasingly heterogeneous and pluralistic in their structure and discontinuous in time. In consequence, while public communications have become increasingly conventional in order to be understood by an extremely broad and diverse audience, the intellectual elites have placed ever higher valuation on invention out of a sense that rapid cultural changes require continually new perceptions of the world. Thus we have arrived at a situation in which the model great work of literature is Joyce's *Finnegan's Wake*, a creation which is almost as far as possible along the continuum toward total invention as it is possible to go without leaving the possibility of shared meanings behind. At the same time, there has developed a vast amount of literature characterized by the highest degree of conventionalization.

This brings us to an initial definition of formula. A formula is a conventional system for structuring cultural products. It can be distinguished from form which is an invented system of organization. Like the distinction between convention and invention, the distinction between formula and form can be best envisaged as a continuum between two poles; one pole is that of a completely conventional structure of conventions – an episode of the Lone Ranger or one of the Tarzan books comes close to this pole; the other end of the continuum is a completely original structure which orders inventions – *Finnegan's Wake* is perhaps the best example of this, though one might also cite such examples as Resnais' film "Last Year at Marienbad," T.S. Eliot's poem "The Waste Land," or Becket's play "Waiting for Godot." All of these works not only manifest a high degree of invention in their elements but unique organizing principles. "The Waste Land" makes the distinction even sharper for that poem contains a substantial number of conventional elements – even to the point of using quotations from past literary works – but these elements are structured in such a fashion that a new perception of familiar elements is forced upon the reader.

I would like to emphasize that the distinction between form and formula as I am using it here is a descriptive rather than a qualitative one. Though it is likely for a number of reasons that a work possessing more form than formula will be a greater work, we should avoid this easy judgment in our study of popular culture. In distinguishing form from formula we are trying to deal with the relationship between the work and its culture, and not with its artistic quality. Whether or not a different set of aesthetic criteria are necessary in the judgment of formal as opposed to formulaic works is an important and interesting question, but necessarily the subject of another series of reflections.

We can further differentiate the conception of formula by comparing it to genre and myth. Genre, in the sense of tragedy, comedy, romance, etc., seems to be based on a difference between basic attitudes or feelings about life. I find Northrop Frye's suggestion that the genres embody fundamental archetypal patterns reflecting stages of the human life cycle, a very fruitful idea here. In Frye's sense of the term genre and myth are universal patterns of action which manifest themselves in all human cultures. Following Frye, let me briefly suggest a formulation of this kind – genre can be defined as a structural pattern which embodies a universal life pattern or myth in the materials of language; formula, on the other hand is cultural; it represents the way in which a culture has embodied both mythical archetypes and its own pre-occupations in narrative form.

An example will help clarify this distinction. The western and the spy story can both be seen as embodiments of the archetypal pattern of the hero's quest which Frye discusses under the general heading of the mythos of romance. Or if we prefer psychoanalytic archetypes these formulas embody the oedipal myth in fairly explicit fashion, since they deal with the hero's conquest of a dangerous and powerful figure. However, though we can doubtless characterize both western and spy stories in terms of these universal archetypes, they do not account for the basic and important differences in setting, characters, and action between the western and the spy story. These differences are clearly cultural and they reflect the particular preoccupations and needs of the time in which they were created and the group which created them: the western shows its nineteenth century American origin while the spy story reflects the fact that it is largely a twentieth century British creation. Of course, a formula articulated by one culture can be taken over by another. However, we will often find important differences in the formula as it moves from one culture or from one period to another. For example, the gunfighter Western of the 1950's is importantly differ-ent from the cowboy romances of Owen Wister and Zane Grey, just as the American spy stories of Donald Hamilton differ from the British secret agent adventures of Eric Ambler and Graham Greene.

The cultural nature of formulas suggests two further points about them. First, while myths, because of their basic and universal nature turn up in many different manifestations, formulas, because of their close connection to a particular culture and period of time, tend to have a much more limited repertory of plots, characters, and settings. For example, the pattern of action known generally as the Oedipus myth can be discerned in an enormous range of stories from Oedipus Rex to the latest Western. Indeed, the very difficulty with this myth as an analytical tool is that it is so universal that it hardly serves to differentiate one story from another. Formulas, however, are much more specific: Westerns must have a certain kind of setting, a particular cast of characters and follow a limited number of lines of action. A Western that does not take place in the West, near the frontiers, at a point in history when social order and anarchy are in tension, and that does not involve some form of pursuit, is simply not a Western. A detective story that does not involve the solution of a mysterious crime is not a detective story. This greater specificity of plot, character, and setting reflects a more limited framework of interest, values, and tensions that relate to culture rather than to the generic nature of man.

The second point is a hypothesis about why formulas come into existence and enjoy such wide popular sue. Why of all the infinite possible subjects for fictions do a few like the adventures of the detective, the secret agent, and the cowboy so dominate the field.

I suggest that formulas are important because they represent syntheses of several important cultural functions which, in modern cultures have been taken over by the popular arts. Let me suggest just one or two examples of what I mean. In earlier more homogeneous cultures religious ritual performed the important function of articulating and reaffirming the primary cultural values. Today, with cultures composed of a multiplicity of differing religious groups the synthesis of values and their reaffirmation has become an increasingly important function of the mass media and the popular arts. Thus, one important dimension of formula is social or cultural ritual. Homogeneous cultures also possessed a large repertory of games and songs which all members of the culture understood and could participate in both for a sense of group solidarity and for personal enjoyment and recreation. Today, the great spectator sports provide one way in which a mass audience can participate in games together. Artistic formulas also fulfill this function in that they constitute entertainments with rules known to everyone. Thus, a very wide audience can follow a Western, appreciate its fine points and vicariously participate in its pattern of suspense and resolution. Indeed one of the more interesting ways of defining a western is as a game: a western is a three-sided game played on a field where the middle line is the frontier and the two main areas of play are the settled town and the savage wilderness. The three sides are the good group of townspeople who stand for law and order, but are handicapped by lack of force; the villains who reject law and order and have force; and the hero who has ties with both sides. The object of the game is to get the hero to lend his force to the good group and to destroy the villain. Various rules determine how this can be done; for example, the hero cannot use force against the villain unless strongly provoked. Also like games, the formula always gets to its goal. Someone must win, and the story must be resolved.

This game dimension of formulas has two aspects. First, there is the patterned experience of excitement, suspense, and release which we associate with the functions of entertainment and recreation. Second, there is the aspect of play as ego-enhancement through the temporary resolution of inescapable frustrations and tensions through fantasy. As Piaget sums up this aspect of play:

> Conflicts are foreign to play, or, if they do occur, it is so that the ego may be freed from them by compensation or liquidation, whereas serious activity has to grapple with conflicts which are inescapable. The conflict between obedience and individual liberty is, for example, the affliction of childhood [and we might note a key theme of the Western] and in real life the only solutions to this conflict are submission, revolt, or cooperation which involves some measure of compromise. In play, however, the conflicts are transposed in such a way that the ego is revenged, either by suppression of the problem or by giving it an acceptable solution... it is because the ego dominates the whole universe in play that it is freed from conflict.

Thus, the game dimension of formula is a culture's way of simultaneously entertaining itself and of creating an acceptable pattern of temporary escape from the serious restrictions and limitations of human life. In formula stories, the detective always solves the crime, the hero always determines and carries out true justice, and the agent accomplishes his mission or at least preserves himself from the omnipresent threats of the enemy.

Finally, formula stories seem to be one way in which the individuals in a culture act out certain unconscious or repressed needs, or express in an overt and symbolic fashion certain latent motives which they must give expression to, but cannot face openly. This is the most difficult aspect of formula to pin down. Many would argue that one cannot meaningfully discuss latent contents or unconscious motives beyond the individual level or outside of the clinical context. Certainly it is easy to generate a great deal of pseudo-psychoanalytic theories about literary formulas and to make deep symbolic interpretations which it is clearly impossible to substantiate convincingly. However, though it may be difficult to develop a reliable method of analysis of this aspect of formulas, I am convinced that the Freudian insight that recurrent myths and stories embody a kind of collective dreaming process is essentially correct and has an important application on the cultural as well as the universal level, that is, that the idea of a collective dream applies to formula as well as to myth. But there is no doubt that we need to put much more thought into our approach to these additional dimensions of formula and about their relation to the basic dimension of a narrative construction.

My argument, then, is that formula stories like the detective story, the Western, the seduction novel, the biblical epic, and many others are structures of narrative conventions which carry out a variety of cultural functions in a unified way. We can best define these formulas as principles for the selection of certain plots, characters, and settings, which possess in addition to their basic narrative structure the dimensions of collective ritual game and dream. To analyze these formulas we must first define them as narrative structures of a certain kind and then investigate how the additional dimensions of ritual, game and dream have been synthesized into the particular patterns of plot, character and setting which have become associated with the formula. Once we have understood the way in which particular formulas are structured we will be able to compare them, and also to relate them to the cultures which use them. By these methods I feel that we will arrive at a new understanding of the phenomena of popular literature and new insights into the patterns of culture.

16 The Task of the Translator: An Introduction to the Translation of Baudelaire's *Tableaux Parisiens*

Walter Benjamin

In the appreciation of a work of art or an art form, consideration of the receiver never proves fruitful. Not only is any reference to a certain public or its representatives misleading, but even the concept of an "ideal" receiver is detrimental in the theoretical consideration of art, since all it posits is the existence and nature of man as such. Art, in the same way, posits man's physical and spiritual existence, but in none of its works is it concerned with his response. No poem is intended for the reader, no picture for the beholder, no symphony for the listener.

Is a translation meant for readers who do not understand the original? This would seem to explain adequately the divergence of their standing in the realm of art. Moreover, it seems to be the only conceivable reason for saying "the same thing" repeatedly. For what does a literary work "say"? What does it communicate? It "tells" very little to those who understand it. Its essential quality is not statement or the imparting of information. Yet any translation which intends to perform a transmitting function cannot transmit anything but information – hence, something inessential. This is the hallmark of bad translations. But do we not generally regard as the essential substance of a literary work what it contains in addition to information – as even a poor translator will admit – the unfathomable, the mysterious, the "poetic," something that a translator can reproduce only if he is also a poet? This, actually, is the cause of another characteristic of inferior translation, which consequently we may define as the inaccurate transmission of an inessential content. This will be true whenever a translation undertakes to serve the reader. However, if it were intended for the reader, the same would have to apply to the original. If the original does not exist for the reader's sake, how could the translation be understood on the basis of this premise?

Translation is a mode. To comprehend it as mode one must go back to the original, for that contains the law governing the translation: its translatability. The question of whether a work is translatable has a dual meaning. Either: Will an adequate translator ever be found among the totality of its readers? Or, more pertinently: Does its nature lend itself to translation and, therefore, in view of the significance of the mode, call for it? In principle, the first question can be decided only contingently; the second, however, apodictically. Only superficial thinking will deny the independent

Original publication: Benjamin, Walter, "The Task of the Translator: An Introduction to the Translation of Baudelaire's *Tableaux Parisiens*," from *Illuminations* by Walter Benjamin (Suhrkamp Verlag, Frankfurt am Main. English translation by Harry Zohn, 1968).

meaning of the latter and declare both questions to be of equal significance.... It should be pointed out that certain correlative concepts retain their meaning, and possibly their foremost significance, if they are referred exclusively to man. One might, for example, speak of an unforgettable life or moment even if all men had forgotten it. If the nature of such a life or moment required that it be unforgotten, that predicate would not imply a falsehood but merely a claim not fulfilled by men, and probably also a reference to a realm in which it *is* fulfilled: God's remembrance. Analogously, the translatability of linguistic creations ought to be considered even if men should prove unable to translate them. Given a strict concept of translation, would they not really be translatable to some degree? The question as to whether the translation of certain linguistic creations is called for ought to be posed in this sense. For this thought is valid here: If translation is a mode, translatability must be an essential feature of certain works.

Translatability is an essential quality of certain works, which is not to say that it is essential that they be translated; it means rather that a specific significance inherent in the original manifests itself in its translatability. It is plausible that no translation, however good it may be, can have any significance as regards the original. Yet, by virtue of its translatability the original is closely connected with the translation; in fact, this connection is all the closer since it is no longer of importance to the original. We may call this connection a natural one, or, more specifically, a vital connection. Just as the manifestations of life are intimately connected with the phenomenon of life without being of importance to it, a translation issues from the original – not so much from its life as from its afterlife. For a translation comes later than the original, and since the important works of world literature never find their chosen translators at the time of their origin, their translation marks their stage of continued life. The idea of life and afterlife in works of art should be regarded with an entirely unmetaphorical objectivity. Even in times of narrowly prejudiced thought there was an inkling that life was not limited to organic corporeality. But it cannot be a matter of extending its dominion under the feeble scepter of the soul, as Fechner tried to do, or, conversely, of basing its definition on the even less conclusive factors of animality, such as sensation, which characterize life only occasionally. The concept of life is given its due only if everything that has a history of its own, and is not merely the setting for history, is credited with life. In the final analysis, the range of life must be determined by history rather than by nature, least of all by such tenuous factors as sensation and soul. The philosopher's task consists in comprehending all of natural life through the more encompassing life of history. And indeed, is not the continued life of works of art far easier to recognize than the continual life of animal species? The history of the great works of art tells us about their antecedents, their realization in the age of the artist, their potentially eternal afterlife in succeeding generations. Where this last manifests itself, it is called fame. Translations that are more than transmissions of subject matter come into being when in the course of its survival a work has reached the age of its fame. Contrary, therefore, to the claims of bad translators, such translations do not so much serve the work as owe their existence to it. The life of the originals attains in them to its ever-renewed latest and most abundant flowering.

Being a special and high form of life, this flowering is governed by a special, high purposiveness. The relationship between life and purposefulness, seemingly obvious yet almost beyond the grasp of the intellect, reveals itself only if the ultimate purpose toward which all single functions tend is sought not in its own sphere but in a higher one. All purposeful manifestations of life, including their very purposiveness, in the final analysis have their end not in life, but in the expression of its nature, in the representation of its significance. Translation thus ultimately serves the purpose of expressing the central reciprocal relationship between languages. It cannot possibly reveal or establish this hidden relationship itself; but it can represent it by realizing it in embryonic or intensive form. This representation of hidden significance through an embryonic attempt at making it visible is of so singular a nature that it is rarely met with in the sphere of nonlinguistic life. This, in its analogies and symbols, can draw on other ways of suggesting meaning than intensive – that is, anticipative, intimating – realization. As for the posited central kinship of languages, it is marked by a distinctive convergence. Languages are not strangers to one another, but are, a priori and apart from all historical relationships, interrelated in what they want to express.

With this attempt at an explication our study appears to rejoin, after futile detours, the traditional theory of translation. If the kinship of language is to be demonstrated by translations, how else can this be done but by conveying the form and meaning of the original as accurately as possible? To be sure, that theory would be hard put to define the nature of this accuracy and therefore could shed no light on what is important in a translation. Actually, however, the kinship of languages is brought out by a translation far more profoundly and clearly than in the superficial and indefinable similarity of two works of literature. To grasp the genuine relationship between an original and a translation requires an investigation analogous to the argumentation by which a critique of cognition would have to prove the impossibility of an image theory. There it is a matter of showing that in cognition there could be no objectivity, not even a claim to it, if it dealt with images of reality; here it can be demonstrated that no translation would be possible if in its ultimate essence it strove for likeness to the original. For in its afterlife – which could not be called that if it were not a transformation and a renewal of something living – the original undergoes a change. Even words with fixed meaning can undergo a maturing process. The obvious tendency of a writer's literary style may in time wither away, only to give rise to immanent tendencies in the literary creation. What sounded fresh once may sound hackneyed later; what was once current may someday sound quaint. To seek the essence of such changes, as well as the equally constant changes in meaning, in the subjectivity of posterity rather than in the very life of language and its works, would mean – even allowing for the crudest psychologism – to confuse the root cause of a thing with its essence. More pertinently, it would mean denying, by an impotence of thought, one of the most powerful and fruitful historical processes. And even if one tried to turn an author's last stroke of the pen into the *coup de grâce* of his work, this still would not save that dead theory of translation. For just as the tenor and the significance of the great works of literature undergo a complete transformation over the centuries, the mother tongue of the translator is transformed as well. While a poet's words endure in his own language, even the greatest translation is destined to become part of the growth of its own language and eventually to be absorbed by its renewal. Translation is so far removed from being the sterile equation of two dead languages that of all literary forms it is the one charged with the special mission of watching over the maturing process of the original language and the birth pangs of its own.

If the kinship of languages manifests itself in translations, this is not accomplished through a vague alikeness between adaptation and original. It stands to reason that kinship does not necessarily involve likeness. The concept of kinship as used here is in accord with its more restricted common usage: in both cases, it cannot be defined adequately by identity of origin, although in defining the more restricted usage the concept of origin remains indispensable. Wherein resides the relatedness of two languages, apart from historical considerations? Certainly not in the similarity between works of literature or words. Rather, all suprahistorical kinship of languages rests in the intention underlying each language as a whole – an intention, however, which no single language can attain by itself but which is realized only by the totality of their intentions supplementing each other: pure language. While all individual elements of foreign languages – words, sentences, structure – are mutually exclusive, these languages supplement one another in their intentions. Without distinguishing the intended object from the mode of intention, no firm grasp of this basic law of a philosophy of language can be achieved. The words *Brot* and *pain* "intend" the same object, but the modes of this intention are not the same. It is owing to these modes that the word *Brot* means something different to a German than the word *pain* to a Frenchman, that these words are not interchangeable for them, that, in fact, they strive to exclude each other. As to the intended object, however, the two words mean the very same thing. While the modes of intention in these two words are in conflict, intention and object of intention complement each of the two languages from which they are derived; there the object is complementary to the intention. In the individual, unsupplemented languages, meaning is never found in relative independence, as in individual words or sentences; rather, it is in a constant state of flux – until it is able to emerge as pure language from the harmony of all the various modes of intention. Until then, it remains hidden in the languages. If, however, these languages continue to grow in this manner until the end of their time, it is translation which catches fire on the eternal life of the works and the perpetual renewal of language. Translation keeps putting the hallowed growth of languages to the test: How far removed is their hidden meaning from revelation, how close can it be brought by the knowledge of this remoteness?

This, to be sure, is to admit that all translation is only a somewhat provisional way of coming to terms with the foreignness of languages. An instant and final rather than a temporary and provisional solution of this foreignness remains out of the reach of mankind; at any rate, it eludes any direct attempt. Indirectly, however, the growth of religions ripens the hidden seed into a higher development of language. Although translation, unlike art, cannot claim permanence for its products, its goal is undeniably a final, conclusive, decisive stage of all linguistic creation. In translation the original rises into a higher and purer linguistic air, as it were. It cannot live there permanently, to be sure, and it certainly does not reach it in its entirety. Yet, in a singularly impressive manner, at least it points the way to this region: the predestined, hitherto inaccessible realm of reconciliation and fulfillment of languages. The transfer can never be total, but what reaches this region is that element in a translation which goes beyond transmittal of subject matter. This nucleus is best defined as the element that does not lend itself to translation. Even when all the surface content has been extracted and transmitted, the primary concern of the genuine translator remains elusive. Unlike the words of the original, it is not translatable, because the relationship between content and language is quite different in the original and the translation. While content and language form a certain unity in the original, like a fruit and its skin, the language of the translation envelops its content like a royal robe with ample folds. For it signifies a more exalted language than its own and thus remains unsuited to its content, overpowering and alien. This disjunction prevents translation and at the same time makes it superfluous. For any translation of a work originating in a specific stage of linguistic history represents, in regard to a specific aspect of its content, translation into all other languages. Thus translation, ironically, transplants the original into a more definitive linguistic realm since it can no longer be displaced by a secondary rendering. The original can only be raised there anew and at other points of time. It is no mere coincidence that the word "ironic" here brings the Romanticists to mind. They, more than any others, were gifted with an insight into the life of literary works which has its highest testimony in translation. To be sure, they hardly recognized translation in this sense, but devoted their entire attention to criticism, another, if a lesser, factor in the continued life of literary works. But even though the Romanticists virtually ignored translation in their theoretical writings, their own great translations testify to their sense of the essential nature and the dignity of this literary mode. There is abundant evidence that this sense is not necessarily most pronounced in a poet; in fact, he may be least open to it. Not even literary history suggests the traditional notion that great poets have been eminent translators and lesser poets have been indifferent translators. A number of the most eminent ones, such as Luther, Voss, and Schlegel, are incomparably more important as translators than as creative writers; some of the great among them, such as Hölderlin and Stefan George, cannot be simply subsumed as poets, and quite particularly not if we consider them as translators. As translation is a mode of its own, the task of the translator, too, may be regarded as distinct and clearly differentiated from the task of the poet.

The task of the translator consists in finding that intended effect [*Intention*] upon the language into which he is translating which produces in it the echo of the original. This is a feature of translation which basically differentiates it from the poet's work, because the effort of the latter is never directed at the language as such, at its totality, but solely and immediately at specific linguistic contextual aspects. Unlike a work of literature, translation does not find itself in the center of the language forest but on the outside facing the wooded ridge; it calls into it without entering, aiming at that single spot where the echo is able to give, in its own language, the reverberation of the work in the alien one. Not only does the aim of translation differ from that of a literary work – it intends language as a whole, taking an individual work in an alien language as a point of departure – but it is a different effort altogether. The intention of the poet is spontaneous, primary, graphic; that of the translator is derivative, ultimate, ideational. For the great motif of integrating many tongues into one true language is at work. This language is one in which the independent sentences, works of literature, critical judgments, will never communicate – for they remain dependent on translation; but in it the languages themselves, supplemented and reconciled in their mode of signification, harmonize. If there is such a thing as a language of truth, the tensionless and even silent depository of the ultimate truth which all thought strives for, then this language of truth is – the true language. And this very language, whose divination and description is the only perfection a philosopher can hope for, is concealed in concentrated fashion in translations. There is no muse of philosophy, nor is there one of translation. But despite the claims of sentimental artists, these two are not banausic. For there is a philosophical genius that is characterized by a yearning for that language which manifests itself in translations. *"Les langues imparfaites en cela que plusieurs, manque la suprême: penser étant écrire sans accessoires, ni chuchotement mais tacite encore l'immortelle parole, la diversité, sur terre, des idiomes empêche personne de proférer les mots qui, sinon se trouveraient, par une frappe unique, elle-même matériellement la vérité."*[1] If what Mallarmé evokes here is fully fathomable to a philosopher, translation, with its rudiments of such a language, is midway between poetry and doctrine. Its products are less sharply defined, but it leaves no less of a mark on history.

If the task of the translator is viewed in this light, the roads toward a solution seem to be all the more obscure and impenetrable. Indeed, the problem of ripening the seed of pure language in a translation seems to be insoluble, determinable in no solution. For is not the ground cut from under such a solution if the reproduction of the sense ceases to be decisive? Viewed negatively, this is actually the meaning of all the foregoing. The traditional concepts in any discussion of translations are fidelity and license – the freedom of faithful reproduction and, in its service, fidelity to the word. These ideas seem to be no longer serviceable to a theory that looks for other things in a translation than reproduction of meaning. To be sure, traditional usage makes these terms appear as if in constant conflict with each other. What can fidelity really do for the rendering of meaning? Fidelity in the translation of individual words can almost never fully reproduce the meaning they have in the original. For sense in its poetic significance is not limited to meaning, but derives from the connotations conveyed by the word chosen to express it. We say of words that they have emotional connotations. A literal rendering of the syntax completely demolishes the theory of reproduction of meaning and is a direct threat to comprehensibility. The nineteenth century considered Hölderlin's translations of Sophocles as monstrous examples of such literalness. Finally, it is self-evident how greatly fidelity in reproducing the form impedes the rendering of the sense. Thus no case for literalness can be based on a desire to retain the meaning. Meaning is served far better – and literature and language far worse – by the unrestrained license of bad translators. Of necessity, therefore, the demand for literalness, whose justification is obvious, whose legitimate ground is quite obscure, must be understood in a more meaningful context. Fragments of a vessel which are to be glued together must match one another in the smallest details, although they need not be like one another. In the same way a translation, instead of resembling the meaning of the original, must lovingly and in detail incorporate the original's mode of signification, thus making both the original and the translation recognizable as fragments of a greater language, just as fragments are part of a vessel. For this very reason translation must in large measure refrain from wanting to communicate something, from rendering the sense, and in this the original is important to it only insofar as it has already relieved the translator and his translation of the effort of assembling and expressing what is to be conveyed. In the realm of translation, too, the words ἐν ἀρχῇ ην ὁ λόγος [in the beginning was the

word] apply. On the other hand, as regards the meaning, the language of a translation can – in fact, must – let itself go, so that it gives voice to the *intentio* of the
original not as reproduction but as harmony, as a supplement to the language in
which it expresses itself, as its own kind of *intentio*. Therefore it is not the highest
praise of a translation, particularly in the age of its origin, to say that it reads as if it
had originally been written in that language. Rather, the significance of fidelity as
ensured by literalness is that the work reflects the great longing for linguistic
complementation. A real translation is transparent; it does not cover the original,
does not block its light, but allows the pure language, as though reinforced by its
own medium, to shine upon the original all the more fully. This may be achieved,
above all, by a literal rendering of the syntax which proves words rather than
sentences to be the primary element of the translator. For if the sentence is the wall
before the language of the original, literalness is the arcade.

Fidelity and freedom in translation have traditionally been regarded as conflicting
tendencies. This deeper interpretation of the one apparently does not serve to
reconcile the two; in fact, it seems to deny the other all justification. For what is
meant by freedom but that the rendering of the sense is no longer to be regarded as
all-important? Only if the sense of a linguistic creation may be equated with the
information it conveys does some ultimate, decisive element remain beyond all
communication – quite close and yet infinitely remote, concealed or distinguishable,
fragmented or powerful. In all language and linguistic creations there remains in
addition to what can be conveyed something that cannot be communicated; depending on the context in which it appears, it is something that symbolizes or something
symbolized. It is the former only in the finite products of language, the latter in the
evolving of the languages themselves. And that which seeks to represent, to produce
itself in the evolving of languages, is that very nucleus of pure language. Though
concealed and fragmentary, it is an active force in life as the symbolized thing itself,
whereas it inhabits linguistic creations only in symbolized form. While that ultimate
essence, pure language, in the various tongues is tied only to linguistic elements and
their changes, in linguistic creations it is weighted with a heavy, alien meaning. To
relieve it of this, to turn the symbolizing into the symbolized, to regain pure language
fully formed in the linguistic flux, is the tremendous and only capacity of translation.
In this pure language – which no longer means or expresses anything but is, as
expressionless and creative Word, that which is meant in all languages – all information, all sense, and all intention finally encounter a stratum in which they are
destined to be extinguished. This very stratum furnishes a new and higher justification for free translation; this justification does not derive from the sense of what is to
be conveyed, for the emancipation from this sense is the task of fidelity. Rather, for
the sake of pure language, a free translation bases the test on its own language. It is
the task of the translator to release in his own language that pure language which is
under the spell of another, to liberate the language imprisoned in a work in his recreation of that work. For the sake of pure language he breaks through decayed
barriers of his own language. Luther, Voss, Hölderlin, and George have extended the
boundaries of the German language. – And what of the sense in its importance for
the relationship between translation and original? A simile may help here. Just as a
tangent touches a circle lightly and at but one point, with this touch rather than with
the point setting the law according to which it is to continue on its straight path to

infinity, a translation touches the original lightly and only at the infinitely small point of the sense, thereupon pursuing its own course according to the laws of fidelity in the freedom of linguistic flux. Without explicitly naming or substantiating it, Rudolf Pannwitz has characterized the true significance of this freedom. His observations are contained in *Die Krisis der europäischen Kultur* and rank with Goethe's Notes to the *Westöstlicher Divan* as the best comment on the theory of translation that has been published in Germany. Pannwitz writes: "Our translations, even the best ones, proceed from a wrong premise. They want to turn Hindi, Greek, English into German instead of turning German into Hindi, Greek, English. Our translators have a far greater reverence for the usage of their own language than for the spirit of the foreign works.... The basic error of the translator is that he preserves the state in which his own language happens to be instead of allowing his language to be powerfully affected by the foreign tongue. Particularly when translating from a language very remote from his own he must go back to the primal elements of language itself and penetrate to the point where work, image, and tone converge. He must expand and deepen his language by means of the foreign language. It is not generally realized to what extent this is possible, to what extent any language can be transformed, how language differs from language almost the way dialect differs from dialect; however, this last is true only if one takes language seriously enough, not if one takes it lightly."

The extent to which a translation manages to be in keeping with the nature of this mode is determined objectively by the translatability of the original. The lower the quality and distinction of its language, the larger the extent to which it is information, the less fertile a field is it for translation, until the utter preponderance of content, far from being the lever for a translation of distinctive mode, renders it impossible. The higher the level of a work, the more does it remain translatable even if its meaning is touched upon only fleetingly. This, of course, applies to originals only. Translations, on the other hand, prove to be untranslatable not because of any inherent difficulty, but because of the looseness with which meaning attaches to them. Confirmation of this as well as of every other important aspect is supplied by Hölderlin's translations, particularly those of the two tragedies by Sophocles. In them the harmony of the languages is so profound that sense is touched by language only the way an aeolian harp is touched by the wind. Hölderlin's translations are prototypes of their kind; they are to even the most perfect renderings of their texts as a prototype is to a model. This can be demonstrated by comparing Hölderlin's and Rudolf Borchardt's translations of Pindar's Third Pythian Ode. For this very reason Hölderlin's translations in particular are subject to the enormous danger inherent in all translations: the gates of a language thus expanded and modified may slam shut and enclose the translator with silence. Hölderlin's translations from Sophocles were his last work; in them meaning plunges from abyss to abyss until it threatens to become lost in the bottomless depths of language. There is, however, a stop. It is vouchsafed to Holy Writ alone, in which meaning has ceased to be the watershed for the flow of language and the flow of revelation. Where a text is identical with truth or dogma, where it is supposed to be "the true language" in all its literalness and without the mediation of meaning, this text is unconditionally translatable. In such case translations are called for only because of the plurality of languages. Just as, in the original, language and revelation are one without any tension, so the translation must be one with the original in the form of the interlinear version, in which literalness and freedom are united. For to some degree all great texts contain their potential translation between the lines; this is true to the highest degree of sacred writings. The interlinear version of the Scriptures is the prototype or ideal of all translation.

Note

1 "The imperfection of languages consists in their plurality, the supreme one is lacking: thinking is writing without accessories or even whispering, the immortal word still remains silent; the diversity of idioms on earth prevents everybody from uttering the words which otherwise, at one single stroke, would materialize as truth."

17 Intertextuality

John Fiske

The theory of intertextuality proposes that any one text is necessarily read in relationship to others and that a range of textual knowledges is brought to bear upon it. These relationships do not take the form of specific allusions from one text to another and there is no need for readers to be familiar with specific or the same texts to read intertextually. Intertextuality exists rather in the space *between* texts. Madonna's music video *Material Girl* provide us with a case in point: it is a parody of Marilyn Monroe's song and dance number "Diamonds are a Girl's Best Friend" in the movie *Gentlemen Prefer Blondes*: such an allusion to a specific text is not an example of intertextuality for its effectiveness depends upon specific, not generalized, textual knowledge – a knowledge that, incidentally, many of Madonna's young girl fans in 1985 were unlikely to possess. The video's intertextuality refers rather to our culture's image bank of the sexy blonde star who plays with men's desire for her and turns it to her advantage. It is an elusive image, similar to Barthes's notion of myth, to which Madonna and Marilyn Monroe contribute equally and from which they draw equally. The meanings of *Material Girl* depend upon its *allusion* to *Gentlemen Prefer Blondes* and upon its intertextuality with *all* texts that contribute to and draw upon the meaning of "the blonde" in our culture. Intertextual knowledges pre-orient the reader to exploit television's polysemy by activating the text in certain ways, that is, by making some meanings rather than others. Studying a text's intertextual relations can provide us with valuable clues to the readings that a particular culture or subculture is likely to produce from it.

We can envisage these intertextual relations on two dimensions, the horizontal and the vertical. Horizontal relations are those between primary texts that are more or less explicitly linked, usually along the axes of genre, character, or content. Vertical intertextuality is that between a primary text, such as a television program or series, and other texts of a different type that refer explicitly to it. These may be secondary texts such as studio publicity, journalistic features, or criticism, or tertiary texts produced by the viewers themselves in the form of letters to the press or, more importantly, of gossip and conversation.

Horizontal Intertextuality

The most influential and widely discussed form of horizontal intertextuality is that of genre, and it is this that we will concentrate on first. But there are other axes of horizontal intertextuality such as character: B. A., for instance, one of the characters of the adventure series *The A-Team*, is also a hero of a cartoon series, and the actor

Original publication: Fiske, John, "Intertextuality," from John Fiske *Television Culture* (Methuen, London, 1987).

who plays him, Mr T, not only introduces the cartoon series but also appears on television as a wrestler or a guest on talk shows. The meaning of Mr T/B. A. (for the character and actor are almost indistinguishable) does not reside in any one of his screen appearances but in the intertextuality which is the aggregate of all and an essential part of the reading of any one. Of course, different viewers will have different intertextual aggregates of Mr T/B. A. according to the variations in their intertextual experience of him. Adult viewers of *The A-Team* may well not see the cartoon series and so "their" B. A. will differ from that of their children who do watch it. Madonna is similarly a web of intertextual meanings crossing media boundaries, "she" is a sign formed by television, film, records, the press, and the publicity industry.

Williams's (1974) analysis of television's *flow* has shown how intertextual relations of content can easily cross genre boundaries: the meaning of a traditional western is intertextually inflected by its juxtaposition with a news item about American Indians protesting their place in a white-dominated society. Adventure films taking place in unspecified Third World countries run by corrupt regimes relate all too readily with news reports from Africa or Latin America. But despite the ease with which intertextual relations cross genre boundaries, genre still organizes intertextual relations in particularly influential ways.

Genre

Genre is a cultural practice that attempts to structure some order into the wide range of texts and meanings that circulate in our culture for the convenience of both producers and audiences. Television programs appear to fall "obviously" into clear generic categories – cop shows, soap operas, sitcoms, hospital dramas, quiz and game shows, and so on. Television is a highly "generic" medium with comparatively few one-off programs falling outside established generic categories. Even single dramas typically have their generic characteristics emphasized: on British television, for example, they are screened under generic titles such as *Play for Today* whose title sequence consists of a rapid montage of stills from previous plays in the series – a sort of intertextual memory jogger.

Thinking of television generically requires us to prioritize the similarities between programs rather than their individual differences. The conventions shared between different programs or series in a genre are often disparaged by being referred to as "a formula," and popular art is then labeled "formula art."

Cawelti (1970) opposes formula art to art with invented or original structures:

> Like the distinction between convention and invention, the distinction between formula and structure can be envisaged as a continuum between two poles; one pole is that of a completely conventional structure of conventions – an episode of the Lone Ranger or one of the Tarzan books comes close to this pole; the other end of the continuum is a completely original structure which orders inventions – *Finnegans Wake* is perhaps the ultimate example. (p. 29)

The distinction is not just between the poles of convention and invention, but between highbrow and lowbrow art with all the value judgments that those metaphors imply. Highbrow, elitist works of art are typically valued for their unique qualities, and a whole critical practice is devoted to detailing and praising these elements that differentiate one particular work of art from others, for it is in its uniqueness that its value is believed to reside. Understanding works of art generically, however, locates their value in what they have in common, for their shared conventions form links not only with other texts in the genre, but also between text and audiences, text and producers, and producers and audiences. Generic conventions are so important in television because they are a prime way of both understanding and constructing this triangular relationship between producer, text, and audience.

Conventions are the structural elements of genre that are shared between producers and audiences. They embody the crucial ideological concerns of the time in which they are popular and are central to the pleasures a genre offers its audience. Conventions are social and ideological. A formula, on the other hand, is an industrial and economic translation of conventions that is essential to the efficient production of popular cultural commodities and should not be evaluated by aesthetic criteria that dismiss it as mere lack of imagination. Getting the right formula that transforms the right conventions into a popular art form is no easy task, but given the high cost of cultural production and the unpredictability of the cultural marketplace, formula art is an integral part of the culture industries and needs to be investigated, not dismissed.

Feuer (1987) suggests there are three main strategies for constructing generic categories. The first is the *aesthetic*, which confines itself to textual characteristics. The second she calls the *ritual*, which sees genre as a conventional repeated "exchange between industry and audience, an exchange through which a culture speaks to itself." Generic conventions allow the negotiation of shared cultural concerns and values and locate genres firmly within their social context. The third approach she calls *ideological* and this is her most problematic one. At one level, this view of genre accounts•for the way that genres can be called upon to deliver audiences to advertisers, and structure the dominant ideology into their conventions. More productively, however, Feuer suggests that the meanings of programs for viewers are influenced, even manipulated, by the genres they are fitted into.

The least productive is the aesthetic or textual:

> Genres are not to be seen as forms of textual codifications, but as systems of orientations, expectations and conventions that circulate between industry, text and subject.
>
> *(Neale 1981: 6)*

Genres are intertextual or even pre-textual, for they form the network of industrial, ideological, and institutional conventions that are common to both producer and audiences out of which arise both the producer's program and the audiences' readings. As Kerr (1981: 73) points out, genres predetermine texts and readings.

The difficulty with a purely textual definition of genre is that it tends to fix characteristics within genre boundaries in a way that rarely fits any specific instance. The characteristics of the crime thriller listed by Kerr (1981) are a good distillation of the genre, but any one crime thriller is unlikely to exhibit all of them, and is equally likely to include others:

Briefly the realist crime thriller is comprised of a network of conventional practices including a teleological and formulaic narrative structure (an equilibrium posed, fractured by villainy and recovered by heroism); credible characterisation (a family allegory peopled by coherent, plausibly motivated, racial, sexual and class stereotypes, cruder in the background than the foreground); identifiable iconographic elements (as illustrated, for example, by the discussion in both studies of the imagery of the title sequence, emphasising costume, decor and the tools of the hero's trade); milieu (the use of "authentic" locations, the contrast between class settings, etc.); and finally the film and video conventions for the construction of these fictions (conventions of framing, shooting, lighting, editing, sound recording, composing, narrating, plotting, casting, acting, writing and directing). *(p. 74)*

A genre seen textually should be defined as a shifting provisional set of characteristics which is modified as each new example is produced. Any one program will bear the main characteristics of its genre, but is likely to include some from others: ascribing it to one genre or another involves deciding which set of characteristics are the most important. *Hill Street Blues* and *Cagney and Lacey* are either cop shows with characteristics of soap opera, or vice versa. *Remington Steele* and *Scarecrow and Mrs King* are cop shows with characteristics of the sitcom, *Miami Vice* a cop show with characteristics of music video. Each new show shifts genre boundaries and develops definitions. There is an intergeneric network of conventions with various points of convergence that form the foci but not the boundaries of the various genres when defined textually.

The difficulty of tying down the textual dimension of genre leads us to predict that a greater value will lie in the ritual approach which spans the realms of the producers/distributors and of the audiences; here genre acts as an agreed code that links the two. For the producers its advantages are primarily economic. The market response to a cultural commodity is notoriously hard to predict, and updating or modifying a previously successful genre can minimize this unpredictability. Genres rise and fall in popularity as popular taste shifts with social and historical changes. The rise of Reaganism and the rehabilitation of the US experience in Vietnam has modified the cop show and reasserted its popularity. Not only do many shows have heroes who learned their ideologically validated skills in Vietnam (e.g. *Magnum p.i., The A-Team, Simon and Simon*) but the narratives continually reenact the right of those in control of "The Law" to impose that law upon others. When this law is related to Lacan's "Law of the Father," the links between Reaganism, masculinity, the exercise of social power, and the form of the genre in the 1980s become clearer:

Miami Vice and its moment in American TV history comes at the end of a decade of attempts to reconstruct the credibility of male institutional authority from the vacuum created by Vietnam – a process of reconstruction that has, in a sense, been concomitant with the rewriting of the history of that war. *(Ross 1986: 150)*

Genres are popular when their conventions bear a close relationship to the dominant ideology of the time.

The overlap between the ritual and ideological approaches to drama should not lead us to the view that changes in sociocultural conditions produce changes in generic conventions directly. The industry plays a vital mediating role in identifying potential shifts in the culture and "testing" them with a new inflection of a genre. Feuer (1987) gives a good account of how MTM Enterprises in the 1970s produced sitcoms that picked up and developed cultural concerns with shifting definitions of femininity, and produced shows like *The Mary Tyler Moore Show*, *Rhoda*, and *The Bob Newhart Show*.

This higher profile given to the rights of women also began to influence cop shows, and modified the genre with the introduction of female cop heroines (*Charlie's Angels*, *Police Woman*), and the male/female hero couple of *MacMillan and Wife*: the masculine control of the Law was joined by more feminine values, but by the 1980s, the swing to the right and the reassertion of masculinity began to stress the contradictions more clearly.

These contradictions occasionally resulted in shows like *Cagney and Lacey* where they were dealt with seriously as a mainspring of the drama, but more often in shows that dealt with them humorously like *Remington Steele* or *Scarecrow and Mrs King*. The ideological contradictions between the rise of feminism and the reassertion of masculine power required the mixing of genres (cop show with soap opera or cop show with sitcom): the genre mix was also a gender mix – cop shows are a mainly masculine genre, sitcoms and soap operas are more feminine.

This market-driven desire to predict and produce popularity lies behind scheduling practice as well. By a careful mix of genres – news, soap opera, cop shows, and sitcoms – the scheduler hopes to build an audience for the network or channel that is of maximum size and that contains the right mix of social groups to be sold to advertisers.

The scheduling of *Cagney and Lacey* provides a good example not only of its ability to build an audience, but also to affect meanings and popularity by influencing a show's generic affiliations. When CBS scheduled *Cagney and Lacey* after *Magnum* on a Thursday evening, it rated poorly. But when rescheduled on a Monday to follow *Scarecrow and Mrs King*, *Kate and Allie* and *Newhart* it topped the ratings. Monday became known as "women's night" and *Cagney and Lacey* was shifted away from the masculine generic relations with *Magnum* and towards more feminine ones. Because *Cagney and Lacey* shows a particularly even mix of generic characteristics, its prime genre was in some doubt, and so scheduling was able to tip the balance away from masculine cop show towards soap opera or woman's show. The cultural practices of producers and audiences are finally more influential than textual characteristics in determining genre.

A more extreme example of genre-shifting is given by Jenkins (1986) in his study of the fans of *Star Trek*. The numerous fan clubs consist mainly of women who run a whole secondary publication industry of newsletters and fanzines, and Jenkins finds ample evidence in these publications that the fans have changed *Star Trek's* genre to that of the romance. The popularity of the show for its female fans is centered around the personal, especially romantic, relationships of the spaceship's crew and the women fans were explicitly critical of the way that the masculine generic conventions of science fiction neglected this feminine focus. Reascribing the genre of a text is a tactic of popular reading that takes pleasure in its ability to evade or redirect the cultural strategy that serves the interests of the dominant economic or gender power structures.

Shows are conventionally marketed to networks and advertisers, and presented to reviewers and the public, as new inflections of a popular genre. Genre serves the dual needs of a commodity: on the one hand standardization and familiarity, and on the other, product differentiation.

But the work of genre is more than economic, it is cultural as well, and this is another aspect of Feuer's (1987) ideological approach. Genre spells out to the audience the range of pleasures it might expect and thus regulates and activates memory of similar texts and the expectations of this one.

For Davies (1978/9) genre knowledge is crucial to the pleasure of the mystery/thriller/adventure film, for it works to compensate for potential unpleasures in the plot structure:

> The mystery/thriller/adventure plot works through otherness. We have less knowledge and control as the narrative progresses and the mystery is compounded with further mystery. Why, then, are we not deeply disturbed by such a narrative pattern? . . . In such plots the reader finds generic rather than psychological points of reference. The disturbing effect of mystery and suspense is balanced by a confidence in the inevitability of genre.
> *(p. 62)*

Genre works to promote and organize intertextual relations, particularly amongst primary texts.

It also works within the practice of reading. Neale (1981) argues that it limits and conditions the audience response, and works to contain the possibilities of reading. Genre is part of the textual strategies by which television attempts to control its polysemic potential. As Hartley (1985) puts it:

> Audiences' different potential pleasures are channeled and disciplined by genres, which operate by producing recognition of the already known set of responses and rules of engagement. Audiences aren't supposed to judge a western for not being musical enough, a musical for not being very horrific, or a sitcom for not being sufficiently erotic.
>
> Such is the "contract" of genre. It entails a loss of freedom of desire and demand in order to achieve efficiency and properly labeled packaging.
> *(p. 18)*

Genre is a means of constructing both the audience and the reading subject: its work in the economic domain is paralleled by its work in the domain of culture; that is, its work in influencing which meanings of a program are preferred by, or proffered to, which audiences. It does this by preferring some intertextual relations and their associated meanings over others and in so far as the relations it prefers are those proposed by the industry, its work is likely to be reactionary. Reading the progressive meanings of *Hill Street Blues* or *Cagney and Lacey* requires the reader to distance them from their apparent genre of cop show, and to read them as a contradictory mix of the masculine and feminine, of the cop show and soap opera, of bourgeois realism and social realism.

Inescapable Intertextuality

Generically driven intertextuality is finally constraining and does little to open the text up to the reader: similarly, it does little to advance our understanding of the inevitability of intertextuality, of the intertextual as the prime site of culture. This is the view proposed by Barthes (1975) who argues that intertextual relations are so pervasive that our culture consists of a complex web of intertextuality, in which all texts refer finally to each other and not to reality. None of the five codes that structure all narratives and our understanding of them refer to "the real" or relate the narrative to it. For Barthes "the real" is never accessible in its own terms, and is therefore not part of the study of meaning or of narrative. He replaces the notion of the real with that of culture's construction of the real, which can be found only in cultural products (such as texts) and not in reality itself. Every text, in this theory, refers not to reality but to all the other texts in a culture for the sense that it makes, even if this sense is a sense of reality. Codes are the bridges between texts that enable this constant intertextual interplay to take place. For Barthes, then, the knowledge of reality, and therefore, for practical purposes, reality itself, is intertextual; it exists only in the interrelations between all that a culture has written, spoken, visualized about it. In this sense, all texts refer to "what has been written, i.e. to the Book (of culture, of life, of life as culture), it (the code) makes the text into a prospectus of this book" (pp. 20–1). In this view, a television program can only be understood by its relationship to other television programs, not by any relationship to the real. So a representation of a car chase only makes sense in relation to all the others we have seen – after all, we are unlikely to have experienced one in reality, and if we did, we would, according to this model, make sense of it by turning it into another text, which we would also understand intertextually, in terms of what we have seen so often on our screens. There is then a cultural knowledge of the concept "car chase" that any one text is a prospectus for, and that is used by the viewer to decode it, and by the producer to encode it.

There is, according to Barthes, an adequate but limited number of such cultural knowledges, which he usually identifies by verbal nouns, because they are forms of action. Examples of these are "The Kidnapping," "The Meeting," "The Seduction," and so on. Each narrative is a rewriting of these already written "knowledges" of the culture and each text makes sense only in so far as it rewrites and re-presents them for us. Literary and high art critics, who set a high value on originality and creativity, may be offended by this theory, but those of us concerned with as conventional and repetitious a medium as television, should find it more readily acceptable.

Barthes was interested exclusively in literature as he developed his theory, and literature differs from television in that it is, in general, explicitly fictional. It is provocative, then, to apply these ideas to "factual" television, such as news. This would explain our understanding of a news item not in terms of its relation to the "real event" but as a prospectus of the already written (and thus already read) "Book." So a news item of politicians meeting a dignitary at an airport is encoded and decoded according to our cultural knowledge of "The Greeting." An earthquake, a fire, and a famine are similarly understood as specific transformations of "The Disaster" with all its connotations of the fragility of culture's control over nature. The intertextuality of news is not merely generic (in which all "economic" stories refer to each other) but is also more broadly cultural: news, as a narrative, refers to all other narratives and their knowledges. Representation, then, becomes a rewriting, rather than a specific response to a specific event or to an original, creative "idea."

Stuart Hall (1986) has noted that the twentieth century's massive development of the means of reproducing and circulating images has pushed representation into the center of the cultural arena. The nineteenth-century's empiricist concern with the reproduction of the real has receded as the real has faded behind the imperative, incessant images of our culture. Images are clearer, more impressive than the reality they claim to represent, but they are also fragmented, contradictory and exhibit a vast variety that questions the unity of the world of experience. Images are made and read in relation to other images and the real is read as an image. Television commercials are not "about" products, but are images of desire and pleasure that overwhelm the product they are attached to. TV news is a mosaic of images of elite persons, horrific nature, and human violence. TV sport is a kaleidoscope of images of muscle, of skill, of pain. The images are what matter, they exist in their own flickering domain and never come to rest in a firm anchorage in the real. Postmodernism posits the rejection of meaning in its affirmation of the image as signifier with no final signified; images exist in an infinite chain of intertextuality.

This denial of a final meaning for images has similarities with the deconstructionists' reading of Derrida: the infinitely receding signified reduces language to a free play of signifiers that denies the possibility of any fixed or final meaning. What is welcome in these views is their emphasis upon the instability of symbolic systems and the absence of a final authoritative "meaning" against which the "correctness" or "truth" of specific readings can be judged. What is unproductive, however, is the belief in the impossibility of a meaning, because meaning is necessarily infinitely elusive and thus the search for it is misdirected. To counteract this we need to shift our focus from the text to its moments of reading; points of stability and anchored meanings (however temporary) are to be found not in the text itself, but in its reading by a socially and historically situated viewer. Such a meaning is, of course, not fixed in a universal, empirical "reality," but in the social situation of the viewer. Different readings may stabilize texts differently and momentarily, but they do achieve moments of stability, moments of meaning.

Vertical Intertextuality: Reading the Secondary Text

Denying any final textual meaning anchored in reality is only pushing the notion of polysemy to its extreme. It is part of the same view of the text which stresses its inability to police or fix its own meanings. Polysemy works through textual devices which admit of a variety of readings. This variety is not anarchic, but is delimited by the structure of the text, and the readings that comprise it are always made in relation to those preferred by the text itself. Because television is institutional art with a strong economic motive, this preferred reading will normally bear the dominant ideology, and the relation of any one subculture's reading to the preferred reading reproduces the relation of that subculture to the dominant ideology. Reading relations and social relations reproduce each other.

The social situation of viewers influences the readings they make of television, and thus how they mobilize its polysemy to serve their cultural interests. Mobilizing its polysemy involves activating one set of meanings rather than any of the others, or responding to some contradictions rather than others. This selection is rarely a conscious or intentional process, but it is none the less an active one, so the phrase "activating a set of meanings" is apt. But besides being polysemic, the television text has leaky boundaries, and viewers bring to bear on it not only their material social existence, but also their cultural experience of other texts into which it leaks.

Vertical intertextuality consists of a primary text's relations with other texts which refer specifically to it. These secondary texts, such as criticism or publicity, work to promote the circulation of selected meanings of the primary text. The tertiary texts are the final, crucial stage of this circulation, for they occur at the level of the viewer and his/her social relations. Studying them gives us access to the meanings that are in circulation at any one time.

This vertical intertextuality works not only to provide the analyst with evidence of how television's polysemic potential is specifically mobilized, but also to serve as an agent of this mobilization for the viewer. As Hodge and Tripp (1986) say:

> Discourse about television is itself a social force. It is a major site of the mediation of television meanings, a site where television meanings fuse with other meanings into a new text to form a major interface with the world of action and belief.   *(p. 143)*

An essential element of television is its intertextuality with what is written and spoken about it.

Secondary texts play a significant role in influencing which of television's meanings may be activated in any one reading. Television's pervasiveness in our culture is not due simply to the fact that so much of it is broadcast and that watching it is our most popular leisure activity, but because it pervades so much of the rest of our cultural life – newspapers, magazines, advertisements, conversations, radio, or style of dress, of make-up, of dance steps. All of these enter intertextual relations with television. It is important to talk about their relations with television, and not to describe them as spin-offs from it, for the influence is two-way. Their meanings are read back into television, just as productively as television determines theirs.

To illustrate this I wish to concentrate on the role played by journalistic writing about television. It may be helpful to imagine examples of this writing arranged on a scale whose two ends represent the producers' interests and the viewers' interests. At the producers' end lie program publicity and articles heavily dependent on studio press releases. At the viewers' end, there is independent criticism which seeks to serve the interests of the viewer, either by helping him or her to choose and discriminate, or by providing a response to a program to confirm or challenge his or hers. Somewhere in the middle come the fan magazines that purport to be independent of the studios, but obviously rely on studio press releases and cooperation for their material and access to the players for interviews. Studio gossip, commentary, interviews in magazines whose main subject matter is other than television will also fall somewhere towards the middle of the scale.

Bennett (1982, 1983) and Bennett and Woollacott (1987) have theorized the role that secondary texts from the producers' end of the scale play in helping to promote certain readings of the primary text. In their case, the primary text was that intertextual phenomenon, James Bond. They show how promotional material has inflected the meanings of Bond differently in the different periods of his popularity. Their emphasis diverges slightly from ours, because their interest lies in how the dominant or preferred readings can change over time, whereas ours, more appropriate to the transience of television than to the more permanent forms of novel and film, is concerned with how the primary text can simultaneously give rise to different readings, corresponding to the different audience groups. But their work still shows how secondary texts can activate the primary text in different ways. Thus, in the late 1950s and early 1960s, Bond was seen as the Cold War warrior – the publicity and bookjackets foregrounded guns and paraphernalia of spying – but a decade later Bond became the definer of the new sexuality. In this period the publicity for the films and novels emphasized the Bond girl, and the important enigma of the narrative became if, or how, Bond would win the girl rather than defeat the villain. Bond, at this time, liberated the bachelor from the ideal of marriage, and the girl liberated the new woman from the restriction of sexuality to marriage.

Criticism and publicity are, according to Bennett, an ideological system of bids and counterbids for the meanings of texts: they act as textual shifters for "Bond," who has no stable set of meanings discernible in the primary texts themselves. One of the most influential of these secondary texts was Sean Connery himself (the star of the early Bond films), whose "real" biography and opinions were read into the primary texts to flesh out the character of the fictional Bond. But it is important to note here how much attention these secondary texts devote to the lives and opinions of the actors and actresses who play the characters in television drama, and how these real-life biographies are mobilized to make the fictional characters appear more real.

The concern of Hobson's (1982) subjects with the realisticness of *Crossroads* focused primarily on the believability of the characters and their actions or reactions. Ang's (1985) viewers of *Dallas* expressed a similar concern in their evaluation of various characters' "genuineness." The way that viewers relate to characters is not as straightforward as the "cultural dope" fallacy would have us believe, but it is certainly a common desire of viewers that characters should appear "real." So it is no surprise to find in soap opera fanzines, for example, photographs that are ambiguously of the player or the character, as though the two were indistinguishable.

This promotion of a reading strategy that plays with the boundary between the fictional and the real occurs in the words of these secondary texts as well:

> It seems odd, doesn't it, that one day a Hardy boy would end up marrying a Vulcan? It's not really as strange as it sounds, but it is entirely true! Handsome Parker Stevenson, the evil and dirty Joel McCarthy of *Falcon Crest*, has found happiness in the arms of an alien. The ex-Hardy boy (he starred with Shaun Cassidy) met his wife-to-be while she was filming the feature *Star Trek: the Wrath of Khan*.
> (*Daytime/Nighttime Soap Stars* No. 7, February 1985: 75)

The language slips easily, with no sense of strain, between that of representation, which separates player from character – "starred," "filming" – and that which identifies player with character – "a Hardy boy marrying a Vulcan," "Parker Stevenson, the evil and dirty Joel McCarthy." *Daytimers* (May 1985) carried an article "written" by the character about the player, which is only carrying to its logical extreme the common practice of having the player talk about his or her character as if it were a real person. This sort of secondary text, according to Bennett (1983), constructs "a series of micro-narratives in which the 'real' biographies, views and values of the stars fill out, but are also filled out by, the character of the hero (or heroine)" (p. 216). We must be careful not to let the "cultural dope" fallacy lead us to believe that the soap fans are incapable of distinguishing between character and player: the jokey tone of the piece about the Hardy boy marrying a Vulcan is typical, and indicates that this is an intentional illusion, a conspiracy entered into by viewer and journalist in order to increase the pleasure of the program.

This deliberate self-delusion is fun: it involves playing with the boundary between the representation and the real, and playing with the duality of the viewers' reading position as it switches between involvement and detachment. Both Hobson (1982) and Ang (1985) found this to be a common reading strategy which allowed viewers to enjoy the pleasure of the illusion without surrendering themselves totally to it.

The nature of television as representation is never lost sight of despite the deliberate denial. These secondary texts are equally concerned to celebrate the hard work and the professionalism of the actors and actresses. They frequently take the reader on to the set to show how the program is made, they frequently trace the personal history of the actor or actors through a number of different roles in different soap operas, and they frequently draw attention to the acting skills required to produce this illusion of the real.

These secondary texts, then, are no more univocal than the primary ones. Though they promote a realistic reading of television, they are shot through with clear references to television as a system of representation. When we are reminded which character a particular player plays the tone is factual and objective in contrast to the excessiveness of the language when the fictional is treated as though it were the real. These magazines encourage the reader to enter into the delusion of realism not just to increase the pleasure of that delusion, but also to increase the activeness and sense of control that go with it. An article that was headed by photos of soap opera actors Michael Knight and Steve Caffrey begins:

> Competition. It's something *All My Children*'s Michael Knight and Steve Caffrey have been locked into for over a year now. On-screen their popular characters, playboy Tad Martin and man-about-town Andrew Preston, are in hot pursuit of the same Pine Valley cutie – Dottie Thornton. Off-screen Michael and Steve were recently vying for the same daytime Emmy award....
>
> But when you get down to basics, just which one of these *AMC* heroes is really the hottest guy in town? Perhaps an indepth look at both these fine actors and what makes them tick can help you decide.   (Daytime TV, *November 1985: 16*)

This is quite typical – the biographies of the actors, in real competition, are mobilized to authenticate the fictional competitiveness of the characters, so evaluating the sexiness of the character involves an in-depth study of the actor. There is also an attempt to mobilize the activity of the reader. These magazines abound with questions addressed to the reader asking his or her opinion on characters, on plotlines, or on incidents. Fans are asked both to evaluate and predict: "Will Shana's (Susan Kelly) love for Father Jim (Peter Davies) ruin any chance of happiness she may have with Mike (James Kilberd)?" (*Soap Opera Digest*, August 27, 1985: 71).

These opinions are frequently formalized into polls, so that fans can compare their opinions with those of others. Thus the article about the rival *AMC* heroes quoted above ends with a ballot form so that every reader can contribute to answering the question "Who is the sexiest guy in Pine Valley?". Fans are encouraged both to "gossip" and to "write" their own scripts:

> The identity of the mysterious priest (played by Ken Olin) in *Falcon Crest* next season is a secret, but we suspect he will turn out to be Julia's (Abby Dalton) illegitimate son. Think of the possibilities.   (Soap Opera Digest, *August 27, 1985: 73*)

Polls can be used to make this solitary imaginative activity into a collective public one and thus use it to help construct a sense of the community of viewers. These magazines do not create this activity, but they know it is there, encourage it, and give it a public status in their letter columns and polls in order to enhance the pleasures of the active viewer. They also enhance the producerly activity of the viewer, for the industrial producers do read them and do take account of them in their decisions about the development of plotlines.

The Tertiary Text

This leads us on to the third level of the intertextuality of television. These are the texts that the viewers make themselves out of their responses, which circulate orally or in letters to the press, and which work to form a collective rather than an individual response. This is then read back into the program as a textual activator. These third-level texts form much of the data for the ethnographic study of audiences, they are "ethno-semiological data" (Katz and Liebes 1985: 189). They can be public, such as letters to the papers or the results of opinion polls, or private, such as the conversation between members of the family, or gossip between friends. Or they can be somewhere in between such as the responses given to researchers like Morley (1980), Hobson (1982), Ang (1985), Katz and Liebes (1984, 1985), Hodge and Tripp (1986), or Tulloch and Moran (1986). Studying them can give us insights into how the primary and secondary texts are read and circulated in the culture of the viewers.

The following letter gives us some clues as to how a *General Hospital* fan reads her favorite program:

> They are the shining stars of *General Hospital* and I couldn't imagine the show without them. On the other hand, when Luke and Laura left Port Charles, their departure seemed like the natural conclusion to a pair of previously beloved characters who, for whatever reason, had begun to fizzle out. I admit I missed Tony Geary and Genie Francis at first, but I'm glad they got out before their characters became such overpowering bores that we former fans would begin to despise them on sight. They had so many unreal adventures, what else was left for them to do or say? Holly and Robert, by comparison, have their feet planted firmly on the ground. We viewers can experience their true romance. Their chemistry is so right-on and their love scenes so believable that I really envy Emma Samms. I *never* wanted to step into Genie Francis' shoes! All she ever got was grief.   (Daytimers, *June 1985: 56*)

This letter shows the familiar desire to see the fictional as real, a desire that both primary and secondary texts play on, and is an example of a tendency noted by both Hobson and Ang in which what is liked is seen as real, and what is disliked as unreal. But it also shows an awareness of the representational conventions of soap opera realism, that characters and stories have only so much life or interest in them, that they are, in other words, created to entertain the viewers rather than to represent the real in a transparent or objective way.

The pleasure of *General Hospital*, for this fan at least, is the pleasure of "implication", a controlled identification with characters that necessarily involves "believability" and "truth." The two words are almost interchangeable, but the criteria upon which their values are judged are not the objective ones of empiricism but the subjective ones of internalized norms of feeling and behavior. These norms derive primarily from the conventions of soap opera realism which require, for instance, that when a pair of characters begin to "fizzle out" their plotline should reach a "natural conclusion." These conventions produce an impression of "truth" resulting in a "believability" that may well be stronger than that produced by actual social experience, because the social norms are more clearly encoded in the conventions than in social experience. Where the conventions deviate from social experience is a point of possible interrogation of that experience, or of the norms, or of other, possibly more dominant and less "popular," values.

Ethnographic studies provide us with numerous examples of these tertiary texts, but ethnography typically tends to read these texts as responses, that is, as the *result* of viewing: it does not see them as being read back into the program and activating its meanings in a particular way. Any activity it finds in them, any ability to initiate consequences, is confined to social experience, not television. Yet the way that Hodge and Tripp's (1986) school children, for example, read *Prisoner* must have worked upon their continuous viewing of the program just as much as it did upon their experience of school, and Katz and Liebes (1984, 1985) found many examples of gossip helping viewers to activate certain meanings of *Dallas* in preference to others.

In a study of the cultural meanings of Madonna (Fiske 1987), I used two sorts of tertiary texts as evidence of young girl fans' ability to make *their* subcultural meanings out of the primary text of Madonna herself. In a discussion between fans, one 14-year-old girl said:

> She's tarty and seductive . . . but it looks alright when she does it, you know what I mean, if anyone else did it, it would look right tarty, a right tart you know, but with her it's OK, it's acceptable . . . with anyone else it would be absolutely outrageous, it sounds silly, but it's OK with her, you know what I mean.

In this we can see her struggle to express her meanings of Madonna that contradict the dominant patriarchal ones of tartiness and to find ones "acceptable" to the girl fans, whose interests are clearly different from those of the dominant patriarchy, but who lack a formal language in which to express them: the texts of Madonna fill this lack for them.

A less direct tertiary text that serves the same purpose, is the words of other Madonna fans quoted in *Time* (May 27, 1985: 47):

She's sexy and she doesn't need men … she's kind of there all by herself

or

She gives us ideas. It's really women's lib, not being afraid of what guys think.

The contradictions in the primary texts of Madonna, her music videos, are expressed in the opposition between these fans' comments and that of *Playboy* (September 1985: 122) on behalf of its readers (a very different subcultural group):

Best of all, her onstage contortions and Boy Toy voice have put sopping sex where it belongs – front and center in the limelight.

Intertextuality and Polysemy

It is the polysemy of Madonna that allows her to appeal to such different audiences as young girls and *Playboy* readers, the first a resistive subculture, the second one that accommodates easily and exactly to the dominant patriarchal ideology. Intertextual criticism shows how the one primary text can be articulated (Hall 1986) with others, or with other cultural domains, to exploit its polysemy. Hall uses the term "articulation" in its dual senses of "speaking" and "linkage". When Madonna's primary texts are "linked" to the subordinate culture of young girls in patriarchy they "speak" quite differently from when they are "linked" with the sexist masculine culture of *Playboy*. Reading the secondary and tertiary texts can help us see how the primary text can be articulated into the general culture in different ways, by different readers in different subcultures.

The plurality of these meanings and articulations is not, of course, a structureless pluralism, but is tightly organized around textual and social power. The fact that *Dallas* has more meanings than Hollywood can control or any one audience group can activate, does not negate television's struggle to control its meanings, and prefer some over others. The preferred meanings in television are generally those that serve the interests of the dominant classes: other meanings are structured in relations of dominance-subordination to those preferred ones as the social groups that activate them are structured in a power relationship within the social system. The textual attempt to contain meaning is the semiotic equivalent of the exercise of social power over the diversity of subordinate social groups, and the semiotic power of the subordinate to make their own meanings is the equivalent of their ability to evade, oppose, or negotiate with this social power. Not only is the text polysemic in itself, but its multitude of intertextual relations increases its polysemic potential.

References

Allen, R. (ed.) (1987) *Channels of Discourse: Television and Contemporary Criticism*, Chapel Hill: University of North Carolina Press.
Ang, I. (1985) *Watching Dallas*, London: Methuen.

Barthes, R. (1975) *S/Z*, London: Cape.

Bennett, T. (1982) "Text and Social Process: The Case of James Bond," *Screen Education* 41: 3–15.

Bennett, T. (1983) "The Bond Phenomenon: Theorizing a Popular Hero," *Southern Review* 16: 2, 195–225.

Bennett, T. and Woollacott, J. (1987) *Bond and Beyond: Fiction, Ideology and Social Process*, London: Macmillan.

Cawelti, J. (1970) *The Six Gun Mystique*, Bowling Green: Bowling Green University Press.

Davies, G. (1978/9) "Teaching about Narrative," *Screen Education* 29: 56–76.

Feuer, J. (1987) "Genre Study and Television" in R. Allen (ed.) (1987) *Channels of Discourse: Television and Contemporary Criticism*, Chapel Hill: University of North Carolina Press, 113–33.

Fiske, J. (1987) "British Cultural Studies" in R. Allen (ed.) (1987) *Channels of Discourse: Television and Contemporary Criticism*, Chapel Hill: University of North Carolina Press, 254–89.

Hall, S. (1986) "On Postmodernism and Articulation: An Interview with Stuart Hall" (edited by L. Grossberg), *Journal of Communication Inquiry* 10: 2, 45–60.

Hartley, J. (1985) "Invisible Fictions, Television Audiences and Regimes of Pleasure," unpublished paper, Murdoch University, Perth, WA.

Hobson, D. (1982) *Crossroads: the Drama of a Soap Opera*, London: Methuen.

Hodge, R. and Tripp, D. (1986) *Children and Television*, Cambridge: Polity Press.

Jenkins, H. (1986) "*Star Trek:* Rerun, Reread, Rewritten," unpublished paper, University of Wisconsin–Madison.

Katz, E. and Liebes, T. (1984) "Once upon a Time in Dallas," *Intermedia* 12: 3, 28–32.

Katz, E. and Liebes, T. (1985) "Mutual Aid in the Decoding of *Dallas:* Preliminary Notes from a Cross-Cultural Study" in P. Drummond and R. Paterson (eds) (1985) *Television in Transition*, London: British Film Institute, 187–98.

Kerr, P. (1981) "*Gangsters:* Conventions and Contraventions" in T. Bennett, S. Boyd-Bowman, C. Mercer, and J. Woollacott (eds) (1981) *Popular Television and Film*, London: British Film Institute/Open University, 73–8.

Morley, D. (1980) *The Nationwide Audience: Structure and Decoding*, London: British Film Institute.

Neale, S. (1981) "Genre and Cinema" in T. Bennett, S. Boyd-Bowman, C. Mercer, and J. Woollacott (eds) (1981) *Popular Television and Film*, London: British Film Institute/Open University, 6–25.

Ross, A. (1986) "Masculinity and *Miami Vice*: Selling In," *Oxford Literary Review* 8: 1 & 2, 143–54.

Tulloch, J. and Moran, A. (1986) *A Country Practice: "Quality Soap"*, Sydney: Currency Press.

Williams, R. (1974) *Television: Technology and Cultural Form*, London: Fontana.

18 On Reading Soaps: A Semiotic Primer

Robert C. Allen

Until very recently the analysis of soap operas has been the domain of elitist aesthetic criticism and mass media "content analysis." To the elitist critic, conducting an analysis of soap operas constitutes a contradiction in terms. Art works are the products of individual artistic genius; they are self-contained and autonomous; they make intellectual demands on the spectator. Soap operas, on the other hand, are assembly-line products, comic-book-like in their lack of closure, and (it is supposed) formally transparent. At most, soap operas are sources of puzzlement for elitist critics. How, they implicitly ask, can anyone with an I.Q. exceeding that of a turnip subject herself (female viewership is presumed) to a daily diet of what Renata Adler has called "sustained morbidity and dread"?[1]

Content analysts, at least, take soap operas seriously enough as a social phenomenon to go beyond simply dismissing them as garbage. To them, soap operas are pseudo-realities that present curiously distorted reflections of empirical social reality – the "world" of the soap opera is more violent than the real world, is more concerned with sex and parentage, suffers more from amnesia, mental illness, and coma-producing maladies. Content analysts assume that *what* a soap opera means can be separated from *how* a soap opera means, that the production of meaning in soap operas is simple and unproblematic.

This paper argues first, that the lack of serious aesthetic attention given soap operas has less to do with their simplemindedness than with the inability of many critics to read them as texts; and second, that soap operas should be studied as social phenomena (any media product that is consumed by 14 million persons daily and generates $700 million for its producers annually is an important social phenomenon), but that the analysis of social and cultural aspects of soap operas and soap opera viewing must be predicated upon a better understanding of how soaps work as producers of meaning and pleasure.

The Soap Opera As Text

The first problem the soap opera presents the textual analyst is one of defining his/her object of study. The analyst examining *Ulysses* or *Strangers on a Train* or *Love Story* has no difficulty in specifying the text under scrutiny, since each of these works is, in narrative terms, self-contained, autonomous, and closed-off. What, however, constitutes the soap opera as aesthetic object? A single episode? Surely not, since the

Original publication: Allen, Robert C., "On Reading Soaps: A Semiotic Primer," from E. Ann Kaplan (ed.), *Regarding Television* (University Publications of America, Frederick, MD, 1983).

meaning of any one episode is clearly dependent upon those which have preceded it. A week's worth of episodes? Why a week? Why not a month? A year's worth?

A central aesthetic characteristic of the soap opera is its absolute resistance to narrative closure. While subplots are regularly resolved, the "story" of the soap itself is never completed and never can be. Even when soaps have been cancelled (as was *Love of Life* in 1980), their final episodes have not tied all the narrative threads together – they were not closed down so much as they expired defiantly *in media res*.

The soap opera's open-endedness makes it resistant to many types of narrative textual analysis in that the textual models from which these analyses work presume narrative closure. They assume that one of the chief operations of the text is the solving of the enigma/s posed at the beginning of the work (in Barthes' terminology, the operation of the hermeneutic code),[2] bringing the text to resolution, audience satisfaction and closure. How, then, to deal with a form in which audience satisfaction cannot possibly be derived from the telos at the end of the work (since there is none), a form in which the operation of the hermeneutic code is perpetually retarded?[3]

I would argue that the soap opera as text can be specified only as the sum of all its episodes broadcast since it began. Hence what we are dealing with is a huge meta-text which has, in some cases, taken shape over the course of 30 – or more – years, a saga which, if all its episodes to the present were broadcast sequentially, would take 780 hours (or 32.5 days) to run (assuming an average episode length of one-half hour). But even at the end of this marathon screening, the critic could still not claim to have "read" the entire text of the soap, since during the 32.5 days of continuous viewing, 16 additional hours of textual material would have been produced.

Hence, to approach the soap narratively is to push oneself into the embarrassing corner of not being able to specify the text one is studying and to be forced to admit that the narrative under scrutiny lacks closure – one of the defining characteristics of narrative.

If we turn to the broader field of semiotics, we find an analytical framework better able to deal with the peculiar problems presented by the soap opera. Such a shift allows us to consider narrative as but one of several aspects of the soap opera as text. In "The Role of the Woman Reader: Eco's Narrative Theory and Soap Operas," Ellen Seiter has proposed Umberto Eco's *The Role of the Reader* as the basis for a possible feminist reading of popular culture, particularly the soap opera. I should like to use Seiter's and Eco's works to open up the soap opera to textual analysis, while at the same time diverging somewhat from their interpretations of the soap opera's semiotic operation.[4]

Seiter's feminist consideration of the soap opera is based upon Eco's distinction between open and closed texts. For Eco, soap operas are closed texts in that the reader's response has been carefully and precisely governed by the text's author. Closed texts, says Eco:

> apparently aim at pulling the reader along a predetermined path, carefully displaying their effects so as to arouse pity or fear, excitement or depression at the due place and at the right moment. Every step of the "story" elicits just the expectation that its further course will satisfy. They seem to be structured according to an inflexible project.[5]

The open text, on the other hand, has built into it multiple levels of inter-pretation. Whereas the closed text is a straightforward linear pathway of stimulus and anticipated response, the open text is a "structural maze" of possible readings. Because of the one-dimensionality of the closed work, because it aims at an "aver-age" reader,

> it is enough for these texts to be interpreted by readers referring to other conventions or oriented by other presuppositions ["other" than those of the author] and the result is incredibly disappointing (or exciting – it depends on the point of view).

In other words, ironically, the "closed" text is open to all sorts of aberrant readings – its textual "path," to use Eco's metaphor, is so narrow that the reader for whom the text was not intended finds it easy to stray. In the open work, while the possibility of pluri-signification is built in, so is the notion of the model reader – the person with sufficient knowledge of codes at work in the text to be able to read it competently.

The open work is not entirely open to any interpretation. The reader, says Eco, is "strictly defined by the lexical and syntaxical organization of the text." So while the possible aberrant interpretations of the closed text remain always open, the multiple interpretations of the open text have been foreseen by the author and are hence to some extent closed off. "You cannot use the [open] text as you want, but only as the text wants you to use it."[6]

Seiter accepts Eco's inclusion of the soap opera in the category of closed texts and in her own work suggests "possible ways that women can read soap operas subversively – ways which do not exclude or negate the widespread negative inter-pretation of soap opera viewing as escapist fantasy for women working in the home."[7]

But to see reader response to soap operas in terms of a single anticipated response and the possibility of a number of alternative, even subversive, readings is to sell short the semiological complexity of the soap opera. A careful examination of the semiological operation of the soap opera shows that it shares much more with Eco's model of the open text than it does with that of the closed texts of Superman or James Bond. Further, the openness of the soap opera is supported by empirical audience analysis and helps to explain the wide appeal and longevity of the soap opera form.

Reading the Soap Opera

What is involved in reading a soap opera? Commentators and television critics have long made soap opera viewing the *sine qua non* of a mindless mass media passivity requiring little more thought than the act of munching all the bonbons we are told "housewives" consume while being consumed by their "stories." In fact, what occurs is a complex exchange between viewer and text, in which a number of distinct codes engage the reader in the interpretive process.

A full description of the semiotic structure of soap operas is not possible here. However, in order to suggest the complexity of that structure, let me at least mention the codes by which meaning in soap operas is achieved.

1   Video-cinematic code

This is the complex of codes television has borrowed from the classical Hollywood narrative cinema, which the soap opera shares with most other narrative television forms. Indeed, it might well be that in the soap opera the "zero-degree" style of Hollywood films (as Noël Burch has called it), has reached its apex. A device such as an unmotivated camera movement, which would probably go unnoticed in the average Hollywood film, is such a departure from the norm in soap opera style that its use immediately privileges the content of the shot for the audience – the viewer "reads" this device as "something important is about to happen."

2   Codes of the soap opera form

There is another set of codes derived in large measure from the soap opera form itself – although, obviously, some of them overlap with other forms of narrative as well. Included in this category would be the soap opera's use of time and space: the prolongation of events (rather than their compression as in most other narrative forms), and the construction of a world that is for the most part an interior one. Also included would be codes of soap opera acting (a style in which facial expression carries as much semiotic weight as dialogue), the use of multiple, inter-secting narratives, the use of a certain type of non-diegetic music, the use of commercials as a structuring device in each episode (a large and very important topic in itself), and a very high degree of both inter-episode and intra-episode narrative redundancy. There are certainly other soap opera codes which could be enumerated as well as these, and any one of the above could be explored much further.

3   Textual codes

There are currently 13 soap operas being broadcast on network commercial television. While they all share the above codes, each is different. To know that these differences are significant to their respective audiences, all one need do is ask a soap opera viewer about his/her preference. You will find that far from being indiscriminate, most soap opera viewers express strong likes and dislikes for certain soaps. They can also tell you immediately when they feel something is "wrong" with their soap – a plot line is headed in the wrong direction, a character is behaving in an uncharacteristic manner, etc. In other words, each soap sets up its own set of expectations, its own parameters in terms of content and style recognized by the audience and used by them to derive meaning from each episode. An important aspect of this textual coding is the network of interpersonal relationships among characters in a given soap. The longtime soap viewer can recognize not only appropriate and inappropriate behavior in a given character, but appropriate responses of a given character to another, based on the two characters' often varied relationships in the show's past. The knowing wink that Joe gives Mary might escape the novice viewer, but it would carry great signification to the experienced viewer. Such a viewer would know Mary once carried on a secret love affair, which resulted in Mary giving birth to a child who everyone thought was really fathered by her then husband Frank, etc., etc., even though the "baby" might now be grown and involved in clandestine affairs himself.

4   Intertextual codes

All cultural products exist within networks of other texts to which they inevitably in some way refer. Soap operas are no exceptions. The reader is constantly comparing the text under consideration with the encyclopedia of other texts he/she has experienced. Intertextuality is sometimes used quite explicitly by soap opera writers in their never-ending search for new plot twists. Soap opera subplots have been based on the Mafia, the occult, the kidnapping of a wealthy heiress by a fringe political group, messianic religious figures, another television show (*Dallas*), the movie *Jaws*, etc. Sometimes intertextual reference will take the form of the appearance in the soap of a television or movie star as him/herself. In each case, a level of meaning is produced by reference to another text or set of texts.

5   Ideological codes

Quite often in making sense of an action in a soap opera, the viewer will rely upon his/her own experience of the world, sense of right and wrong, truth and realism. Eco calls this set of codes "common frames."[8] The viewer constantly compares soap opera actions with "what should" happen in such a situation – what is plausible, veristic, morally correct, etc., not in terms of the world of the soap but in terms of the viewer's own world of experience and values.

The Semiotic Operation of the Soap Opera Text

Having listed the codes involved in the reading of soap operas, I want to suggest that the operation of the soap opera text opens up multiple levels of meanings, making of the soap if not an open text, at least not a closed one.

I first realized the possible openness of soaps because I was puzzled by the universal use of redundancy. What we might call inter-episodic redundancy – that is the reiteration on Tuesday of plot developments on Monday – is to a large degree explicable as a device to keep non-daily viewers "up" on narrative developments. Soaps always walk a thin line between moving the narrative along too quickly, and thus "using it up" too soon, and stretching subplots out for too long, and thereby risking boring the audience. But I was also struck by the great deal of intra-episodic redundancy – that is, the repetition of information from character to character within each daily episode. The latter can hardly be explained in the same way as the former. For example: Judy is having an affair with Alan. In scene one, Judy confides to her friend Sylvia that she is having the affair. In scene three, Sylvia through a verbal slip hints of the affair to Fred. In scene five, Fred, a friend of Alan, warns him (Alan) of becoming too involved with Judy. Such reference to the affair might continue for days or weeks, without anything "happening" to alter the state of affairs – the same information is passed along from character to character to character. In terms of the syntagmatic (in this case narrative) dimension of the soap, such exchanges *are* redundant, since the audience already knows that Judy is having an affair with Alan, and since such redundant dialogue scenes do not move the plot forward. Paradigmatically, however, such exchanges are far from redundant, and are, in fact, quite meaningful to the experienced viewer. As such a viewer knows, Sylvia was once married to Alan – their marriage breaking up because of Alan's impotence. Furthermore, the reader knows that Sylvia still loves Alan, although she has kept this hidden for many years, and, in fact, refuses offers of marriage from Jack because of her romantic nostalgia. The reader also knows that it was Fred who paid for Judy's abortion, the result of a one-night fling with Dr. Bates, and who further believes her to be self-destructive, etc., etc.

In discussing the musical film, Charles Altman and Jane Feuer have pointed out that when regarded syntagmatically the musical is a particularly uninteresting genre – 95 percent of its plots can be summarized as "boy meets girl; boy loses girl; boy gets girl back." Their paradigmatic structures, however, often turn out to be surprisingly complex – the oppositional structure of characters and the values they represent providing a source of meaning much richer than that of the "plot."[9] Similarly, if regarded as a series of episodes of unmitigated suffering or an interminable rehashing of hackneyed subplots, then the soap opera must also seem extremely one-dimensional. But the soaps' elaborate paradigmatic structure of character relationships opens up whole new avenues of possible meaning. Not only do soap operas contain 30 or more characters, most of whom are related to each other in various ways, but this network of relationships has a history. Soap operas, unlike prime-time series, have memories, and, in fact, frequently encourage the viewer's recognition of that memory through references to departed characters or past relationships. Several characters on *As The World Turns* – Penny, in particular – have not been seen on the screen for years (their parts were written out long ago) but are still fondly remembered.

One of the reasons critics treat soap operas with such disdain is that, as naive viewers, they are unable to decode this paradigmatic textual code. To them the reiteration of the fact of Judy's affair is redundant, because they can read along the syntagmatic axis only. They are, in fact, incompetent readers of soaps just as much as the lexically and literarily impoverished high school student is an incompetent reader of *Ulysses*. The complex paradigmatic structure of the soap opera outlines its model reader "as a component of its structural strategy" – even though "model reader" is a term Eco reserves for open works; it is just that the model reader of *The Guiding Light* is more apt to be a 50-year-old woman than a male semiotician.

I would further argue that soap operas are "over-coded" – that is, their visual and auditory signifiers are coded not just as narrative elements, but in a number of other ways, allowing for multiple audience appeal. It is this over-coding that helps to account for the increasing diversity of the soap opera viewing audience. Since the days of Herzog's study of radio serial listeners, researchers have presumed that the soap opera audience consisted of lower middle class married women between the ages of 18 and 49. While this group still constitutes a large part of the audience, the past five years have seen a steady broadening of the demographics of soap opera viewing. A study conducted in March 1981 at the University of North Carolina, using a randomly selected sample of nearly 800 undergraduate and graduate students, found that nearly half (47 percent) considered themselves to be soap opera viewers, with another 17 percent stating that they would watch if they had the time. Twenty-one percent of the college soap viewers were male.[10] It has also been noted in the general press that pre-college age individuals constitute a significant portion of the audience for soaps such as *General Hospital*, which are aired in most markets in the late afternoon.

Just as interesting as this broadening of the audience for soaps is the diversity of functions soap opera viewing provides for its audience. A comparison of college soap opera viewers with a random sample of urban non-college viewers conducted in the spring of 1980 found that for members of both groups soap opera viewing served a number of functions: it acted as a time-filler; served as the basis for social intercourse; compensated for a lack of social intercourse in the everyday lives of some viewers; provided a source of information on the outside world (information on law, medicine, clothing styles, dealing with social situations, etc.); and enabled some viewers to escape into a fantasy world and thus be temporarily diverted from problems in their own lives. In other words, soap operas were decoded and used in a variety of sometimes seemingly contradictory ways (reality counseling/fantasy; social facilitating/social compensatory).[11]

Over-coding helps to account for both the diversity of the soap opera audience and the concomitant variety of functions viewing serves. To give but a very simple example: the character Noah Drake in *General Hospital* is "read" by adolescent girls in the audience as teen-idol rock star Rick Springfield ("I've Done Everything For You," "Jesse's Girl,") playing Noah Drake; to others he is read as the person having the relationship with Bobbie; to still others as a character with a particular function in one or more subplots; to another as a set of behaviors which correspond to a "real-life" situation, etc., etc. And, of course, none of these readings of Springfield/Drake is mutually exclusive. Indeed, the model reader is able to decode him as all of these, and possibly more.

In 1975, Sari Thomas conducted extensive interviews with sample of 40 soap opera viewers. Working from a theoretical distinction made by Worth and Gross, Thomas found that soap opera viewers seemed to make sense of soap operas by decoding them according to two frames of reference or orientations: what Worth and Gross have called "attributional" and "inferential" and which we might call "fictive" and "realistic." According to this model, when the reader encounters what he/she believes to be a fictional text, he/she decodes it by attempting to assign the patterns of signification (the "message") found in the text to its author. When the reader encounters what seems to be a non-authored text (a natural phenomenon, a piece of unedited new film, etc.), he/she decodes it by inferring meaning from it by reference to "real life," or, more accurately his/her experience of real life[12] Thomas does *not* suggest that soap opera viewers with an attributional frame of reference regard soaps as "reality," but that they tend to rely more on what I have called "ideological" codes in their decoding; that is, soap opera characters and situations are "made sense of" by integrating them into the viewer's own field of knowledge, values and experience. For example, Thomas asked her respondents to predict what would happen in a given plotline in the soap opera *All My Children*. One woman responded:

I think Chuck and Tara will stay together for the sake of the baby. Even if it is Phil's child, Chuck has really acted as the father. I don't go for that. I mean irregardless of who actually made the baby, it's the parents who raise the child that counts.

Other viewers tended to project the plotline according to non-ideological codes: those of narrative expectation, acting conventions, intertextual codes, etc.:

Chuck and Tara will stay together because this way there's always room for complication later on. If Tara and Phil actually did stay together, the whole story there would be kaput.

Thomas concludes:

It is clear that in the first case, the viewer only takes real-life stereotypes into consideration when formulating her prediction (attribution). In the second case, the respondent bases her judgment on her explicit familiarity with soap opera story-telling conventions.[13]

Integrating Thomas's finding into the critical framework of this paper, I would argue that attributional/inferential orientations of soap opera readers do not represent correct/aberrant decoding practices applied to a closed work. Rather, the semiotic operation of the soap opera text not only allows for but actually encourages both these orientations, or, more accurately, the soap opera text is encoded in such a way that there is considerable slippage among codes, particularly between the ideological and others. The narrative openness, episodic structure, and the nature of the plot situations themselves (many of which overlap into the daily experience of the viewer herself) all encourage a reading of the soap within a common frame of reference, whereas the rigidity of some soap opera conventions encourages a different sort of decoding operation.

The soap opera consciously walks the line between texts that can be read as fiction and those which, for various reasons, constantly spill over into the experiential world of the viewer as few, if any, other fictions do. Eco remarks that fiction is marked by a distance from the reader; the author uses certain devices by which "the reader is invited not to wonder whether the reported facts are true."[14] The soaps, however, use devices which both distance the world of the soap from that of the viewer and make quite explicit connections with it.

Conclusion

Many critics like to talk of the "world of the soap opera" in comparison to that of the "real world," or at least that of the viewer, as if the social significance of the soap lay in the comparison between the two. But rather than offering a simple message, soaps offer amazingly complex fields of semiotic possibilities which a variety of audience members can use in a variety of ways. It is precisely this openness that makes the soap opera historically unique as a form of television programming, but which also makes the "message" or "ideology" of the soap very difficult to specify. It seems less important to argue that the soap is a closed or open text, in Eco's scheme, than to recognize that in soaps we are dealing with extremely significant economic, aesthetic and cultural products of a complexity just now, after nearly half a century, being recognized by mass communications scholars.

Notes

1 Renata Adler, "Afternoon Television: Unhappiness Enough, and Time," in *Television: The Critical View*, ed. Horace Newcomb (New York: Oxford University Press, 1979), p. 76.
2 Roland Barthes, *S/Z* (New York: Hill and Wang, 1974).
3 To give but one further example of the problems soap operas present to narratological analysis, in his book *Story and Discourse: Narrative Structure in Fiction and Film* (Ithaca, NY: Cornell University Press, 1978), Seymour Chatman makes a useful distinction between essential and non-essential narrative events. A "kernel," he says, is an event crucial to the narrative, one without knowledge of which the discourse would cease to be meaningful to the reader. By constructing a chain of kernels we can reduce the discourse to its bare-bones, but still narratively meaningful, set of events. What fleshes out the text are "satellites" – events that might add color, dimension, flavor to the narrative, but which could be removed from the discourse without disturbing the basic causal chain of events constituting the narrative. This distinction, useful as it is in discussing traditional narratives, is nevertheless dependent upon narrative closure to give it meaning, since the significance of any event in a narrative is dependent upon its relationship to narrative resolution. While kernels and satellites might be specified in a given soap opera subplot, determining which events are essential or non-essential in terms of the soap's meta-narrative is much more problematic, since there is no ultimate closure to generate criteria by which they can be judged.
4 Ellen Seiter, "The Role of the Woman Reader: Eco's Narrative Theory and Soap Operas," *Tabloid* No. 6 (1981), (I am grateful to Ms. Seiter for making her work available to me prior to publication); Umberto Eco, *The Role of the Reader: Explorations in the Semiotics of Texts* (Bloomington, IN: Indiana University Press, 1979).
5 Eco, p. 8.
6 Ibid., p. 9.
7 Seiter, p. 3.
8 Eco notes that "common frames come to the reader from his storage of encyclopedic knowledge and are mainly rules for practical life." (pp. 20–1.)
9 Charles F. Altman, "The American Film Musical: Paradigmatic Structure and Mediatory Function," *Wide Angle* Vol. 2 No. 2 (November 1978), pp. 10–17; Jane Feuer, "The Self-Reflective Musical and the Myth of Entertainment," *Quarterly Review of Film Studies* Vol. 2 No. 3 (August 1977), pp. 313–26.
10 Robert C. Allen, et al., "The College Student Soap Opera Viewer," unpublished paper (University of North Carolina, April 1981).
11 Sally M. Johnstone and Robert C. Allen, "The Audience for Soaps: A Comparison of Two Populations," paper presented at the 1981 Conference on Communication and Culture (University of Pennsylvania, April 1981).
12 Sol Worth and Larry Gross, "Symbolic Strategies," *Journal of Communication* Vol. 24 No. 4 (Autumn 1974), pp. 27–39.
13 Sari Thomas, "The Relationship between Daytime Serials and their Viewers," (Ph.D. Dissertation, University of Pennsylvania, 1977).
14 Eco, p. 12.

19 "Don't Have to DJ No More": Sampling and the "Autonomous" Creator

David Sanjek

"[T]he street finds its own use for things – uses the manufacturers never imagined."
(William Gibson)[1]

Musical language has an extensive repertoire of punctuation devices but nothing equivalent to literature's " " quotation marks. Jazz musicians do not wiggle two fingers of each hand in the air, as lecturers sometimes do, when cross-referencing during their extemporizations, as on most instruments this would present some technical difficulties. *(John Oswald)*[2]

Get hyped, c'mon we gotta
Gather around – gotcha
Mail from the courts and jail
Claim I stole the beats that I rail
Look at how I'm livin' like
And they're gonna check the mike, right? Sike
Look at how I'm livin' now, lower than low
What a sucker know
I found this mineral that I call a beat
I paid zero
I packed my load cause it's better than gold
People don't ask the price but its [sic] sold
They say I sample but they should
Sample this my pit bull
We ain't goin' for this
They say I stole this
Can I get a witness?
  (Public Enemy, "Can We Get A Witness")[3]

It is a longstanding practice for consumers to customize their commodities, command their use and meaning before they are commanded by them. The Puerto Rican poet, Victor Hernandez Cruz, comments on this practice in his prose poem *The Low Writers*, where he describes how the inhabitants of the San Jose barrio inscribe meaning upon their vehicles:

When I am in this room that flies it is as if I invented rubber. Like San Jose Low riders interiors, fluffy sit back, unwind, tattoo on left hand, near the big thumb a cross with four sticks flying, emphasizing its radiance, further up the arm skeletons, fat blue lines,

Original publication: Sanjek, David, "'Don't Have to DJ No More': Sampling and the 'Autonomous' Creator," from Martha Woodmansee and Peter Janszi (eds.), *The Construction of Authorship: Textual Appropriation in Law and Literature* (Duke University Press, 1994).

Huichol designs on the copper flesh, the arm of the daddy-o on the automatic stick. A beautiful metal box which many call home. It doesn't matter if the manufacturer was Ford or General Motors, their executives in the suburbs of Detroit watching home movies, vacationing in weird Londons, when the metal is yours you put your mark on it, buying something is only the first step, what you do to it is your name, your history of angles, your exaggeration, your mad paint for the grand scope of humanity, the urbanites will see them like butterflies with transmissions.[4]

Similarly, the consumers of recorded music possess a range of options for the recontextualization of preexisting compositions: they can take material from one format and transfer it from a given context to another, thereby creating their own "mixes"; alter speed or pitch or juxtapose distinct recordings through mixers, variable speed turntables, or filters; or manipulate the recording on an adaptable turntable. Without doubt, while "[p]assivity is still the dominant demographic," a recording can be "played like an electronic washboard."[5] As Cruz states, the purchase of a commodity is only the first step; it can become the means of declaring your "exaggerations," your "mad paint for the grand scope of humanity."[6]

The range of options available either to the consumer or the creator for the recontextualization of existent recordings has been substantially enlarged by computer technology, specifically the Musical Instrument Digital Interface, or MIDI. A MIDI converts any sound into a series of retrievable signals which, since they can be stored on a computer, may be manipulated as one would manipulate any computer program. In effect, if one can type, one can compose; the programmer and the composer are now synonymous. Since one is able to retrieve any compositional element at will, as well as store any musical phrase, rhythmic device, or vocal effect one desires, the range of compositional possibilities is endless. This has undeniably enlarged, if not "democratized," the ranks of potential creators. Instrumental dexterity is no longer a prerequisite for creation. As John Leland has written:

> The digital sampling device has changed not only the sound of pop music, but also the mythology. It has done what punk rock threatened to do: made everybody into a potential musician, bridged the gap between performer and audience.... Being good on the sampler is often a matter of knowing what to sample, what pieces to lift off what records; you learn the trade by listening to music, which makes it an extension more of fandom than musicianship.[7]

However, it should be evident that the elevation of all consumers to potential creators thereby denies the composer or musician an aura of autonomy and authenticity. If anyone with an available library of recordings, a grasp of recorded musical history, and talent for ingenious collage can call themselves a creator of music, is it the case that the process and the product no longer possess the meanings once assigned them? Also, how is one to guarantee the livelihood of the composer of the sampled material, and insure that it is accorded the protection of copyright, if the sampling does not appear to infringe upon the original material under the protection of the "fair use" clause of the 1976 Copyright Act? The question of sampling's propriety remains open, but it is a process whose presence in the recording of music is increasing, not decreasing. It is my purpose, therefore, to address three questions. First, what is sampling's history and how is it connected to other common practices in the recording process; are the ideological presuppositions of rock history, which see technology as directly opposed to self-expression, no longer operative? Second, how has the sampling process necessitated a reexamination of copyright law and infringement litigation; has the "fair use" clause been rendered more elastic or called into question altogether? Finally, is sampling the postmodernist artistic form par excellence, and, if so, does it demand that we reexamine certain ideologies of performance, composition, and authenticity that have driven rock history for most of its duration? And, when considering these questions, we must not forget the dominant society's demonization of much contemporary popular music as well as the fact that the very technology that permits the process of sampling is manufactured by conglomerates that demean their employees and pollute our environment.[8] It is all too easy to fall prey to a vision of a technological utopia of unfettered creativity while forgetting the workers who construct the chips that drive MIDI synthesizers, or that the dominant culture feels it needs to defend itself against the ideological contestation in some sampled music.

While sampling is most often associated with the genre of rap and hip-hop, it has in fact become common in the recording of all forms of music. Sampling is a process with a distinct history, a developed aesthetic, and a set of auteurs who have defined the parameters of its use. Rather than engaging in rock's traditional distinction between technology and art, the romantic assumption that any overindulgent use of technology diminishes not only individual "feel" or "touch" but also the very idea of self-expression, sampling proceeds from a belief in the innovative potentialities of technology and the use of a recording *itself* as a musical instrument. It legitimizes the belief that technological devices can be utilized by musicians and audiences alike (two distinguishable constituencies that sampling effectively unifies, as the technology can make any audience member a potential musician) to appropriate the products of capital and the recording industry to serve their own devices.

Sampling began as a manual procedure and gained in sophistication and precision with the invention and marketing of inexpensive computer technologies that transferred the work of the DJ to the programmer. The performing modes it largely, but not exclusively, serves – rap and hip-hop – have their origins in various black vocal performance styles including acapella work songs, skip-rope and ring game songs, doo-wop vocalizing, Cab Calloway and other jazz vocalists (including Leo Waton and Slim Gaillard), and the aggressive braggadocio of Bo Diddley.[9] However, technique and technology came together in Jamaica when portable sound systems allowed DJs such as Prince Buster, Duke Reid, Sir Coxsone, and Lee "Scratch" Perry to establish mobile discotheques and, using records by all manner of Jamaican and non-Jamaican artists alike, engage in audio combat with one another. They began to chant over the records, scatting or toasting improvised sets of lyrics. At first, this was an exclusively live phenomenon. Later, producer/engineer King Tubby discovered that by manipulating the elements of a recording through reverb and echo or emphasizing bass tracks and phasing elements of the vocal in and out of the mix, one could create a multitude of versions from the raw components of any given recording.[10] Henceforth, what was once a purely vocal performance-based form became a technological creation, *dub*. It allowed for the process Dick Hebdige has called "versioning," whose beauty is that "it implies that no one has the final say.

Everybody has a chance to make a contribution. And no one's version is treated as Holy Writ."[11] Performers adapted King Tubby's discovery to their own ends, and dub performers such as U Roy, I Roy, Big Youth, Tapper Zukie, Dr. Alimentado, Prince Far I, Augustus Pablo, and Eek a Mouse chanted their lyrics over the booming bass and echoing guitar and drums of the dub mix.

Dub most likely made its way to the United States through the Kingston, Jamaica-born Kool DJ Herc who emigrated in 1967 and purchased a sound system in 1973.[12] He soon, along with such other early key DJs as Theodor, Afrika Bambaataa, and Grandmaster Flash, began to establish the techniques that would lead to sampling: emphasizing the "break-beat" passages of a given record by cueing and extending a particular rhythmic break until the crowd was virtually exhausted; spinning or "scratching" a record very quickly on a single groove so that the vinyl itself becomes a percussion instrument; switching adeptly from one record to another or "punch phasing" so one musical passage flows seamlessly to the next; and emphasizing the pulse of the records by adding an electronic beat box. DJs engaged in style wars, a veritable form of aesthetic combat in which the audio auteurs attempted to outdo one another by providing the freshest sounds, the hardest beats, and the widest range of tracks. The result was, in the words of Houston A. Baker, Jr.:

> Discotechnology was hybridized through the human hand and ear – the DJ turned wildman at the turntable. The conversion produced a rap DJ who became a post-modern, ritual priest of sound rather than a passive spectator in an isolated DJ booth making robots turn. A reverse cyborgism was clearly at work in the rap conversion. The high technology of advanced sound production was reclaimed by and for human ears and the human body's innovative abilities. A hybrid sound then erupted in seemingly dead urban acoustical spaces.[13]

However, as DJing was a manual technology, its range of effects was as limited as the manual dexterity of a lone individual. That all changed with the MIDI synthesizer, first engineered by the American company Sequential Circuits in 1981 and marketed by Sequential in conjunction with Roland and Yamaha in 1983. The MIDI works by taking an analog audio signal and converting it into a string of computer digits which can be held in random-access memory, retrieved, and introduced into a given recording. The process of recording a sample requires only that one set a level and press a record button. Playback is accomplished by connecting a piano-style keyboard to the sampler; striking a key on the keyboard "triggers" the sample.[14] Anything can be sampled, from a melody to a rhythmic accent, or even a vocal ejaculation. At first, a MIDI synthesizer unit could cost as much as $20,000, and, therefore, its use was beyond the economic reach of the live DJ. However, as prices fell (the unit nowadays costing as little as $2,000) the technology not only fell into the hands of a wider range of individuals but also cost far less to maintain and took far less time to master than standard instruments. Thus, it has led us to enter what some have called an Age of Plunder and Orgy of Pastiche, as the MIDI permits the possibility of deconstructing any available recording or any recordable material into a novel construction. It furthermore permits "the increasingly oligopolistic control of musical media [to be] countered by the consumer preference for devices that can, in some sense, increase their control over their own consumption."[15]

The range of possible uses for sampling is wide, but the forms it has taken can roughly be broken down into four general areas, each of which is distinguishable by the amount of sampling included, its placement in the material, and the effect the sampler has accomplished by the use of computer technology.

First, there are those records which sample known material of sufficient familiarity so that the listener may recognize the quotation and may, in turn, pay more attention to the new material as a consequence of that familiarity. Examples of the practice include Run DMC's "Walk This Way," which incorporates Aerosmith's original recording; Hammer's "U Can't Touch This," which is built around a repeating riff from Rick James' "Super Freak"; and Vanilla Ice's "Play That Funky Music," which incorporates as its bridge that line as sung in the song of the same name by Wild Cherry. In addition, there is the quoting of material not immediately recognizable to the listener, but whose sampling is so frequent and widespread that it attains a measure of familiarity to the listener. The chief example of this practice is the drumming of Clyde Stubblefield, percussionist for James Brown from 1965 to 1971; his playing on the 1971 minor hit "Funky Drummer" has been sampled by various artists including Sinead O'Connor, Fine Young Cannibals, Big Daddy Kane, the Good Girls, Grace Jones, Mantronix, Michel'le, Seduction, Todd Terry Project, Alyson Williams, and most notably at the beginning of Public Enemy's "Fight The Power," on which Chuck D. raps "1989 the number another summer/Sound of the funky drummer."[16]

Secondly, there are those records which sample from both familiar and arcane sources, thereby attracting a level of interest equal to the lyrical content. Most often the amount of sampling, particularly on rap recordings, is minimal, the emphasis being laid on the rap itself and the beat supporting it; excessive sampling might be felt to intrude upon the vocal performance. However, other artists crowd their work with an intentional and at times oppressive amount of sound, sampled and otherwise. They act as what Simon Reynolds has called "chaos theoreticians," for their work reflects the chaos of society by metronomically replicating the din and collisions of a traumatized civilization.[17] Principal amongst these artists is Public Enemy, whose three albums to date – "Yo! Bum Rush the Show," "It Takes A Nation of Millions To Hold Us Back," and "Fear Of A Black Planet" – pile up layers of ingenious wordplay, ideological agitation, and some of the densest mixing imaginable to "Bring The Noise" to a resistant public. Their records, like Radio Raheem's boom box in Spike Lee's "Do The Right Thing" (itself playing Public Enemy's "Fight the Power"), are meant to be aurally agitating. Of equal interest is the work of the British producer/mixer and director of the On-U Sound record label, Adrian Sherwood. In addition to found sound and polemical quotations from various sources, Sherwood's releases (over forty in all) incorporate and sample materials and performances from the realms of rock, reggae, dub, punk, and hip-hop. In his work with the performer Gary Clail and the ensemble Tackhead (which includes the rhythm section, Keith LeBlanc and Doug Wimbush, that propelled the recordings of one of the pioneering rap labels, Sugarhill Records), Sherwood aims for what has been called "sonic terrorism."[18] However, not all these samplers, who maximize their use of appropriated materials, aim to antagonize their listeners. A number of them playfully and wittily utilize the technology to more peaceful ends, including De La Soul, A Tribe Called Quest, and Digital Underground. They make it clear that one is able to maintain street credibility without losing a sense of humour. Like the technology it employs, sampling can be adaptable.

Finally, in a process dubbed "quilt-pop" by critic Chuck Eddy, recordings can be constructed wholecloth from samples to create a new aesthetic.[19] The landmark recording that laid the groundwork for this form was the 1980 "Adventures Of Grandmaster Flash On The Wheels Of Steel" on which the DJ joined together elements of Chic's "Good Times," Queen's "Another One Bites The Dust," Blondie's "Rapture," and three raps, Sugarhill Gang's "8th Wonder," Furious Five's "Birthday Party," and Spoonie Gee's "Monster Jam." The result was a recording about "taking sound to the very edge of chaos and pulling it back from the brink at the very last millisecond. On this record Flash is playing chicken with a stylus."[20] The technology Grandmaster Flash used to create these audacious and spectacular results is primitive compared to that available to contemporary samplers. Today, more sophisticated forms of montage encompass not only musical sources, but all manner of sounds in what might be described as instances of musical onomatopoeia. These would include S'Express, M/A/R/R/S, Cold Cut, and the Jams, whose album "The History Of the Jams a.k.a. The Timelords" sarcastically details on its sleeve all the legal and journalistic brouhaha left in their wake.[21] Certainly one of the most exciting and prolific creators of sampled collage is the young mixer/producer Todd Terry. Under various names, including Masters at Work, Black Riot, Swan Lake, and Royal House, Terry's "aggressive appropriation and recycling of breaks, hooks, shouts, and choruses from all corners of clubland combine with a rhythmic propulsion for another sort of postrap noise: raw, reckless, risky jams as exhilarating as they are brutal."[22]

Finally, sampling has been utilized in the ever proliferating domain of "mixes." As new dance forms or performance styles come into fashion, mixers – many of whom began, and on occasion still act as club DJs – are hired to produce alternate versions of a given recording in that style. Now it is uncommon to find a 12-inch release that does not include any number of versions, including the dance, dub, acid, house, and new jack swing mixes in addition to the ubiquitous bonus beats. (One wonders which amongst the various versions would be considered the Ur-Mix?). Mixers such as Arthur Baker, Trevor Horn, Rick Rubin, and Jellybean Benitez (in whose footsteps younger mixers such as Scott Blackwell, "Little" Louis Vega, and Freddie Bastone hope to follow) have found that their careers as DJs opened the path to full-time producing.[23] The degree to which these individuals deconstruct the original texts they mix can be so extreme that Arthur Baker was once named "Rock Critic Of The Year."[24]

It should come as no surprise that the practitioners of sampling have been accused of sheer pilferage, of appropriating the work of others because they are incapable of creating any of their own. Jon Pareles, popular music critic of the New York Times, in a piece entitled "In Pop, Whose Song Is It, Anyway?" wrote, "[I]t sometimes seems that sophisticated copying has overtaken innovation, that an exhausted culture can only trot out endless retreads."[25] He and other critics would like us to believe that if, as Marvin Gaye and Tammi Terril sang, "Ain't Nothin' Like The Real Thing," then sampling is a mere reflection of the real thing.

However, it is absurd to assert that we are living in an audio echo chamber, cycling and recycling the same sounds without adding to our stock of materials. Samplers engage in the practice for a number of reasons, only one of which (and any honest sampler will admit to it) is their lack of instrumental expertise. Part of it is surely their fascination with a form of technology whose cost and use is easily within their grasp. Additionally, technology is now so developed it has made the manual practice of DJing outmoded. But, even more important is the belief that sampling is not so much ransacking the past as reanimating it. As Greg Tate writes, "[M]usic belongs to the people, and sampling isn't a copycat act but a form of reanimation. Sampling in hip-hop is the digitized version of hip-hop DJing, an archival project and an artform unto itself. Hip-hop is ancestor worship."[26] No better illustration of hip-hop's sense of its own geneology exists than the persistent inclusion of lists of inspirations of the genre as well as those current practitioners who are hardcore and those who deserve to be dissed. Self-serving as the posture may seem to some, sampling in many cases resurrects material the conglomerates in charge of record companies have allowed to languish in their back catalog (those recordings kept in print but not customarily released to record sellers unless upon request) or taken out of print. As Stetsasonic argue in "Talkin' All That Jazz," "James Brown was old/Till Eric & Rak came out with 'I Got Soul'/Rap brings back old R&B."[27] Sampling, one could also argue, only benefits the conglomerates, as much of the CD market has been dedicated to just that archival material. However, one final reason individuals sample, as I was told by Prince Paul, former member of Stetsasonic and producer of De La Soul, is that the advances in recording technology have not necessarily improved the sound of recording, and he, therefore, often samples older records because, despite the resources available to him in the contemporary studio, he cannot recreate that original sound. Therefore, rather than denigrate the practice of sampling as Jon Pareles does, calling it "appropriationist art," we might instead examine what it allows artists to accomplish.[28]

We need also to realize that, while writers like Pareles focus almost exclusively upon rap and hip-hop music, sampling practices now pervade all elements of modern music recording. The magnetic recording tape that recording companies began to use in the 1950s has, from the start, made possible all manner of cutting/splicing/dubbing/multi-track recording. To assume that studio-produced recording is "natural," while the sampling of recorded material is "artificial," is splitting hairs. Producers and artists who belittle sampling see nothing wrong in availing themselves of the same technological resources – which range from digital delay to string and drum machines, emulators, and synclaviers – when it will save them the cost of hiring a live string section. As Evan Eisenberg has written, "The word 'record' is misleading. Only live recordings record an event; studio recordings, which are the great majority, record nothing. Pieced together from bits of actual events, they construct an ideal event. They are like the composite photograph of a minotaur."[29]

And yet, if one may not photograph a minotaur, one can market a recording and sample it too; but what then is the legal status of that sampled record? Is it now a new composition and how should its authorship be credited, royalties be judged, and proper monetary distribution of earnings be made? Such questions are complex and it must be admitted that the Copyright Act of 1976 fails to apply in any direct way to the administration of sampled material.[30] Furthermore, it can be argued, and samplers have done so, that the very nature of copyright is inexorably West European, in that it recognizes the melodic and lyrical components of any given piece, but fails to encompass its rhythmic components. And if rap and hip-hop are, like all

Afro-American music, rhythmic in nature – as Max Roach states, "The thing that frightened people about hiphop was that they heard people enjoying rhythm for rhythm's sake" – can a rhythm be protected under the statutes as they now stand?[31] Charles Aaron focuses on the legal peculiarity of sampling's status when he writes:

> An experienced lawyer would advise any sampler to ask himself the following questions before seeking a license or selling a composition: Is the sample melodically essential to both the original and new work? Is it readily recognizable in its new context? Is it crucial to the financial success of both the original and the new work? But questions based on melodies or "hooks" or "key phrases" often don't apply to hip-hop, which is a *rhythmic* construct of patched-together drum beats and bass fragments, animated by snatches of melodic figures.[32]

What then is the legal status of a sampler and his use of digital technology for the appropriation of other artists' material? Is it merely, as J. C. Thom asserts, "[N]othing but old fashioned piracy dressed in sleek new technology"?[33] Clearly, any number of performers and writers have felt themselves to be abused, and therefore, pressed their cases in the courts. The most publicized of cases have been the Turtles' $1.7 million suit against De La Soul for using part of "You Showed Me" in the rappers' "Transmitting Live From Mars" and Jimmy Castor's suit against the Beastie Boys for using drum beats and the words "Yo Leroy" from his hit recording "The Return of Leroy (Part I)." Both suits were settled despite the heated publicity, yet not all negotiations have been acrimonious. Hammer split his publishing royalties 50–50 with Rick James for the use of the passage from "Super Freak," and 2 Live Crew worked out an arrangement for a payment of 5.5 cents per sale with Bruce Springsteen for material incorporated in "Banned in the USA."[34]

Despite the variety of settlements, the legal status of a sample involves three key issues: the nature of the appropriation, the amount in bars or length in number of seconds, and the intention of use, either to compliment or parody and in some way damage the status of the original recording. At present, any legal resolution of these questions must refer back to the 1971 Sound Recording Act,[35] as a sample is always the transfer of an element of a recording to another recording. The 1971 Act, itself enacted in response to the marketing of audio cassettes and the recording industry's panic over home taping,[36] supplemented the 1907 Copyright Act[37] which did not legislate protection of recordings. Its writers felt they were not tangible entities, as is a piece of sheet music or a score, and they received no protection until the 1971 Act. However, due to a mistake, the Act protects only those recordings made subsequent to 1972, any earlier recording being protected by individual state statutes.[38]

The 1971 Act protects the work of the writer, the artists, and all performers, engineers, and manufacturers involved in a recording. Under the Copyright Act, authors control how their work is used, and any individual who wishes to appropriate the piece in some fashion must apply for a mechanical license through the Harry Fox Agency, sole agent in charge of such transactions, at the rate of 5.25 cents per composition per record sold or one cent per minute, whichever is larger. The 1971 Act extends the protection from the writer to include the other prior mentioned individuals involved in the recording of that piece of material. It asserts a recording to be as much a "work" as a documented composition, thereby updating the 1907 law.[39] Although the recording industry customarily pays each of the "authors" of a recording, thereby allowing the record label to be the sole possessor of copyright, the Act nonetheless names performers, engineers, and manufacturers as co-authors. In the Senate Committee hearings drafting the 1971 Act, the following statement was made:

> The copyrightable elements in a sound recording will usually, though not always, involve "authorship" both on the part of the performers whose performance is captured and on the part of the record producer responsible for setting up the recording session, capturing and electronically processing the sounds, and compiling and editing them to make the final sound recording. There may be cases where the record producer's contribution is so minimal that the performance is the only copyrightable element in the work.... [T]he bill does not fix the authorship, or the resulting ownership, of sound recordings, but leaves these matters to the employment relationship and bargaining among the interests involved.[40]

The problem with this supposed resolution of the issue of pirated recordings, the immediate worry being the practice of home taping, is that it is meant to protect the reproduction of a whole recording, not the appropriation of separate sounds on that recording which digital technology permits. As is often the case with copyright legislation, the law must catch up with advancing technology. Nonetheless, the burden of proof of piracy is upon the plaintiff, who must prove that the accused party had access to the recording and that the new work is "substantially similar" to the original. Proving this can be difficult if the original work has been so mechanically altered as to be unrecognizable. The defendant can try, in turn, to apply the "fair use" component of copyright law and assert that he appropriated neither the "hook" nor the "essence" of the original composition, that his borrowing of a sound, rhythm, or stock musical phrase is so insignificant or *de minimus* as not to damage the original recording, make light of its substance, or affect its marketability. Aside from these qualitative measures, he may also apply the quantitative tests posited in legal decisions but which are not necessarily outcome determinative. These include the limits to infringement stated in the 1915 *Boosey v. Empire Music Co.*[41] settlement that indicated that borrowings of six notes or more are an infringement when accompanied by phraseology similar to that sung in the original and the 1952 *Northern Music Corp. v. King Record Distribution Co.*[42] settlement that indicated that the appropriation of any more than four bars can indicate piracy. However, these presumed precedents were complicated by the 1974 case, *United States v. Taxe*,[43] that involved a defendant who pirated tapes of hit records produced and distributed by major record companies; the defendants changed the originals through alteration of speed, frequencies, or tones and addition of echoes or other sounds produced by a Moog synthesizer. They claimed the result was a "derivative" work, but the court was not persuaded by that defense. One commentator summarized the holding of the case as stating that "even though the right to reproduce is limited to the recapture of original sounds, that right can be infringed by an unauthorized re-recording which, despite changes in the sounds duplicated, results in a work of substantial similarity."[44] The significance of the *Taxe* decision can be found in the court's instructions to the jury which seemed to foreshadow the type of problem that would crop up repeatedly with the advent of digital technology. Thus the court instructed the jury that "[a]n infringement which recaptures the actual sounds by re-recording remains an infringement even if the re-recorder makes changes in the speed or tone of the original or adds other sounds or deletes certain frequencies, unless the final product is no longer recognizable as the same performance."[45]

Clearly, the law has begun to reflect the possibilities open to creators through digital technology, but it has not yet fully resolved the substance of sampling. A possible solution is for Congress to amend copyright legislation to establish some specific restrictions on duration, but this might affect the mechanical rate structure and raise the wrath of music publishers and songwriters. Another alternative is for the record companies to establish an industry-wide rate structure for licensing of and royalty payments for samples, but that could lead to complaints of price fixing. The likely resolution is outlined in the proposals of Steven R. Gordon and Charles J. Sanders.[46] Samplers should apply for the appropriate licenses, respect the rights of copyright holders, and be respected in turn as equal creators. Responsibility for obtaining clearance should fall to either the artist, the label, or both. Samplers realize that in the litigious environment of the United States, there is nothing to be gained and much money potentially to be lost by being a renegade. Surely some obscure materials will be sampled and overlooked, but the process should proceed devoid of recrimination and with the opportunity for money to be made by both the sampler and those whom he samples.

However, all too often the process has become embroiled in accusation and litigation even when the sampler operates outside the commercial mainstream, acknowledges his sampling, and in no way intends the new work to act as a detriment to that which it appropriates. Such was the case for John Oswald, a Canadian musician, operator of the Mystery Laboratories project, and a professor of music at York University, Toronto. Over the last several years, Oswald has spoken and published about the sampling process as a means of composition he calls "Plunderphonics," the practice of "electroquoting" or "audioquoting." Although Oswald uses sampling techniques, he has always been entirely aboveboard in his procedures and has in no way attempted to hide behind fair use protection. He stated in an interview, "My overall game plan was to try not to be covert about anything," and further indicated he wished all records came with footnotes or bibliographies of who they quoted.[47] Oswald saw his work as being in the avant-garde tradition that treated all forms of sound, recorded and otherwise, as potential compositional elements. In a March 1988 guest editorial in *Keyboard* Magazine he wrote:

> If creativity is a field, copyright is the fence. . . . When writers borrow ideas, they enclose the material in quotation marks and credit the source by name. There's a similar solution for musicians: credit all sources in print on albums and recital programs. . . . By definition, sampling is a derivative activity. Samples won't replace all pianos; they will continue to refer to pianos. Similarly, a sample or quote from an existing composition refers to, rather than steals from, the original. It's not necessary to tear down the copyright fence when you can enter from the gate.[48]

Despite Oswald's straightforwardness about his practices, he had the gate rather rudely slammed behind him. In 1987 he released a vinyl EP of four treated pieces by

Stravinsky, Count Basie, Elvis Presley, and Dolly Parton that was followed by the 24 piece, 73 minute Plunderphonics CD with its sampled cover design of the head of Michael Jackson attached to a scantily clothed female body. As stated on the packaging, "Any resemblance to existing recordings" – or existing individual – "is unlikely to be coincidental. This disc is absolutely not for sale."[49] Furthermore, it includes a circled S, the computer term for programs that can be reproduced indefinitely by anyone with access to them. Unfortunately, the Canadian legislation against duplication and piracy is staggering, and when Bruce Robertson, president of the Canadian Recording Industry Association (CRIA) was presented with the CD, he responded by stating, "My immediate and deep reaction was not to the music, but to the gross distortion of Michael Jackson's image.... It was the combination of the music being played around with that only added insult to injury."[50] Yet, in the end, the injured party was not Jackson, but Oswald, for Robertson threatened to prosecute him to the full extent of the Canadian law despite the CD's disclaimer, its being not for sale, and general lack of publicity (until the prosecution that is) outside the avant-garde music community. Oswald was threatened with exorbitant infringement fines, a six year prison term, and required to surrender all remaining CDs and master tapes. He did so, and, in a compromise, agreed to surrender all materials, thereby erasing the master tapes and ceasing distribution of the materials, which one can only obtain through copies being made of the original CD. What Jackson and others gained from the action is vague, but what is lost is the work of a thoughtful artist who may well be extending the potential uses of recorded sound.

Oswald's fate brings us to the question of how sampling has transformed our notions of composition and authenticity. Some have designated sampling, with its emphasis upon appropriation, replication, and simulation, as the Postmodernist artistic form par excellence. Others less rhapsodically remind us that our emphasis upon the autonomous creator might well be a romantic artifact, and technology has so pervaded the creative process that the rhetoric of co-option lacks substance. True, sampling disrupts our long-cherished notions of the autonomous creator, but the technology that permits it allows consumers to appropriate not only the technology of mass culture but also the ideology that surrounds it for their own purposes. Sampling reminds us that our notions of mimesis have an aural component, for when we distinguish between "real" and sampled sound, it forces us to reconsider notions we have lazily allowed to abide in a virtual pre-technological avoidance of what sound means.

Furthermore, the fury sampling has given rise to in some people must be connected to the demonization of much popular music, particularly the rap and hip-hop genres. When *Newsweek* denigrates the "attitude" of much contemporary Afro-American music as a debasement of civilized standards, we must not only recognize that a diverse and complex community is being painted with too broad a brush but also wonder how much of its work the dominant society has sampled?[51]

Finally, sampling must be seen as a tactic, not the means of a technological utopia of unfettered creation by disenfranchised cultures. Is it as important to focus upon the process of pastiche as the ends which pastiche might serve? Too often the discussion of sampling has led to either exaggerated cultural pessimism or a facile polemical overenthusiasm. While too many voices bemoan the process of pop eating itself, might it be better to turn to the work and recognize that we have only begun to discover the potential sampling holds for the disposition of sound rather than focus on whose music is this anyway?

Notes

1 Mirrorshades: The Cyberpunk Anthology at xiii (Bruce Sterling ed., 1988).
2 John Oswald, *Bettered by the Borrower: The Ethics of Musical Debt*, Whole Earth Rev., Winter 1987, at 104, 106.
3 Public Enemy, *Caught Can We Get a Witness, on* It Takes A Nation Of Millions To Hold Us Back (Def Jam/Columbia Records 1988).
4 Victor Hernández Cruz, *The Low Writers, in* By Lingual Wholes (1982).
5 John Oswald, *Plunderphonics: Or, Audio Piracy as a Compositional Prerogative*, 34 Musicworks 5, 7 (1986).
6 Cruz, *supra* note 4.
7 John Leland, *Singles*, Spin, Aug. 1988, at 80.
8 For documentation of the hazards to the environment, their workers, and the economy wrought by the computer manufacturers of Silicon Valley, see Dennis Hayes, Behind The Silicon Curtain: The Seductions of Work in A Lonely Era (1989).
9 David Toop, The Rap Attack: African Jive to New York Hip-Hop 83 (1984).
10 Dick Hebdige, Cut 'N' Mix Culture, Identity, and Caribbean Music 83 (1987).
11 *Id.* at 14
12 Toop, *supra* note 9, at 19; *see also* B. Adler, Rap! – Portraits and Lyrics of a Generation of Black Rockers 15 (1991).
13 Houston A. Baker, Jr., *Hybridity, the Rap Race, and Pedagogy for the 1990s, in* Techno-culture 197, 200 (Constance Penley & Andrew Ross eds., 1991).
14 J. D. Considine, *Larcenous Art*, Rolling Stone, June 14, 1990, at 107–9.
15 Simon Frith, *Art Versus Technology: The Strange Case of Popular Music*, 8 Med., Culture & Soc'y 263, 275 (1986).
16 Harry Weinger, *The Ghost in the Machine is a Drummer*, Rolling Stone, June 14, 1990, at 105.
17 Simon Reynolds, Blissed Out: The Raptures of Rock 160 (1990).
18 MC, *Chaos Theory: Tackhead*, I-D Magazine, Oct. 1990, at 73–4.
19 Chuck Eddy, *Quilt-Pop: Reap What You Sew*, Village Voice, Oct. 24, 1988, at 86.
20 Hebdige, *supra* note 10, at 142.
21 A striking illustration of how rich and complex mixing can be is the transcription of M/A/A/R/S's re-mix of Erick B. and Rakim's "Paid in Full – Seven Minutes of Madness." *See* Mark Costello & David Foster Wallace, Signifying Rappers: Rap and Race in the Urban Present (1990).
22 Vince Aletti, *The Single Life: Can We Party?*, Village Voice, Jan. 10, 1989, at 67.
23 Rusty Cutchin, *The Sons of Jellybean*, Working Musician, Aug. 1989, at 81–2, 84, 86, 116.
24 Andrew Goodwin, *Sample and Hold: Pop Music in the Digital Age of Reproduction*, 30 Critical Q. 34, 47 (1988).
25 Jon Pareles, *In Pop, Whose Song Is It, Anyway? N.Y. Times*, Aug. 27, 1989 (Arts & Leisure), at 1.
26 Greg Tate, *Diary of a Bug*, Village Voice, Nov. 22, 1988, at 73.
27 Stetsasonic, *Talkin' All That Jazz, on* In Full Gear (Tommy Boy Records 1988).
28 Pareles, *supra* note 25, at 1.

29 Evan Eisenberg, The Recording Angel: The Experience of Music from Aristotle to Zappa 109 (1987).

30 *See generally* Copyright Act of 1976, Pub. L. No. 94–553, at 101, 90 Stat. 2541 (1976).

31 Tate, *supra* note 26, at 73.

32 Charles Aaron, *Gettin' Paid. Is Sampling Higher Education, or Grand Theft Audio?*, Village Voice Rock & Roll Quarterly, Fall 1989, at 22, 23.

33 J. C. Thom, Comment, *Digital Sampling: Old-Fashioned Piracy Dressed Up in Sleek New Technology*, 8 Loy. Ent. L. J. 297, 336 (1988).

34 Jeffrey Resner, *Sampling Amok?*, Rolling Stone, June 14, 1990, at 105.

35 Sound Recording Act of 1971, Pub. L. No. 92–140, 85 Stat. 391 (1971).

36 *See* H. R. No. 92–487, 92d Cong., 1st Sess. 2 (1971).

37 The Copyright Act of 1907, ch. 320, 35 Stat. 1075 (codified as amended at 17 U.S.C. §§ 1–215 (1909)).

38 See Thom, *supra* note 33, at 308.

39 *Id.* at 306–7.

40 H. R. Rep. No. 487, 92d Cong., 1st Sess. (1971), *reprinted in* 1971 U.S.C.C.A.N. 1566, 1570.

41 224 F. 646, 647 (S.D.N.Y. 1915).

42 105 F. Supp. 393, 397 (S.D.N.Y. 1952).

43 380 F. Supp. 1010 (C.D. Cal. 1974), *aff'd, vacated, and remanded in part*, 540 F.2d 961 (9th Cir. 1976), *cert. denied*, 429 U.S. 1040 (1977).

44 Thom, *supra* note 33, at 327.

45 *Id.* at 328 (quoting *Taxe*, 380 F. Supp at 1017).

46 "Practical Guidelines of Phonorecord Sampling Etiquette and Ethics"

1 Samplers should apply for mechanical and master licenses for any sample whose source is in any way recognizable by an informed listener as it appears on the new recording.

2 Copyright owners of both the sampled underlying musical composition and the master sound recording should give due consideration to licensing requests made by samplers, and if no philosophical or practical bar to such licensing is harbored by the petitioned licensor, license the use at a fair and reasonable rate.

3 Samplers should respect the rights of copyright owners both to receive fair compensation for sampling uses, or to deny the use if the owner so sees fit. In instances in which the material being sampled may not be copyrightable, but the final sampling use represents a recognizable taking of the style of the particular artist who created the sound which was sampled, similar consideration should be extended to such artist.

4 Sampling license applications should be made by samplers in writing "without prejudice," and potential licensors should accept the "without prejudice" nature of the request in all cases, in order to encourage the licensing process on the whole.

5 Mutual respect for the artistic integrity of both the sampler's work and the work being sampled should characterize all negotiations and discussions between the parties.

- Edward P. Murphy, president and CEO of The National Music Publishers' Association, Inc. and The Harry Fox Agency, Inc., in New York, reports that the Fox Agency is always willing to pass along licensing requests from samplers to the Agency's publisher principals, and to issue such licenses for use of the underlying song being sampled on instructions from the publisher, in a timely manner.

- Joel Schoenfeld, general counsel to the Record Industry Association of America in Washington, D.C. states that RIAA staff are available to help samplers seeking licenses to get in contract with the master licensing departments of its record company members in order to speed the licensing request process.

Steven R. Gordon & Charles T. Sanders, *The Rap on Sampling: Theft, Innovation, or What, in* Entertainment, Publishing, and the Arts Handbook 211 (1988).

47 Mark Hosler, *Plunderphonics*, Mondo 2000, Summer 1990, at 102, 103–4.

48 Gerry Belanger, *Plunderphonics – Who Owns the Music?*, Option, Jul./Aug. 1990, at 16 (citing John Oswald's guest editorial, Neither a Borrower nor a Sampler Prosecute, Keyboard, Mar. 1988).

49 John Oswald, Plunderphonics (Mystery Laboratories 1987).

50 Belanger, *supra* note 47, at 18.

51 The questionable analysis of rap and hip-hop music was included in two articles, Jerry Adler et al., *The Rap Attitude*, Newsweek, Mar. 19, 1990, at 56–9, and David Gates, *Decoding Rap Music*, Newsweek, Mar. 19, 1990, at 60–3. The best judgment of these two pieces is contained in the January 1991 issue of *The Source. The Magazine of HipHop Music, Culture & Politics*, the principal journal on that scene, where it states:
> DON'T BELIEVE THE TYPE: The good news is that Tone-Loc was on the cover. The bad news is everything else inside. *Newsweek*'s March 19 issue fronted as a fair representation of our art form and our culture but really was a one-sided, vicious attack which ignored the positive value of rap and portrayed rappers and rap fans as threatening to mainstream culture. With this story, *Newsweek* confirmed that much of the media has *no clue* about what rap music really is.

The 1990 Hip-hop Year in Pictures, The Source, Jan. 1991, at 48.

Part V

Celebrity and Fandom

20 The Assembly Line of Greatness: Celebrity in Twentieth-Century America

Joshua Gamson

"It is, we are sure," wrote the editor of the movie fan magazine *Silver Screen* in the 1930s, "impossible to be great part of the time and revert to commonplaceness the rest of the time. Greatness is built in" ("Final Fling," 1970, p. 39). In the late 1960s, a *TV Guide* writer (Efron, 1967) took issue with this claim, describing a "peculiar machine" in American culture. "It was conceived by public-relations men," she wrote, "and it is a cross between a vacuum cleaner and a sausage maker. It sucks people in – it processes them uniformly – it ships them briskly along a mechanical assembly line – and it pops them out at the other end, stuffed tight into a shiny casing stamped 'US Celebrity'" (p. 16). Decades later, Andy Warhol's claim that "in the future everyone will be world famous for fifteen minutes" has become the most famous statement on fame. "Well, Andy, the future is now," wrote the editors of "How Fleet It Is," a 1988 *People Weekly* report. "Fame's spotlight darts here and there, plucking unknowns from the crowd, then plunging them back into obscurity" (p. 88). How did this central American discourse migrate from fame as the natural result of irrepressible greatness to celebrity as the fleeting product of a vacuum cleaner/sausage maker?

This is the story of two stories. In one, the great and talented and virtuous and best-at rise to the top of the attended-to, aided perhaps by rowdy promotion, which gets people to notice but can do nothing to actually make the unworthy famous. Fame – from the Latin for "manifest deeds" – is in this story related to achievement or quality. In the other story, the publicity apparatus itself becomes a central plot element, even a central character; the publicity machine focuses attention on the worthy and unworthy alike, churning out many admired commodities called celebrities, famous because they have been made to be. Contrary to ahistorical popular mythology, these two stories have actually coexisted for more than a century, usually in odd but harmonious combinations. Over the course of this century, however, the balance between them has shifted. In this paper, I trace and attempt to make sense of changes in the popular discourse of celebrity – in particular, the implicit and explicit explanations in popular magazines of why and how people become famous.[1] I argue in closing that these stories, built on a long-standing tension between aristocratic and

Original publication: Gamson, Joshua, "The Assembly Line of Greatness: Celebrity in Twentieth-Century America," *Critical Studies in Mass Communication* 9, 1992.

democratic models of fame, raise important questions about public visibility in democratic, consumer-capitalist society.

This is not simply the story of texts, however. Tracing the discourse on celebrity involves tracing as well the history of the mechanisms available and used for garnering attention. A system for celebrity-creation, at times much less systematic than at others, has been in place firmly since the birth of mass commercial culture. Changes both in the concrete organization of publicity and in the technology and media through which recognition is disseminated have had a profound impact on the operation of celebrity in this century.

As technology and publicity apparatuses grew, they became more and more publicly visible, integrated into discussions of celebrity. This visibility increasingly posed a threat, I will argue, to the reigning myth that fame was a natural cream-rising-to-the-top phenomenon. In the first half of the century this threat was largely controlled. It was not entirely muted, however, and a number of changes in the discourse developed, seemingly defusing the challenge. Audiences began to be invited inside the "real lives" of celebrities. Texts affirmed meritocratic fame by "training" audiences in discerning the reality behind an image and by suggesting that publicity apparatuses were in the audience's control. Beginning around 1950, changes in the celebrity-building environment – the breakdown of studio control, the rise of television, a boom in the "supply" of celebrities – significantly destabilized what had been a tightly integrated celebrity system. The publicity enterprise then began a move toward center stage in the celebrity discourse, with manufacture becoming a serious competitor to the organic explanation of fame. A new coping strategy began to show itself in texts: audiences were now invited not only behind the image, but behind the scenes to image *production*. The relationship between image and reality gradually became less a problem than a source of engagement. Previously flattered as the controllers of the direction of publicity spotlights, audiences were now flattered as cynical insiders to the publicity game.

Early Fame: Growth of a Fault Line

As Braudy (1986) amply demonstrates in his history of fame, *The Frenzy of Renown*, the ambition to stand out from the crowd is not at all new in Western culture. One dynamic in particular is relevant here: the long-standing and intertwined strains of aristocratic and democratic fame. At its very early stages, fame-seeking was limited to those with "the power to control their audiences and their images" (p. 28) – that is, to political and religious elites. The early discourses firmly established fame – whether the Roman "fame through public action" (p. 117), the Christian "fame of the spirit" (p. 121), or the literary "fame of the wise" (p. 152) – as the province of the top layer of a natural hierarchy.

Yet with the development of technologies and arts to which many more had access (printing, portraiture, engraving, all widespread by the late sixteenth century), public prominence was gradually detached from an aristocratic social status. "Faces," Braudy (1986) writes, "were appearing everywhere" (p. 267). Both the producers of and audiences for images broadened dramatically, opening "a whole new market in faces and reputations" (p. 305). Discourse began to recognize this as well, suggesting that fame is not the "validation of a class distinction" (p. 371) but the personal possession of any worthy individual. In its democratized version, particularly strong in early America, the discourse is characterized by what Braudy calls "paradoxical uniqueness" (p. 371), a sort of compromise between an elitist meritocracy of the personally distinguished and an egalitarian democracy in which all are deserving. "Praise me because I am unique," went the logic, "but praise me as well because my uniqueness is only a more intense and public version of your own" (p. 372). The "great man" was generally one of distinctive inner qualities, but qualities that could potentially exist in any man. (Women, almost entirely excluded from public life, were also generally excluded from this early mythology of public greatness.)

What is important in this vastly boiled-down history is the existence of a fault line, a pull between aristocracy (in modern form, usually meritocracy) and democracy, that is *built into* modern discourses on fame. The two stories we will be examining are constructed on this fault.

The Sucker as Expert: Barnum and Nineteenth-Century Celebrity

In the middle of the nineteenth century, a series of dramatic changes in the media of publicity and communication established celebrity as a "mass" phenomenon. Newspapers began to spread with the invention of the steam-powered cylinder press in the early 1800s. By mid-century, new technologies – the telegraph in particular – allowed information to move without necessarily being constrained by space. The idea of "context-free information" began to solidify, such that the value of information was no longer necessarily "tied to any function it might serve in social and political decision-making and action, but may attach itself merely to its novelty, interest, and curiosity" (Postman, 1985, p. 65). Information was now transportable through space and, thus freed, could be bought or sold. With the arrival of the rotary press in the mid-1840s, the subsequent growth of widely available "penny press" papers, the founding of the news wire services, and the professionalization of reporting (Schudson, 1978), encounters with the names and activities of unknown people became a daily experience – and a business. In the meantime, photography was taking a strong hold in the latter half of the century, with the halftone print perfected by the 1880s. Photography, of course, meant encountering not only a name and a description of a stranger, but a realistic image. Imaging was now at nearly everyone's disposal.[2]

If anyone brought the publicity of surfaces to the American cultural arena, it was P. T. Barnum. Publicity stunts were standard early journalistic fare, and often revealed (Fuhrman, 1989, p. 14); but with Barnum and his claim to cater to the "sucker born every minute," the showman-publicist and the publicity system became active parts of the discourse on fame. Barnum was, first of all, an innovator in the activity of press agentry. His subjects were superlatives – the best, the strangest, the biggest, the only – made superlative through image management. Throughout, "by turning every possible circumstance to [his] account," his main instrument was the press, to which he was "so much indebted for [his] success" (Barnum, 1981 [1869], p. 103).

Barnum was not simply publicly promoting the performers, however; he was publicly performing the promotion. He himself became an international figure for the *way* he focused attention, the way he created fame, and the way he created illusion. "First he humbugs them," a ticket-seller once observed (Toll, 1976) "and then they pay to hear him tell how he did it" (p. 26). His multivolume autobiography was one of the most widely read books of the latter nineteenth century (Bode, 1981, p. 23). There, as in many of his shows, he revealed the tricks of attention-gathering and image-creation, behind-the-scenes with the humbug. As Braudy (1986) points out, the activity involved playing with reality more than definitively marking it off. Barnum's was an active audience, "willing to be manipulated but eager to convey how that ought to be done more expertly" (p. 381). Shuttling his audiences between knowing the tricks and believing the illusions, Barnum brought publicity mechanisms and questions of artifice to the forefront.

Film and the Early Twentieth-Century Star System

Barnum, however, was extraordinary. Although they were common activities, attention-getting and image-management were still relatively unsystematic until the growth of professional public relations and film technology in the early twentieth century. As industrial power grew in the first quarter of the century, so did conscious policies of managing public attitudes in order to retain that power. Corporations "began to *recognize* a public for the first time" (Schudson, 1978, p. 133; see also Carey, 1987). Ivy Lee relentlessly promoted "the art of getting believed in" (Olasky, 1987, p. 49). By the 1920s, led by Edward Bernays (1952), the profession of "counsel on public relations" was well established.

The new publicity professional represented a departure from showman press agentry. The "art" was not simply getting attention (any publicity is good), but "getting believed in" (only publicity that promotes the desired image is good). The public relations counsel, Bernays argued, "is not merely the purveyor of news, he is more logically the *creator* of news" (quoted in Schudson, 1978, p. 138). The growth of public relations thus involved radical changes in the ideology and practice of news as well. "What had been the primary basis for competition among journalists – the exclusive, the inside story, the tip, the scoop," writes Schudson (1978), "was whisked away by press releases and press conferences" (p. 140). Image management, which had earlier been haphazard, was now a profession, and newspapers, which "had once fought 'the interests,' now depended on them for handouts" (p. 140).

This period also marked the birth of modern American consumer culture (see Fox and Lears, 1983) and, with newly expanded markets (urban, female), a boom in the business of leisure. As celebrity became systematized in early twentieth-century America, the leisure-time business of "show" was its primary arena: famous people as entertainment and entertainers as famous people. This new system grew up, of course, around the new technologies of film. In 1894, the world's first Kinetoscope parlor opened in New York City. Within a few years, short moving films had been integrated into the preeminent popular entertainment of the time, vaudeville, then moved rapidly into widespread "nickelodeon" exhibition, which dominated until around 1912 (Balio, 1985, part I). The possibilities for mass, industrial production of film entertainment quickly became clear.

Using featured players to attract audiences had been the custom in stage theater, touring companies, burlesque, and vaudeville but had not made the transition to early film.[3] The first steps toward the breakdown of film anonymity came from economic necessity and the new requirements of the developing mass production system. Early on, the Motion Picture Patents Company essentially controlled the industry, and independent producers were searching for means to challenge the monopoly. By the early teens, competition from independents had pushed important innovations, among them the replacement of single-reel with feature-length programs. The feature film, with higher production costs, required "a special and individualized promotional effort" and a new marketing and distribution system not met by nickelodeons (Balio, 1985, p. 111). Studios began to draw on established actors from the stage to promote these new, more expensive films.[4] The first movie fan magazine, *Photoplay*, was founded in 1910, followed quickly by others.

Despite challenges from independent producers, power was in the hands of studios, which were firmly committed to a mass production system. Movie manufacturers adapted the star system to the industry's needs. After unsuccessfully trying to distinguish their products through trademarks and storylines, Klaprat (1985) argues, producers shifted strategies with the discovery that audiences distinguished films by stars (pp. 351–4).

The advantages of the star system had become abundantly clear to film manufacturers, and the studios moved quickly to institutionalize it.[5] By the 1920s, film performers were essentially studio owned-and-operated commodities. The system was extensive and very tightly controlled – successfully so because of the high integration of the industry (see Balio, 1985; Powdermaker, 1950) – encompassing production, distribution, and exhibition of films. Through testing and molding, studios designed star personalities; through vehicles, publicity, promotion, public appearances, gossip, fan clubs, and photography, they built and disseminated the personalities; through press agents, publicity departments, and contracts, they controlled the images.

Controlling a contracted actor, of course, did no good unless he or she could become a semi-guaranteed draw. The strategies developed during this time for manufacturing and using celebrity remained essentially intact until the early 1950s. Some celebrity-building was conducted through simple fabrication. For example, with no established on-screen reputation, Theda Bara was given a name and an exotic background to establish her off screen, making her a film star before she had made a film (Walker, 1970, pp. 51–2). For the most part, though, celebrity was built systematically and deliberately through publicity and grooming that merged on-and off-screen personae.

Like the new public relations professionals, the studios turned not only on manipulating attention but on manipulating belief. Critical to the early building of stars was the building of an image that did not *appear* to emanate from the studio. Thus, after test-marketing the image; promoting the personality through advertising, stunts, rumors, and feature stories and photos; and releasing and exhibiting films in premieres and opulent theaters that underlined the stars' larger-than-life images, the studio publicity departments took over to match a star's personal life with the traits of the screen character. The "audience was assured that the star acted identically in both her 'real' and 'reel' lives" (Klaprat, 1985, p. 360). Publicity, advertising, and "exploitation" crews – organized together like newspaper city rooms and with 60 to 100 employees at their height – would actively create and manipulate the player's image:

> To begin, the department manufactured an authorized biography of the star's personal life based in large part on the successful narrative roles of the star's pictures. The department would disseminate this information by writing features for fan magazines, press releases, and items for gossip columns. A publicist would then be assigned to handle interviews and to supervise the correct choice of makeup and clothing for public appearances. Finally, the department had glamour photographs taken that fixed the important physical and emotional traits of the star in the proper image.   *(p. 366)*

These activities took place within the power-from-the-top studio, with vertical integration allowing firm, though not seamless, jurisdiction.

The appetite for films, film stars, and their movie and private lives had by the 1920s become voracious. By the 1930s, Hollywood was the third largest news source in the country, with some 300 correspondents, including one from the Vatican (Balio, 1985, p. 266). The most important outlets for entertainment celebrity stories were the film fan magazines – *Photoplay, Modern Screen*, and *Silver Screen* had monthly circulations of nearly half a million – and the columns of gossip writers such as Hedda Hopper and Louella Parsons (and, publicizing a broader range of people, Walter Winchell in New York). With an eager and sensationalizing press in place by the 1920s, and a fully integrated oligopolistic film industry – by 1930, dominated by the "Big Five" studios – image and information control was not difficult to manage.

Early Celebrity Texts

Other routes to public visibility still existed, of course, but the process had entered a period of industrialization. This, then, was the state of celebrity in the first half of the twentieth century: the entry of visual media as "the prime arbiters of celebrity and the bestowers of honor" (Braudy, 1986, p. 551), a developed profession of public image-management, and an elaborate and tightly controlled production system mass-producing celebrities for a widely consuming audience. The discourse on celebrity[6] remained in this period, for the most part, in line with the interests of its producers. The theme of the discovery of greatness, earlier termed a greatness of character, was translated into the discovery of a combination of "talent," "star quality," and "personality." The claim was in a different vocabulary – the "culture of personality" (Susman, 1984, pp. 273–7) of consumer capitalism had overtaken the "culture of character" of producer-capitalist republic – but it was still one of an organic, merited rise.

The story of the press agent was alive and well, nearly always harking back to the image of Barnum. The new publicity profession slowly began to get some attention, but in these stories publicity was not a mechanism for creating celebrity but simply a means of bringing the deserving self to the public. At times, however, the new power of publicity media (and studios) to artificially produce fame asserted itself, deepening ambiguities in explanations of claims to fame. The visibility of a publicity "machine" stood as a threat to the notion of naturally derived celebrity status. The simultaneous promotion of audiences to controllers of the publicity machine defused this challenge. Celebrities at the service of the audience, however, brought a new problem: the suspicion that the images presented were constructed to gain an audience. The constant textual exposure of the "real lives" of celebrities – in their more believable, "ordinary" form, supported by a closer audience-celebrity "relationship" – kept this threat at bay.

Discovering the Gift: Fame Explanations in Early Texts

These changes were gradual and never seamless. Greatness in its more traditional, aristocratic formulation – virtue, genius, character, or skill that did not depend on audience recognition – remained a strong model in many early magazine texts. "Greatness," asserted Ludwig (1930) in *American Magazine*, "is always productive, never receptive. It is both imagination and will which give the genius his strength" (p. 15). The notion of a correspondence between greatness and fame, however, was clearly threatened in the early consumer culture. The elitist *Vanity Fair*, for example, was forever striving to distinguish the truly "great" from the commercially successful (see Amory and Bradlee, 1960).

These postures were defensive, and understandably so. As Lowenthal (1968) demonstrated, by the 1920s the typical idols in popular magazines were those of consumption (entertainment, sport) rather than production (industry, business, natural sciences). By the 1940s, almost every hero biography featured a hero either "related to the sphere of leisure time" or "a caricature of a socially productive agent" (p. 115). Most writing about famous people reported on their private lives, personal habits, tastes, and romances. Fan magazines took this sort of story to its extreme, reporting on the specifics of "How Stars Spend Their Fortunes"; exhibiting his home, her pets, their swimming pools; providing their beauty secrets, dietary preferences, expenses, travel plans, advice (see Gelman, 1972; Levin, 1970). In typical stories, Ginger Rogers explained "Why I Like Fried Potatoes" while Hedy Lamarr explained why "A Husband Should Be Made to Shave."

Not only did attention shift to entertainers and their personal lives, but these famous entertainers also underwent a gradual demotion of sorts over the first half of the century. Early on, the stars had been depicted as democratic royalty (with Mary Pickford and Douglas Fairbanks reigning), popularly "elected" gods and goddesses. Lifestyle reports focused on "the good life," the lavish Hollywood homes, the expensive clothing, the glamour those watching could not touch. But, pushed by the development of sound and film realism – and, I will argue below, by deeper difficulties – the presentation by the 1930s had become more and more mortal, "prettified versions of the folks who lived just down the block" (Schickel, 1985, p. 99). Rather than the ideal, celebrity was presented in the pages of magazines such as *Life* and *Look* as containing a blown-up version of the typical. "Stars now build homes, live quietly and raise children," a *Life* article ("The New Hollywood," 1940) explained. "Their homes, once gaudy and too ornate, are now as sensible and sound in taste as any in the country" (p. 65). And, as always, *Life* had the pics to prove it: "candid" shots of Merle Oberon playing blind man's bluff with her nephews on a suburban lawn, Brenda Marshall eating her "frugal breakfast" in a simple, bachelor-ette kitchen (pp. 65–7).

Such ordinariness promoted a greater sense of connection and intimacy between the famous and their admirers. Crucial to this process was the ubiquitous narrative principle of the "inside" journey into the "real lives" of celebrities, lives much like the readers'. Other common themes in entertainment celebrity texts of the time – love lives, the "price they pay for fame," the desire to be just like the reader, the hard work of gaining and retaining success – further tightened the narrative links between the audience and the celebrated.[7]

Decreasing the distance between the celebrated and the celebrators creates a difficulty: If celebrities were so much like the reader, why were they so elevated and so watched? Early celebrity texts updated the American paradox of egalitarian distinction. Rather than for public virtue or action, the celebrity rose due to his or her *authentic, gifted self*. A fame meritocracy was reinscribed in the new consumerist language: the celebrity rises, selected for his personality (revealed through lifestyle choices), an irrational but nonetheless organic "folk" phenomenon. The luck of the lucky star, for example, is that she got the "break" that allowed her to rise. "Nobody knows," an *American Magazine* (Eddy, 1940) article told its readers, "when or where one of these will bob up" (p. 162). Jean Harlow, driving some friends to a studio luncheon, came to fame "quite by accident," moving "from extra to star" (Lee, 1970, p. 43). The stories in their purest form thus suggested that a star would not rise, or bob up, even with a lucky break – unless he had what it took. As Morin (1960) found in how-to-be-a-star handbooks, "luck is a break, and a break is grace. Hence, no recipe.... What matters is the *gift*" (p. 51). It could be cultivated, certainly, and for that reason hard work was important; without it, one might never find out if one had the gift that would be demonstrated by the break. Hard work, however, could do nothing to actually *create* the qualities that might make one famous. Sometimes – as in the lucky break's corollary, the discovery story – one did not need to work, just *be* (Lana Turner sitting in the soda shop). Fame, apparently, would come to those destined to be famous and pass over the doors of the undeserving.

This tautology (how do we know the famous deserve fame? because they have it) is the core of the dominant early story of fame. Talent was often mentioned but rarely treated as sufficient. The only stars who survived, *Photoplay* suggested (Cohn, 1972), were the ones "who had that rare gift designated as screen charm or person-ality, combined with adaptability and inherent talent" (p. 33). Clark Gable "deserves his pre-eminent place" because "there's no one else exactly like him" (Maddox, 1970, p. 174). What it took to rise – "star quality," "charisma," "appeal," "person-ality," or simply "It" – was never defined beyond a label, even "ineffable" (Eddy, 1940, p. 25). Whatever it was, though, the texts made it clear that stars had always had it. Fame, based on an indefinable internal quality of the self, was natural, almost predestined.

The celebrity's background thus took its place as a demonstration that, put simply, a star is born. Ruby Keeler was "born with dancing feet" (Hoyt, 1970, p. 51). Greta Garbo had "a certain force within her" that explained her position "in the vaulted and resplendent cathedral of fame" (Joel, 1970, pp. 172–3). Look back at Greta's childhood and you'll see that the "urge" was always "in her," that "she was a born actress." This presentation of childhood did not build a personal history so much as locate a nebulous *essence* in the famous that explained their fame. Lowenthal's (1968) description of consumption-idol biographies aptly sums up fan and general magazine portrayals as well:

> Childhood appears neither as prehistory and key to the character of an individual nor as a stage of transition to the growth and reformation of the abundant diversity of an adult. Childhood is nothing but a midget edition, a predated publication of a [person's] profession and career. *A [person] is an actor, a doctor, a dancer, an entrepreneur, and [she or] he always was.*   *(pp. 124–5)*

Greatness is built in; it is *who you are*. If one works at it, or gets a lucky break, it may be discovered. If it is discovered, one becomes celebrated for it, which is evidence that one had it to begin with.

What do we make of the characteristics of these texts – the focus on leisure idols and leisure habits, the gradual move toward ordinariness, the logic of the discovered gift? In many ways these early texts simply reassert in a new cultural vocabulary that those in the public eye are there because they deserve to be. But why not continue to focus on glamorous and extravagant consumption habits? Why increase the intimacy between star and reader through inside stories? A large part of the answer becomes clear when we examine the place of the new publicity professions and the studio system in these early texts.

Exposing the Gift: Publicity in the Early Texts

The publicity system was clearly visible and commonly noted in these texts. Writing in *Collier's*, Ferber (1920) observed, "Everyone thinks he knows everything there is to know about moving pictures. Small wonder. The knowledge has been poured down our not unwilling throats by the photoplay magazines, the press agents, the newspapers, the censors, the critics" (p. 7). Initially, this knowledge was not a problem. The studio star system was, for the most part, accommodated quite comfortably into most stories as the final step up the ladder. If the ineffable quality was discovered *and properly publicized*, the story often added, one became celebrated. Like hard work, the studio could not create a star from the ungifted. *Life* reported ("Starlets," 1940), for example, that starlets spent their days in training "that would wilt all but the most determined" (hard work). They were "told what to do, what to say, how to dress, where to go, whom to go with" (studio control). Yet the studio couldn't make them into something they were not: "Only if they obey implicitly and only if, *in addition, by some magic of beauty, personality or talent* [italics added], they touch off an active response in millions of movie fans, will a few of them know the full flower of stardom" (indefinable essence) (p. 37).

The management of publicity was itself generally presented in a way that posed hardly a threat to the notion of natural, deserved celebrity. Stories of Barnum-like "ballyhoo" press agents persisted, claiming that "the old hokum still gets newspaper space better than anything else" (Lockwood, 1940, p. 180); behind each movie premiere, *Reader's Digest* reported (Costello, 1941), was "a group of harried, sardonic studio press agents... [pulling] the strings" (p. 88). This Barnumesque figure was portrayed as a harmless, amusing promoter – harmless because of the visibility of his tricks. The new public relations counselor had, according to most stories, the same aim as the old showman press agent: to "boost the fame" of public figures. Only his style differed: he wore a suit instead of "a sun-struck plug hat and molting fur-lined overcoat" and depended "more upon his typewriter and truth and less upon the imagination" (O'Malley, 1921, p. 56). Since he favored building on facts rather than fiction, he could only *amplify* a preexisting condition. While new inventions meant "an engine of publicity such as the world has never known before," Lippmann (1960) wrote in *Vanity Fair*, that machine "will illuminate whatever we point it at.... The machine itself is without morals or taste of any kind, without prejudice or purpose, without conviction or ulterior motive" (p. 121). This new publicity machine had taken a permanent place in the discussion of celebrity by the 1930s.

Although Lippmann pointed out that "newspapermen" were the ones doing the pointing, the dominant notion of publicity in early celebrity texts was of a neutral machine illuminating what "we," the public, wanted to see in the spotlight. The standing model of celebrities as rising organically from the populace would otherwise be jeopardized: if the studios or the newspapers controlled the "machine," people could enter the spotlight not because of popular election but because of manufactured attention by interested elites. The "public" in these stories, modeled as a unified, powerful near-person forever casting its votes for its favorite personalities, became a crucial character in its own right. The notion of the public as an entity that "owned" both space and the public figures inhabiting it runs consistently through both general and fan magazines. In a 1932 *Vanity Fair* (in Amory and Bradlee, 1960), Mussolini, the Prince of Wales, George Bernard Shaw, William Randolph Hearst, and others romp in bathing suits "On the Public's Beach." The public, forever "fickle," was increasingly credited with *control* of celebrity.

As celebrities were being demoted to ordinariness in narratives, then, the audience was being promoted from a position of religious prostration. The public became the final discoverer, the publicity machine shifting the spotlights according to the public's whims. Myrna Loy tells "all you little Marys and Sues and Sarahs who wish you could be movie stars" (Service, 1970) that she is, in fact, *at their service*.

> I'd like to tell her in good plain English that I am not my own boss. I'd like to tell her that I serve not one boss but several million. For my boss is – the Public. My boss is that very girl who writes me herself and thousands like her. It is the Public that first hired me, and it is the Public that can fire me. The Public criticizes me, reprimands me.
>
> *(p. 142)*

The celebrity-as-public-servant displaces difficult questions in the relationship between "authentic" greatness and publicity activities. It affirms the notion that celebrities are cream risen to the top while allowing the vague criterion of "personality" to coexist with the newly visible power of the publicity "machine." *You* control the machine, it says. If *you* don't like me, *you* can grab the spotlight and throw it onto someone else more worthy. The anti-democratic implications of both a celebrity elite and elite-controlled publicity are tempered by the emphasis on audience control. Desert and publicity live together.

In a remarkably obsequious, and revealing, rumination on the question of "Why Did I Slip?" Robert Taylor (1970) turned to the fans in control. "Maybe temperament is the trick that captures the public imagination. Should an actor be erratic and difficult, or should he be business-like, stable, and quiet?" (p. 124). Taylor's article, while it contained the characteristic direct apostrophe and bow to the power of the public, also revealed a theme that grew in early texts along with that of public control. What image should I put on? he asks. The assumption that people are famous because of *who they are*, an authentic self, gets left behind as Taylor suggests that he will be *who you want me to be*. In one, audiences discover; in the other, audiences dictate.

Indeed, as the power of the audience to create stars to their liking became a stronger narrative ingredient, an alternative storyline also developed. The more active the audience, the more celebrity is suspect as an artificial image created and managed to pander to that audience. Terms of commerce began to enter the discourse, although still subordinated to terms of greatness and quality. Commercial creation and the marketing of false public images (as opposed to publicizing of true selves) began to surface as an explanation of fame. Myrna Loy, significantly slipping between public-as-boss and studio-as-boss, complained that

> I daren't take any chances with Myrna Loy, for she isn't my property. . . . I couldn't even go [to the corner drugstore] without looking "right," you see. Not because of personal vanity, but because the studio has spent millions of dollars on the personality known as Myrna Loy. And I can't let the studio down by slipping off my expensive mask of glamor. I've got to be, on all public occasions, the personality they sell at the box office.
>
> *(Service, 1970, p. 214)*

Marlene Dietrich, a 1930s *Motion Picture* writer argued, was nothing but manufactured glamour. Through the use of publicity stunts, lighting effects, photography, and Dietrich's single talent – "simulating glamour" – she became famous. "The difference between Miss Dietrich in real life and Miss Dietrich in the photograph," Boehnel (1970) argued, "was the difference between a handsome woman and one built up by studio artifice into a glamorous idol" (p. 218). Here a story was taking shape that gained steam as the century progressed: studio artifice, in search of box office sales, created images that had little or nothing to do with the actual persons behind them. As early as 1931, *The Nation* ("Fame," 1931), wrote that fame "is largely manufactured and that those best known are those who have seen to it that they should be" (p. 450). By 1944, an *American Mercury* writer ("Celebrity Unlimited," 1944) was arguing that celebrity had become a "lush, weedy thing" choking "many a rare plant of genuine accomplishment" (pp. 204–5) – a perspective that would become more popular in the following decades.

This rising skepticism about the connection between celebrity and authenticity was, however, largely muted in most celebrity stories. To a degree, this was simply accomplished through studio control. When Clark Gable suggested in a 1933 *Photoplay* interview, for example, that "I just work here. . . . The company has an investment in me. It's my business to work, not to think," his statement was considered "frank enough to be dangerous and the studio thereafter began to 'protect' Gable from unguarded utterances" (King, 1986, p. 174).

But the skepticism heightened by increasingly visible publicity activities was contained more commonly by being acknowledged: by pulling down "the expensive mask of glamor." By embracing the notion that celebrity images were artificial products and inviting readers to visit the real self *behind* those images, popular magazines partially defused the notion that celebrity was really derived from *nothing but* images. Celebrity profiling became parked in expose gear, instructions in the art of distinguishing truth from artifice, the real Dietrich from the fake one. Once you get to know the real one, the texts implied, you'll see why you were right to have made her famous. The at-home-with-the-famous "inside story" was central to this process. The glamorous celebrity was thus sacrificed for the more "realistic" down-to-earth one. Intimacy, bolstering belief, was offered up. Manufactured images, then, would be harmless to allegiances. The public discovers and makes famous certain people because it (with the help of the magazines) *sees through* the publicity-generated, artificial self to the real, deserving, special self. The story of celebrity as a natural phenomenon was shakily joined with the story of celebrity as an artificial one.

Self-Owned Commodities: Late Twentieth-Century Celebrity

In the late 1940s and early 1950s, the film industry was jolted from several sides. In 1948 the Supreme Court unanimously sided with the Department of Justice in its charges against the industry, breaking the Big Five's production–distribution–exhibition monopoly (Balio, 1985, p. 402). The industry was also facing a box office crisis: by 1950, the movie audience had shrunk by two-thirds. The crisis was much aggravated by television, which was fast displacing film as the dominant leisure-time activity.[8]

This shake-up of the movie studio system meant changes in industry organizational structure and new entrants in the field. Independent production companies began to grow. Studios shifted to contracting on a picture-by-picture basis rather than "owning" workers for longer periods. Talent agents, whose role earlier had been marginal, moved in, taking on tasks abandoned by the studios: cultivating "talent," selecting "properties" to develop, taking "the long view." Agents began to be important power-brokers, and the "packages" they offered – a writer, script, a star or two, sometimes a director – became (and remain) the currency of the industry (Balio, 1985, pp. 418–19). Eventually, despite changes in ownership patterns, the system stabilized in its new form: the majors still dominating, collaborating with the television industry and with talent agents and agencies, absorbing independent production. While the economic drive toward a star system remained in this changed environment, new players entered the game from the now-dispersed sub-industries of star-making and from the new television industry, and strategies began to shift to meet the new environmental requirements.

As studio control was necessarily relaxed and the studio image-maintenance activities became dispersed into an independent publicity profession, film stars in the 1950s became "proprietors of their own image," which they could sell to filmmakers, and subsequently began "to show a distance from their own image" (King, 1986, pp. 169–70). Independent publicists, assistants in the management of public images (and often the controllers in place of the celebrities themselves), became powerful players.

In the meantime, the publicity profession was taking new, more sophisticated shapes. Since World War II, public relations (PR) has grown "from a one-dimensional 'press agentry' function into a sophisticated communications network connecting the most powerful elements of our society" (Blyskal and Blyskal, 1985, p. 27). This growth contained several components that affect celebrity. First, the overall trend toward delineating and targeting specialized market niches in product development, advertising, and sales has made the task of garnering and shaping attention progressively more "scientific." Strategies attempt to zero in on the perceived needs, desires, and knowledge of particular publics, seeking to attract and then sell the attention of segments of the mass markets, matching certain populations to specific messages and vehicles.[9] Second, as the daily practices and interests of PR operatives and journalists, aligned since the 1920s, moved closer over these decades, arenas traditionally perceived as non-entertainment (news in particular) have come to depend on the practices of the entertainment industry, and celebrity in particular. Third, the technologies for providing a visual image that *imitates the representation* of an activity, event, or person, rather than representing it directly, have become highly developed.[10] Finally, the outlets for publicity have exploded with the success, beginning in the early 1970s, of magazine and newspaper writing about "people" and "personality" and, more recently, broadcast "infotainment." This has meant a need for more subject matter, and more opportunities for recognition: literally more editorial space for those aspiring to fame or to regain faded recognition, for star-for-a-day ordinary people,[11] and for celebrities from untapped fields.

Television, with its constant flow, enormous reach, and vast space-filling needs, has from its initial boom provided the most significant new outlet for image-creation.[12] In this world of massive exposure to television's sophisticated image-production, it has become increasingly possible *in a practical sense* to create familiarity with images without regard to content. Boorstin (1961) noted the effect: the celebrity has become familiar for being familiar, "a person who is known for his well-knownness" (p. 57). The economic push to make people known for themselves rather than for their actions remains at the heart of the now-decentralized star system: as sales aids, celebrities are most useful if they can draw attention regardless of the particular context in which they appear. Name recognition in itself is critical for commerce. In fact, the less attached a name is to a context, the more easily it transfers to new markets. As the prime outlet for, disseminator of, and certifier of public images, television has made decontextualized fame a ubiquitous currency.

Celebrity Texts in the Late Twentieth Century

The changes in the apparatuses and practices of publicity in the post-glamour, television-dominated era have seeped into celebrity texts. In the later twentieth century several new elements entered gradually into the celebrity discourse. First and most generally, the mechanisms by which images are made and by which celebrity is built have been increasingly exposed. Second, celebrity as a commercial enterprise has been not only acknowledged but often embraced. Third, the audience has been invited to increase its knowledge and its power. Finally, the discourse has brought about an increasing self-consciousness and irony about celebrity.

Although the narratives about and explanations of fame developed in the earlier part of the century have remained commonplace, the challenge from the manufacture-of-fame narrative has been greatly amplified. No longer under institutional guard, it has become a very serious contender in explaining celebrity. Invitations into the process and an ironic stance about it, I argue, operate much like the invitations into the "real lives" of the famous (which continue from the 1920s). They partially defuse the threats the process makes to the notion that fame is rooted in character traits, that admiration of celebrities is grounded in merit.

Celebrity-Making Revealed

With *TV Guide*, which began in 1948, then quickly grew in circulation and has since the early 1970s been one of the two top-selling magazines in the United States, celebrity-making as a business moved from a peripheral to a central theme. "Why," an article ("Does TV Drama Need a Star System?" 1953), asked, "is there a lack of star-studded names in TV dramas?" (p. 6). The answer is simply that "building a 'star'" costs too much, and "few, if any, performers make the top without the Big Buildup. It's a selling job that requires an organized bunch of legmen, plenty of time and lots of cash" (p. 6). The presence or lack of stars was not, in this story, a question of talent resources, but of sales resources. A few years later, one performer's summary of the "feeling among performers" ("For the Stars," 1956, p. 6) about answering fan mail stands in stark contrast to earlier treatments of mail-answering and autographing as a sort of public service. "Stardom is a business," she says matter-of-factly. "It would be bad business to ignore a fan" (p. 6). A "shrewd agent," an agent tells readers in a later article, "knows how to make Hollywood pay, what image is wanted on the market, where shortages exist, how to fill niches" (Hobson, 1968, p. 6).

Visible links between celebrity and selling were certainly not new. Fame as a sales device had been evident within advertising very early on, primarily through endorsements. Beginning in the 1950s, however, celebrity began to be commonly represented not only as *useful to* selling and business, but as a business itself, *created by* selling. Along with the old-style "what success does to the stars" and "life at home with the stars" stories, for example, *TV Guide* showed stars bickering over billing ("Television's Biggest Struggle," 1958), arguing that "I'm a piece of merchandise. The bigger they make my name, the more important I am. And, the more important I am, the more money I'm worth" (p. 21). This stance, which in the early days of studio celebrity was rare and sometimes punished, rapidly became fairly common-place. Terms began to change: the celebrity was becoming "merchandise," "inventory," "property," a "product," a "commodity," and the fans "markets." Star production, said Kendall (1962) in a *New York Times Magazine* article, "is as ritualistic in its way as a fire dance" (p. 37). Celebrities are an "investment" – "like all raw materials, they often require a good deal of processing before they are marketable" – and that investment "must be protected" (p. 38).

As the treatment of fame as produced and the famous as commercial products took hold, the question of how exactly that production worked became central. By the 1960s, *TV Guide* was offering instructions in "how to manufacture a celebrity" (Efron, 1967, p. 16). Detailing the case of Barbara Walters, the author demonstrated how the "mechanical assembly line" created celebrities from raw human material: Walters was picked up in small feature stories, then profiled in *Life* and *TV Guide*, provided with professional recognition, then "piped into the lecture circuit" and into commercials, which turned her into a "personality" (p. 17). Then "certain character- istic things began to happen to her – *none of which had anything to do with her professional skills*" (p. 17). She was now "being courted as a 'name'" (p. 17). Her wardrobe, home, and cosmetic habits became women's magazine topics; she appeared on talk shows and at "fancy" parties. Even Walters can recognize her own manufacture, chatting "candidly about the meaningless mechanics of fabricated fame" (p. 19). Several years later, a press agent was quoted saying that his client, Ann-Margret, could initially have been "sold... as anything"; "She was a new product. We felt there was a need in The Industry for a female Elvis Presley. We mounted her on a billboard on Sunset Strip with her legs around a motorcycle. I saw emerge a star without the benefit of major industry achievement" (Hobson, 1969, p. 10). A 1967 article (Amory, 1967) quoted the coordinator of a star-grooming program: The "whole thing nowadays" is "just a big machine. When they push the button, they grind out the name" (p. 33).

"Make no mistake," that article continued, "the people who push the button nowadays... are primarily publicity people" (Amory, 1967, p. 33). As the focus on the celebrity-making machine continued, publicity people became central characters, as named sources and as profile subjects. In many cases, the publicity system has remained in the same place it had been earlier, subordinated to innate characteristics – sometimes talent, usually the same vague notions of "star quality" and "person- ality" – and guided by public desires. In 1988, Geraldo Rivera asked a personal manager and two television producers to tell his TV-show audience what "star quality" was. Their typical answers echo the 1930s and 1940s texts: "I would say it's potential," said one; "it's the ability to feel," said another; it's "the ability to light a television up or a movie screen" ("How to Make It in Hollywood," 1988, pp. 3–4). In these cases, image managers have continued to be represented (often by them- selves) as giving the public what they want, not by creating it but by discovering and publicizing it.

Also commonly, though, celebrity-production and -control activities have been explicitly discussed, with "quality" as a concept absent, irrelevant, old-fashioned. "Image" has itself become a common term in the texts. In earlier days, an agent was typically shown discovering star quality that simply demanded to be brought to the public, and the subsequent adoration was proof of the quality. Now, a shrewd agent was shown discovering a market and manufacturing a celebrity-product around it. A 1963 series on "Gentlemen of the Pressure" (Morgan, 1963) opened with an illustra- tion of a giant hand holding a television screen on which the word "images" is written. Behind the hand, operating it through a panel marked "networks," is a messy, motley group of people; in front of it, a happy, smiling audience looks at the screen. "A mixed breed of nonobjective salesmen have found a home in the house of TV," the author warned, selling "affection for personalities, products, corporate entities and ideas" (p. 6). Their effects are "a little frightening," and "although they prefer to work in the shadows, they leave their traces on every TV screen in America" (p. 6).

The interview process itself began to be dissected for its control aspects. "The impresario of the Hollywood interview is the press agent," wrote one journalist, "who is trained to assess the writer and publication and then cut off at the pass embarassing situations" (Bell, 1966, p. 115). Another described how "stars and their press agents will arrange a location that will fortify the basic image they wish to present to the public," will "channel the discussion into those very few areas where the star can excel conversationally," and "look upon The Interview as an opportunity to convince the world at large that they are something quite different than they seem to be" (Bart, 1966).

Publicity agents and managers have been drawn into the narrative, coaching the public figure in "how to look cool in talk-show hot seats" (Shaw, 1982, p. 56), sitting next to (or even replacing) the celebrity during an interview, and overseeing the touching-up of photos. "Publicists rule the day," a *Rolling Stone* (Hirschberg, 1986) article explained. "The bigger the star, the more power the publicist wields. And this power enables publicists to choose the photographer for a fashion shoot, pick a sympathetic writer for an interview or demand the cover of a magazine" (p. 28). Several years later, *Time* (Henry, 1990) outlined how celebrity is "available to any Manhattan couple with about $100,000 to squander," by adopting the right charities, being photographed at the right spots, and hiring public relations counselors, who "now serve everybody from models and movie stars to lawyers and landlords" (p. 48). These are not the harmless "ballyhoodlums" revealed in some early twentieth-century texts, but sophisticated business operators. Throughout these texts, then, is a tremendously heightened self-consciousness about the systematic production of celebrity and celebrity-images for commercial purposes.

Enjoy the Hype: Instruction and Irony

With such increased visibility, the problem that had surfaced occasionally in the first half of the century has deepened during the second: if celebrities are artificial creations, why should an audience remain attached and lavish attention on their fabricated lives? Along with the gradual foregrounding of artifice have come new narrative elements that, I argue, temper this problem. Texts have brought in what amount to instructions to readers and a new ironic knowingness.

Many such texts have brought to fruition the behind-the-scenes, inside-dope style begun earlier, instructing the reader further in reading performances, finding the "real" behind the "image." This writing acknowledges that a gap between image and reality exists, but denies that bridging it is a problem, especially with television, a medium that can't help but transmit an "accurate, searching image" (Javits, 1960, p. 11). "The TV camera has an X-ray attachment," Arlene Francis told *TV Guide* readers in 1960. "It pierces, it penetrates, it peels away the veneer. It communicates the heart and mind of man" (p. 6). Not surprisingly, this argument runs with the older-style emphasis on a person's "genuine," internal characteristics. If there is a problem peeling away the veneer, viewers need simply be given better viewing tools, and readers can depend on the writer to provide the person underneath. This remains the most common stance in what is still the standard celebrity text, the profile. With the proper guides, one can distinguish true personality from false.

Many texts, though, have become more up-front and unapologetic about artificial authenticity, instructing readers in how to be more sophisticated in recognizing and using it themselves. Groucho Marx's "You Bet Your Life," *TV Guide* disclosed ("The Truth," 1954), "represents the finest *manufactured spontaneity* television has yet known" (p. 5). That, the article claims, is simply professionalism, the business of "concocting entertainment." One 1950s article ("Familiar Gestures," 1954) prompted readers to pay attention to television stars' familiar, unconscious gestures which, converted into conscious performances like Eddie Cantor's eye-popping, could "serve as trademarks." By the 1980s, *Rolling Stone* (Martel, 1987) was sardonically claiming that the key to everyone's inevitable encounter with fame is preparation: "No self-respecting modern person should be without fifteen minutes' worth of the props, costumes and condiments that are vital to the maintenance of fame" (p. 91).

A final set of "instructions" has taken the inside-story theme a small, subtle step further. As stories of how the publicity system works both to manufacture celebrity and to fabricate sincerity have become more common (especially with the growth of "infotainment" in the 1970s and 1980s), the audience has been instructed not simply in viewing the self behind the image (what the star really thinks, wears, does) but in viewing the fabrication process (how the celebrity is being constructed to amuse). Armed with knowledge about the process, the audience doesn't need to believe or disbelieve the hype, just enjoy it. Barnum, disembodied and ubiquitous, has reappeared as a central character: the celebrity industry.

An ironic, winking tone in these revelatory texts is one of the clearest later twentieth century developments, not only in "hipster" magazines[13] but also in more mainstream "middle American" ones. The audience has been invited to take its power further with a new, cynical distance from the production of celebrity and celebrity images. In a 1977 report on overcrowding in the "celebrity industry," *Newsweek* ("The People Perplex," 1977) waxed sarcastic, suggesting the foundation of a "National Celebrity Commission to select, at the earliest possible age, a rotating galaxy of Designated People" who would be "scientifically schooled in the art of outrageous behaviour" (p. 90). A decade later, an *Esquire* writer (Ephron, 1989) claimed that the strategy of cloaking oneself in goodness by "[buying] a lesser disease, preferably one that primarily affected children," no longer works, since "all the lesser diseases were taken" (p. 104). *Life* magazine ("The Making of Billy Gable," 1989) consulted "industry bigfoots" on how Clark Gable would fare starting out today. The experts recommended plastic surgery ("deflating those wind socks"), publicity control ("a spin doctor"), image building ("have him sitting at ringside for fights and Laker games"), and television series and talk shows. "Were Gable a young actor today," the article concluded, "he would require careful packaging to make him the King of this era" (pp. 53–4). A *TV Guide* article (Warga, 1982) traced the "three stages" of stardom, each turning on the manipulation of image and publicity apparatus. In stage one, the performer is eager, and "you see, hear and read about him or her everywhere"; in stage two, the successful celebrity is temperamental, and appearances now "depend on the publication, the subjects *not* to be discussed, who else will be in the story, whether or not the cover will be included"; in stage three, "the great holdout," the star exists, because "nothing is right" (pp. 4–5). Each stage is a pose. The reader, armed with a cynical knowledge about image manipulation strategies, is being told how to read the pose as a pose. Instructively, what lies behind the pose is not taken up.

Irony has also become a common piece of celebrity public personae. "A self-mocking sense of humor," according to casting directors in a *TV Guide* story (Stauth, 1988), "is a key ingredient in star quality" (p. 5). Celebrities are often caught "simultaneously mocking and indulging their icon status," Gitlin (1989) says, describing a collection of *Rolling Stone* photographs. "New-style stars flaunt and celebrate stardom by mocking it, camping it up, or underplaying it (in public!). . . . . The star now stands apart from glamour, and comments (often ironically) on it" (p. 14). In *Esquire* (June 1989), then-Republican Party leader Lee Atwater, joining the posing of entertainment celebrities, saluted the audience with his pants around his ankles.

Why this combination of exposure of the celebrity-and image-manufacturing processes and mockery of it? On one level, the mocking of glamour by celebrities is another star turn, much like tabloid revelations of the "true self," updated to accommodate the visibility of glamour-production: Celebrities invite their admirers to revere them for being "too hip to be reverent or revered" (Gitlin, 1989, p. G14). The constant visibility of publicity mechanisms works similarly on another level, defusing a threat to admiration by offering the audience the position of control. Celebrity audiences are treated to the knowledge of how they, and others, become the "sucker born every minute" – and thus avoid becoming the sucker.

In Barnum, though, the source of tricks was simple and visible. In the later twentieth century texts everyone is a potential trickster, and image-makers and hypesters are everywhere, including in the audience. Who is real? Who really has "star quality" or "talent" or "greatness"? Who actually deserves attention? These questions, still circulating from the earlier fame story, are unanswered – this time because they are largely rendered moot. The notion that fame is based in artifice challenges not only the economics of the celebrity system (if no one is more deserving, consumer loyalty is extremely unstable) but potentially readers as well (if artifice and reality are indistinguishable, one's grounding is extremely unstable). The cynical, knowing, sometimes mocking stance keeps the tension from cracking the story; indeed, it can serve to engage. Miller's comments (1988) about televisual irony have more general application here:

> TV seems to flatter the inert skepticism of its own audience, assuring them that they can do no better than to stay right where they are, rolling their eyes in feeble disbelief . . . . [Each] subtle televisual gaze . . . offers not a welcome but an ultimatum – that we had better see the joke or else turn into it. . . . [The] TV viewer does not gaze up at the screen with angry scorn or piety, but – perfectly enlightened – looks down on its images with a nervous sneer which cannot threaten them and which only keeps the viewer himself from standing up.   *(pp. 326, 331)*

Through irony, these celebrity texts reposition their readers, enlightened about the falseness of celebrity, to "see the joke" and avoid the disruptive notion that there is nothing behind a fabricated, performed image but layers of other fabricated, performed images.

Conclusion: Democratic Celebrity?

The overall history sketched here is of a position switch between two twentieth-century takes on the famous. The struggle by many involved in representing celebrity has been to keep the economics of stardom intact by making celebrity-admiration a coherent enterprise. The economic interests of celebrity producers push toward certain textual characteristics (a coincidence of public and private personae, an explanation of fame as naturally derived and deserved). Celebrity production, when revealed, contains its own potential threat: the explanation of fame as artificially derived. In the early part of the century, the organization of production allowed tight control over the texts. To the degree that the story of artificial production did assert itself, it was accompanied by narrative elements that quieted it (audience control of publicity, the inside story, de-glamorizing). As production organization changed mid-century and "authorship" of the texts was decentralized, the notion of artificial fame was released and intensified in texts. Through discussions of images as images, flattery of audiences' notions of their own knowledge and power, and an ironic stance, celebrity texts have continued to negotiate the tension between the two claims-to-fame stories.

Embedded in these two stories is the long-standing pull between the democratic and the aristocratic in fame discourse. Ought attention go to a naturally deserving elite, or is everyone and no one more deserving? The struggles between these stories described raise important questions about the dynamics of public visibility in democratic, consumer-capitalist society. Do commercial industries dependent on the production of celebrity push in anti-democratic directions by building mystifying myths of meritocratic fame and offering pseudo-participation? Or do they push in democratic directions by empowering audiences, generally in the form of markets, to shape celebrities?[14] Does the embrace of artifice undermine democratic discourse by pushing toward the replacement of reason with image? Or does it support democratic involvement by opening up participation – with lip-synching, anyone can be a star – and decreasing the social gap between the admired and the admirer? The strained and often paradoxical coexistence of the two major storylines examined here does not answer these questions. It may, however, suggest an interesting and critical oddity: that the answer to all of these questions may be yes.

Notes

1 Articles from early fan magazines were drawn primarily from two compilations (Gelman, 1972; Levin, 1970). Articles from general-interest periodicals and newspapers were derived from selected years in the *Reader's Guide to Periodicals* and from the archives of the Margaret Herrick Library, Academy of Motion Picture Arts and Sciences, Los Angeles.

2 The perceived interests of the burgeoning newspaper industry, especially in the circulation wars and "yellow journalism" in the latter quarter of the nineteenth century, in fact made

stories about *people* a central feature of journalism. In particular, newspapermen like William Randolph Hearst used "human symbols whose terror, anguish, or sudden good fortune, whatever, seemed to dramatically summarize some local event or social problem or social tragedy" (Schickel, 1985, p. 40) to provide them with a competitive edge in the increasingly information-dense environment. Names, in short, began to make news.

3 Filmmakers in the first decade of this century referred to players by "singling out a striking physical feature of the nameless owner" – such as "the girl with the curls," "the sad-eyed man," "the fat guy" (Walker, 1970, p. 29). In part, players were not named and advertised because "names" cost money. In part, May suggests, early film directors "saw their art as separate from the entertainment popular with the rich and the immigrants," and subordinated character to the "larger message of the plot" (May, 1980, pp. 99–100). Finally, exhibition in nickelodeons – 20-to 60-minute programs, morning to midnight, often changing daily – was a handicap to the emergence of film stars since, with "no time for word-of-mouth publicity to build up a following" for players, "they might not be available for very long when the fans wanted to see them" (Walker, 1970, pp. 29–30).

4 In 1909 the Edison Company began publicizing its acquisition of theatrical players from Broadway producers; in 1910, Leman and Vitagraph introduced lobby-card photo displays of their acting companies (Balio, 1985, p. 114). At the same time, independent producers drew on Barnumesque techniques to manufacture film star celebrity (p. 115). In March of 1910, Carl Laemmle, in an attempt to give his independent production company an edge, demonstrated the possibilities of star-building. He hired Florence Lawrence, who was already recognizable as "the Biograph Girl," and apparently planted a story of her tragic, untimely death. He subsequently denounced the story as a lie and as proof announced Lawrence's appearance in St. Louis – the first public appearance in film history – where she made a tremendous publicity splash.

5 The early star system was aided in its development by innovations in the use of film as a medium. In particular, the close-up, brought into film by D. W. Griffith around 1908, allowed the face to take over the screen. The close-up provided the star system with two critical characteristics. The focus on the face, with signs of emotion greatly magnified, established a sense of intimacy between audience and stranger-performer. And, by "isolating and concentrating the player's looks and personality, sometimes unconnected with his or her abilities," it provided a means to establishing a performer's "unique" personality (Walker, 1970, p. 21). The apparent revelation by the close-up of the "unmediated personality of the individual," (Balazs, quoted in Dyer, 1979) has pointed out, "and this *belief* in the 'capturing' of the 'unique' 'person' of a performer" (p. 17), is essential for the star phenomenon. The coming of sound in the late 1920s further shortened the psychological distance between performer and audience, and further increased the apparent uniqueness and "realness" of the apprehended performer. "What seemed to be their last significant secret, their tones of voice," writes Schickel (1985), "was now revealed – or so it seemed" (p. 99). No longer pantomimed emotion, performance was less stylized; with voices, performers were less unlike the audiences.

6 The celebrity production systems and the discourse examined here are primarily those connected with visual entertainment. Celebrity certainly exists in other sectors, and certainly the characteristics of its production and the discourse surrounding it differ in the various sectors. In sports, for example, the link between exposure and achievement or talent may be tighter (though perhaps much less tight than many people assume); in politics and religion, the tolerance for exposure of image-manipulation may be lower (though perhaps much higher than many people assume). Although these instructive differences are important, I work from two simple premises that suggest visual entertainment is the most important case. First, film and television have been and continue to be this century's major popular media, those that figure most constantly in daily lives and consciousnesses. Second,

other sectors have become increasingly dependent on visual media and have taken on many of the strategies and characteristics of entertainment-celebrity production.

7 Celebrities, in fact, began to address readers directly, often as confidantes: "I regret more than I can say that my marriage with Hal Rosson did not work out," wrote Jean Harlow to her "*Screen Book* Friends" (in Levin, 1970, p. 25). Joan Crawford confessed in a 1928 *Photoplay* that she hadn't told her life story because "I was afraid to tell it to you. You have one idea of Joan Crawford, now you are going to have another" (p. 88).

8 The spread of American television was notoriously rapid: the number of sets in use in 1947 was around 14,000 and by the next year had shot to 172,000; by 1950, it reached 4 million, by 1954 eight times more, and by the late fifties television was in 90 percent of American homes (Balio, 1985, p. 401).

9 Beginning in the early 1960s, with the "values and life styles" research of the Stanford Research Institute, the advertising industry has slowly abandoned class-based marketing for marketing that "hones in on a consumer's 'lifestyle' (marital status, education, region, sex) and 'attitudes' (religion, ambition, optimism, etc.)" (Sullivan, 1989, p. 37). In the world of television, this trend is well captured by the "Performer Q," issued since the early 1970s by a company called Marketing Evaluations. Ranking some 500 celebrities according to a survey of American families, it provides subscribers with "a demographic road map" for each celebrity, breaking down his or her audience appeal by sex, age, income, education, and occupation (Barber, 1974).

10 Publicity practitioners, especially by making use of new video technology, have become masters at delivering entertaining news to news organizations. The electronic press release, "imitation news," is now commonplace. Originating in the film industry, these releases have "the feel of a genuine news story, right down to the imperfect oratory as the interview subjects gather their thoughts on camera." In entertainment PR, these releases are often highly advanced and widely used: some include multiple stories (personality profiles, "news features," etc.) on a dual soundtrack that allows a reporter to dub in his or her own voice, art work, scripts, and "teaser" commercials for the news program to use. Universal Studios sends video interviews into which local reporters can insert tapes of themselves asking questions, thus appearing to "be rubbing elbows with the Hollywood elite" (Blyskal and Blyskal, 1985, pp. 99–102).

11 "We're scouring every facet of American life for stars," said *People* magazine editor Richard Stolley in 1977 ("The People Perplex", 1977). "We haven't changed the concept of the magazine. We're just expanding the concept of 'star'" (p. 90).

12 It is an environment, moreover, with new characteristics: tremendous repetition, allowing increased familiarity; a literal down-sizing of the celebrity due to television's small size and living-room location, bringing, as Schickel (1985) points out, "famous folks into our living room in psychically manageable size"; an increased "illusion of intimacy" (p. 13) between celebrities and audience built through "reality" programming, most significantly talk shows; and a near-total ratings dependence with pressure to hold onto the few perceived "hit" elements and replace the elements that may not be selling, leading to rapid turnover. Focus, though repeated, is diffuse; turnover is rapid. Television's attention is easier to get and more difficult to hold onto.

13 At least one magazine, *Spy*, has made its name and its money from this combination of inside dope and mockery. A regular feature lists the number of mentions given particular people in Liz Smith's gossip column. An April 1989 cover story on "celebrity garbage" offers "coffee grounds of the rich and famous – a scientific, sanitary and not at all unseemly SPY investigation"; in June, "the current bull market for selling one's soul." A 1990 cover story ("The State of Celebrity 1990") on "building a better celebrity" reports on "what America thinks about celebrities, what celebrities will do to keep themselves celebrated, what nobodies will do to become famous" (p. 59) and features a

mock-scientific survey and analysis of public opinion, with percentages of people believing that Drew Barrymore is dead, agreeing that "nearly every celebrity has been to the Playboy mansion" (p. 61), or willing to sacrifice a limb to win an Oscar. The accompanying list, a "surgical history of celebrity," includes the celebrity's name, rumored cosmetic surgery – and their "publicist's denial" (pp. 66–7).

14 Schudson (personal communication, May 30, 1991) points out that contemporary objections to the phenomenon of celebrity, usually attacking celebrity-manufacturing institutions and/or the divorce of fame and achievement (for example, see Boorstin, 1961; Goldsmith, 1983), contain a nostalgic longing for "heroism" along aristocratic lines, perhaps amounting to veiled attacks on democracy. In *High Visibility* (Rein, Kotler and Stoller, 1987), a remarkably unapologetic how-to book that "applies marketing science to the quest for celebrity" (p. 6), the authors make a similar point about their detractors. Social critics, whose "conception of a perfectly ordered hierarchy is under relentless attack by the celebrity world" (p. 10) and believe that "society elevates precisely the wrong people into popular acclaim" (p. 9), are really angry "that they themselves don't control the process" (p. 29).

References

Amory, C. (1967, November 25). Who killed Hollywood society? *TV Guide*, pp. 32–6.

Amory, C., and Bradlee, F. (eds.). (1960). *Vanity Fair: Selections from America's most memorable magazine*. New York: Viking.

Balio, T. (ed.). (1985). *The American film industry*. Madison: University of Wisconsin Press.

Barber, R. (1974, August 10). Just a little list. *TV Guide*, pp. 4–8.

Barnum, P. T. (1981). *Struggles and triumphs*. In C. Bode (ed.), *Struggles and triumphs*. Middlesex: Penguin Books. [Original work published 1869].

Bart, P. (1966, March 27). Well, what's an interview for? *The New York Times*, p. X13.

Bell, J. N. (1966, October 8). Canonizing the superficial. *Saturday Review*, p. 115.

Bernays, E. L. (1952). *Public relations*. Norman, OK: University of Oklahoma Press.

Blyskal, J., and Blyskal, M. (1985) *PR: How the public relations industry writes the news*. New York: William Morrow.

Bode, C. (1981). Introduction to Barnum's *Struggles and triumphs*. In C. Bode (ed.), *Struggles and triumphs*. Middlesex: Penguin Books.

Boehnel, W. (1970). Dietrich is still selling glamour. In M. Levin (ed.), *Hollywood and the great fan magazines* (p. 158). New York: Arbor House.

Boorstin, D. J. (1961). *The image: A guide to pseudo-events in America*. New York: Harper and Row.

Braudy, L. (1986). *The frenzy of renown: Fame and its history*. New York: Oxford University Press.

Carey, A. (1987). Reshaping the truth: Pragmatists and propagandists in America. In D. Lazare (Ed.), *American media and mass culture* (pp. 34–42). Berkeley, CA: University of California Press.

Celebrity unlimited. (1944, February). *American Mercury*, pp. 204–5.

Cohn, A. (1972). What every girl wants to know. In B. Gelman (ed.), *Photoplay treasury* (pp. 32–5). New York: Bonanza Books. [Original work published 1919]

Costello, M. (1941, February) They pronounce it pre-meer. *Reader's Digest*, pp. 88–92.

Crawford, J. (1972). The story of a dancing girl. In B. Gelman (ed.), *Photoplay treasury* (pp. 86–8). New York: Bonanza Books. [Original work published 1928]

Does TV drama need a star system? (1953, October 30). *TV Guide*, pp. 5–7.

Dyer, R. (1979). *Stars*. London: British Film Institute.

Eddy, D. (1940, July). Hollywood spies on you. *American Magazine*, pp. 24–5.

Efron, E. (1967, August 11). How to manufacture a celebrity. *TV Guide*, pp. 16–19.

Ephron, N. (1989, June). Famous first words. *Esquire*, pp. 103–5.

Fame. (1931, October 28). *The Nation*, p. 450.

Familiar gestures. (1954, March 26). *TV Guide*.

Ferber, E. (1920, December 4). They earn their millions. *Collier's*, pp. 7–8.

The final fling. (1970). In M. Levin (ed.), *Hollywood and the great fan magazines* (p. 39). New York: Arbor House.

For the stars, the postman always rings more than twice . . . (1956, December 29). *TV Guide*, pp. 4–6.

Fox, R. W., and Lears, T. J. J. (eds.). (1983). *The culture of consumption: Critical essays in American history 1880–1980*. New York: Pantheon.

Francis, A. (1960, September 3). Just be yourself. *TV Guide*, pp. 4–7.

Fuhrman, C. J. (1989). *Publicity stunt!* San Francisco: Chronicle Books.

Gelman, B. (ed.). (1972). *Photoplay treasury*. New York: Bonanza Books.

Gitlin, T. (1989, December 3). Review of *Rolling Stone: The photographs*. *The New York Times*, p. G14.

Goldsmith, B. (1983, December 4). The meaning of celebrity. *The New York Times Magazine*, pp. 75–83.

Henry, W. A. (1990, March 5). Pssst . . . did you hear about? *Time*, pp. 46–51.

Hirschberg, L. (1986, May 22). The power of hot. *Rolling Stone*, pp. 25–8.

Hobson, D. (1968, December 18). The ten percenter. *TV Guide*, pp. 4–9.

Hobson, D. (1969, April 12). The Hollywood flack. *TV Guide*, pp. 6–11.

How fleet it is! (1988, December 28-January 4). *People Weekly*, pp. 88–91.

How to make it in Hollywood [transcript of television program *Geraldo*]. (1988, March 17). Investigative News Group.

Hoyt, C. S. (1970) It's Ruby's turn now! In M. Levin (ed.), *Hollywood and the great fan magazines* (p. 51). New York: Arbor House.

Javits, J. K. (1960, October 1). You can't fool the camera. *TV Guide*, pp. 8–11.

Joel, P. (1970). The first true story of Garbo's childhood. In M. Levin (ed.), *Hollywood and the great fan magazines* (pp. 14–15). New York: Arbor House.

Kendall, E. (1962, September 30). Success (?) secret of the starmakers. *The New York Times Magazine*, pp. 37–40.

King, B. (1986). Stardom as an occupation. In P. Kerr (ed.), *The Hollywood film industry* (pp. 154–84). London: Routledge & Kegan Paul.

Klaprat, C. (1985). The star as market strategy: Bette Davis in another light. In T. Balio (ed.), *The American film industry* (pp. 351–76). Madison, WI: University of Wisconsin Press.

Lee, S. (1970). Jean Harlow – from extra to star. In M. Levin (ed.), *Hollywood and the great fan magazines* (pp. 43–44). New York: Arbor House.

Levin, M. (ed.) (1970). *Hollywood and the great fan magazines*. New York: Arbor House.

Lippmann, W. (1960). Blazing publicity: Why we know so much about "Peaches" Browning, Valentino, Lindbergh and Queen Marie. In C. Amory & F. Bradlee (eds.), *Vanity Fair* (pp. 121–2). New York: Viking Press. [Original work published 1927]

Lockwood, A. (1940, February). Press agent tells all. *American Mercury*, pp. 173–80.

Lowenthal, L. (1968). The triumph of mass idols. In L. Lowenthal, *Literature, popular culture and society* (pp. 109–40). Palo Alto, CA: Pacific Books.

Ludwig, E. (1930, May). What makes a man stand out from the crowd? *American Magazine*, p. 15.

Maddox, B. (1970). What about Clark Gable now? In M. Levin (ed.), *Hollywood and the great fan magazines* (pp. 20–1, 173–4). New York: Arbor House.

The making of Billy Gable. (1989, Spring). *Life*, pp. 53–4.

Martel, J. (1987, May 21). Sweet fifteen. *Rolling Stone*, p. 91.

May, L. (1980). *Screening out the past: The birth of mass culture and the motion picture industry*. New York: Oxford University Press.

Miller, M. C. (1988). *Boxed in: The culture of TV*. Evanston, IL: Northwestern University Press.

Morgan, T. (1963, October 19). Gentlemen of the pressure. *TV Guide*, pp. 6–9.

Morin, E. (1960). *The stars*. New York: Grove Press.

The new Hollywood. (1940, November 4). *Life*, pp. 65–7.

Olasky, M. N. (1987). *Corporate public relations: A new historical perspective*. Hillsdale, NJ: Lawrence Erlbaum.

O'Malley, F. W. (1921, June 25). Hot off the press agent. *The Saturday Evening Post*, p. 56.

The people perplex. (1977, June 6). *Newsweek*, pp. 89–90.

Postman, N. (1985). *Amusing ourselves to death: Public discourse in the age of show business*. New York: Penguin.

Powdermaker, H. (1950). *Hollywood the dream factory*. Boston: Little, Brown.

Rein, I. J., Kotler, P., and Stoller, M. R. (1987). *High visibility*. New York: Dodd, Mead.

Schickel, R. (1985). *Intimate strangers: The culture of celebrity*. New York: Fromm International.

Schudson, M. (1978). *Discovering the news: A social history of American newspapers*. New York: Basic Books.

Service, F. (1970). So you'd like to be a star: Myrna Loy shows you what is back of Hollywood's glamor front. In M. Levin (ed.), *Hollywood and the great fan magazines* (pp. 142–3). New York: Arbor House.

Shaw, E. (1982, October 2). Never get riled, don't knock women, chefs – and bring your own pillow. *TV Guide*, pp. 56–60.

Starlets are world's most envied of girls. (1940, January 29). *Life*, pp. 37–9.

The state of celebrity 1990. (1990, January). *Spy*, pp. 59–69.

Stauth, C. (1988, April 2). The secrets of Hollywood's casting directors. *TV Guide*, pp. 2–6.

Sullivan, A. (1989, May 8). Buying and nothingness. *The New Republic*, pp. 37–41.

Susman, W. (1984). *Culture as history*. New York: Pantheon.

Taylor, R. (1970). Why did I slip? In M. Levin (ed.), *Hollywood and the great fan magazines* (pp. 124–5). New York: Arbor House.

Television's biggest struggle: The battle of billings. (1958, October 4). *TV Guide*, pp. 21–3.

Toll, R. C. (1976). *On with the show: The first century of show business in America*. New York: Oxford University Press.

The truth about Groucho's ad libs. (1954, March 19). *TV Guide*, pp. 5–7.

Walker, A. (1970). *Stardom: The Hollywood phenomenon*. New York: Stein and Day.

Warga, W. (1982, October 9). The three stages of Hollywood stardom. *TV Guide*, pp. 4–10.

21 Mountains of Contradictions: Gender, Class, and Region in the Star Image of Dolly Parton

Pamela Wilson

Dolly Parton has achieved broad popularity over the past twenty years as an exceptional country musician who successfully "crossed over" into pop music and is now perceived as one of the industry's most respected and prolific singer/songwriters. Her distinctive voice is noted for its lilting clarity and "shimmering mountain tremolo," and her repertoire ranges from Appalachian ballads to African-American gospel tunes to hard-driving rockabilly numbers. Parton was one of the first female country musicians whose career developed in front of the television cameras: first as Porter Wagoner's partner on *The Porter Wagoner Show* (1967–74), then as the first woman to host her own country and western variety show, *Dolly* (1976–77). Securing her position as a multimedia star, Parton has played major roles in a number of notable Hollywood films, including *9–to–5*, *The Best Little Whorehouse in Texas*, and *Steel Magnolias*. In addition to her musical fame and her starring roles on television and in films, Dolly Parton has become well-known through the popular media as an icon of hyperfemininity and as a hero to or role model for women of varying class and cultural backgrounds.[1] As Mary A. Bufwack and Robert K. Oermann explain, "Dolly Parton is the most famous, most universally beloved, and most widely respected woman who has ever emerged from country music," making her "a role model not only for other singers and songwriters, but for working women everywhere."[2]

Dolly Parton has fashioned her star image visually to accentuate her ample, voluptuously overflowing body, particularly her large breasts, a body image that she has embellished with showy, garish costumes and an exaggeratedly sculptured blond wig. This persona is a caricature that juxtaposes the outlandish style of the country singer (in a predominantly male tradition of gaudy costuming) with the stereotypical self-display of the "painted woman," or prostitute, whose sexuality is her style. In ironic contrast to the parodic nature of her visual style, the articulate Parton has perpetuated an image that has gained her respect as a smart, wholesome, sincere person with traditional rural values (Christianity, family, rootedness, and "old-fashioned" integrity) who has managed, through perseverance and resourcefulness, to transcend the disadvantaged economic and social circumstances into which she was born and to use her talents to realize many of her dreams. These "dreams,"

Original publication: Wilson, Pamela, "Mountains of Contradictions: Gender, Class, and Region in the Star Image of Dolly Parton," *South Atlantic Quarterly*, 94:1 (Spring 1995) pp. 109–34.

when materialized and activated, entail another set of contradictions since they represent a lifestyle which, on the surface, is decidedly nontraditional for someone with any combination of her social identities: female, Southern, rural, Appalachian, working-class. Yet, through the construction of her persona, Parton manages and actively exploits the contradictory meanings associated with the social categories of gender, class, ethnic, and regional identity.[3]

Parton is often compared to Mae West, Marilyn Monroe, Bette Midler, and Madonna for her manipulation and burlesquing of femininity. In fact, she has incorporated an acknowledgment of her place in this tradition of subversive white femininity into her 1990s persona through mimetic references in her costumes, makeup, and performances.[4] Yet there is something about Parton that distinctively resonates with a rural and/or working-class audience and that seems to strengthen her appeal as a popular role model rather than a mere visual icon. As a fluent and savvy promoter of "Dolly," Parton provides a fascinating case study in the construction of a star image, specifically one that mediates the often contradictory ideals of gender, region, and class.[5]

An examination of national magazine stories about Dolly Parton reveals that different popular periodicals, the discourses of which strategically target different demographic constituencies, have appropriated Parton for their own discursive realms or purposes and have contributed to the construction of her persona in a number of different ways.[6] Music and musical technology magazines (e.g., *High Fidelity, Stereo Review, Crawdaddy*) have depicted her as a musician and songwriter, tending to focus on her extraordinary talent and her status in the music industry. Men's magazines (e.g., *Esquire, Playboy*) have claimed her as an icon for the desiring male gaze, focusing on her body and sexual image. Supermarket tabloids (e.g., *The Star, National Examiner, National Enquirer,* and *The Globe*) have variously portrayed her as a sexual icon, as a transgressor of patriarchal conventions, and as the occasional victim of personal crisis. They have also focused on her body and the unconventionality of her long-distance marriage and have offered projections of various scandals that lurk on the horizon of her life, so to speak. Middlebrow women's magazines (e.g., *Good Housekeeping, Ladies Home Journal, Redbook*) have promoted Parton's womanliness, speaking of her as if she were a potential friend and focusing on Parton's "private side": her personal history, her family and her home, her nurturing motherliness, her problems with her weight, her emotions, and her ability to balance an "ordinary" marriage and homelife with an extraordinary career. The feminist magazine *Ms.* has promoted what it reads as Parton's feminism, praising her as an empowering agent for women and the working class: "a country artist, a strong businesswoman, and a mountain woman with loyalty and love for her roots."[7] Finally, mainstream news magazines (e.g., *Newsweek, Time*) have billed Parton as a phenomenon of popular culture, focusing on her astute financial management in the entertainment industry and business world.

Dolly Parton's appearance, notably, the images of her body and especially her breasts, has become the terrain for a discursive struggle in the popular press over the social meaning of the female body and the associated ideologies that compete for control over the meaning of "woman" in our society.[8] Parton has consciously and strategically created a star persona that incorporates and even exploits many of the gender contradictions that currently circulate in society. Her complex encoding of these contested meanings via multiply accentuated signifiers defies any easy or uniform interpretation and categorization – in fact, her image encourages a plurality of conflicting readings, which she seems to relish playfully.

The Dolly persona *embodies* (there being no other word for it) excessive womanliness, in any interpretation. Parton displays this excess through her construction of a surface identity (her body and appearance) and through her representation of interiority, or a deeper identity (her emotions, desires, and "dreams"). As one interviewer noted, "Dolly built overstatement into what she calls her 'gimmick,' that is, looking trashily sexy on the surface while being sweet, warm and down-to-earth on the inside."[9] Parton openly discusses the strategies she employs for the construction of her image in almost every interview, and she makes no secret of the fact that the Dolly image is a façade she has created to market herself. This "masquerade" might be interpreted in the psychoanalytic terms theorized by Mary Ann Doane (based on the work of Lacan and Joan Riviere). Yet it might also be seen, following Claire Johnston, as a social parody, a hyperbolic stereotype, a tongue-in-cheek charade that playfully and affectionately subverts the patriarchal iconography of female sexuality.[10] As Parton has explained.

> When I started out in my career, I was plainer looking. I soon realized I had to play by men's rules to win. My way of fighting back was to wear the frilly clothes and put on the big, blonde wigs. It helped that I had a small voice that enabled me to sing songs of pain and loneliness and love and gentle things like butterflies and children. I found that both men and women liked me.[11]

Parton's construction of the "inner" Dolly, though just as carefully controlled, is not as readily evident since she attempts to elide the constructedness of the Dolly persona by conflating it with public perceptions of the "real" Dolly Parton, thus diverting attention from the aim of such strategies (i.e., as marketing ploys) as well:[12]

> I'm careful never to get caught up in the Dolly image, other than to develop and protect it, because if you start believing the public persona is you, you get frustrated and mixed up.... I see Dolly as a cartoon: she's fat, wears a wig, and so on.... Dolly's as big a joke to me as she is to others.[13]

In many ways, it is difficult to deconstruct the issues of gender, class, regionalism, and ethnicity as distinct facets of Dolly, since many of the signifiers Parton uses connote and connect two or more. Parton never decontextualizes herself from her rural, working-class, Southern Appalachian identity; from her interviews it is clear that she does not distinguish the abstract condition of being female from her personal experience as a Southern Appalachian, working-class woman. Parton "plays herself," constructing an image from the very contradictions of her own culturally grounded experience and social identity. However, many popular discourses (particularly those addressed to a gendered audience, either masculine or feminine) foreground gender issues. They focus on Dolly as a (more abstract) "woman," buying into her image without necessarily considering the relationship between her "woman-ness" and her class and regional/ethnic origins.

In a 1977 issue of *High Fidelity*, a country music columnist addressed Parton's corporeal contradictions:

> Inevitably, the recent national notice accorded Dolly Parton has focused more on the improbability of her image than on her art. A voluptuous woman with a childish giggle, she finger-picks the guitar, the banjo and the mountain dulcimer with inch-long, painted nails. She composes delicate lyrics of Tennessee mountain innocence and performs them in finery a stripper would happily peel. And through layers of lipstick, she pushes a voice fervent with fundamentalist religion. . . . Today she would like to be a little more listened to and a little less ogled. But the reams of copy about her fashion and physiognomy can hardly be blamed on anyone but herself; she donned the gaudy garb and high-piled hair specifically to make us stare.[14]

Critic Ken Tucker has also addressed the tactical strategy of Parton's self-marketing:

> Now, there is no doubt that the major reason non-country fans initially took an interest in Parton was the outer package – "People will always talk and make jokes about my bosom," was the way she put it with typical forthrightness. This, combined with her Frederick's of Hollywood high heels . . . and cartoonish hairpieces ("You'd be amazed at how expensive it is to make a wig look this cheap"), transformed Parton into the country version of Mae West, and made her a highly telegenic figure.[15]

The traditional masculine perspective that fetishizes the female body (particularly large breasts and an hourglass figure) for the male gaze has long been a visual staple of men's magazines. However, the fact that Parton's appearance is such an exaggeration of that aesthetic (plus, I suspect, the fact that she has maintained such a mystique about her sexuality) seems to make her male admirers too uncomfortable to directly address this fetish, relying instead on nervous puns, laughter, jokes, and euphemisms to communicate their desire. For example, humorist and *Esquire* columnist Roy Blount, Jr., once wrote:

> Folks, I am not going to dwell on Dolly's bosom. I am just going to pass along a vulgar story: "They say old Dolly's gone women's lib and burned her bra. Course it took her three days." Dolly's bosom, horizontally monolithic in its packaging, is every bit as imposing as her hair. And then abruptly her waist goes way in. . . . And she wears very tight clothes over it. . . . I imagine you would have to know Dolly a good while before you could say hello to her without suddenly crying, "Your body!"[16]

Prefacing his extended 1978 interview with Parton in *Playboy*, Lawrence Grobel remarked:

> Although she appears larger than life, she is actually a compact woman – dazzling in appearance; but if you took away the wig and the Frederick's of Hollywood five-inch heels, she'd stand just five feet tall. Of course, her height isn't the first thing one notices upon meeting her. As she herself kids onstage, "I know that you-all brought your binoculars to see me; but what you didn't realize is you don't need binoculars."[17]

Grobel continued with another anecdote about a little girl whose parents brought her backstage to greet Dolly; it too articulates the discourse of male desire:

The picture I'll always remember was of the father telling his wife to take a shot of him behind Dolly. He had this crazy gleam in his eyes, his tongue popped out of his mouth, and I was sure he was going to cop a feel. But he restrained himself, as most people do around her. Because she is so open and unparanoid, she manages to tame the wildest instincts of men.[18]

What the *Playboy* interview reveals is Parton's complicity in (and ultimate control of) this discourse of male desire. Several factors enter into the carefully constructed mystique that Parton maintains. First, her long-distance, part-time marriage to the mysterious, never-interviewed Carl Dean of Tennessee has generated questions about outlets for her sexual energy. There is an implicit assumption that since she appears to be hyperfeminine, she must be hypersexual. One of the most prevalent topics in "Dolly" discourse is speculation about her relationship with her husband, about how much time she spends with him, and, often implicitly, about the terms of their marriage vis-à-vis fidelity (about which questions are posed but evaded in several interviews). The tabloids have linked her sexually to a number of singing partners and leading men; there have also been suggestions of a lesbian relationship with her best friend and companion. This obsessive concern with the intimate details of Parton's sex life is found primarily in men's magazines and the tabloids. In contrast, when women's magazines have addressed the issue of her marriage, the focus has primarily been on her interpersonal/emotional relationships in general.

Throughout the *Playboy* interview, Grobel repeatedly raised questions about Parton's sexuality, to which she responded teasingly and unabashedly, but always stopping short of any personal disclosures. She admitted that she frequently flirts; however, the reader can observe her flirtations with the interviewer as her way of tactically taking control of the situation; her witty and manipulative comebacks frequently seemed to take Grobel by surprise and usually served to keep the ball in her court. The late Pete Axthelm once wrote about this aspect of Parton's persona:

> What Dolly is, it seems to me, is more than the sum of her attractive parts. Aside from her talent, she represents a vanishing natural resource – the mountain woman who understood independence and manipulation of men long before the first city girl got her consciousness raised. Dolly has a seldom-seen husband . . . she also employs a number of men to help build her career. But there is no doubt about who's boss. "I need my husband for love," she says, "and other men for my work. But I don't depend on any man for my strength."[19]

Although some feminists have spoken out against the objectification of women's bodies as fetishes of male desire, on the grounds that such objectification reduces women to a passive state that victimizes them, one counterargument attributes power to the woman who controls – and controls the use of – her own image. Dolly Parton, by managing and manipulating her sexual image in such a way as to attain the maximum response from the male gaze while maintaining her own dignity and self-esteem, is making patriarchal discourse work to her own advantage. She is keeping the upper hand and stage-managing her own "exploitation."

If Dolly's appearance seems to signify excessive femaleness in the discourse of male desire and the magazines that articulate it, in such women's magazines as *Good Housekeeping* and *Ladies Home Journal* it is identified with a different kind of excess: exaggerated womanliness. There, Parton's literal embodiment of excessive womanliness is represented in two domains: that of her attitudes about her weight and body image, and that of her reproductive capabilities and speculations about whether her future holds motherhood. Both domains function as grounds for identification with Dolly by many female readers. While the evocation of male desire constructs Dolly as an object of voyeurism and aggressive sexual fantasy, the emphasis on female identification constructs Dolly as an ordinary woman who has the same types of physical and emotional problems as other women. In contrast to the physiological oddity constructed by men's magazines, in women's magazines Dolly becomes "Everywoman," and efforts are made to minimize her exceptionalness.[20]

The first discursive domain of women's magazines deals respectfully with the *imperfections* of Dolly's body, as noted by Parton herself, and the associated psychological aspects (a very different reading of the same physical "text" on which the masculine reading of sexuality is based):

> I look better fat, though, don't you think? Skinny, my face looks too long. I'm just very hefty. People are always telling me to lose weight, but being overweight has certainly never made me less money or hurt my career. . . . Besides, everybody loves a fat girl. . . . See, I know I'm not a natural beauty. I got short legs, short hands, and a tiny frame, but I like the way I am. I am me. I am real.[21]

After an extended illness and gynecological surgery in the early 1980s, Parton lost a good deal of weight. This generated a surge of interest in – and a number of women's magazine articles about – her body and her relationship to it:

> Dolly admits she was overeating. Although she confesses, "I'm a natural-born hog. . . . I also eat when I'm happy," the protracted illness added more pounds to an already overloaded five-foot frame. "See, I'd always had this eating problem. I'd gain twenty pounds, lose it, gain it back the next week. In ten days I'd put on ten pounds. . . . I'd binge, diet, gain, start all over again. . . . Overeating is as much a sickness as drugs or alcoholism."

> To the suggestion she's too thin, that she looks anorexic, Dolly guffaws, "Honey, hogs don't get anorexia."

> Boy, it burns me up to see people look at a fat person and say, "Can you believe anybody would let herself get into that kind of shape?" That's easy for someone who looks like Jane Fonda to say. When I see a really overweight person, I feel sorry for her, because I've been there. . . . I know I could gain the weight back any minute, and it scares me to death."[22]

Through this admission, Parton brings herself down from any pedestal on which her star status might have placed her and aligns herself with the everyday concerns of ordinary women. Yet she also specifically identifies with working-class women, sarcastically criticizing the class-based aesthetic of thinness among the upwardly mobile:

> My doctors would tell me, "Okay, you have about twenty pounds to lose, but you can do that easily. Just eat right." Well, that's easy to say, I just love those beautiful people

who tell you, "I *cahn't* see how anybody could let themselves get in that awful shape. Oh, my dear. That's gross," says Dolly, aping a fancy society voice.[23]

The other discursive domain of women's magazine articles about Dolly, the intense interest in her childbearing potential, has included speculation about her desire and possible plans for motherhood:

> Dolly doubts whether they'll have children because of the demands of her career. "I'm not saying women can't do both, but I'm on the road so much that it wouldn't be fair to the child. I love children so much that I'd want to be a mother all day long if I was going to be one. . . . But remember, I was one of the oldest in my family. I've been raising babies all my life. . . . There's no shortage of kids around our home."[24]

This interest in the nurturing, maternal side of Dolly continued after her hysterectomy, shading into curiosity about her emotional reactions to the loss of her childbearing potential:

> Dolly had a partial hysterectomy and can no longer become pregnant. "Carl and I wanted children for years," she says. "I used to grieve after the hysterectomy, but since I turned forty, it doesn't bother me as much. I think God meant for me not to have children. My songs are my children, and I've given life to three thousand of them." Had she had kids, Dolly admits, most of those songs would never have been written.[25]

This metaphoric link between childbearing and the cultural production of songs recalls the Appalachian folk tradition (as described by Bufwack and Oermann) of women's collecting and amassing huge repertoires of ballads and other songs that were then shared and exchanged among themselves.[26] Songs, like stories, have been a vital part of the cultural economy of Appalachian women; producing songs, like producing children, has been important to their social identities.

In contrast to women's magazines, recent tabloid articles have created masculinist scenarios, such as this one:

> Dolly Parton wants a baby. The country music star, who's pushing 43, always insisted motherhood wasn't for her. But now she's pining for the patter of little feet. Though she knows she can't become pregnant – surgery has eliminated that possibility – she wants to tear a page out of 44-year-old Loni Anderson's book and adopt a child.[27]

Tabloid discourse thus works hard at trying to "push" Parton back into a normative patriarchal structure, to contain and/or deny the creative potential of other forms of cultural production for women.

One of the contradictions between Parton's Dolly persona and her "real-life" image is that while the former has attained wealth and fame, the latter is projected as a humble Tennessee housewife who merely puts up with the demands of fame and fortune until she can get home and relax, slip into something more comfortable – her private life – which is just like everyone else's, well, almost. These conflicting images are paralleled by the dualistic roles that Parton models for women. On the one hand, she represents the modern, nonrepressed woman who can "have it all" – marriage, strong family ties and friendships, and a successful, self-managed business/career that has brought her financial independence and a commensurate degree of social power; on the other hand, she represents the traditional values of rural American womanhood. The women's magazine articles reflect both a strong interest in how she manages to balance all of these aspects of her life and an intense curiosity about what that life entails/who that woman is – hence their focus on the private, emotional side of the star. By contrast, articles in mainstream, business-oriented news and music magazines (as well as in *Ms.*) have charted the (nontraditional) economic accomplishments of Dolly Parton. Particular interest has been paid to her business acumen and to her success as a crossover, both of which are associated with overcoming institutional and social obstacles. Parton has been successful as a country music singer and songwriter, a Hollywood actress, and a television performer in both specials and series. She has also proved to be an extremely successful entrepreneur as the owner of several production companies, publishing companies, toy companies, and music studios, and as the developer of Dollywood – the theme park she created to strengthen the economy of her native Tennessee county, which celebrates both her own career and the culture of the Appalachian region where she began.[28]

Dolly Parton's star image is the terrain for a struggle over not only the contested meanings of gender – the social construction of "woman" – but also the nature of and relations among class, regional culture, and ethnicity.[29] The Dolly persona, as an intersection of multiple social categories, raises the question of what it means to be Southern, Appalachian, rural, working-class, and female – or any one of these social identity categories.

In today's cosmopolitan, rapidly globalizing society, the construction of cultural identities is increasingly becoming a symbolic process rather than a result of geographic positioning. Although the role of the media in this symbolic construction needs further exploration, I want to suggest that the country music industry contributes to it by constructing notions of "Southernness" or "country-ness" to which consumers can subscribe. Today, many cultures are geographically situated in or otherwise associated with the American South, such as the cultures of black, rural, working-class Southerners; the "old South's" white aristocracy; urban black Southerners; urban Southern Jews; Southern Appalachian whites; urban/suburban white Southerners; Louisiana Cajuns; Southern Mennonites; and Cherokee, Choctaw, and Seminole Indians. All are distinct, but their cultural boundaries are permeable, and social agents may be associated with more than one of these subcultures. Class, race, ethnicity, and place are the most significant markers of cultural group identity. As a result, "Southern" is clearly a generic construct rather than a label for a distinct culture. It is used as a classifying and stereotyping term by outsiders; the signifiers of Dolly Parton's distinctive white Southern Appalachian culture are collapsed into a nonspecific "Southernness" and "country-ness" by the popular culture discourses relating to country music.

"Southernness," as a symbolic and discursive construction, has acquired distinct connotations and cultural referents that are usually associated with white Southern cultures.[30] The political history of the Southern states, beginning with their secession from the United States during the Civil War period, through the stark, Depression-era WPA images of impoverished sharecroppers, to the civil rights movement of the 1960s, has generated a host of internal and external discourses and stereotypes about the "South," which are reproduced and further fueled by conflicting images and representations of the region in literature, the media, and popular culture.

The specific subculture represented by Dolly Parton (Southern Appalachian mountain culture) has also been subject to stereotyping in popular culture, from the socially inept and "primitive" hillbillies of the "L'il Abner" comic strip and television's *Beverly Hillbillies* to the violent, sexually deviant villains of James Dickey's novel *Deliverance* and its 1972 film adaptation. Parton parodies these popular images in her persona, even as she promotes the more "authentic" cultural elements that reflect her heritage, particularly the culture of Appalachian women. Historically and culturally, kinship has been the central organizing principle of Southern Appalachian society, and a matrilineal orientation has resulted in strong affective ties among women.[31] Each rural community tended to form an independent, kinship-oriented, egalitarian social group, without clear social-class differences (most group antagonism stemmed from tensions between a social group and the outside world – meaning, since the mid-nineteenth century, the northern industrial society – as well as from minor tensions between communities or between families). Relationships between women have been primarily kin-and neighbor-oriented, and a strong women's culture has been maintained. Members of a traditional mountain community have tended to share a common history and ideology, with their code of morality primarily informed by localized inflections of fundamentalist Christianity.

In the traditional, preindustrial economy, there was a gendered division of labor: the woman's domain was her household, where she was responsible for raising food and children and for serving as a repository of cultural knowledge (history, genealogy, and the moral code). As industrialization overtook the agrarian mode of life in this century, mountaineers have been gradually assimilated into this economy as working-class laborers, and both men and women now participate in the wage-labor force.[32] Although this culture is generally perceived as strongly patriarchal (a perception largely due to the work of early male "ethnographers," such as John C. Campbell), studies by women who have examined the culture challenge that assumption; they see instead a gender-based system of coexisting models for cultural practice, whereby Appalachian women maintain a great deal of power within and through a facade of patriarchal control.

On the matter of the oppositional relationship between Southern Appalachian culture and the dominant American social order, some readings of Gramsci's work on early twentieth-century rural and urban societies in Italy are especially useful.[33] Gramsci describes rural intellectuals as "for the most part 'traditional,' . . . linked to the social mass of country people and the town (particularly small town) petite bourgeoisie, not as yet elaborated and set in motion by the capitalist system."[34] Anne Sassoon's explanation is significant:

> These intellectuals are considered traditional from . . . the point of view of the dominant, capitalistic mode of production. They are still linked to a world which is pre-capitalist. In this terrain they weld together a sub-bloc which has its own particular coherence. Although they are traditional *vis-à-vis* the dominant bloc, they can at the same time have *organic* links to surviving pre-capitalist modes and classes. They live, as it were, in two different historical times.[35]

The dualistic historical inscription of Southern Appalachian culture – one inscribing mountaineers as residual remnants of the past and the other transposing them to contemporary lower-or working-class status – is an important key to understanding the multiple sources of oppositional sentiment represented in Southern Appalachian cultural expression: the traditional agrarian mode versus postindustrial capitalism, and rural working-class culture versus mainstream/middle-class American culture (especially as constructed by film and television).

A great deal of the "Dolly" discourse in popular magazines has been devoted to authenticating her "country" life history and cultural roots, particularly the conditions of poverty, rural isolation, and familial heritage in which she developed.[36] In interviews, Parton herself has emphasized her working-class background:

> I can think like a workingman because I know what a working-man goes through.... Where I came from, people *never* dreamed of venturing out. They just lived and died there. Grew up with families and a few of them went to Detroit and Ohio to work in the graveyards and car factories. But I'm talking about venturing out into areas that we didn't understand.[37]

Parton has also discussed the farming/working-class mentality of her husband, an asphalt contractor:

> He's really bright. He's not backward at all. I just really wish that people would let him be. He's a home-lovin' person. He works outside, he's got his tractor and his grader, he keeps our farm in order. He wouldn't have to work no more, because I'm making good money now, but he gets up every morning at daylight. If he ain't workin' on our place, he'll take a few jobs, like grading somebody's driveway or cleaning off somebody's property, to pick up a couple of hundred bucks.... He'll say, "Well, I ain't in show business, I got to work."[38]

Many magazine articles underscore Parton's refusal to be assimilated into a Hollywood celebrity lifestyle and her preference for maintaining a home near Nashville. However, this brings up the complex issue of the subcultural hegemony represented by the Nashville-based country music industry.

In relation to the mainstream music and entertainment industries centered in Los Angeles and New York, the Nashville industry represents a successful regional-cultural force that has gained a national audience, yet remains independent and appears somewhat radical in its advocacy of Southern, white, working-class culture. In the course of being disseminated nationally through radio and, most recently, cable television, the "country" culture has been appropriated by a generalized working-class audience, both urban and rural, that represents various racial and ethnic backgrounds.[39] As a result of its folk music origins, country music has long been a genre of self-defined "ordinary folks," whose sense of humor has frequently generated both oppositional satire and a somewhat self-mocking tone (often read as straight by outsiders, but recognized as ironic and self-parodying by insiders).[40] Since the 1950s, country music has increasingly become a genre for female artists, who have aligned themselves with rural and working-class women.

However, the country music industry has recently changed, shifting away from its folk roots (though still incorporating them in the construction of "country-ness") and moving into the postmodern popular-music mainstream market. In an insightful essay, Patrick Carr discusses the changing social image of and audience for country music in the 1980s:

> Historically in America, the rural working class has been the object of prejudice, of stereotyping amounting to contempt, on the part of the urban population.... Not long ago, to "be country" meant that you had been cast by a geo-socio-economic accident of birth with an almost automatically adversarial relationship with the dominant urban/ suburban culture; in effect, you belonged in a cultural ghetto. Now it's a matter of free consumer choice.[41]

Carr argues that the country music industry has structured its current place in the entertainment industry in such a way as to commercialize those adversarial voices, thereby economically insinuating them into a capitalist order to which they have been traditionally opposed.[42] This is indeed a major paradox of country music in general and of stars like Parton in particular. The bristling tension between the proudly rebellious, rough-hewn rural style of "authentic" country music culture and the glossy, slickly packaged commercialized style of the mainstream entertainment industry has become the defining mark of the country music industry today.[43]

I find Raymond Williams's insights on "residual" cultural elements helpful in analyzing how Southern Appalachian and rural Southern subcultural elements are incorporated into the dominant economy and culture: "The residual, by definition, has been effectively formed in the past, but is still active in the cultural process, not only and often not at all as an element of the past, but as an effective element of the present."[44] This notion of "the residual" illuminates the active role that the past plays, not just in subcultures, but in their incorporation into the dominant culture:

> A residual cultural element is usually at some distance from the effective dominant culture, but some part of it, some version of it...will in most cases have had to be incorporated if the effective dominant culture is to make sense in these areas.... It is in the incorporation of the actively residual – by reinterpretation, dilution, projection, discriminating inclusion and exclusion – that the work of the selective tradition is especially evident.[45]

In constructing her star persona, Dolly Parton has played with and exploited cultural stereotypes of style and taste – not only in terms of femininity, but also with respect to Southern Appalachian, rural and/or working-class culture – often exaggerating them in her persona or emphasizing them in interviews:

> I always liked the looks of our hookers back home. Their big hairdos and makeup made them look *more*. When people say that less is more, I say *more* is more. Less is *less*; I go for more.

> Dolly, who commands $350,000 a week in Las Vegas – making her the highest paid entertainer there – says she prefers shopping at K-Mart or Zayre's, where she can get several articles of clothing for the price she'd pay for one at a more upscale establishment.

> I'd much rather shop in a mall and buy some cheap clothes than go into some fine store and buy something that costs a fortune.... I want to design something for the average woman, something that could be sold at Sears or Penney's.[46]

By foregrounding such stereotypes, Parton not only celebrates working-class tastes and values, but also parodies her male predecessors in the country music world of the 1950s and 1960s, particularly her former partner, Porter Wagoner, and others who perpetuated country music's most distinctive visual symbol – the extravagantly expensive, gaudy, spangled-and-rhinestoned stage costume, which became the *haute couture* of male country music performers of that era.[47] The "down-home" side of Dolly thus advocates "authenticity" by making fun of the superficial stylistic elements that have encrusted the dominant society's image of (and that have been internalized as identificatory values by) women on display, country music performers, Southerners, and the rural working class. As Gloria Steinem points out, "Her flamboyant style has turned all the devalued symbols of womanliness to her own ends. If feminism means each of us finding our unique power, and helping other women to do the same, Dolly Parton certainly has done both."[48] If we extend Steinem's statement to include the other categories of social identity and oppression that the "Dolly" image enunciates, Parton can be understood as a self-empowered woman whose image, challenging social stereotypes through parody, becomes empowering and counter-hegemonic.

My main interest here is in the type of feminism Dolly Parton represents, which seems to be "organically" rooted in and intertwined with the multiply oppressive conditions of class, regional ethnicity, and gender. Through her practices and her discourse, Parton has made public what had previously been tacit or private strategies used by rural, working-class, Southern Appalachian women to negotiate power for themselves within patriarchy and the capitalist class structure. Nevertheless, Parton is not an anomaly, but is instead drawing upon a model of feminine action in which women subvert, and gain strength from within, the dominant patriarchal system.[49] The apparent purpose of this subversion is not to overthrow patriarchy altogether, but to create opportunities for women to control their lives within it.

Michel de Certeau's theories of the resistance practiced by working classes within a capitalist class structure, or by subcultures resisting assimilation into dominant culture, provide insights that can be extended to gender negotiations of power within patriarchy:

> [She] creates for [herself] a space in which [she] can find *ways of using* the constraining order of the place. . . . Without leaving the place where [she] has no choice but to live and which lays down its law for [her], [she] establishes within it a degree of *plurality* and creativity. By an art of being in between, [she] draws unexpected results from [her] situation.[50]

De Certeau's model is one of subversion from within an order of power: not overthrowing or necessarily transforming it, but exploiting its resources (time and materials) for one's own purposes, constructing one's own space and strategies for action within the boundaries, and tactically identifying and exploiting the loopholes in the structure of dominance to acquire power for oneself. Both de Certeau's model and the case of Southern Appalachian women illustrate the dual operations of orders of power – a top-down presumption that the legitimately powerful are in control, complemented by a bottom-up pretense of endorsing that presumption: although "they" think they are in control of "us" (and "we" pretend to be controlled by "them"), "we" are in fact manipulating the structure for our own purposes, taking advantage of every opportunity to informally (and quietly) exploit the system. In the coalescence of multiple oppressions (gender, social class, economic group, etc.), these mechanisms operate on multiple levels, against a variety of "systems" of power.

Feminism, class, and regional/ethnic consciousness become personal rather than political, rhetorical, or structural issues for women like Dolly Parton. She represents a type of popular feminism that has little knowledge of or use for the political rhetoric of the women's movement, although Parton herself has never publicly opposed its goals and has always aligned herself with other strong, self-sufficient women. In citing the qualities that Parton hails in her 1991 song "Eagle When She Flies," Bufwack and Oermann describe this type of feminism among female country artists of the 1960s and 1970s, who "sang proudly of the enduring strength of womanhood": "They portrayed the country woman as the powerful life force, the resilient mother, the source of love, and the rock of support."[51] In a May 1991 (week of Mother's Day) appearance on *The Tonight Show*, Parton introduced "Eagle When She Flies" with these comments:

> I wanted to do a song for all the mamas out there. This is a song I actually wrote about my own mother, and about myself – about people like Mother Teresa, Amelia Earhart, Harriet Tubman, Eleanor Roosevelt, Ann Richards, and all the great women who've helped make this world more wonderful. I hope maybe you guys will appreciate this, too.

In spite of this tribute to female humanitarians, politicians, and adventurers, Parton dissociates herself from the rhetoric of mainstream feminism, insistently personalizing and individualizing feminist ideology in terms of lived experience, as in this segment of the 1978 *Playboy* interview:

> *Grobel*: Do you support the Equal Rights Amendment?
> *Parton*: Equal rights? I love everybody....
> *Grobel*: We mean equal rights for women.
> *Parton*: I can't keep up with it.
> *Grobel*: Do you read any books on the women's movement?
> *Parton*: Never have. I know so little about it they'd probably be ashamed that I was a woman. Everybody should be free: if you don't want to stay home, get out and do somethin'; if you want to stay home, stay home and be happy.[52]

And, in another interview:

> I think if women, or people in general, would just listen and not think they're still listening to their father or to their mother or their husband, or to this or to that, but listen to what *they* think they can do.... I always said, with my accountants, with my managers, or my bankers or agents: "Look, I don't need advice, I need information. I will make my own decisions."[53]

Parton applies her belief system to the management of her own life and career. She openly discusses her determination to control the construction of her image, even as she also chooses to express herself in language that marks her by class and region:

> People have thought I'd be a lot farther along in this business if I dressed more stylish and didn't wear all this gaudy get-up. Record companies have tried to change me. I just refused. If I am going to look like this, I must have had a reason. It's this: if I can't make it on my talent, then I don't want to do it. I *have* to look the way I choose to look, and this is what I've chose.[54]

She has also exhibited a strong-willed determination to master and manipulate the social codes and conventions of the patriarchal and capitalist systems, deploying these codes to her own advantage without transgressing them.[55] This is a key to her acceptance as a non-threatening but powerful influence. Parton, in forging new traditions from old ones, is serving as a model for others to do the same. As one music magazine describes her, she is "a woman taking possession of her destiny."[56] Or, as Parton's occasional collaborator Linda Ronstadt puts it:

> I think Dolly is a girl who was born with an amazing amount of insight into people. It's like an intelligence of compassion. Shakespeare really understood human behavior. Tolstoy could write the greatest novel ever because he really understood what makes people tick. And I think Dolly Parton is one of those kinds of people. She has that kind of intelligence; she is amazingly perceptive.[57]

Basing her feminism and class consciousness on cultural knowledge and emotion rather than intellectual rhetoric, Parton's impassioned, popular feminism speaks to segments of the working class who are probably beyond the reach of liberal feminist rhetoric. It is also significant, I believe, that she reaches this population through the vehicle of musical expression (and its attendant discourses) rather than through political or intellectual rhetoric. As Gramsci articulated the dichotomy:

> The popular element "feels" but does not always know or understand: the intellectual element "knows" but does not always understand and in particular does not always feel.... The intellectual's error consists in believing that one can know without understanding and even more without feeling and being impassioned.... One cannot make politics-history without this passion, without this sentimental connection between intellectuals and people-nation.[58]

As a popular feminist and an advocate of the rural working class, Parton employs a counter-hegemonic rhetoric that seems sentimental, emotional, and nonthreatening to those in the power bloc, who often perceive it as comical and ineffectual. Yet her subversive strategies are powerful. Far from serving as a vehicle for the dominant ideology, Parton's star image provides a rich, multidimensional configuration of signifiers that exploit the contradictory meanings inherent to that image. "Dolly" may well make Parton's fans aware of their own social positioning and thereby encourage alternative readings and practices.

Acknowledgments

Many thanks to Lynn Spigel, Julie D'Acci, John Fiske, David Morley, Greg Smith, and Cecelia Tichi for their insights and suggestions at various stages in this paper's development.

Notes

1 Mary Bufwack and Robert K. Oermann's *Finding Her Voice: The Saga of Women in Country Music* (New York, 1993) provides a thorough and fascinating account of the central, though often overlooked, role of women in the growth of country music throughout this century. See also Joan Dew's *Singers and Sweethearts: The Women of Country Music* (Garden City, NJ, 1977); and scattered references in Bill C. Malone's *Southern Music, American Music* (Lexington, 1979); and in John Lomax III, *Nashville: Music City USA* (New York, 1985). Patrick Carr also provides an insightful look at the industry; see "The Changing Image of Country Music," in *Country: The Music and the Musicians*, ed. Paul Kingsbury, Country Music Foundation (New York, 1988), 482–517.

2 Bufwack and Oermann, *Finding Her Voice*, 360.

3 See Richard Dyer, *Stars* (London, 1979).

4 During the US military engagement in the Persian Gulf ("Operation Desert Storm"), a story on Parton in *Vanity Fair* featured photos of Dolly attired in the style of various 1940s pin-up queens and posing atop the shoulders of American fighter pilots. Another stylized image mimetically invoked Dolly "doing" Madonna "doing" Marilyn Monroe: A photo in *People*, taken during a concert performance shows Parton with a brassiere-like contraption of two huge cones – a mocking parody of Madonna's contemporaneous act. The caption reads "Dolly Parton finally found a way to contain herself and still delight fans at the Brady Theater in Tulsa, where she sang 'Like a Virgin' with a pointed reference to the originator." See Kevin Sessums, "Good Golly, Miss Dolly!" *Vanity Fair* (June 1991): 106–11, 160–6; and *People*, 29 June 1992, 7.

5 To clarify my terminology here, since it has potential political implications, I use the name "Dolly" to refer to the constructed persona or image and "Parton" to refer to the social agent responsible for the act of constructing. I realize, however, that even this distinction is problematic since Parton's construction and representation of her "authentic" self amounts to creating a media persona as well. Admittedly, it is difficult to refer to her as "Parton" because in almost all of the literature (with the exception of three articles, two in music magazines and one in *Ms.*) she is referred to as "Dolly" with a familiarity that I suspect would be less acceptable in journalistic writing about a man.

6 These magazine articles represent only a small portion of the available media coverage of this star, which also addresses her recordings, films, two television series and numerous specials, as well as other promotional coverage.

7 Gloria Steinem, "Dolly Parton," *Ms.* (January 1987): 95.

8 Consider the dual cultural meaning of women's breasts in our society: as characteristics of sexual attractiveness, and as sites of maternal life-giving, nourishment, nurturance, and mother-child bonding.

9 Cliff Jahr, "Golly, Dolly!" *Ladies Home Journal* (July 1982): 85.

10 See Mary Ann Doane, "Film and the Masquerade: Theorizing the Female Spectator," *Screen* (September–October 1982): 74–87; Joan Riviere, "Womanliness as a Masquerade,"

Formations of Fantasy, ed. Victor Burgin et al. (London, 1986 [1929]), 35–44; and Claire Johnston, "Feminist Politics and Film History," *Screen* 16 (Autumn 1975): 115–24.

11 "Love Secrets That Keep the Magic in Dolly's Marriage," *The Star*, 27 November 1990, 12.

12 For example, regarding the emphasis on family and traditional rural values in much of the popular discourse about Parton, Ken Tucker notes that "the invocation of family is an emotional button that country stars like to push – it seems to produce instant sympathy among tradition-minded fans." See his "9 to 5: How Willie Nelson and Dolly Parton Qualified for 'Lifestyles of the Rich and Famous,'" in Kingsbury, ed., *Country*, 386.

13 Jahr, "Golly, Dolly!" 85, 139.

14 Jack Hurst, "You've Come a Long Way, Dolly," *High Fidelity* (December 1977): 122.

15 Tucker, "9 to 5," 383.

16 Roy Blount, Jr., "Country's Angels," *Esquire* (March 1977): 131.

17 Lawrence Grobel, "Dolly Parton: A Candid Conversation with the Curvaceous Queen of Country Music," *Playboy* (October 1978): 82.

18 Ibid.

19 Pete Axthelm, "Hello Dolly," *Newsweek*, 13 June 1977, 71.

20 See Dyer, *Stars*, on "ordinariness" as an important aspect of star-image construction, especially among women (49–50).

21 Jahr, "Golly, Dolly!" 142.

22 Cindy Adams, "Dolly's Dazzling Comeback," *Ladies Home Journal* (March 1984): 153; Nancy Anderson, "Dolly Parton: A Home Town Report," *Good Housekeeping* (February 1988): 186; and Mary-Ann Bendel, "A Different Dolly," *Ladies Home Journal* (November 1987): 120.

23 Adams, "Dolly's Dazzling Comeback," 153.

24 Joyce Maynard, "Dolly," *Good Housekeeping* (September 1977): 60.

25 Bendel, "Different Dolly," 182.

26 Bufwack and Oermann, *Finding Her Voice*, 7.

27 Gary Graham, "Dolly Parton to Adopt Baby," *The Star*, 14 April 1989, 6.

28 See Charles Leehrsen, "Here She Comes, Again," *Newsweek*, 23 November 1987, 73–4; see also Hurst, "You've Come a Long Way," 122; Grobel, "Candid Conversation," 108; and Alanna Nash, "Dollywood: A Serious Business," *Ms.* (July 1986): 12–14.

29 I use the term "ethnicity" in the anthropological sense established by Barth and by de Vos and Romanucci-Ross, that is, as referring to cultural groups within a pluralistic and hegemonic society who define themselves (through a perception of common origins or common beliefs and values) as culturally distinct from the dominant group and who use a variety of mechanisms to maintain symbolic boundaries and delineations from other groups. In this sense, I perceive Southern Appalachian culture to be one of regional ethnicity, but I do not perceive "Southernness," as an external construction of regionality, to be a kind of ethnicity in itself, although it incorporates many. See Fredrik Barth, *Ethnic Groups and Boundaries* (Boston, 1969); and *Ethnic Identity: Cultural Continuities and Change*, ed. George De Vos and Lola Romanucci-Ross (Palo Alto, 1975).

30 In the working-class South, the races (white, black, and American Indian) have lived in relative isolation from each other, maintaining fairly separate but parallel cultures. The black population in the Appalachian region has always been much smaller than that of the lowland South, according to Phillip J. Obermiller and William W. Philliber, *Too Few Tomorrows: Urban Appalachians in the 1980's* (Boone, NC, 1987), 11. For useful over-views of Southern cultural issues, see Carole Hill, "Anthropological Studies in the American South: Review and Directions," *Current Anthropology* 18 (1987): 309–26; Marion Pearsall, "Cultures of the American South," *Anthropological Quarterly* 39 (1966):

476–87; and John S. Reed, *The Enduring South: Subcultural Persistence in Mass Society* (Chapel Hill, 1974).

31 Relevant works on the Southern Appalachian culture of Parton's region include John C. Campbell's 1921 classic. *The Southern Highlander and His Homeland* (Lexington, 1969 [1921]); *Appalachian Ways: A Guide to the Historic Mountain Heart of the East*, ed. Jill Durrance and William Shamblin (Washington, DC, 1976); Elmora Messer Matthews, *Neighbor and Kin: Life in a Tennessee Ridge Community* (Nashville, 1965); and Jack Weller, *Yesterday's People: Life in Contemporary Appalachia* (Lexington, 1965). For insights into the culture of Southern and Appalachian women, see Margaret Jarman Hagood, *Mothers of the South: Portraiture of the White Tenant Farm Woman* (New York, 1977 [1939]); and Pamela Wilson, "Keeping the Record Straight: Conversational Storytelling and Gender Roles in a Southern Appalachian Community" (Master's thesis, University of Texas at Austin, 1984). Obermiller and Philliber, *Too Few Tomorrows*, also provide insights into Appalachian ethnicity.

32 With this century's increasing economic dependence upon industry and the corresponding breakdown of the agricultural economy, many farmworkers have been integrated into the dominant capitalist system as part of the working class and now tend to fill that slot in the social and economic structure (although it is important to point out that this rural working-class society exhibits characteristics that are quite different from those of an urban/industrial working-class society). In addition, as Obermiller and Philliber report in *Too Few Tomorrows*, from 1940 through 1970, over three million people migrated from the Southern Appalachian region to industrial urban centers in the Midwest (primarily Cincinnati, Detroit, and Chicago) to find work as unskilled laborers; some returned after a few years, but many stayed and created cultural ghettos of Appalachian people in these cities.

33 My understanding of Gramsci is based on the interpretations of Anne Showstack Sassoon, as well as on the neo-Gramscian interpretations of Raymond Williams, John Fiske, and Dick Hebdige. See Sassoon, *Gramsci's Politics* (Minneapolis, 1987); Williams, *Marxism and Literature* (Oxford, 1977); Fiske, *Television Culture* (London, 1987); and Hebdige, *Subculture: The Meaning of Style* (London, 1979).

34 Antonio Gramsci, *Selections from the Prison Notebooks*, ed. and trans. Quintin Hoare and Geoffrey Nowell Smith (London, 1971), 14.

35 Sassoon, *Gramsci's Politics*, 144.

36 Parton's family history and the photographs that visually document her rags-to-riches story feature prominently in women's magazine articles (see, e.g., Anderson, "Home Town Report"; and Jahr, "Golly, Dolly!"). Grobel's 1978 *Playboy* interview also extensively investigates the details of Parton's life growing up, and the two articles in *Ms.* (by Nash and by Steinem) focus on the rootedness of Parton's life and image in her region and hometown community. See also Willadeene Parton, "My Sister, Dolly Parton," *McCall's* (July 1985): 74–125; and Connie Berman, "Dolly Parton Scrapbook," *Good Housekeeping* (February 1979): 140–3, 203–9.

37 Grobel, "Candid Conversation," 88, 102.

38 Ibid., 88.

39 On the predominance of working-class and female consumers in the composition of country music audiences, as well as the prevalence of working-class backgrounds among country music performers, see Mary A. Bufwack and Robert K. Oermann, "Women in Country Music," in *Popular Culture in America*, ed. Paul Buhle (Minneapolis, 1987), 91–101.

40 On the folk origins of country music, see Hurst, "You've Come a Long Way," 123. He traces Parton's musical style to the convergence of three components: (1) Elizabethan ballads preserved for centuries by isolated Appalachian mountaineers; (2) the wildly emotional religious music of Protestant fundamentalist churches; and (3) the country music on early 1950s radio.

41 Carr, "Changing Image," 484.

42 Ibid.; see also George Lipsitz, *Time Passages* (Minneapolis, 1990), esp. 99–160; and Bufwack and Oermann's "Women in Country Music."

43 This is particularly true of country music videos; see Mark Fenster, "Country Music Video," *Popular Music 7* (1988): 285–302.

44 Williams, *Marxism and Literature*, 122.

45 Ibid., 123.

46 Jahr, "Golly, Dolly!" 85; Kingsbury, ed., *Country*, 258; and Bendel, "Different Dolly," 182.

47 Carr, "Changing Image," 494.

48 Steinem, "Dolly Parton," 66.

49 Willadeene Parton, in "My Sister," 125, tells of vacations that all the women of the Parton family take together each year ("It's so secret that not even our husbands and children know what we do"), and she articulates the patriarchal myth: "For the first years of their life together, we were sorry for Mother because Papa's word was law; and the last years, we were sorry for Papa because Mother keeps breaking the law."

50 Michel de Certeau, *The Practice of Everyday Life*, trans. Steven Rendell (Berkeley, 1984), 30.

51 Bufwack and Oermann, *Finding Her Voice*, 320–21. The lines from "Eagle When She Flies" that seem particularly relevant in this context are as follows:

> She's been there. God knows, she's been there.
> She has seen and done it all.
> She's a woman. She knows how to dish it out or take it all.
> ....
> She's a lover, she's a mother, she's a friend and she's a wife.
> ....
> Gentle as the sweet magnolia, strong as steel, her faith and pride.
> She's an everlasting shoulder, she's the leaning post of life.
> ....
> And she's a sparrow when she's broken,
> But she's an eagle when she flies.
> (For recording information, see Selected Discography.)

52 Grobel, "Candid Conversation," 110.

53 Susan McHenry, "Positively Parton," *Ms.* (July 1986): 14.

54 Grobel, "Candid Conversation," 82.

55 On Parton's tenacious control over her own business affairs, see Noel Coppage, "Dolly," *Stereo Review* (September 1979): 82–4; Scott Isler, "Where Town Meets Country," *Crawdaddy* (February 1978): 74; Karen Jaehne, "CEO and Cinderella: An Interview with Dolly Parton," *Cineaste* 17 (1990): 16–19; and Leehrsen, "Here She Comes," 73–4.

56 Hurst, "You've Come a Long Way," 124.

57 Quoted in Bufwack and Oermann, *Finding Her Voice*, 429.

58 Gramsci, *Prison Notebooks*, 418.

22 Fandom as Pathology: The Consequences of Characterization

Joli Jensen

The literature on fandom is haunted by images of deviance. The fan is consistently characterized (referencing the term's origins) as a potential fanatic. This means that fandom is seen as excessive, bordering on deranged, behavior. This essay explores how and why the concept of fan involves images of social and psychological pathology.

In the following pages I describe two fan types – the obsessed individual and the hysterical crowd. I show how these types appear in popular as well as scholarly accounts of fans and fandom. I consider why these two particular characterizations predominate – what explains this tendency to define fans as, at least potentially, obsessed and/or hysterical fanatics?

I suggest here that these two images of fans are based in an implicit critique of modern life. Fandom is seen as a psychological symptom of a presumed social dysfunction; the two fan types are based in an unacknowledged critique of modernity. Once fans are characterized as deviant, they can be treated as disreputable, even dangerous "others."

Fans, when insistently characterized as "them," can be distinguished from "people like us" (students, professors and social critics) as well as from (the more reputable) patrons or aficionados or collectors. But these respectable social types could also be defined as "fans," in that they display interest, affection and attachment, especially for figures in, or aspects of, their chosen field.

But the habits and practices of, say, scholars and critics are not deemed fandom, and are not considered to be potentially deviant or dangerous. Why? My conclusion claims that the characterization of fandom as pathology is based in, supports, and justifies elitist and disrespectful beliefs about our common life.

Characterizing the Fan

The literature on fandom as a social and cultural phenomenon is relatively sparse. What has been written is usually in relationship to discussions of celebrity or fame. The fan is understood to be, at least implicitly, a result of celebrity – the fan is defined as a *response* to the star system. This means that passivity is ascribed to the fan – he or she is seen as being brought into (enthralled) existence by the modern celebrity system, via the mass media.

Original publication: Jensen, Joli, "Fandom as Pathology: The Consequences of Characterization," from Lisa A. Lewis (ed.), *The Adoring Audience: Fan Culture and Popular Media* (Routledge, London, 1992)

This linking of fandom, celebrity and the mass media is an unexamined constant in commentary on fandom. In a *People Weekly* article on the killing of TV actress Rebecca Schaeffer by an obsessive fan, a psychologist is quoted as saying:

> The cult of celebrity provides archetypes and icons with which alienated souls can identify. On top of that, this country has been embarking for a long time on a field experiment in the use of violence on TV. It is commonplace to watch people getting blown away. We've given the losers in life or sex a rare chance to express their dominance.[1]

In one brief statement, cults, alienation, violence, TV, losers and domination (themes that consistently recur in the fandom literature) are invoked. A security guard, also quoted in the article, blames media influence for fan obsessions: "It's because of the emphasis on the personal lives of media figures, especially on television. And this has blurred the line between appropriate and inappropriate behavior."[2]

In newspaper accounts, mental health experts offer descriptions of psychic dysfunctions like "erotomania" and "Othello's Syndrome," and suggest that the increase in fan attacks on celebrities may be due to "an increasingly narcissistic society or maybe the fantasy life we see on television."[3]

This same blending of fandom, celebrity and presumed media influence in relation to pathological behavior can be found in more scholarly accounts. Caughey describes how, in a media addicted age, celebrities function as role models for fans who engage in "artificial social relations" with them. He discusses fans who pattern their lives after fantasy celebrity figures, and describes at some length an adolescent girl, "A," who in 1947 shot Chicago Cubs first baseman Eddie Waitkus. He argues that her behavior cannot simply be dismissed as pathological, because up to a point her fan activity resembled that of other passionate fans. The model of fandom Caughey develops is one in which pathological fandom is simply a more intense, developed version of more common, less dangerous, fan passion.[4]

This is also Schickel's explicit claim. He ends his book on the culture of celebrity by comparing deranged fans and serial killers to "us." He concludes that we "dare not turn too quickly away" from "these creatures" who lead "mad existences" because "the forces that move them also move within ourselves in some much milder measure."[5] These academically-oriented accounts develop an image of the pathological fan who is a deranged version of "us."

One model of the pathological fan is that of the obsessed loner, who (under the influence of the media) has entered into an intense fantasy relationship with a celebrity figure. These individuals achieve public notoriety by stalking or threatening or killing the celebrity. Former "crazed" acts are referenced in current news stories of "obsessive" fans: Mark David Chapman's killing of ex-Beatle John Lennon, and John Hinckley's attempted assassination of President Ronald Reagan (to gain and keep the attention of actress Jodie Foster) are frequently brought up as iconic examples of the obsessed loner type.

This loner characterization can be contrasted with another version of fan pathology: the image of a frenzied or hysterical member of a crowd. This is the screaming, weeping teen at the airport glimpsing a rock star, or the roaring, maniacal sports fan rioting at a soccer game. This image of the frenzied fan predominates in discussions of music fans and sports fans.

Since the 1950s, images of teens, rock "n" roll and out-of-control crowds have been intertwined. In press coverage, the dangers of violence, drink, drugs, sexual and racial mingling are connected to music popular with young people. Of particular concern are the influences of the music's supposedly licentious lyrics and barbaric rhythms. Crowds of teen music fans have been depicted as animalistic and depraved, under the spell of their chosen musical form. Heavy Metal is the most recent genre of youth music to evoke this frightening description of seductive power: Metal fans are characterized, especially by concerned parents, as vulnerable youngsters who have become "twisted" in response to the brutal and Satanic influence of the music.[6]

The press coverage of rock concerts almost automatically engages these images of a crazed and frantic mob, of surging crowds that stampede out of control in an animalistic frenzy. When 11 teenagers were crushed to death in Cincinnati's River-front Coliseum (before a 1979 concert by The Who) press coverage was instantly condemnatory of the ruthless behaviour of the frenzied mob. In his Chicago-based syndicated column, Mike Royko vilified the participants as "barbarians" who "stomped 11 persons to death [after] having numbed their brains on weeds, chemicals and Southern Comfort."[7]

Yet, after investigation, the cause of the tragic incident was ascribed not to a panic or a stampede of selfish, drug-crazed fans, but instead to structural inadequacies of the site, in combination with inadequate communication between police, building workers and ticket-takers. Apparently, most crowd members were unsuccessfully (but often heroically) trying to help each other escape from the crush, a crush caused by too few doors into the arena being opened to accommodate a surge of people pressing forward, unaware of the fatal consequences at the front of the crowd.

In other words, the immediately circulated image of mass fan pathology (a crazed and depraved crowd climbing over dead bodies to get close to their idols) was absolutely untrue. As Johnson concludes, "the evidence ... is more than sufficient to discount popular interpretations of 'The Who Concert Stampede' which focus on the hedonistic attributes of young people and the hypnotic effects of rock music."[8] Nonetheless, the "hedonistic and hypnotic" interpretation was widely made, an interpretation consistent with the iconic fans-in-a-frenzy image historically developed in connection with musical performances.

Concern over fan violence in crowds also appears in relation to sports. There is an academic literature, for example, on football hooliganism.[9] This literature explores the reasons for violence at (mostly) soccer games, where "hard-core hooligans" engage in violent and destructive acts, often against the opposing teams' fans. These incidents have become cause for social concern, and have been researched in some depth, especially in Britain. Even though, obviously, not all soccer fans engage in spectator violence, the association between fandom and violent, irrational mob behaviour is assumed. In this literature, fans are characterized as easily roused into violent and destructive behavior, once assembled into a crowd and attending competitive sports events.[10]

To summarize, there is very little literature that explores fandom as a normal, everyday cultural or social phenomenon. Instead, the fan is characterized as (at least potentially) an obsessed loner, suffering from a disease of isolation, or a frenzied crowd member, suffering from a disease of contagion. In either case, the fan is seen as being irrational, out of control, and prey to a number of external forces. The influence of the media, a narcissistic society, hypnotic rock music, and crowd contagion are invoked to explain how fans become victims of their fandom, and so act in deviant and destructive ways.

Fans as Socially Symptomatic

What explains these two iconic images? One possibility is that they genuinely embody two different aspects of the fan /celebrity interaction – individual obsessions, privately elaborated, and public hysteria, mobilized by crowd contagion. But *do* these models accurately or adequately describe the ways in which fandom is manifested in contemporary life? *Are* they appropriate representations of fandom? Do fans *really* risk becoming obsessed assassins or hysterical mobs? Do they (we) too easily "cross the line" into pathological behavior, as Schickel suggests, because "we suffer to some degree from the same confusion of realms that brings them, finally, to tragedy?"[11]

I suspect not, and the crux of my argument here is that these particular pathological portrayals exist in relation to different, unacknowledged issues and concerns. I believe that these two images tell us more about what we want to believe about modern society, and our connection to it, than they do about actual fan–celebrity relations.[12]

What is assumed to be true of fans – that they are potentially deviant, as loners or as members of a mob – can be connected with deeper, and more diffuse, assumptions about modern life. Each fan type mobilizes related assumptions about modern individuals: the obsessed loner invokes the image of the alienated, atomized "mass man"; the frenzied crowd member invokes the image of the vulnerable, irrational victim of mass persuasion. These assumptions – about alienation, atomization, vulnerability and irrationality – are central aspects of twentieth-century beliefs about modernity.

Scholars as well as everyday people characterize modern life as fundamentally different from pre-modern life. Basically, the present is seen as being materially advanced but spiritually threatened. Modernity has brought technological progress but social, cultural and moral decay. The modernity critique is both nostalgic and romantic, because it locates lost virtues in the past, and believes in the possibility of their return.

In the early twentieth century, mass society terms (like alienation and atomization) took on added resonance in the urbanizing and industrializing United States, where the inevitable beneficence of progress (celebrated by technocrats and industrialists) was being increasingly questioned by intellectuals and social critics. Two aspects were of particular concern to American critics – the decline of community, and the increasing power of the mass media.

These concerns are related. Communities are envisioned as supportive and protective, they are believed to offer identity and connection in relation to traditional bonds, including race, religion and ethnicity. As these communal bonds are loosened, or discarded, the individual is perceived as vulnerable – he or she is "unstuck from the cake of custom" and has no solid, reliable orientation in the world.

The absence of stable identity and connection is seen as leaving the individual open to irrational appeals. With the refinement of advertising and public relations campaigns in the early twentieth century, along with the success of wartime propaganda, and the dramatic rise in the popularity of film and radio, fears of the immense and inescapable powers of propaganda techniques grew. It seemed that "mass man" could all too easily become a victim of "mass persuasion." And under the spell of propaganda, emotions could be whipped into frenzies, publics could become crowds and crowds could become mobs.

This conceptual heritage, which defines modernity as a fragmented, disjointed mass society, is mobilized in the two images of the pathological fan. The obsessed loner is the image of the isolated, alienated "mass man." He or she is cut off from family, friends and community. His or her life becomes increasingly dominated by an irrational fixation on a celebrity figure, a perverse attachment that dominates his or her otherwise unrewarding existence. The vulnerable, lonely modern man or woman, seduced by the mass media into fantasy communion with celebrities, eventually crosses the line into pathology, and threatens, maims or kills the object of his or her desire.

The frenzied fan in a crowd is also perceived to be vulnerable, but this time to irrational loyalties sparked by sports teams or celebrity figures. As a member of a crowd, the fan becomes irrational, and thus easily influenced. If she is female, the image includes sobbing and screaming and fainting, and assumes that an uncontrollable erotic energy is sparked by the chance to see or touch a male idol. If he is male, the image is of drunken destructiveness, a rampage of uncontrollable masculine passion that is unleashed in response to a sports victory or defeat.

Dark assumptions underlie the two images of fan pathology, and they haunt the literature on fans and fandom. They are referenced but not acknowledged in the relentless retelling of particular examples of violent or deranged fan behavior. Fans are seen as displaying symptoms of a wider social dysfunction – modernity – that threatens all of "us."

Fandom as Psychological Compensation

The modernity critique, with its associated imagery of the atomized individual and the faceless crowd, is mostly social theory – it does not directly develop assumptions about individual psychology. Nonetheless, it implies a connection between social and psychological conditions – a fragmented and incomplete modern society yields a fragmented and incomplete modern self. What we find, in the literature of fan – celebrity relationships, is a psychologized version of the mass society critique. Fandom, especially "excessive" fandom, is defined as a form of psychological compensation, an attempt to make up for all that modern life lacks.

In 1956, Horton and Wohl characterized the media – audience relationship as a form of "para-social interaction."[13] They see fandom as a surrogate relationship, one that inadequately imitates normal relationships. They characterize the media mode of address as a "simulacrum of conversation" and demonstrate how it tries to replicate the virtues of face-to-face interaction.

They also examine the structure and strategies of celebrity public relations, noting how they function to create what they call the celebrity "persona." They suggest that "given the prolonged intimacy of para-social relations...it is not surprising that many members of the audience become dissatisfied and attempt to establish actual contact.... One would suppose that contact with, and recognition by, the persona transfers some of his prestige and influence to the active fan." This implies that the fan, unable to consummate his desired social relations "normally," seeks celebrity contact in the hope of gaining the prestige and influence he or she psychologically needs, but cannot achieve in anonymous, fragmented modern society.

This statement is followed by commentary on a letter written to Ann Landers by a female fan (another "Miss A."), who says she has "fallen head over heels in love with a local television star" and now can't sleep, finds other men to be "childish," and is bored by her modeling job. Miss A. is said to reveal in this letter "how narrow the line often is between the more ordinary forms of social interaction and those which characterize relations with the persona." Even worse, "persona" relations are deemed to have "invaded" Miss A.'s life, "so much so that, without control, it will warp or destroy her relations with the opposite sex" (p. 206).

Horton and Wohl suggest, however, that "it is only when the para-social relationship becomes a substitute for autonomous social participation, when it proceeds in absolute defiance of objective reality, that it can be regarded as pathological" (p. 200). These extreme forms of fandom, they claim, are mostly characteristic of the socially isolated, the socially inept, the aged and invalid, the timid and rejected. For these and similarly deprived groups, para-social interaction is an attempt by the socially excluded (and thus psychologically needy) to compensate for the absence of "authentic" relationships in their lives.

Schickel suggests that celebrities act to fulfill our own dreams of autonomy (the famous appear to have no permanent allegiances) and dreams of intimacy (the famous appear to belong to a celebrity community). The psychopathic fan-turned-assassin, he implies, similarly uses mediated celebrities to form an identity, although he kills in order to share their power and fame. To be a fan, Schickel and others imply, is to attempt to live vicariously, through the perceived lives of the famous. Fandom is conceived of as a chronic attempt to compensate for a perceived personal lack of autonomy, absence of community, incomplete identity, lack of power and lack of recognition.

These vague claims, bolstered by various strains of social and psychological research, parallel, strikingly, the claims made about the reasons for fanaticism. Milgram defines a fanatic as "someone who goes to extremes in beliefs, feelings and actions."[14] He suggests that fanatics use belief systems as a "therapeutic crutch...staving off a collapse of self worth." Any challenge to the fanatic's belief system is seen as a "threat to his self-esteem," and thus to his "ego-defensive system."

Interestingly, deviants are also seen by researchers as lacking in self-worth, or as having weak "ego-boundaries."[15] This characteristic may even be linked to "role engulfment," where the identity of deviance becomes a way to organize a "concept of self."[16] Thus in all three concepts (fan, fanatic and deviant) a psychological portrait of fundamental inadequacy, and attempted compensation, is developed.

The inadequate fan is defined as someone who is making up for some inherent lack. He or she seeks identity, connection and meaning via celebrities and team loyalties. Like the fanatic and the deviant, the fan has fragile self-esteem, weak or non-existent social alliances, a dull and monotonous "real" existence. The mass media provide (the argument goes) ways for these inadequate people to bolster, organize and enliven their unsatisfying lives.

Fandom, however, is seen as a risky, even dangerous, compensatory mechanism. The fan-as-pathology model implies that there is a thin line between "normal" and excessive fandom. This line is crossed if and when the distinctions between reality and fantasy break down. These are the two realms that must remain separated, if the fan is to remain safe and normal.[17]

The literature implies that "normal" fans are constantly in danger of becoming "obsessive loners" or "frenzied crowd members." Ann Lander's curt response to Miss A. ("you are flunking the course of common sense") is figuratively given to all fans – as long as the fan shows "good common sense," remains "rational" and "in control", then he or she will be spared. But if the fan ceases to distinguish the real from the imaginary, and lets emotion overwhelm reason and somehow gets "out of control," then there are terrible consequences. These consequences are referenced in the cautionary tales of fans who go "over the edge" into fanaticism, and thus pathology.

Aficionados as Fans

The literature on fandom, celebrity and media influence tells us that: Fans suffer from psychological inadequacy, and are particularly vulnerable to media influence and crowd contagion. They seek contact with famous people in order to compensate for their own inadequate lives. Because modern life is alienated and atomized, fans develop loyalties to celebrities and sports teams to bask in reflected glory, and attend rock concerts and sports events to feel an illusory sense of community.

But what happens if we change the objects of this description from fans to, say, professors? What if we describe the loyalties that scholars feel to academic disciplines rather than to team sports, and attendance at scholarly conferences, rather than Who concerts and soccer matches? What if we describe opera buffs and operas? Antique collectors and auctions? Trout fisherman and angling contests? Gardeners and horticulture shows? Do the assumptions about inadequacy, deviance and danger still apply?

I think not. The paragraph makes sense only if it is believed to describe recognizable but nebulous "others" who live in some world different from our own. Fandom, it seems, is not readily conceptualized as a general or shared trait, as a form of loyalty or attachment, as a mode of "enacted affinity." Fandom, instead, is what "they" do; "we," on the other hand, have tastes and preferences, and select worthy people, beliefs and activities for our admiration and esteem. Furthermore, what "they" do is deviant, and therefore dangerous, while what "we" do is normal, and therefore safe.

What is the basis for these differences between fans like "them" and aficionados like "us"? There appear to be two crucial aspects – the objects of desire, and the modes of enactment. The objects of an aficionado's desire are usually deemed high culture: Eliot (George or T.S.) not Elvis; paintings not posters; the *New York Review of Books* not the *National Enquirer*. Apparently, if the object of desire is popular with the lower or middle class, relatively inexpensive and widely available, it is fandom (or a harmless hobby); if it is popular with the wealthy and well educated, expensive and rare, it is preference, interest or expertise.

Am I suggesting, then, that a Barry Manilow fan be compared with, for example, a Joyce scholar? The mind may reel at the comparison, but why? The Manilow fan knows intimately every recording (and every version) of Barry's songs; the Joyce scholar knows intimately every volume (and every version) of Joyce's *oeuvre*. The relationship between Manilow's real life and his music is explored in detail in star biographies and fan magazines; the relationship between Dublin, Bloomsday and Joyce's actual experiences are explored in detail in biographies and scholarly monographs.

Yes, you may say, there are indeed these surface similarities. But what about the fans who are obsessed with Barry, who organize their life around him?[18] Surely no Joyce scholar would become equally obsessive? But the uproar over the definitive edition of *Ulysses*[19] suggests that the participant Joyceans are fully obsessed, and have indeed organized their life (even their "identity" and "community") around Joyce.

But is a scholar, collector, aficionado "in love" with the object of his or her desire? Is it the existence of passion that defines the distinction between fan and aficionado, between dangerous and benign, between deviance and normalcy?

So far we have established that one aspect of the distinction between "them" and "us" involves a cultural hierarchy. At least one key difference, then, is that it is normal and therefore safe to be attached to elite, prestige-conferring objects (aficionadohood), but it can be abnormal, and therefore dangerous to be attached to popular, mass-mediated objects (fandom).

But there is another key distinction being made between the fan and the aficionado. Fans are believed to be obsessed with their objects, in love with celebrity figures, willing to die for their team. Fandom involves an ascription of excess, and emotional display – hysterics at rock concerts, hooliganism at soccer matches, autograph seeking at celebrity sites. Affinity, on the other hand, is deemed to involve rational evaluation, and is displayed in more measured ways – applause and a few polite "Bravos!" after concerts; crowd murmurs at polo matches; attendance of "big-name" sessions at academic conferences.

This valuation of the genteel over the rowdy is based in status (and thus class) distinctions. It has been described in nineteenth-century parades,[20] public cultural performances,[21] and turn of the century newspaper styles.[22] Unemotional, detached, "cool" behavior is seen as more worthy and admirable than emotional, passionate, "hot" behavior. "Good" parades are orderly and sequential and serious (not rowdy, chaotic or lighthearted); "good" audiences are passive and quiet and respectful (not active, vocal or critical); "good" newspapers are neutral, objective and gray (not passionate, subjective and colorful). Congruently, then, "good" affinities are expressed in a subdued, undisruptive manner, while "bad" affinities (fandom) are expressed in dramatic and disruptive ways.

The division between worthy and unworthy is based in an assumed dichotomy between reason and emotion. The reason–emotion dichotomy has many aspects. It describes a presumed difference between the educated and uneducated, as well as between the upper and lower classes. It is a deeply rooted opposition, one that the ascription of intrinsic differences between high and low culture automatically obscures.

Apparently, the real dividing line between aficionado and fan involves issues of status and class, as they inform vernacular cultural and social theory. Furthermore, the Joyce scholar and the Barry Manilow fan, the antique collector and the beer can collector, the opera buff and the Heavy Metal fan are differentiated not only on the basis of the status of their desired object, but also on the supposed nature of their attachment. The obsession of a fan is deemed emotional (low class, uneducated), and therefore dangerous, while the obsession of the aficionado is rational (high class, educated) and therefore benign, even worthy.

These culturally-loaded categories engage Enlightenment-originated ideas based on rationality. Reason is associated with the objective apprehending of reality, while emotion is associated with the subjective, the imaginative, and the irrational. Emotions, by this logic, lead to a dangerous blurring of the line between fantasy and reality, while rational obsession, apparently, does not. But does this reason–emotion dichotomy, complete with dividing line, hold up? Let me give you some examples from my own life, to suggest that the line is inevitably and constantly crossed, without pathological consequences, by respectable professorial types like me.

Anyone in academia, especially those who have written theses or dissertations, can attest to the emotional components of supposedly rational activity. A figure or topic can become the focal point of one's life; anything even remotely connected to one's research interests can have tremendous impact and obsessive appeal. For example, while I was writing my dissertation (on the commercialization of country music in the 1950s), the chance to touch Patsy Cline's mascara wand, retrieved from the site of her 1963 plane crash, gave me chills.

Similarly, (but far more respectably) the handling of a coffee cup made by William Morris was deeply moving. I have also envied a colleague who once owned a desk that had been used by John Dewey, and I display a framed copy of a drawing of William James in my office. I would be thrilled if I could own any memorabilia associated with Lewis Mumford, to whom I regret not having written a letter of appreciation before he died.

Am I, then, a fan of Patsy Cline, William Morris, William James, John Dewey and Lewis Mumford? Or of country music, the pre-Raphaelites, the pragmatists and iconoclastic social critics? Yes, of course I am, if fandom is defined as an interest in, and an attachment to, a particular figure or form. Would I write a fan letter to these figures? Yes, if fan letter includes (as it does, in academic circles) review essays or appreciative quotation. Would I read a fanzine? Again yes, but in the scholarly versions – heavily footnoted biographies and eloquent critical appreciations. Would I seek autographs? Yes, if I could do so without losing face, via auctions or books or scholarly correspondence. Would I collect memorabilia? Well, I confess here to having at least one version of all 100 of Patsy Cline's recordings; calendars and a piece of cloth designed by Morris; and as many books as I can afford to purchase by James, Dewey and Mumford, along with miscellaneous biographies, reviews and commentaries.[23]

Would I defend my "team," the pragmatists, against the attacks on them by, say, Hegelians, neo-Marxists and/or post-structuralists? You bet. Would I do so in a rowdy, rambunctious or violent way? Of course not. I would respond instead with respectable rowdiness (acerbic asides in scholarly articles) and acceptable violence (the controlled, intellectual aggression often witnessed in conference presentations).

Would I claim to be "in love" with any of these individuals, would I offer to die for any of these preferences? Not likely, and certainly not in public. I would lose the respect of my peers. Instead, I will say that I "admire" William James, I "read with interest" Lewis Mumford, I "enjoy" pre-Raphaelite design and "am drawn to" aspects of pragmatism. In short, I will display aficionado-hood, with a vengeance. But, as I hope my confessions have made obvious, my aficionado-hood is really disguised, and thereby legitimated, fandom.

The pejorative connotations of fans and fandom prevent me from employing those terms to describe and explore my attachments. While my particular affinities may be somewhat idiosyncratic, everyone I've ever met has comparable ones. Most of us seem to have deep, and personal, interests, and we enact our affinities by investing time, money and "ourselves" in them. I have even been fortunate enough to make a living in relation to my interests. Does that mean I am truly "obsessed" by them? Am I, perhaps, even more dysfunctional than most because I force others (like students) to listen, even temporarily to participate, in my predilections?

Were I to call myself a fan, I would imply that I am emotionally engaged with unworthy cultural figures and forms, and that I was risking obsession, with danger- ous consequences. I would imply that I was a psychologically incomplete person, trying to compensate for my inadequate life through the reflected glory of these figures and forms. My unstable and fragile identity needs them, they are a "ther- apeutic crutch," a form of "para-social relations," functioning as "personas" in my life. I must have these relationships because my lonely, marginal existence requires that I prop myself up with these fantasy attachments to famous dead people, and these alliances with abstract, imaginary communities.

Obviously, I find these ascriptions of dysfunction, based on my affinities, to be misguided and muddleheaded, as well as extraordinarily insulting. I assume that others would, too, whether they call themselves aficionados or fans. The pejorative association of fandom with pathology is stunningly disrespectful, when it is applied to "us" rather than "them."

The Consequences of Circumscription

There are consequences to defining fans as abnormal "others," irrationally obsessed with particular figures or cultural forms, capable of violent and destructive behavior. To consider these consequences, we need first to discuss why this kind of stigmatizing definition has been developed, and why it continues to dominate the literature. What purposes does such a conceptualization serve?

Stigmatization of a persona or group can be seen as a way of relieving anxiety[24] by a display of hostility or aggression. It is a form of displacement, a blaming, a scapegoating that allows explanation in ambivalent or contradictory circumstances.

By conceiving of fans as members of a lunatic fringe which cracks under the pressure of modernity, as the canaries in the coal mines whose collapse indicates a poisonous atmosphere, we tell ourselves a reassuring story – yes, modernity is dangerous, and some people become victims of it by succumbing to media influence or mob psychology, *but we do not.* "We" are not these unstable, fragile and therefore vulnerable people. We are psychologically stable and solid ("normal") and we will not crack. We recognize and maintain an equilibrium. Unlike obsessed and frenzied fans, we are in touch with reality. We have not crossed that line between what is real and what is imaginary.

To summarize, one outcome of the conceptualization of the fan as deviant is reassurance – "we" are safe, because "we" are not as abnormal as "they" are, and the world is safe, because there is a clear demarcation between what is actual and what is imagined, what is given and what is up for grabs.

Defining disorderly and emotional fan display as excessive allows the celebration of all that is orderly and unemotional. Self-control is a key aspect of appropriate display. Those who exhibit charged and passionate response are believed to be out of control; those who exhibit subdued and unimpassioned reaction are deemed to be superior types. Thus the "we" who write about, and read about, "them," the fans, get to be allied with the safe and superior and worthy types. "We" get to be thoughtful, educated and discriminating, if we assume that "they" are obsessed, uneducated and indiscriminate. Not only do "we" get to be safe, in spite of the perceived dangers of modernity, but we also get to be better than this group of inferior types – fans.

Defining fandom as a deviant activity allows (individually) a reassuring, self-aggrandizing stance to be adopted. It also supports the celebration of particular values – the rational over the emotional, the educated over the uneducated, the subdued over the passionate, the elite over the popular, the mainstream over the margin, the status quo over the alternative. The beliefs evidenced in the stigmatization of fans are inherently conservative, and they serve to privilege the attributes of the wealthy, educated and powerful. If these are indeed the attributes and values that the critic or researcher seeks to celebrate, then they should be disentangled from their moorings in objective research or critical inquiry, and directly addressed.

Treating people as "others" in social and psychological analysis risks denigrating them in ways that are insulting and absurd. The literature on deviance, fanaticism and fandom has a thinly veiled subtext – how are "we" not "them"? The "others" become interesting cases, that tell us about life on the margin, or in the wild, under duress, or on the edge. Like primitive tribes to be saved by missionaries, or explained by anthropologists, we too easily use social and psychological inquiry to develop and defend a self-serving moral landscape. That terrain cultivates in us a dishonorable moral stance of superiority, because it makes others into examples of extrinsic forces, while implying that we somehow remain pure, autonomous, and unafflicted.

Much social analysis gets conducted from this savannah of smug superiority, particularly research on media effects. Whether researchers are concerned with the media uses and gratifications, or the circulation of ideology, or the reasons for fandom, "they" (viewers, consumers and fans) are seen as victims of forces that somehow can not and will not influence "us." The commentator on fandom is protected by reason or education or critical insight: thanks to these special traits, "we" don't succumb to whatever it is we believe applies to "them."

This is not only a dishonorable stance, individually, but it is a severely truncated basis for inquiry. It means that the perceived-to-be deviant, exotic and dramatic, is studied with zeal, while the normal, everyday, and accepted is ignored. Little is known, for example, about the variety of ways people make meaning in everyday ways. We know far too little about the nature – and possibilities – of varieties of affection, attachment, sentiment and interest, *as they are manifested in people's lives*. How and why do we invest meaning and value in things, lives, ideals? Does our selection of particular figures and forms connect with other aspects of ourselves?

How does sentiment work? How and why do things mean? These are not trivial or uninteresting questions, but so far they have barely been studied, except perhaps in the humanities as "aesthetics," and in the social sciences as functions of other (economic or psychological or demographic) forces.

I am arguing here that social inquiry and criticism can and should proceed very differently. They should not define people as collections of preferences to be analyzed and controlled, any more than they should define them as unwitting victims of ideology or advertising or media or mob mentalities or ego-fragmentation. Social inquiry can and should be a form of respectful engagement. It can and should illuminate the experiences of others *in their own terms*, because these "others" are us, and human experiences intrinsically and inherently matter. Constantly to reduce what other people do to dysfunction or class position or psychic needs or socio-economic status is to reduce others to uninteresting pawns in a game of outside forces and to glorify ourselves as somehow off the playing field, observing and describing what is really going on.

If we instead associate ourselves with those "others," assume that there are important commonalities as well as differences between all individuals, communities and social groups, and believe that we are constantly engaged in a collective enter-prise of reality creation, maintenance and repair, then we are less likely to succumb to the elitism and reductionism that so far has characterized the research and literature on fans and fandom. What I am suggesting is that we respect and value other people as if they were us, because they always are. I ask that we avoid, assiduously, the seduction of separateness that underlies the description of fans as pathological.

The moral iconography of the deviant other fosters a belief that modernity hurts "them" and (for now) spares us, that the habits and practices of the wealthy and educated are to be valued and emulated, and that "we" are inevitably separate from, and superior to, "them." To the extent that we stigmatize fandom as deviant, we cut ourselves off from understanding how value and meaning are enacted and shared in contemporary life. If we continue to subscribe to the dominant perspective on fandom – pathology – inquiry on fandom cannot help us understand how we engage with the world. Instead, we will continue to conceptualize the fan as desperate and dysfunctional, so that he or she can be explained, protected against, and restored to "normalcy."

I believe what it means to be a fan should be explored in relation to the larger question of what it means to desire, cherish, seek, long, admire, envy, celebrate, protect, ally with others. Fandom is an aspect of how we make sense of the world, in relation to mass media, and in relation to our historical, social, cultural location. Thinking well about fans and fandom can help us think more fully and respectfully about what it means today to be alive and to be human.

Notes

1 Marilyn Robinette Marx, quoted in Axthelm (1989).
2 Gavin de Becker is described in Axthelm (1989, p. 66) as "an L. A. security expert who helps stars ward off unwanted attentions."

3 Jack Pott, Assistant Clinical Director of Psychiatry for Maricopa County Health Services, quoted in Rosenblum (1989), an *Arizona Daily Star* article kindly provided to me by Lisa Lewis.

4 Caughey (1978a). See also Caughey (1978b).

5 Schickel (1985). See especially the final pages.

6 See Miller (1988).

7 Quoted in Johnson (1987).

8 Johnson, ibid.

9 See, for example: Ingham (1978); Lee (1985); and Marsh *et al.* (1978).

10 See Dunning, Murphy and Williams (1986, p. 221), where they say that many fans are "drawn into hooligan incidents – fans who did not set out for the match with disruptive intent... [by contact with] hard-core hooligans."

11 Schickel (1985, p. 285).

12 The argument in this essay draws on my belief that vernacular social theory is accessible through the analysis of the narrative strategies of popular and scholarly accounts. I develop this belief, as well as the associated notion of the displacement of ambivalence, or scapegoating, in Jensen (1990).

13 Horton and Wohl (1956). Subsequently reprinted in Gumpert and Cathcart (eds) (1982).

14 Milgram (1977).

15 See, for example, the model developed by S. Giora Shoham (1976).

16 See the brief summary of this and other claims in Schur (1971).

17 The mass media, in conjunction with modern society, are believed somehow to blur this necessary distinction. The media are defined as dangerous precisely because they are believed to disrupt people's ability consistently and reliably to separate fantasy from reality. This account of media influence is pervasive, but fails to recognize the historical presence of narrativity in cultures, and that the insistence on distinctions between "objective" fact and "subjective" fiction is an historically recent development.

18 Vermorel (1985).

19 Probably best recorded in the *New York Review of Books* letters, in 1988 and 1989.

20 See Davis (1986).

21 Levine (1988).

22 Schudson (1978).

23 In the case of William James, my fandom extends to an interest in his parents and siblings, and I wish I knew something about his descendants. I have considered taking a vacation that would include visits to places he lived and worked. I disagree with some of the interpretations of some of his biographers, and am infuriated by Leon Edel's "unfair" portrayal of William in his biography of Henry James.

24 See, for example, the conclusion of Shoham (1976).

References

Axthelm, Pete. 1989. An Innocent Life, A Heartbreaking Death. *People Weekly* 32(5): 60–6.

Caughey, John L. 1978a. Artificial Social Relations in Modern America. *American Quarterly* 30(1).

Caughey, John L. 1978b. Media Mentors. *Psychology Today* 12(4): 44–9.

Davis, Susan. 1986. *Parades and Power: Street Theatre in Nineteenth-Century Philadelphia*. Philadelphia: Temple University Press.

Dunning, Eric, Patrick Murphy, and John Williams. 1986. Spectator Violence at Football Matches: Towards a Sociological Explanaion. *The British Journal of Sociology* 37(2).

Gumpert, Gary and Robert Cathcart. 1982. *Inter/Media: Interpersonal Communication in a Media World*, 2nd edn. New York: Oxford University Press.

Horton, David and R. Richard Wohl. 1956. Mass Communication and Parasocial Interaction: Observation on Intimacy at a Distance. *Psychiatry* 19(3): 188–211.

Ingham, Roger (ed.). 1978. *Football Hooliganism: The Wider Context*. London: Inter-Action.

Jensen, Joli. 1990. *Redeeming Modernity: Contradictions in Media Criticism*. Beverly Hills: Sage Publications.

Johnson, Norris R. 1987. Panic at "The Who Stampede": An Empirical Assessment. *Social Problems* 34(4): 362.

Lee, Martin J. 1985. From Rivalry to Hostility Among Sports Fans. *Quest* 37(1): 38–49.

Levine, Lawrence W. 1988. *Highbrow/Lowbrow: The Emergence of Cultural Hierarchy in America*. Boston: Harvard University Press.

Marsh, Peter, Elizabeth Rosser, and Rom Harre. 1978. *The Rules of Disorder*. London: Routledge & Kegan Paul.

Milgram, Stanley. 1977. The Social Meaning of Fanaticism. *Et Cetera* 34(1): 58–61.

Miller, Dale. 1988. Youth, Popular Music and Cultural Controversy: The Case of Heavy Metal. PhD thesis, University of Texas at Austin.

Rosenblum, Keith. 1989. Psychiatrists Analyze Fantasies, Fixations that Lead to Crimes Against Celebrities. *Arizona Daily Star* July 21, Section A: p. 2.

Schickel, Richard. 1985. Coherent Strangers. In *Intimate Strangers: The Culture of Celebrity*. Garden City, New York: Doubleday.

Schudson, Michael. 1978. *Discovering the News: A Social History of American Newspapers*. New York: Basic Books.

Schur, Edwin M. 1971. New York: Harper & Row.

Shoham, S. Giora. 1976. *Social Deviance*. New York: Gardner Press.

Vermorel, Fred and Judy. 1985. *Starlust: The Secret Fantasies of Fans*. London: W. H. Allen.

23 Scottish Fans, not English Hooligans! Scots, Scottishness, and Scottish Football[1]

Gerry P. T. Finn and Richard Giulianotti

Scotland, England, and Football

Scotland has one of the world's oldest footballing traditions. This sporting history owes much to Scotland's complex relationship to England, whether in Unionist fraternity, cultural rivalry or nationalist animosity. Imitation of England was behind the early organisation of Scottish football and the administration of its affairs (Rafferty 1975), in a process that was then thought to strengthen the British nation and the union. For a nation of only five million inhabitants, Scotland still exercises a disproportionate power within football, through officials like UEFA's Technical Director (Andy Roxburgh), the Vice President of FIFA (David Will), and the Chairman of UEFA's Stadium Committee (Ernie Walker). Scotland also has one of eight seats on the International Football Association Board, a legacy of its links with England and the British role in the early evolution of football.[2]

On the park, Scottish players have shown a greater sense of their cultural subsidiarity. They instructed English neighbours in the aesthetics and benefits of the "passing" game, and helped export and teach the game overseas (Forsyth 1990). Scotland is the only nation to compete and qualify for the World Cup Finals on five consecutive occasions (1974–90). In the European Championships Scotland has been much less successful, having previously qualified only for the 1992 finals in Sweden. Qualification for Euro 96 was achieved only through the tournament's expansion to accommodate sixteen rather than eight teams. Euro 96 also provided several other new departures for Scottish football. It was the first time Scotland had participated in a major international tournament held in England. Although Scotland also played Holland and Switzerland (in Birmingham) as part of its Group D matches, Scottish supporters were mainly focused on the match at Wembley against England, the first against the "Auld Enemy" since 1989. According to the traditions of Scotland's football culture, the match against England furnishes players and supporters alike with the greatest anticipation and highest levels of adrenaline. The curious ambivalence, sometimes downright hostility, of Scotland towards England is so culturally and historically embedded as to lend credence to the argument that this truly

Original publication: Finn, Gerry, P.T. and Richard Giulianotti, "Scottish Fans, not English Hooligans! Scots, Scottishness, and Scottish Football," from Adam Brown (ed.), *Fanatics! Power, Identity and Fandom in Football* (Routledge, London, 1998).

represents world football's most intense "derby match" at any level – civic, national or international.

Fan Styles: Social Identities and Culture

Recently, international football identities have been located in heavily contrasting styles: the "carnival" and "hooligan" styles of support. "Carnival" supporters display sociable, indeed gregarious, behaviour that is best described as boisterous. Although carnival behaviour is strongly associated with alcohol use, it remains decidedly non-violent. Qualifiers for Euro 96 with supporter groups falling into this category included Scotland's "Tartan Army", the Dutch "Oranji", and the Danish "Roligans" (Giulianotti 1991; 1995a; Peitersen 1991; cf. van den Brug 1994. "Hooligan" supporters engage in competitive violence with other fan groups. Usually a "moral code" is claimed by these supporters, who say they target their violence only on similar groups of opposing fans (Allan 1989: 23; Finn 1994b: 114). Germany, Holland and Scotland each have a hooligan contingent that can appear among their fans, particularly when opposing teams are thought to possess a comparable grouping.

The carnival and hooligan categories have heuristic and self-identifying value. They are important analytical categories for examining the cultural structures of the Scottish fans' activities. The carnival–hooligan differentiation also provides a consciously nurtured resource through which these supporters develop and publicly sustain their distinctive social identities. The appearance of Scotland and Holland in both carnival and hooligan categories indicates how this binary opposition of fan categories can be crudely manufactured. For example, previous research with the Tartan Army has shown that in certain circumstances the apparently opposed categories of carnival and hooligan can be submerged within a common Scottish social identity (Giulianotti 1991; 1995a).

Social identities are complex, incorporating multiple dimensions. Different facets of an individual's social identity can be made more or less salient as a result of different forms of social exchange, and this can produce quite different forms of behaviour. In some instances the identity may remain at the personal level and not be group oriented, so inter-group behaviour would not be expected. However, if the inter-group dimension is made situationally dominant, the ensuing exchange will involve participants' respective social identities.

The social dynamics of an inter-group exchange are strongly influenced by the pre-existing relationship between the social identities involved. Even when social actors have mutually opposed categories of social identity, antagonistic inter-group behaviour does not have to take place. The "opposing" groups may, for example, share another social identity. Clearly, the behaviour that then ensues will strongly depend on which aspect of inter-group differentiation is made most salient. In the case of Scotland's supporters, rival club identities are largely submerged within a crossed and common Scottish identity, which adopts a carnivalesque pattern of behaviour as its group norm. However, the social identity of Scottish fans is complicated by the existence of other, earlier variants of Scotland fan behaviour (which are more easily associated with "hooligan" behaviour). The interpretation and evaluation of Scottish fan behaviour is given greater complexity by the continuing uncertainty over how they should respond, and how they will respond, when they are confronted by "hooligan" international fans, particularly those from England. For some years this uncertainty has provided an undercurrent of unease that occasionally appears in statements from Scottish officials or the Scottish media.

To understand the enactment and interplay of Scottish supporter identities, it is necessary to look in greater detail at how the carnival and hooligan identities are engendered by Scottish fans. Carnival fans are typically presented by the media and football authorities as "ambassadors" for the game. Their public persona of gregariousness and friendliness represents good publicity for tournament organisers and football as a sport. The Scottish "Tartan Army" has acquired an international reputation as carnival fans *par excellence*. In part, this fan identity has a long cultural history in Scotland, being rooted in the popular Scottish working-class carnival that has surrounded events such as seaside holiday outings or Hogmanay gatherings. Behaviourally, carnivals are characterised by an abandonment to hedonistic excesses, and the psycho-social *jouissance* of eating, drinking, singing, joking, swearing, wearing of stylised attire and costumes, engaging in elaborate social interplay, enjoying sexual activity, etc. (Hall 1993: 6, on Bakhtin). Modern carnival tends to be comparatively circumscribed, in being permitted to occur only within specific times and places (Eco 1984: 6). However, since by definition the carnivalesque involves the turning upside-down of hierarchical orders, in which bourgeois senses of propriety may be symbolically or physically assaulted, there is always the danger for those in authority that the carnival might become unruly or "get out of hand".

Like Irish fans, through the extension of this carnivalesque to football, Scotland's Tartan Army have self-consciously developed and presented a positive Scottish persona when abroad (see Giulianotti 1996a; 1996b). At Italia '90, over 20,000 Scots attended the three group matches in Genoa and Turin, and developed a "mutual appreciation society" with the local Italians. In Genoa, Scotland fans broke the Ferraris Stadium's decibel record at the match against Sweden. Even more remarkably, while on the park the Scottish team behaved very aggressively to the Swedes, off the park Scottish and Swedish fans behaved like reunited long lost friends (Finn 1994b; Giulianotti 1991). At Euro '92, 5,000 Scottish fans were awarded the "Fair Play Award" for their behaviour by UEFA (Giulianotti 1994a; 1995a).

The Swedish campaign was a key moment in the image-reconstruction of Scottish football supporters. The Tartan Army have made deliberate efforts to "behave" at fixtures outside Britain since 1981. A positive impression is manufactured by the fans for other nationalities, through social rituals with a truly Goffmanesque form. A degree of "self-policing" now occurs: supporters who become abusive or aggressive towards others tend to be "quietened" through the intervention of fellow Scots, acting by persuasion or by force. For "self-policing" to occur, the Tartan Army needs to have already generated a sense of shared identity within its ranks. Like any other supporter group, Scottish fans are separated by the sociological "facts" of class, age and ethnic stratification, and regional divisions.[3] More seriously, there are fundamental cleavages within Scottish football culture, in particular those relating to club affiliation and, in some cases, club fan identities tied to ethnic divisions overlaid with religious sentiments (like those found to quite varying degrees around the

"Protestant" Rangers or Hearts, and the "Catholic" Celtic or Hibernian (Finn 1991a; 1991b; 1994a; 1994c)). But as Cohen (1993: 129) points out, carnival can "bring together in amity people from different classes and ethnic and religious groupings". To achieve this unity, there is an informal "ban" throughout the Tartan Army on the wearing of potentially divisive Scottish club colours. Special sensitivity is reserved for the wearing of Rangers motifs; as well as dominating Scottish football, the club culture of Rangers is often perceived by rivals to be intolerant, arrogant and rather dismissive of the national team.[4] It has to be noted that the vast majority of Rangers fans who attend Scotland fixtures overseas adhere to the ban on club colours; they also generally avoid voicing the anti-Catholic and anti-Irish epithets which are commonly heard at Rangers' club matches. After overcoming the domestic divisions within the support, the Tartan Army then merges its sense of collective identity with the belief that being a Scottish supporter means entering into positive and exuberantly friendly exchanges with opposing supporters and the local "host" population.

Underpinning the Tartan Army's repertoire is a collective anti-Englishness, strongly associated with the popular typification of English fans as "hooligans" (Giulianotti 1991: 509). This anti-Englishness possesses both a practical and cultural dimension. Scottish supporters deliberately project an image of themselves as being Scottish-not-English, and the stereotype of English fan hooliganism has proved highly efficacious in generating a rapport with the local hosts when they are overseas. The hosts and other fans often make the mistake of confusing Scotland with England, or at least a shared "British" football identity, which means there is an expectation that the Scots may be violent fans. The easiest method through which the Scots may explain their cultural and historical differences from the English, for the benefit of the uninformed, is to stigmatise the English as hooligans and express their contempt for such nationally-defined hooligan behaviour.

Yet there are forms of Scottish identity which are receptive to a shared sense of Britishness with the English. Most germanely, Glasgow Rangers again represent a complicating factor through their Unionism towards England and the UK generally – something blithely ignored by some sociologists and tabloid journalists alike. Ambiguities still remain on the modernisation of Rangers' traditional intolerance towards Catholics. Catholic players signed in recent years have been advised by Rangers not to bless themselves when taking the field. Meanwhile, English internationalists have shown their assimilation into Rangers' club culture, by anti-Irish ranting while with the England team (Terry Butcher), conducting Ibrox fans in these Orange hymns during an Old Firm game (Graeme Roberts), or "playing the flute" in true Orange Order style after scoring (Paul Gascoigne) (Finn 1997).

Within a wider setting, the relationship between Scottish sport and Scottish nationalism is quite perplexing (Jarvie and Walker 1994). Scottish football has been the subject of vexed perorations by cultural nationalists and intellectuals. It is thought that the obsession with football provides the Scots with a "stubborn national neurosis" (McIlvanney 1991: 70), a distraction from the development of a modern nationalist consciousness which should translate into an institutionally autonomous nationhood. The leading Scottish nationalist politician, Jim Sillars, complained that "we have got too many 90-minute patriots in this country" (*Scotsman* 24 April 1992). The critical theorist, Tom Nairn (1981), has argued that Scottish popular culture (including football) fosters a peculiar "sub-nationalism" among the Scottish people, which is politically schizophrenic and ultimately self destructive. Even Scotland's footballing tradition, in snatching defeat from the jaws of victory, is read as a metaphor for its political impotence. (Euro 96 offered further nourishment for this view, as the Scots failed *again* to go beyond the first round of a major international tournament).

These arguments have an historical and ideological appeal. But, they assume that nationalism within popular culture can only deter rather than promote a potentially political sense of Scottishness. Notwithstanding the culturally and nationally unifying features of "Unionist" football in the UK, there are broader and deeper political fissures between Scotland and England. Support for "home rule" was vindicated by the 1997 referendum, in which Scots voted for a Scottish parliament with tax-varying powers. Popular culture *does* reflect some of these emotions. The Scottish National Party has claimed the film *Braveheart* as an inspiration for Scottish political independence.[5] Scotland's football manager claimed the film to be an inspiration for the national team and its supporters in Euro 96. Coach-loads of Scottish supporters watched the epic on video as they travelled south to matches in England. On the eve of the Wembley match, some of the Tartan Army's hard core paid a ceremonial visit to the London site of Wallace's execution by the English in 1304. More commonly, during the long drinking sessions before and after matches, it was a regular sight for a tartan-clad Scot to emerge waving a small-but-life-size cardboard cut-out of Mel Gibson as William Wallace. Mischievous shouts of the battle cry "Freedom!" would be echoed in full by the laughing on-lookers, in an atmosphere more burlesque than bellicose.

More traditionally, the match against England resumed the world's oldest international fixture, and with it a return to the Scottish Wembley "tradition". Since the 1920s, thousands of Scottish fans have enjoyed the carnival excesses of their "Wembley Weekends" (Holt 1989: 260). Mostly, Scottish fans were seen as amiable, if inebriated visitors. But, from the late 1970s, these biennial "northern invasions" had started to attract increasing political and media criticism in which it was the Scottish, not the English, supporter who was typified as "hooligan".

Violence and Scottish Fans

In 1977, after defeating England 2–1 at Wembley, Scotland supporters invaded the pitch, tore down the goal-posts and dug up the grass, to take home as souvenirs of an epic victory. In 1979, after some genuinely violent incidents, the Scots brought the London Underground to a standstill as its workers walked out on strike, rather than transport the visiting fans around the capital. In 1981, the English FA attempted to impose a ticket ban on Scottish supporters, but failed dismally. In 1983, the match was switched to a Wednesday evening, and thus lost much of its sparkle. Nevertheless, in 1985, only days after the Heysel disaster involving Liverpool fans, the Prime Minister Margaret Thatcher insisted that the scheduled Wembley match be transferred to Hampden Park in Glasgow, to stop the "hooliganism" of Scottish fans in London. The switch ignored the change in English fans' relationship to the fixture. Until then, the Scottish fans' tradition had been to greatly outnumber the English, at Hampden (as a matter of course) and at Wembley (as a matter of pride). After

Heysel, English clubs were banned from playing overseas, entailing the near total absence of any hooligan competition at international fixtures in the UK. Matches against Scotland (particularly in Glasgow) provided one of the last tests of English fan "hardness", against even more celebrated opposition. Accordingly, Scotland–England matches between 1985–9 resulted in serious disorder, with over 240 fans arrested at the final fixture in Glasgow. Afterwards, the English and Scottish FAs bowed to police and political pressure by calling off the annual fixture, claiming in the process that this would permit better preparation matches for international tournaments.

Fear of disorder ensured no more meetings occurred. At Italia '90 and Euro '92, the two sides were kept apart in the group draws, while local police and the National Football Intelligence Unit (NFIU) introduced heavy security to prevent the rival fans meeting in transit. In Sweden, the SFA's security adviser had been pessimistic about the Scots' willingness to respond peaceably to any English provocation. Prior to Euro 96, UEFA's President, Lennart Johansson, had considered keeping the two sides deliberately apart in the group draws, while comparing their rivalry to the Balkan situation! But an open draw resulted in the two countries meeting for the first time in seven years.

Since the early 1980s, Scottish hooligan violence at club fixtures has been dominated by the "soccer casuals". The soccer casual style represents a departure from the traditional violence associated with Scottish club fans, and is a special departure from the ethnic violence associated with Rangers and Celtic. It combines football fandom with youth subcultural style (Redhead and McLaughlin 1985; Giulianotti 1993; 1995b); and is thus distinguished by the casuals' almost complete avoidance of club colours in favour of fashionable menswear. The leading casual rivalry involves Aberdeen and Hibernian (also known as Hibs, from Edinburgh); other major casual groups include those who follow the Dundee clubs and Glasgow Rangers. Intriguingly, some casuals attend Scotland matches abroad, but, unlike their English counterparts, they have not transferred their hooligan *club* identity onto the international stage. Instead, their casual identity is usually submerged by full participation in the Scottish carnivalesque.

Nonetheless, some signs of a common *Scottish* casual identity have appeared. For the first time since Hampden 1989, and for the first time ever abroad in modern times, Scotland's friendly match away to The Netherlands in May 1994 led to *mass* arrests of Scottish fans. After some considerable negotiation, an uneasy "alliance" of Hibs, Aberdeen and Dundee casuals had been put together, and totalled approximately 140. Some disorder occurred outside the stadium in Utrecht, police moved in and forty-seven were arrested. At a preliminary meeting of some "top boys" associated with each group, a similar alliance was prepared for Euro 96.

Scotland Fans at Euro 96

In the event, the Scottish "invasion" passed off relatively peacefully. Scottish fans in Birmingham for the fixtures against Holland and Switzerland encountered little trouble. Neither opposing side appeared to have brought a hooligan following (the Dutch being conspicuously absent), while the publicised English assault failed to materialise. Before the first game, a minor skirmish at the campsite involving locals and Scottish fans was turned into a "danger signal" by the Scottish media, partially because a tabloid journalist (and hard core Scottish fan) camping there had chanced upon this newsworthy incident. The pedestrianised city centre was heavily policed, with squad vans and cars habitually parked outside pubs and nightclubs housing Scots drinkers. Supporters staying over in England soon located friendly drinking spots, including those offering the requisite "lock-in", to circumvent uncivilised licensing laws. Small groups of Scottish casuals appeared in Birmingham, neither looking for nor expecting violence; they mixed in with the mainstream Tartan Army, reactivating old friendships with some of the hard core, and discussing freely the issue of violence at the Wembley fixture. Even those Scottish CID officers monitoring the fans in Birmingham expected little action, with some from Aberdeen turning their attentions instead to late-night drinking and local women.

The Birmingham authorities had sought to entertain visiting fans (especially overseas ones), by hiring street theatre artists. Purer moments of the carnivalesque were more appreciated by the Scots when *they* initiated the action; in doing so, they sometimes found themselves near the receiving end of social control. Prior to the Swiss game, a large group of drinking fans were packed into a pedestrianised street, when a light ball was thrown up into the air by a young local. To the accompaniment of constant cheering, the fans kept it aloft by any means possible, with no obstacle too precious, in what passed for a throwback to folk football, in a street lined with "olde worlde" bars. This spontaneous revelry was too much for the attendant police, who insisted that the ball's owner reclaim his property. When, to huge cheers, he threw the returned ball back into play, the police pulled him round the street corner. But a pursuing pack of Scottish fans persuaded them of their humourless indiscretion, the youth was released, and the game continued.

For the Wembley game, the London-Scottish social club had organised some entertainment for compatriots. One bar in Kentish Town doubled as a "flop house" for those without accommodation, while a special "ball" was arranged in Shepherd's Bush. On the morning of the game, Scottish casuals joined the Tartan Army at Trafalgar Square, the Scots' traditional meeting place for Wembley fixtures. In total, around 250 Scottish casuals made the trip south.[6] They soon demonstrated their pursuit of a separate agenda, when a group of over 100, broke off to attack a bar beside Leicester Square containing English hooligans (cf. Brimson and Brimson 1997: 151). *En route* to Wembley, some coaches filled with Scottish fans had their windows smashed while driving past mobs of England fans in central London. Outside the ground, the Scots gathered at the turnstiles to their ground section, which was absurdly small due to the organisers' unjust distribution of tickets. Inside, security was surprisingly lax, as rival fans mingled with one another freely. Yet, the dearth of violence was probably attributable to large numbers of England fans being relative newcomers to the now fashionable game. Their remarkable taciturnity also told its own story, as the outnumbered Scots battled hard to sustain their Wembley tradition, and so out-sang them easily. At full-time, with Scotland defeated, many England fans reached across security cordons to congratulate the Scots fans on their support, shaking hands and swapping some regalia. The home fans' graciousness in victory continued outside the ground, while the visitors morosely speculated on how their hosts would have responded to an England defeat.

After the fixture, the events at Trafalgar Square acquired a ritualistic dimension, as the key players in the drama took up positions in concentric circles. At the epicentre, and controlling the contested space of the square and fountain, were the hard core Tartan Army fans, defiantly drinking and singing their elegies to a beaten team. On the fringes were various groups of Scottish casuals, seeking to move out centrifugally and fight their opposite numbers. Hemming them in was a perimeter of police officers, with batons and shields to the fore, and just as concerned to keep the outer ring of English hooligans on the periphery. The final ring was made up of *de facto* spectators, watching a drama that became London's major tourist attraction for the evening.

While the Scottish media fretted about the incidents, with most newspapers calling for a further ban on the game, it seems likely that the disorder involving the Scottish casuals has done little to affect the image of the Tartan Army abroad. For example, the Italian fan magazine, *Supertifo* (6 August 1996), reported the disorder, but placed the Tartan Army at the top of their league for Euro 96 supporters.

Mediating Scottish Identities

The Scottish media participate in identity construction in intriguing ways. Studies of football fans have argued routinely that the mass media "amplify" football hooliganism: in exaggerating the actual incidence of fan disorder, it is argued, the media promote a climate of fear and intolerance among the authorities and general public towards football fans, while also heightening the expectation of violence among supporters. *Ipso facto*, "amplification" intensifies the very "problem" which the mass media had criticised and set out to eradicate (Hall 1978; Marsh et al. 1978; Whannel 1979; Armstrong and Harris 1991). In Scotland, the "amplification" thesis would appear to have been internalised by the media, to the extent that they would now prefer to "de-amplify" (effectively, to ignore) any disorder involving the Tartan Army at matches overseas. Before the Holland match, the Scottish media typically reported on the "unblemished record" of the Tartan Army, thus ignoring the arrest of a dozen Aberdeen casuals at an international in Paris in 1989, and those other occasions when the carnivalesque of mainstream fans moved from positive impression management to disorderly excess.

The Scottish media adopt several reporting strategies in promoting the ambassadorial image of the Tartan Army. One basic strategy is to collapse the cognitive distance between team, supporters, media and reader, to enable a form of self-celebration between all four categories. Hence, after 5,000 Scotland fans had been publicly "awarded" the Fair Play championship for spectators at Euro '92, the Scottish tabloids proclaimed "We're the finest in Europe" (*Sun* 26 June 1992); and "WE'RE THE TOPS! – And that's official" (*Daily Record* 26 June 1992). This strategy is buttressed by the attempt of the Scottish media to interpolate a sense of national identity through collective differentiation (by reader and media) from an antithetical other: the English. Images of English fans fighting or being arrested at matches overseas, are juxtaposed with pictures of Scottish fans overflowing with bonhomie towards their hosts and opposition fans. When routinely condemning the behaviour of English fans overseas, hapless members of past Conservative governments regularly referred to these miscreants as "British" supporters[7] provoking the ire of Scottish politicians and editorialists, who countered in populist mode that all football offenders hail from south of the border. In heightening this sense of national identification with the supporters, the Scottish media are also legitimising their difference from English-based British-claiming media, which report on the same political and sporting issues, but which are often seen to give only a token coverage of Scottish-orientated news.

These populist and nationalist discourses in the Scottish media have been counterpoised by reporting pressures that would seem to undermine the "ambassadorial" presentation of the Tartan Army. From outwith Scotland, there is the relatively recent attempt by some English politicians and football officials to recontextualise (to the extent of de-amplifying) the violent propensities of English supporters. In arguing that English hooliganism is neither unique nor exceptionally violent, favourable comparisons are drawn with police and press reports of disorder involving Scottish and other European supporters (Giulianotti 1994b). Second, within Scotland, the print media has become increasingly competitive in recent years (Meech and Kilborn 1992). Most "British" newspapers have devolved some editorial and writing power to journalists composing Scottish editions, especially within news and sports sections. Growing pressure is placed on teams of Scottish-based journalists to come up with exclusive reports or new reporting perspectives on particular issues, and the behaviour of Scottish football supporters is no exception. For example, following the disorder in Holland in May 1994, the Scottish newspaper the *Daily Record* and its tabloid rival the *Sun* were involved in an editorial argument surrounding their respective coverage of the story. The *Sun* (30 May 1994) had issued a front page "exclusive", identifying the "leader" of the Scottish hooligans (an individual who, in fact, had not even been to the match in Holland!) (Armstrong and Giulianotti 1998). The *Daily Record* (1 June 1994) responded by accusing its rival of reporting hooliganism irresponsibly and unprofessionally. However, only ten months earlier, the two newspapers had adopted completely opposing positions when reporting a police "dawn raid" in Glasgow.

For Euro 96, the binary opposition between Scottish casuals/hooligans and the Tartan Army/anti-hooligan styles posed problems for the Scottish media. Yet while the Scottish media intermittently reported that the casuals were intending to travel south for violence, the predominant narrative pinpointed English fans *en masse* as the most likely to initiate trouble. This came into some conflict with English media views on hooliganism. Immediately after the group draw, newspaper coverage focused on the England–Scotland match and raised the possibility of fan violence. In discussing this story, the contradictions of advocating dual nationalisms were quickly realised by the *Sun* (18 December 1995). While its Scottish edition compared England fans most unfavourably with the praiseworthy Scots, the English issue portrayed the latter as the likely instigators of disorder. In response, the *Daily Record* (19 December 1995) accused its rival of bad faith, championing its own claim to be the truly Scottish newspaper. This claim was later symbolically strengthened by the *Record*'s announcement of official sponsorship of the Scottish team squad, interpreted as showing that some Scotland players and management "know that *real* Scots read the Record" (3 February 1996). However, on the same day, this proud boast and advertising catchphrase was subverted by the *Sun*, which reported the loss of *Record* jobs to London under the headline, "Real Scots sacked by the Record".

The newspaper circulation war led to continued efforts by tabloids to use Scottish football to position themselves as the newspaper with the truly Scottish identity for a truly Scottish community. Team, fans, newspaper and its readers could be collapsed into one entity, presented as a unity, the *true* Scottish community. For different news purposes different elements of the whole could be topicalised. Yet by the commencement of Euro 96, media reports generally focused at least as much, and arguably more, on the role of Scotland's community of fans as on the players. In the interregnum between the Holland and England fixtures, *Scotland on Sunday*, sister paper to Edinburgh's *Scotsman*, commented:

> This is a crucial time for Scottish football....We hope Scotland wins both matches. If the whole truth be told we hope most of all that Scotland wins at Wembley.... but most of all we hope that the Tartan Army returns from England with its reputation unblemished. It is far better to lose a football match than to gain reputation on the continent for thuggery and xenophobia. Ask England.   (*Scotland on Sunday*, 9 June 1996)

This elevation of the fans above the team also contains within it a gentler expression of anti-English sentiment, and an affirmation of England fans *qua* hooligans (cf. Giulianotti 1995a). But to elaborate our point on the player–fan hierarchy, we may note that Scottish supporters have even come to be used as central representatives of Scottish identity. When the *Daily Record* welcomed the publication of the Home Rule Bill (26 July 1997), the main editorial page was ecstatically titled: "Yes! Yes!" Immediately underneath this slogan, and by way of illustrating an article headed "Scottish and proud of it!", there was a photograph which needed no description: it was the Tartan Army *en fete* in London's Trafalgar Square. The image of Scotland's fans had been appropriated to become the definitive representation of being Scottish, and to herald the new Scotland to come.

Football and Nation into the Millennium

Until now, the limited means for the expression of a Scottish identity has meant that sport, especially the supposed "people's game" of football, has carried much of the burden of expressing a Scottish identity. Recently in the appropriation of any suitable, available images to portray Scotland, it has been real Scottish people, in the form of Scotland's "Tartan Army", that have become a significant representation of that identity. If sports teams can give substance to "imagined communities" (Anderson 1983), then massed supporters can do that as well, or even better – and in the case of Scotland with greater success (Finn 1994b; cf. Hobsbawm 1990). Nonetheless, even the positive carnivalesque Scottish fan identity relies on a binary opposition with English "hooligans", which is then reflected in media coverage of Scottish supporters. Occasionally, a more insightful media analysis is proposed. As *Scotland on Sunday* (25 February 1995) explained, "fighting old battles" with England, in sport or politics, is no substitute for becoming "a modern confident democracy...more concerned about planning for a vibrant future".

Euro 96 was but one of many tests of Scotland and Scottishness, but there was little evidence of real progress towards a less anti-English, more positive Scottish social identity. Scottish supporters' actions have reflected aspects of their nation and its position in the contemporary world: football has been one of the few, and one of the most important, international stages on which the Scottish social identity could be imagined and performed. Both team and supporters, recently especially the supporters, have represented Scotland. The new Scottish parliament may enable other, more significant expressions of Scottishness to be made. A more positive, more inclusive sense of Scottish identities is required and can easily be imagined, but its performance requires much more traditional invention. Two measures of its successful accomplishment will be when Scottish fans can present a truly *Scottish* and *international* carnivalesque social identity, and when that performance is seen in Scotland as being primarily *sporting* rather than quintessentially *Scottish*.

Notes

1 This article extensively revises and develops ideas first tentatively discussed in a paper which has been published in Italian (Finn and Giulianotti 1998).
2 The eight Board seats are taken by England, Scotland, Wales and Northern Ireland (one seat each); and FIFA (four seats). The Board adjudicates on changes to football's rules; a minimum of three-quarters support from its members is required for changes to be made.
3 Gender divisions are less notable within the support, as attendance of women at Scotland's matches abroad is low relative to other fan groups. For example, while Norway's overseas support is roughly equally divided between males and females, we estimate that women constitute less than 20 per cent of the Scottish supporters who travel abroad. Moreover, the carnival culture of the Scottish supporters is strongly masculine in content. During its more excessive moments, female fans are left to choose between screening off traditional perceptions of their "femininity" through participation or, more frequently, by playing a peripheral role in proceedings.
4 At the fixture against Greece in Athens in December 1994, many Scottish fans wore AEK Athens hats, largely in celebration of this side's victory over Rangers in the European Cup four months earlier.
5 The film is rather loosely based on the legend of the eponymous Scottish "freedom fighter" William Wallace, and his vainglorious battles with the English armies in the late thirteenth and early fourteenth centuries.
6 The Scottish casuals comprised mainly lads from Aberdeen (roughly sixty), Dundee (forty), Rangers (thirty), Falkirk (twenty-five), and small groups following Airdrie, Kilmarnock and Celtic. Around fifteen Hibs travelled through to the centre early in the day; a larger number remained in North London.
7 One culprit was David Mellor, then Minister for National Heritage and now head of the Government Football Task Force in England.

References

Allan, J. (1989) *Bloody Casuals: Diary of a Football! Hooligan*, Glasgow: Famedram.
Anderson, B. (1983) *Imagined Communities – Reflections on the Origin and Spread of Nationalism*, London: Verso.

Armstrong, G. and Giulianotti, R. (1998) "Ungentlemanly conduct: football hooligans, the media and the construction of notoriety", in R. De Biasi (ed.) *Il Mito del Tifo Inglese*, Milan: SHEKE.

Armstrong, G. and Harris, R. (1991) "Football hooligans: theory and evidence", *Sociological Review* 39, 3: 427–58.

Brimson, D. and Brimson, E. (1997) *Capital Punishment*, London: Headline.

Brug, H. H. van den (1994) "Football hooliganism in the Netherlands", in R. Giulianotti, N. Bonney and M. Hepworth (eds) *Football, Violence and Social Identity*, London: Routledge.

Cohen, A. (1993) *Masquerade Politics*, Oxford: Berg.

Eco, U. (1984) "The frames of comic freedom", in T. A. Sebeok (ed.) *Carnival!*, New York: Mouton.

Finn, G. P. T. (1991a) "Racism, religion and social prejudice: Irish Catholic clubs, soccer and Scottish society. I – The historical roots of prejudice", *International Journal of the History of Sport* 8, 1: 70–93.

Finn, G. P. T. (1991b) "Racism, religion and social prejudice: Irish Catholic clubs, soccer and Scottish society. II – Social identities and conspiracy theories", *International Journal of the History of Sport* 8, 3: 370–97.

Finn, G. P. T. (1994a) "Sporting symbols, sporting identities: soccer and intergroup conflict in Scotland and Northern Ireland", in I. S. Wood (ed.) *Scotland and Ulster*, Edinburgh: Mercat Press.

Finn, G. P. T. (1994b) "Football Violence: a societal psychological perspective", in R. Giulianotti, N. Bonney and M. Hepworth (eds) *Football, Violence and Social Identity*, London: Routledge.

Finn, G. P. T. (1994c) "Faith, Hope and Bigotry: case-studies of anti-Catholic prejudice in Scottish soccer and society", in G. Jarvie and G. Walker (eds) *Sport in the Making of the Nation: Ninety Minute Patriots?*, Leicester: Leicester University Press.

Finn, G. P. T. (1997) "Scotland, soccer, society: global perspectives, parochial myopia", paper to the *NASSS Annual Conference: Crossing Boundaries*, University of Toronto, Canada.

Finn, G. P. T. and Giulianotti, R. (1998) "La Scozia e Euro 96", in R. De Biasi (ed.) *Il Mito del Tifo Inglese*, Milan: SHEKE.

Forsyth, R. (1990) *The Only Game: The Scots and World Football*, Edinburgh: Mainstream.

Giulianotti, R. (1991) "Scotland's Tartan Army in Italy: the case for the carnivalesque", *Sociological Review* 39, 3: 503–27.

Giulianotti, R. (1993) "Soccer casuals as cultural intermediaries: the politics of Scottish style", in S. Redhead (ed.) *The Passion and the Fashion*, Aldershot: Arena.

Giulianotti, R. (1994a) "Scoring away from home: a statistical study of Scotland football fans at international matches in Romania and Sweden", *International Review for the Sociology of Sport* 29, 2: 171–200.

Giulianotti, R. (1994b) "Social identity and public order: political and academic discourses on football violence", in R. Giulianotti, N. Bonney and M. Hepworth (eds) *Football, Violence and Social Identity*, London: Routledge.

Giulianotti, R. (1995a) "Football and the politics of carnival: an ethnographic study of Scottish fans in Sweden", *International Review for the Sociology of Sport*, 30, 2: 191–224.

Giulianotti, R. (1995b) "Participant observation and research into football hooliganism: reflections on the problems of entrée and everyday risks", *Sociology of Sport Journal* 12, 1: 1–20.

Giulianotti, R. (1996a) "Back to the future: an ethnography of Ireland's football fans at the 1994 World Cup Finals in the USA", *International Review for the Sociology of Sport* 31, 3: 323–48.

Giulianotti, R. (1996b) "'All the Olympians: a thing never known again?' Reflections on Irish football culture and the 1994 World Cup finals", *Irish Journal of Sociology*, 6: 101–26.

Giulianotti, R., Bonney, N. and Hepworth, M. (eds) (1994) *Football, Violence and Social Identity*, London: Routledge.

Hall, S. (1978) "The treatment of football hooliganism in the press", in R. Ingham (ed.) *Football Hooliganism: The Wider Context*, London: Inter-Action Imprint.

Hall (1993) "For Allon White: metaphors of transformation", in A. White (ed.) *Carnival, Hysteria and Writing*, Oxford: Clarendon.

Hobsbawm, E. (1990) *Nations and Nationalism Since 1780*, Cambridge: Cambridge University Press.

Holt, R. (ed.) (1989) *Sport and the British*, Oxford: Oxford University Press.

Jarvie, G. and Walker, G. (eds) (1994) *Scottish Sport in the Making of the Nation: Ninety Minute Patriots?*, Leicester: Leicester University Press.

Marsh, P., Rosser, E. and Harré, R. (1978) *The Rules of Disorder*, London: Routledge and Kegan Paul.

McIlvanney, W. (1991) *Surviving the Shipwreck*, Edinburgh: Mainstream.

Meech, P. and Kilborn, R. (1992) "Media and identity in a stateless nation: the case of Scotland", *Media, Culture & Society* 14: 245–59.

Nairn, T. (1981) *The Break-Up of Britain*, 2nd edn, London: NLB.

Peitersen, B. (1991) "If only Denmark had been there: Danish football spectators at the World Cup finals in Italy", *Report to the Council of Europe*.

Rafferty, J. (1975) *One Hundred Years of Scottish Football*, London: Pan.

Redhead, S. and McLaughlin, E. (1985) "Soccer's style wars", *New Society*, 16 August.

Whannel, G. (1979) "Football crowd behaviour and the press", *Media, Culture & Society* 1:327–42.

Index